SEMIOTICS OF RUSSIAN CULTURE

MICHIGAN SLAVIC CONTRIBUTIONS

General Editor
Ladislav Matejka

Associate Editor
I. R. Titunik

1. B. M. Èjxenbaum, *O. Henry and the Theory of the Short Story.* Tr. by I. R. Titunik.

2. René Wellek, *The Literary Theory and Aesthetics of the Prague School.*

3. Jan Mukařovský, *Aesthetic Function, Norm and Value.* Tr. by M. Suino.

4. Roman Jakobson, *Studies in Verbal Art.* (In Czech and Slovak).

5. Jurij Lotman, *Semiotics of Cinéma.* Tr. by M. Suino.

6. *Sound, Sign and Meaning: Quinquagenary of the Prague Linguistic Circle.* Ed. by L. Matejka.

7. Jurij M. Lotman. *Structure of the Artistic Text.* Trans. from the Russian by Ronald Vroon.

8. *Readings in Russian Poetics: Formalist and Structuralist Views.* Ed. by Ladislav Matejka and Krystyna Pomorska.

9. *Sign: Semiotics Around the World.* Ed. by R. W. Bailey, L. Matejka and P. Steiner.

10. *Semiosis: Semiotics and the History of Culture.* Ed. by Morris Halle *et al.*

11. Ju. M. Lotman and B. A. Uspenskij. *Semiotics of Russian Culture.* Ed. by Ann Shukman.

Department of Slavic
Languages and Literatures
The University of Michigan

Ju.M. Lotman   B.A.Uspenskij

The Semiotics of Russian Culture

edited by
Ann Shukman

Ann Arbor

Front cover:
How the Mice Buried the Cat
Detail of a Russian woodcut
(Early 18th century)

ISBN 0-930042-56-5
Michigan Slavic Contributions, No. 11

CONTENTS

Part Three

Papers by B.A. Uspenskij

EDITOR'S PREFACE

This book has been prepared to celebrate the sixtieth birthday of Jurij Michajlovič Lotman. In marking this occasion we are also honoring a unique scholarly partnership: for together, Jurij Michajlovič Lotman and Boris Andreevič Uspenskij have advanced semiotic theory into the new fields of cultural semiotics, by developing powerful new methods for the description of the motivating values of a culture. These papers, then, illuminate the fundamental values and principles that have made, and still make, Russian culture what it is.

We wish Jurij Michajlovič many happy returns!

Several people have collaborated in the preparation of this volume; the names of the translators appear in the Table of Contents. In addition I should like to thank my colleagues at Birmingham University, David Johnson and Professor R.E.F. Smith, for help with some of the more obscure passages of early Russian. I am especially grateful to Françoise Lhoest of Brussels for her generosity in giving me the benefit of her expert knowledge. For the final shape of the volume I am indebted above all to Sebastian Garrett, who allied a keen sense of style to a deep and sympathetic knowledge of Russian culture and the Russian Orthodox tradition.

The editorial notes at the foot of the pages are designed to fill in the context or elucidate references which would be familiar to a Russian reader but not immediately recognizable to an English-speaking one. Wherever it was felt to be helpful for the understanding of the text, names have been identified, dates given, events or movements explained, and quotations located. The material for these notes was supplied variously by the translators or other collaborators or by myself, but the final versions were written by me. I hope that I have not too frequently omitted the necessary or stated the obvious. It remains to be said that any errors in the translations or notes are my responsibility.

Translations of quotations in the papers are by the translator concerned, unless a standard English version was available, in which case this is referred to.

Transliteration, spelling, and so on: the ISO system has been adopted throughout, except in the case of Russian words which have become familiar in English (e.g., Tsar, Tsarina, Tsarevich). Proper names are given in their transliterated form, except for the Christian names of members of the royal family (Catherine, Peter, Nicholas, etc.), and for Gogol', who loses his soft sign.

Ann Shukman

AUTHORS' INTRODUCTION

The volume here offered to the reader consists of papers written by the authors in the 1970s and early 1980s. Some were written together, others individually, but we believe that the shared features both of the subject matter and of the interpretation give the volume a unity. The features shared by the subject matter of the present volume are the following: firstly, all the papers are devoted to problems of the semiotics of culture; secondly, the selection of the subject matter in one way or another demonstrates the authors' interest in the diachronic aspects of the semiotics of culture – the papers all deal with historical material; thirdly, it is Russian culture that in each case is the topic for investigation. The volume, then, is devoted to the semiotics of Russian culture in the light of history, but the scope of the study is not confined to the subject matter selected by the authors to illustrate a particular point: rather it points to more general theoretical problems. Hence the title of the volume.

The unity of the volume is the result of the authors' shared approach, –one which has been worked out over many years of close collaboration, to several fundamental questions of contemporary semiotics. In this introduction it would seem appropriate briefly to summarize these basic principles.

It is useful to make a distinction between semiotics of the *sign* and semiotics of *language* as a sign system. The first derives from Peirce and Morris, and the second from Saussure. It follows that one may distinguish two tendencies in semiotic research, which may conventionally be defined as the logical tendency and the linguistic one. In the first case the researcher's attention is focussed on the sign in isolation, that is on the relationship of sign to meaning, to addressee, and so on. In this sense we speak of the semantics, syntactics and pragmatics of the sign and of the structure of the sign. We may distinguish iconic signs from symbolic ones and study the process of semiosis, that is, the transformation of the non-sign into the sign. In the second case the researcher concentrates his attention not on the individual sign but on a language, that is, a mechanism which uses a certain set of elementary signs for the communication of content.

The ideas developed in the present volume come genetically from the second point of view. Thus the authors are above all interested in the correlation of a language as a sign system and a text. Each of these concepts is understood in the broad semiotic sense, that is, it is not the sign itself that lies at the center of analysis, but the system of signs and the structural relationship between them. Hence the topic of investigation is as a rule the form and not the content (in the semiotic and not the metaphysical understanding of these terms), i.e. structured, and not non-structured, material. Given this approach, the content of a sign comes down to its structural value; and this is determined by its place in the system, that is by the sign's functional load. There is a crucial difference between the understanding of non-semiotic reality in the Peircean and the Saussurean approaches. If in the former it exists as the object of logical operations, then in the latter it acquires features of empirical reality. For this reason the first approach opens the way only to logical models, while the second affords the hope of reconstructing extratextual empirical reality by means of the text. At this point the aims of semiotics converge with traditional aims of historical research. The Peircean approach proceeds from content to form. The present authors however, proceed from form to content. In this way the first approach sets the task of modelling reality, while the second that of reconstructing it. Reality in its turn is perceived as a text (of a lower level) that also must be decoded.

This, in the most general terms, is how semiotics is understood in the papers of the present volume. What then is culture from the point of view of semiotics? Culture is understood as a system that stands between man (as a social unit) and the reality surrounding him, that is, as a mechanism for processing and organizing the information which comes to him from the outside world. The information may be considered important and significant, or it may be ignored, within a given culture. On the other hand information which is considered not-relevant for the first culture may, in the language of another culture, be extremely important. In this way one and the same texts may be differently read in the languages of different cultures.

Culture, then, is defined as a system of relationships established between man and the world. This system on the one hand regulates human behavior and on the other determines how he models the world. From the social point of view, culture is a system of relationships between man and the collective. In this sense the relationship between man and the social group may be regarded as a communicatory dialogue: the social group reacts to the behavior of the individual, to a considerable extent regulates it, and the individual reacts to the social group (and in general to the reality surrounding him).

This approach moreover, makes it possible to look at history from the semiotic perspective: from this angle the historical process appears as a system of communications between the social group and the reality surrounding it—in particular between various social groups—and, at the same time, as a dialogue between the historical personage and the social group. In this respect conflict situations, when the interlocutors in the communicatory process speak different (cultural) languages, that is when one and the same texts are read in different ways, are of particular interest.

From the point of view of its organization, culture can be regarded as a totality of differing and relatively more individualized languages (sign systems). In this sense culture includes the languages of art (the language of literature, of painting, of cinema), the language of mythology, the language of etiquette and so on and so forth. The functioning of these languages is in complex interdependence, and the nature of this relationship is, to speak in general terms, culturally conditioned, that is, it differs under different actual historical conditions.

In emphasizing the interdependence of the different languages of culture, the authors have the following in mind: in studies of culture as a semiotic object it is very common to describe the separate languages of culture as immanent and self-sufficient. This approach treats culture as a whole as the sum of separate, independently functioning, languages, each of which may be studied on its own. This approach is a possible one and indeed at a certain stage in the development of semiotic methodologies, an essential one. But its limitations must be clearly understood.

The authors have no wish to cast doubt on the usefulness of immanent descriptions of separate languages. The point is to emphasize that even if we tot up these descriptions together we will not arrive at the totality of culture: culture is not the sum of separate languages, rather the separate languages can be isolated from culture through the operation of analysis (or through the self-analysis which a given culture at times carries out on itself). The "atomistic" approach leaves out of account the extent to which the functioning of a particular language depends on other languages and indeed on the whole system of culture: it might be called a semiotic anatomy, a necessary preliminary step in a semiotic study.

In the present volume we are proposing a "semiotic physiology," a study of the functional connection between the different languages in the single functioning whole. By posing the question: "In what way is this particular language essential for the general functioning of culture and what is its special function in the single cultural organism?" we will be able to elucidate what is specific in each language.

Central topics for the semiotician to study are the characteristic features of the separate languages, their functional interdependence, the creolization and reordering of particular languages under the influence of other structures.

Just as life on earth forms a biosphere, the single mechanism of interdependent dynamic life-structures, so the different semiotic phenomena come into the researcher's view not as separate isolated phenomena but forming a vast picture of a single *semiosphere*.

The semiosphere, if pictured in the momentary film-still of a synchronic cross-section, would include in itself all the totality of semiotic acts, from the signals of animals to the verses of poets and the call-signs of artificial satellites. But the semiosphere, because it possesses memory which transforms the history of the system into its actually functioning mechanism, thus includes also the whole mass of texts ever created by mankind as well as programs for generating future texts. This whole mass of semiotic objects not only does not exist as an atomistic accumulation of separate isolated phenomena but cannot even be represented as an immobile hierarchy of statically disposed strata. As against the atomistic static approach we may regard the semiosphere as a *working mechanism* whose separate elements are in complex dynamic relationships. This mechanism on a vast scale functions to circulate information, preserve it and to produce new messages.

A decisive factor in the semiotic (intellectual) creativity of this enormous mechanism is its semiotic diversity—the constant clash of different semiotic structures that takes place within it.

These semiotic conflicts, dialogues, forays by particular texts into what is for them a completely alien semiotic milieu, these processes of transcoding, of the translation of texts from one system of language into another, of drawing equivalences between texts of mutually untranslatable languages, and so on,—all create a picture of exceptional dynamism. In the single mechanism of culture there co-exist semiotic structures with accelerated tempos of development (for example, Russian culture of the nobility in the eighteenth century after the reforms of Peter I), and texts, or whole cultures, oriented towards immutability, and towards total or partial exclusion from temporal dynamics (the culture of the Russian Old Believers, for instance). There is an obvious connection between these phenomena and this makes it necessary to introduce into a semiotic description the factor of cultural time (acceleration/deceleration).

This can be seen, in particular, in the formation of the semiotic diversity of cultural space, and this in its turn creates a different temporal organization in its different sectors. Culture regarded diachronically gives a picture of currents moving at different rates. The dynamic processes typically lack uniformity: sectors with a heightened dynamism are juxtaposed with isolated centers where development is decelerated, or, as in the case of the Russian Old Believers, where cultural time is totally stopped.

It is a well known fact of socio-cultural history that there are isolated collectives with what is, from the point of view of the general tempo of history, a decelerated development. From an internal point of view these collectives may seem to be totally detached from the general process and without any influence on it. Yet from an outside point of view they can be regarded rather as particular mechanisms of the general cultural process, as reserves of movement which, at the next turn of history, will accelerate its tempo.

Two examples will illustrate this: Russian Old Believer culture, which came into being as a result of the schism in the church in the seventeenth century, consciously preserved itself at this point of its cultural development. One might well think that the history of the cultural life of the Europeanized state created by Peter I could ignore the Old Believers and their world or at most refer to them as evidence of the "stagnation" of the consciousness of the masses. But in fact the intense rapidity of the Petrine transformations, the very idea of speed and urgency which gripped the minds of Peter's Europeanized comrades in arms was in complementary correlation with the Old Believer consciousness which was extra-temporal and in principle anti-historical. The one was impossible without the other. Another example: after the reforms of Peter I the culture of the nobility developed at an accelerated tempo. But the Russian clergy formed another cultural current which developed according to different temporal laws. When in the middle of the nineteenth century there started the age of the non-noble intelligentsia [*raznočincy*], this was very largely connected with the fact that the cultural reserve created in the isolated milieu of the clergy overflowed and rapidly accelerated the general movement of culture.

Analogous processes take place on the semiotic level too. From a strictly synchronic point of view they would escape attention and in order to see them new indices have to be introduced: semiotic time, the tension within a structural field of the semiotics of culture, and so on.

In view of the foregoing, the semiotic study of Russian culture is of particular interest. Indeed heterogeneity is a characteristic of Russian culture and has conditioned its constant orientation towards "alien" culture (at first towards Byzantine, later towards the West European cultural model); this orientation has not been manifest uniformly at all stages of culture and naturally it has created the cultural stratification of society. This is the reason why Russian history is so rich in semiotic conflicts and situations of mutual misunderstandings and pseudo-understandings within the framework of a single culture. At the most different historical periods situations have arisen that are typical for Russia: people evidently using the same language (on the expression plane), in fact speak different languages (on the content plane), i. e. they use the same words or phrases but give them different meaning.

Inasmuch as they lead to different kinds of cultural conflicts all these factors make Russian culture rewarding material and at the same time a unique testing ground for semiotic research. This is why we hope that the papers now presented to the reader will be of interest to a wide circle of specialists in the field of semiotics and the history of culture.

Ju. M. Lotman   B. A. Uspenskij

Tartu   Moscow

PART ONE

THE ROLE OF DUAL MODELS IN THE DYNAMICS OF RUSSIAN CULTURE (UP TO THE END OF THE EIGHTEENTH CENTURY)

Ju. M. Lotman, B. A. Uspenskij

0. In the widest sense of the word culture may be understood as non-hereditary collective memory expressed in a definite system of prescriptions and prohibitions.[1] This conception in no way, however, excludes the axiological approach to culture: in fact for the collective itself culture always seems to be a specific system of values. The difference between these approaches can be reduced to that between the external point of view of an outside observer and the internal one of an actual bearer of the culture: the axiological approach inevitably presupposes that it is this internal point of view, i.e. the self-consciousness, of the culture that is taken into account. Anyone investigating a culture in this case too must occupy an alienated position as an external observer: it is the position of the internal observer that is the object of research. The history of culture in this sense is not only the dynamics of the various prescriptions and prohibitions, but it is also the dynamics of the culture's self-consciousness, the dynamics which to some extent explains the corresponding change in the normative regulations (i.e. the prescriptions and prohibitions).

Thus culture, being the system of collective memory and collective consciousness, must at the same time be the unified value structure for that culture. The need for self-description, which is connected with the need at a certain stage to define it as a unit in terms of values and structure, has a vigorous effect on the culture as a phenomenon to be described. In creating for itself its own model of itself the culture actively influences the process of self-organization, organizes itself hierarchically and canonizes some texts and excludes others. This model eventually becomes a fact of cultural history and as a rule influences the ideas of later generations and the conceptions of historians. Our concern, however, is not automatically to apply self-description models of past cultures to a historical research text, but to make these models themselves into a special object for research, regarding them as a kind of cultural mechanism.

Observations of the history of Russian culture in the period we are considering show convincingly that it can be clearly divided into stages[2] which replace one another dynamically; furthermore each new period,

3

whether it is the establishment of Christianity in Russia or Peter I's reforms, is directed towards a decisive break with the preceding one. However, at the same time the investigator is confronted with a series of recurrent or extremely similar events, historical and psychological situations or texts. The regularity of such repetitions means we cannot simply brush them aside as chance occurrences without any deep causation. Nor can they be regarded as fragmentary remnants from preceding cultural periods. This is denied by their persistence and activity in the system of cultures that are contemporary with them. Analysis shows convincingly that new historical structures in Russian culture of this period invariably include mechanisms that regenerate the culture of the past. The more dynamic a culture is, the more active are the memory mechanisms which ensure the homostatic character of the whole.

The specific feature of the aspect of Russian culture of that time, which interests us is its fundamental polarity which is expressed in the dual character of its structure. The basic cultural values (ideological, political, religious) in the system of medieval Russia are arranged in a bipolar value field divided by a sharp line and without any neutral axiological zone. Discussion of a particular case will make it clear what we have in view: in the Catholic Christian West life after death is divided into three zones: paradise, purgatory and hell. Similarly life on earth is thought of as demonstrating three kinds of behavior: definitely sinful, definitely holy and a neutral kind which permits salvation beyond the grave after an ordeal in purgatory. Again in the actual life of the medieval West we find a wide band of neutral behavior and there are neutral social institutions which are neither "holy" nor "sinful," neither "state organized" nor "anti-state" they are neither good nor bad. This neutral sphere becomes a structural reserve from which tomorrow's system develops. Since continuity is obvious here there is no need either to emphasize it structurally or to reestablish it consciously and artificially.

The Russian medieval system was constructed on a marked dualism. To continue our example, we find that the Russian system divides life beyond the grave into heaven and hell. There is no provision for an intermediate zone. And correspondingly, behavior in this life is either sinful or holy. This dualism extended also to concepts unconnected with the Church. The secular authorities might be regarded as divine or demonic, but never as neutral in relation to these concepts.[3]

The existence of the neutral zone in the medieval West led to the development of a sort of subjective continuum between the present, which was regarded negatively, and the future that was awaited. The ideals of anti-feudal thinkers were drawn from particular spheres of the surrounding reality — non-ecclesiastic state institutions and the burgher family — and transposed into the ideal realm of social theories where they underwent heroic and moralistic transformation. The neutral sphere of life became the norm, and the highly semioticized top and bottom of

4

medieval culture were ousted into the zone of cultural anomalies.

In Russian culture of this period a different set of values is prevalent. Dualism and the absence of a neutral axiological zone led to the new being regarded not as a continuation but as an eschatological replacement of everything. In this connection it is significant that the opposition of the positive world of the family to the negative domain of evil, which is normal for Western culture in the Middle Ages, is quite irrelevant in Russian culture. And so at the moment of the break-up of the medieval consciousness, the depiction of the Virgin Mary through the prism of the poetry of private existence and of family life, which is important for Western Renaissance painting, found no echo in Russian art.[4]

Thus in these conditions the dynamic process takes on a fundamentally different character: change takes place as the radical rejection of the preceding stage. The natural result of this was that the new emerged not from the structurally "unexploited" reserve, but as a result of the transformation of the old, as it were, of its being turned inside out. In this way repeated changes could in fact lead to the *regeneration* of archaic forms.

The possibility of progressive development, given such a sequence of cyclically repeated "negation of a negation," is determined by the fact that at each new stage, owing to the changing historical situation and in particular to external cultural influences, a new perspective of cultural development is acquired, which actualizes some semantic parameter. Consequently, the selfsame concepts can at each stage be given a new content depending on what was the initial point of the development.

It is these deep developmental structures which enable us to speak of the unity of Russian culture at the various stages of its history. It is in change that the unchanging is revealed.

What we have been saying in large measure explains the fact that for Russia at its various historical epochs it is not conservatism that is typical, but on the contrary both reactionary and progressive tendencies.

1. One of the most persistent oppositions contributing to the structure of Russian culture throughout its whole history from the introduction of Christianity into Russia until the reforms of Peter I is the opposition "old" ways [starina] ←→"new" ways [novizna]. It proves to be so vigorous and significant that from the subjective standpoint of a bearer of the culture at various stages it absorbs into itself or subordinates to itself other most important oppositions of the type: "Russia ←→ the West," "Christianity ←→ paganism," "true faith ←→ false faith," "knowledge ←→ ignorance," " the social top ←→ the social bottom," etc.

This study will be largely devoted to the difference between the subjective experience of these concepts in the minds of the participants in the historical process, and the meaning which they objectively take on in the whole context of the culture; and also to the complex dialectics

5

of the mutual transitions of these oppositions and their relative values.

1.1. The introduction of Christianity was a decisive landmark in the self-consciousness of ancient Russia. It is in this connection that we meet for the first time in the sources the definition of Russia as "new" and of the Russians as a "new people." In the *Tale of Bygone Years* Vladimir, in a prayer uttered after his baptism says: "Christ our God, who created heaven and earth, look upon these new people."[5] Ilarion in his *Sermon on Law and Grace* describes Russia as a "new wine-skin" into which a new teaching has been poured.[6] In this instance it does not concern us that the epithet "new" with reference to newly Christianized peoples came from a definite external tradition, since ultimately it acquired a much broader and more original meaning in Russian history.

The means by which the "old" was replaced by the "new" is deeply significant. As Aničkov has shown convincingly, the introduction of Christianity into Russia was preceded by an attempt to create an *artificial* pagan pantheon:[7] it might seem that for the creation of the "new" Christian Russia it was psychologically necessary to create a consolidated and largely conventional image of the "old."

The introduction of Christianity itself took the form of a demonstrative change of place between the old (pagan) religion and the new one (Christianity). The external but highly significant manifestation of this was the spatial relocation of the holy objects during this process. The idol Perun was thrown down from the Kiev Hills to Podol, i.e. to where the Christian church of St. Elijah (Perun's Christian counterpart) stood, and a Christian church was built up above where there had previously been a heathen temple.[8] Thus there is a radical switch between the "top" and the "bottom." Vladimir as it were turns the established system of relationships inside out (as Peter did later), changing pluses into minuses. He not only accepts a new system of values, replacing the old with the new, but inscribes the old into the new with a negative sign.

The establishment of Christianity in Russia entailed broad cultural and political changes: it involved, for instance, Russia's entry into Byzantium's zone of influence. All the more remarkable are the very early tendencies to reject Byzantine influence and the attempt to place the Greeks and their empire on a hierarchically lower level than Russia. It is significant that this tendency brings about the qualification of Byzantium as an "old" state in contrast to the "new" Russia. Ilarion, while rejoicing that Russia had joined the worldwide Christian community, already speaks disparagingly of Byzantium which had long been Christian: he equates Byzantium with the Old Testament and with Hagar, both coerced by Law, and contrasts them with Russia, represented by Sarah, who lives by Grace from the New Testament.[9] Subsequently these tendencies were expressed with particular clarity at the time when the notion of "Moscow the third Rome" became prevalent, when, after the fall of Constantinople, Russia became conscious of itself as the only stronghold of Orthodoxy and messianic attitudes grew stronger. It must not be forgotten that the downfall of the Byzantine Empire coincided approximately with the overthrow by the Russians of the Tatar yoke. And so whereas in Byzantium itself Islam was triumphant over Orthodox Christianity, in Russia the opposite was the case and Orthodoxy was victorious over Islam. In effect Byzantium and Russia had changed places and as a result Russia became the center of Orthodoxy and so too of the Christian world.[10]

Even before this the monk Chrabr's views had been popular in Russia: he affirmed that the Slavonic language had a better claim than Greek to holiness since Greek had been created by pagans, whereas Church Slavonic had been created by the holy Apostles. In the original article about the creation of Russian writing which was included in the *Tolkovaja Paleja** but which has also come down to us in other manuscripts, Russian writing, along with the Russian religion, is declared to be a revelation from God, quite independent of Greek mediation. The text says:

Let this be known to all peoples and nations, that the Russian nation did not receive its sacred faith from anywhere and Russian writing was not revealed by anyone, but came from God Himself, the Almighty, the Father, the Son and the Holy Ghost. The Holy Ghost inspired Vladimir to receive the faith, to take baptism and the church ritual from the Greeks. But Russian writing was first revealed by God to a Russian in Chersones and it was from this writing that the philosopher** learned how to compose and write books in the Russian language. [In another version, "words" instead of "language".] This Russian lived reverently, with fasting and virtue in pure faith. He lived alone and was the first of the Russians to be a Christian and no one knows whence he came.[11]

1.2. The constantly maintained view of Russia as "new" is paradoxically combined with the activation of extremely archaic cultural models. The concept of the "new" itself turns out to be the realization of ideas whose roots reach back into the remotest past. Here we may note two models for the construction of the "new culture":

1) The deep structure which evolved in the foregoing period is preserved. But it is subjected to drastic renaming while still maintaining all the basic features of the old structure. In this case *new texts* are created while the archaic cultural framework is retained.

2) The deep structure of the culture is itself changed. But in this process it reveals its dependence on the previous cultural model since it is constructed by turning the old culture "inside out," by rearranging what has previously existed but with a change of signs.

---

*A medieval Russian collection of Old Testament stories with commentaries, literally, "the Interpretative *Palaia.*"
**i.e. St. Cyril.

7

A clear example of this is the way in which pre-Christian pagan ideas penetrated into the cultural system of Christianity. The pagan gods had two possible fates: either they were identified with demons and so occupied a negative but entirely legitimate position in the new religious system; or they were united with the Christian saints who replaced them functionally. As demons they could still keep their names, as saints they only retained their functions. Thus Volos-Veles was transformed into the demon "volosatik," into a wood goblin, or others; and at the same time he was also transformed into St. Vlasij, St. Nicholas or St. George.[12] Mokoš' continued to live on as an evil spirit of the same name (cf. the dialect form *mokoš'* meaning "an evil spirit;"[13] it is interesting that in modern dialects this word means "a loose woman,"[14] cf. urban slang of the eighteenth and nineteenth centuries where *venera* had the same meaning) and at the same time was obviously identified with St. Paraskeva-Pjatnica[15] and even with the Virgin Mary.[16]

In exactly the same way too places where there had been pagan temples might have one of two fates: they might continue in their function as holy places but with the heathen deity replaced by a Christian saint (the deity in fact being renamed), or on the other hand the nature of the deity might be preserved (sometimes the name too), but the function would be totally reversed; the place becoming "evil," the habitation of demons. It is interesting to find an example of how these two points of view, although existing in different cultural environments, might intersect, creating as it were two "readings" for one and the same fact. On the one hand there is the custom established on St. Vladimir's authority of building Christian churches on the sites of pagan temples. On the other, there is a very striking legend from the Kazan' Theological Academy's collection of manuscripts describing how a church was struck by lightning during mass, because it had been built on an "idolatrous place of prayer" [*mol'bišče*] and because behind the altar there were still standing a birch tree and a stone.[17] In exactly the same way in Novgorod a monastery (known as "Perun Monastery") was established at the place where once stood the image of Perun which had been thrown into the Volchov river, and yet even as late as the sixteenth century pagan orgies[18] took place here every year.

Of course the site of a former pagan temple might by tradition still be regarded as holy by the parishioners, while for the priests the construction of a church there implied the expulsion of the demon from his own domain and the sanctification of what had been an evil place.[19] However in either case it is important that the opposition "holy – unholy" applied to the place and that thereby it was contrasted with neutral territories. The possibility of alternating the members of this opposition is confirmed by the fact that what had been holy could be changed into something evil. It is well known that abandoned churches were favorite haunts for the forces of evil (cf. "Vij" by Gogol).

Such buildings as bath-houses, barns and forges are interesting examples of the fate of pagan temples in the Christian world. There are reasons to think that the perception of these places as "unholy" is connected with the fact that they had a special sacred significance in the pre-Christian life of the East Slavs, being used as clan (or family) temples. In other words pagan temples preserved their cult function even in the Christian period, although with a negative sign. Particularly striking is the stubbornly held view that power in the bath-house belongs to the force of evil rather than to the cross. (In the Christian view this is interpreted that the power of the cross as it were turns away from this place as from other "unholy" places. In general, the effectiveness of the force of evil is linked with God's turning a blind eye.) Similarly, those sorcerers who never go to church, at festivals when the people go to church, are said to go off to the *bath-house*.[20] So too the bath-house functions as the traditional place for fortune-telling, sorcery, magical healing and of course for casting spells. The cult role of the bath-house is quite clear in the marriage ritual whereby bathing rites are no less obligatory than the church ceremony: the one complements the other. It is quite natural in view of what has been said that in Russian folklore the term *božena*, meaning "temple," may be applied to the bath-house.[21] No less typical is the widespread idea that people go to the bath-house *to pray* to the force of evil (in effect the spells uttered there may be regarded as a special kind of prayer), as this is expressed, for instance, in this Belorussian song:

In the village of Voučkovskoe,
Ho, ho! [refrain with stamping and thumping]
There stood an oak bath-house:
Hi, hi, hi! [refrain with thumping]
And the young men would come to pray to God,
They embraced the pillar and kissed the stove,
In front of Sopucha they lay down in the form of a cross,
They thought: Thou Most Pure One,
But Sopucha is Evil![22]

Thus in the life of early Orthodox Russia pre-Christian forms of behavior persisted, functioning as legitimized anti-behavior. In certain places and at certain times a Christian *was compelled* to behave "incorrectly" from the point of view of the norms of Christianity. Correct behavior in the wrong place and at the wrong time would be perceived as blasphemous, i.e. sinful. So, for instance, at Christmas time or at certain other points in the calendar cycle of rituals, and also when visiting "evil" places both within Russia and on entry into "infidel" territory, one had to behave in a special way which was opposed to the norms of "correct" behavior.[23] In practice this resulted in the conservation of the norms of pagan behavior.

The new (Christian) culture was largely built up in opposition to its predecessor and in this way the old pagan culture became an essential condition of the culture as such, serving as an anti-culture. So the "new culture," which saw itself as the negation and total destruction of the "old one," in actual fact was a powerful factor in its preservation, incorporating in itself both inherited texts and surviving forms of behavior with their functions changed into their mirror images.

To summarize, the everyday practice of Orthodoxy is an invaluable source for the reconstruction of East Slavonic pagan culture.

1.3. A vital factor in the self-definition of any cultural phenomenon is a polemic with hostile ideologies, since in the process of such a polemic its own position is formulated and the opponent's position is significantly transformed. The introduction of Christianity into Russia not only compelled the "new religion" to define itself in relation to paganism, but also brought the Russians into the polemics between Eastern and Western Christendom. It became necessary to take up a definite position on this the fundamental ideological controversy of the time. Paganism and the "Latin faith" were phenomena of a quite different order from one another. This was clearly recognized by the Old Russian writers who even declared that the Latin heretics were worse than pagans "since you could not be on your guard against them, but you could against the pagans. The Latins have the Gospel and the Apostles and some of the saints too, and they do go to church, but both their religion and their canon are evil; they have defiled the whole earth."[24] In other words the "Latin faith," unlike paganism, was perceived as a blasphemous parody of true Christianity, externally like it, but having a different content: so to speak Orthodoxy turned inside out. Paganism and Catholicism are opposed to one another here as the absence of information (entropy) is opposed to false information.

At the same time, however, a fundamentally different understanding of paganism became possible whereby it was seen as a false religion. In this case it and Catholicism are identified in the Orthodox mind by virtue of their antithetical opposition to true religion. In the eyes of the Orthodox Christians of Kievan Russia, both pagans and "Latins" are bearers of an "alien" faith. They are regarded as identical for polemical purposes and certain common features begin to be attributed to them. Hence there arises a certain syncretic image of "alien faith" in general. Early Russian writers speak of "Chors the Jew" and the "old Greek Perun."[25] Since paganism was thought of as non-Orthodoxy, non-Orthodoxy began to be identified with paganism.

This had some interesting consequences. We have seen how Orthodoxy absorbed certain norms of pre-Christian life in the form of legitimized anti-behavior. Now the reverse happened. Forms of anti-behavior were attributed to the "Latins" whose image was built up from Orthodox ideas about the world of "evil" and of forbidden actions. As a result, along with other "crimes," real features of pagan Russian behavior were attributed to Western Christendom. This circumstance makes polemical writings "against the Latins" another source which should not be ignored in the reconstruction of the East Slavonic pagan world.

Thus an early Russian anti-Catholic polemicist, referring to the familiar Russian expression "mother damp earth" (*mat' syra zemlja*), which sounded to him to be clearly of pagan origin, confidently attributed such ideas to the Catholics: "They call the earth their mother." And from this initial assumption he accurately reconstructs the full text of the myth: "If the earth is their mother, the sky is their father."[26] This example shows exceptionally clearly both what the mechanism was for reconstructing the "Latin world" in early medieval Russian consciousness, and provides evidence that the anti-pagan orientation in early medieval Russian Christianity meant that it had incorporated the mechanisms for independently generating correct pagan texts, i.e. that paganism had been included in the actual cultural memory of early Russian Christianity. So if paganism is understood as an *alien* faith, then Catholicism in its turn acquires in effect features of an *old* faith.

Typical for this identification of Catholicism with paganism is the statement that the "Latins" go to church in "Polovtsian robes" and "Hungarian hats."[27] Aside from the question of the historical authenticity of this report, what is significant is that pagan Polovtsian clothing is equated with the Catholic Hungarian.

A notable example of the same kind is to be found in the attack on the Catholics in the Menology* of Metropolitan Makarij:

> On the first night the priest lies with the bride behind the altar table and having laid her down on the carpet, and making the sign of the cross over her shame, he kisses her shame. And says: before you were my mother and now you are my wife. And so he lies with her, and the evil having come out of the bride onto the carpet, and having washed and burned the carpet, the evil is sprinkled over the people in the church.[28]

It is unnecessary to point out that there were no actual parallels to this ceremony among the Catholics. It is no less obvious that this testimony, along with the fantastic details, contains information about very ancient customs with roots reaching back to the remotest past. Although the possibility cannot be excluded that the author of this work retained some slight memories of such ancient rituals, it is more reasonable to think that these notions were generated independently by the mechanism of prohibitions. In this case it might be supposed that Christianity in Kievan Russia included mechanisms for generating pagan texts for polemical purposes,

---

*Menology (Russian *Mineja*), "book of the month" containing either the services or the readings from the lives of the saints.

i.e. it included a structural memory of the cultural experience of former times.

The "new ways" not only incorporated the "old ways" in a complex way, but also served as generator of the "old ways" while subjectively considering itself as the complete opposite.

1.3.1. Much later on at the most different stages of historical development the polemical or negative orientation could lead to the generation of pagan texts and even to the regeneration of pagan rituals. In a number of cases this is brought about by anti-clerical tendencies.[29] Thus Stepan Razin openly rejected church ritual and made bridal couples dance around a tree, i.e. he effectively revived the corresponding pagan ritual[30] (the memory of which was retained in folklore texts, proverbs, etc.). Similarly after the Revolution,

> there were cases when a couple wishing to avoid a church marriage were afraid to tell the old people about this. They would travel away from their village a few miles as if they were going to church in a neighboring village, but before reaching it they would stop in the forest, get off the cart, and "go around a fir tree with lighted candles."[31]

The behavior of the *Strigol'niki** might well be understood in this sense too: some of their practices demonstrate features of pagan behavior (praying at crossroads,[32] the cult of Mother-Earth,[33] and so on). It could be supposed that what was happening in these cases was not the preservation of a pagan tradition, but precisely the regeneration of such behavior brought about by the rejection of Church organization.

The revival of pagan rituals may be observed among the sectarians, including some extreme groups of priestless Old Believers.** A. F. Belousov has pointed out that in the priestless sects where there is no marriage, the rejection of the church wedding has led to marriage by abduction of the bride, which was practiced until very recently. Further, this custom of "marriage by abduction" may include a ceremony round a tree or lake.[34] No less significant is the fact that some Old Believer sects bury their dead in the *forest*, i.e. where it is usual to bury so-called *"založnye"* ("unhallowed" people).[35] This is the same as the pagan Slavonic custom of burial in the forest or fields which Kozma of Prague wrote about.[36]

Similar rituals occur in those Old Believer sects which consider that the Antichrist has already come. Since the world of the Antichrist is well known to be inverted, rejection of this world may in fact lead back to

---

*Lit. "Shearers," a fourteenth-century heresy which opposed the acquisition of wealth by the Church.
**Those who opposed the reforms of Patriarch Nikon in the mid-seventeenth century.

pagan forms. However the revival (or continuation) of pagan burial is to be found not only among the sectarians. An interesting example of this kind occurs in V. S. Pečerin's memoirs where he describes how a priest refused to bury a suicide in the cemetery: "So he was simply buried in one of the burial mounds," writes Pečerin.[37] Burial in a *mound* here is an alternative to burial in consecrated ground, the mound being regarded as a pagan ("evil") area.[38] In just the same way too in other cases of the burial of "unhallowed people," we again find forms of what is in essence pagan behavior.[39]

2. Russia of the later medieval period as distinct from the earlier one lived largely by the slogan of the "old ways." It was with the concept of "the old" and "the primordial" that the highest axiological criteria began to be associated. However the historian who takes on trust this subjective orientation towards the old ways risks becoming victim of that anachronistic displacement of concepts of which we are already aware.

2.1. Widespread dissatisfaction with the whole pattern of Russian life, which was felt in various strata of the population in the seventeenth century, was expressed in a series of popular movements and took the form of a demand for a return to the old ways. However, this conception of the "old ways" was at times somewhat strange. The idea became widespread that God's beautiful world was in sharp opposition to the terrible lack of order in the world of men. The natural consequence of this was a demand for a return to the primordial natural order. And so we are not surprised to find that in Kirša Danilov's *Anthology* [*Sbornik Kirši Danilova*] (which was compiled in the seventeenth century and written down at the beginning of the eighteenth), the ceremonial opening which declares the breadth, spaciousness and grandeur of the natural world is repeated three times: "High is the height, the height of the sky. . . ." However, the function of this opening is significantly transformed in all three *bylina** texts. In the first, "Concerning Salovij Budimerovič" [*Pro Salov'ja Budimeroviča*], it figures in harmony with the poem's basic content, and presents a picture of epic space.[40] In the second text, the *bylina* "Agafonuška," it is travestied by being turned inside out:

High is the height of the ceiling,
Deep is the depth under the floor,
And the wide open spaces are the patch of hearth in front of the
    stove,
The open field is just the scrap of floor beneath the bench,
And the blue sea is but water in the tub. . .[41]

*Russian heroic poem.

"Space" [*prostor*] in the epic world of the *bylina* is by way of parody contrasted with the "lack of space" [*tesnota*] in the actual world of men's experience. And lack of space for the seventeenth century is a transparent metaphor for social evil. The metaphor is to some extent based on the opposition between the seizure of land in the central provinces of Russia by landlords and the space of the lands and waters "belonging to nobody" in the unknown remote outlying regions. This evokes a third use of the opening—a generalized opposition between the good in nature and the evil prevalent in human society, between the harmony and beauty in the former and the disintegration of all bonds in the latter:

> High is the height of the earth under the sky,
> Deep is the depth of the ocean-sea,
> Wide is the freedom over the whole earth,
> Deep are the pools of the Dnepr,
> Wonderful is the Levanid cross,
> Long are the sandbanks of Čevylec,
> High are the Soročinsk hills,
> Dark are the Brjansk forests,
> Black are the marshes of Smolensk,
> And rapid the lower reaches of the river,
> Under King David, son of Jesse,
> Under the holy man Makarij son of Zacharias,
> There was great misrule:
> Nuns in their cells bore children,
> Monks were robbers of the road,
> The son disputed with his father in the law court,
> Brother assaulted brother,
> Brothers would take their sisters to them.[42]

These ideas were close to those of Archpriest Avvakum:

Around it the mountains were high and the cliffs of rock, fearfully high; twenty thousand versts and more I've dragged myself, and I've never seen their like anywhere. Along their summits are halls and turrets, gates and pillars, stone walls and courtyards, all made by God. Onions grow there and garlic, bigger than the Romanov onion and uncommonly sweet. Hemp grows there too in the care of God, and in the courtyards are beautiful flowers, most colorful and good-smelling. There's no end to the birds, to the geese and swans—like snow they swim on the lake. In it are fish, sturgeon and taimen salmon, sterlet and amul salmon, whitefish, and many other kinds. The sturgeon and taimen salmon are fat as can be; you can't fry them in a pan—there'd be nothing but fat left! The water is fresh, but huge seals and sea lions live in it; in the great ocean sea I never saw their like when I was living at Mezen. The lake swarms with fish. And all this has been done for man through Jesus Christ our Light, so that finding peace he might lift up his praise to God. "But man is like to vanity; his days are as a shadow that passeth away." He cavorts like a goat, he puffs himself out like a bubble, he rages like a lynx, he craves food like a snake; gazing at the beauty of his neighbor he neighs like a colt; he deceives like a devil.[43]

The idea of a divine and beautiful natural order is clearly expressed too in Avvakum's account of how he prayed for the health of the hens: "Everything is of value to God, both bird and beast to His glory."[44]

It is significant that the line of thought which rejected the whole social order in the name of the natural and which objectively speaking contained within itself a most profound negation anticipating Rousseau's and Tolstoj's ideas, was subjectively experienced as an argument in favor of the old ways. The whole of human history was now regarded as the "new ways," whereas the "old ways" were considered to be the primordial divine order.

The image of the "old ways" was deeply anti-historical and aimed at making a break with actual historical tradition.[45]

2.2. The idea that to move forwards was to return to some lost truth (movement into the future being movement into the past) had become so widespread that it was adopted by opposite social groups. Thus the desire of the Nikonians to "correct" the liturgical texts was based on the idea that the Greek order was the primordial and correct one. Later history was conceived as a gradual deterioration and a subsequent revival.

For the Old Believers the inversion of historical time is typical. Instead of the diachronic opposition: "the old and the pagan" vs. "the new and the Christian" there arose in their consciousness a diachronic opposition of another kind: "the old and the Christian" vs. "the new and the pagan," where "pagan" was equivalent to "satanic." This inversion of time among the Old Believers, which was expressed by paganism in their mind being placed *after* Christianity and not *before* it, undoubtedly resulted from the general eschatologism of their thinking which was oriented towards the end, not the beginning of the historical process.[46] Again, since evil was regarded as something brought into Russia from outside, the result of associating with heretics, paganism and heresy are united into the single image of the heretical West. Avvakum is typical in this respect in failing to make any distinction among the internal divisions of the Western world:

The Romans and all the West have behaved adulterously.[47]
But we of the Orthodox Church have three times anathematized this adulterous philosophy of the Roman Church and its bastards the Poles and Kievan Uniats and also our own Nikonians, for all their new-fangled heretical practices.[48]
Everything is in French, that is to say in German.[49]

15

Thus the problem of "the old ←→ the new" is transformed into the antithesis, "the Russian land ←→ the West." Because that which is correct and from God is primordial, while what is sinful and from the Devil is the result of deterioration, i.e. the new ways, the West is thought of as a "new" world. Positive concepts such as piety and Orthodoxy are given the epithet "ancient," and whatever is sinful is perceived as "new-fangled." As a result the polemics with pre-Christian ideas, ancient paganism, loses immediacy. It disappears completely from literature, being replaced on the one hand by attacks on the Nikonians, and on the other by attacks on the Old Believers. However, denunciation of the West becomes extremely lively. The West was finally labelled as the ever "new" world, and also as the "inside-out" or "left-hand" territory, i.e. the devil's territory.[50]

In order to understand the sharply negative attitude to Nikon's reforms among many strata of Russian society, it must be borne in mind that in many cases the new rituals could be regarded as the inverted image of the old ones. Thus procession sun-wise is replaced with procession against the sun, and in the action of the liturgy the right and left sides are switched, and so on. Because the "inside-out," "left" world, in Russian conditions where two faiths coexisted, was perceived as anti-Christian, the Nikon reforms would, in the cultural consciousness, be identified with pagan or magical rites (cf. movement against the sun and the use of the left hand in various magic rituals). At the same time, in so far as the Nikon reforms were associated with Roman Catholicism, Western culture itself might be regarded as sorcery.

From the point of view, however, of the supporters of the new rituals, these ideas, which resulted from "interpreting" the reforms in the light of previous cultural experience, were to be regarded as "ignorance." To retain the link with the accumulated memories of preceding cultural development was called "ignorance," whereas a break with these memories was regarded as "enlightenment." "To remember" meant to be an ignoramus, "to forget"—to be enlightened. It is interesting to note that half a century later Peter I carried through many measures, which he must have known perfectly well were bound to be considered sacrilegious or even marked with the seal of Antichrist. However he deliberately ignored that interpretation on the grounds that it was an expression of ignorance.[51]

It is essential to note that at the very beginning of the Schism* in the Church, both parties to the dispute took up somewhat similar positions. Each camp reproached the other with departing from Orthodoxy. This meant that we find the emotional innovator Avvakum taking his stand for the Old Believers, whereas Nikon's views looked at in the

---

*The Schism was brought about by the imposition of reforms by Patriarch Nikon in the years 1653-57. The reforms were bitterly opposed by the Old Believers.

Josephian* perspective turn out to be fairly traditional. But for each party the opposite group were pagans in the broad sense of the word, although in the one case "ignorance" was emphasized (cf. the traditional term for pagans in Christian polemic literature: *neveglas*, "those who have not heard the voice"),and in the other case, "demonism."

Ultimately the Old Believers' position became fixed in stable traditional forms whereas the ideology of the new ritual was open to new cultural influences. This circumstance made it possible for Renaissance and Baroque ideas to permeate more and more into the church culture of the new believers.[52] This was very noticeable in painting (cf. in particular Iosif Vladimirov's well-known treatise) and in architecture.[53] Of particular significance in this repect was the dispute about *chomovoe* and *narečnoe* singing** on the one hand, and about unison or polyphonic singing on the other, which arises in the middle of the seventeenth century.[54] It is not at all surprising for example to find that the advocates of using ordinary language for singing [*na reč'*] are at the same time against both *chomonija* and polyphony; i.e. these two things, which, generally speaking, are quite distinct, are organically united in the new cultural consciousness. At the same time there is a struggle against all kinds of surviving glossolalic inserts in church singing (e.g. *anenajki* or *chabuvy****). The reasons for this will be clear if we recall that both *chomovoe* and polyphonic singing (recitation) are essentially not addressed to a human audience. The verbal content in these cases may be incomprehensible, and this is evidence that it is directed to the Highest Addressee. The fact of enunciation in the sacred lunage is the important principle. The church service is, so to speak, understood as communication with God, not with man; accordingly, the only thing that is important is the *objective* sense of the text being uttered, and this is in principle abstracted from its *subjective* perception. Whereas the opposite way of performing may be compared with the tendency to translate sacred texts into the vernacular and is oriented precisely towards comprehension by the human audience. From the point of view of the new Renaissance culture both *chomonija* and polyphony cannot but be regarded as unintelligible and ignorant. However, from the historical viewpoint they are the fruit of a long and sophisticated cultural tradition.

In this connection we may note that from the point of view of one of the warring parties, "knowledge" meant the command of a long tradition

---

*Followers of Joseph of Volokolamsk (d. 1515), also known as the "Possessors" since they upheld the right of monasteries to own land. The Josephian tradition was the dominant one in Russian church life throughout the sixteenth century.
**Chomovoe* singing or *chomonija* involves the use of a special pronunciation in church in which an extra vowel is inserted between consonants and after the final one. *Narečnoe* singing is singing using ordinary language.
***Types of glossolalic singing in which extra syllables were inserted as used in old Russian melismatic Church singing. See, N. D. Uspenskij 1965, p. 41; B. A. Uspenskij 1968, pp. 64-65.

elaborated in great detail, while "ignorance" was seen as the rejection of this tradition. In the view of the other party, "knowledge" was thought to be the consignment of that tradition to oblivion in the name of a consciousness that was concise, rational and "clear as the day," whereas "ignorance" was felt to be blind adherence to all the ins and outs of tradition. Again both parties were at one in their initial classification, but diverged only in their evaluations.[55]

3. The eighteenth century came in under the banner of innovation. The "new" was identified with all that was good, valuable and worthy of emulation; the "old" was thought to be bad, due for destruction and demolition. Under Peter people thought of Russia as a being "reborn in a new form" or as a new-born baby. In his *Eulogy on the Battle of Poltava* Feofan Prokopovič addressed himself to "Russia reborn, strengthened and fully matured."[56] He gave expression to the idea of the total and complete transformation of Russia under Peter I in the following well-known words: "The Roman Emperor Augustus when he was dying felt it be the highest praise to say of himself: *I found a Rome built of bricks and leave behind one of marble*. But to say this of our Most Noble Monarch would be no praise at all. It must be acknowledged that he found a Russia made of wood and created one made of gold" (from *The Eulogy on Petr Petrovič's Birthday. . .).*[57] Peter I found another image, that of blindness and the recovery of sight, when in 1724 he sketched an outline ["*sens*"] for a solemn poem for which the poets "were to compose a full set of words." In Peter's words Russia's enemies had sworn to keep her in blindness "in order to prevent us reaching the light of reason in all matters, but worst of all in military affairs." But God had wrought a miracle: they had themselves become blind and had not noticed the wonderful metamorphosis of Russia, "as if this had been concealed from their eyes."[58]

All these images amount to one thing—the instant, miraculous and total transformation of Russia under the Emperor Peter. Kantemir found a synthetic formula:

A wise man does not let Peter's decrees drop out of his hands,
Through these we *have suddenly become a new people. . .* [59]

The image of "the new Russia" and "the new people" became a special kind of myth which came into existence already at the beginning of the eighteenth century and was passed on to the later cultural consciousness. The idea that eighteenth-century culture forms a completely new stage entirely separate from preceding development has become so deeply rooted that it has in fact never been seriously questioned. There may be disputes as to whether the break with the old ways occurred at the end or in the middle of the seventeenth century, whether the break was instantaneous or gradual, and finally whether, in the light of subsequent Russian history, to regard it positively as ensuring rapid cultural progress or negatively as entailing the loss of national character. However the actual fact of a break is generally accepted almost as it was formulated by those living at that time. It is thought that eighteenth-century culture was consistently secular, state-oriented and hostile to the church and in this way in opposition to the pre-Petrine period. At the same time this same process is presented to us as the sytematic Europeanization of Russian culture.

A closer analysis, however, provides convincing evidence that the new (post-Petrine) culture is considerably more traditional than is generally thought. This new culture is not so much constructed on "Western" models (although that was indeed the subjective feeling) as on an "inverted" structural model of the old culture. It was precisely here that a manifest separation of the more superficial and changeable cultural layer from all the deep forms took place, and these forms showed forth all the more clearly in new hypostases of consciousness.

The new culture demonstrated its blasphemous anticlerical character with zeal.[60] It is all the more interesting that the creation of the new culture reveals constant models of the medieval clerical type. (These latter, of course, are only the manifestation of the persistent models which have organized the history of Russian culture over its whole course, including, it may be assumed, the pre-Christian and Christian periods.)

3.1. The determining significance for eighteenth-century culture of the words "enlightenment" and "enlightener" [*prosveščenie* and *prosvetitel'*] is well known. These two words were the basis for the most fundamental ideas of the "Age of Reason." However they were not neologisms—they were known in pre-Petrine Russia. "To enlighten [*prosveščati*] . . . means: to christen, to consider worthy of Holy Baptism."[61] It is in this sense that the word *prosvetitel'* is used in the church canticle addressed to St. Vladimir: "O teacher of Orthodoxy and enlightener of all Rus', you have enlightened all of us with baptism."[62] Joseph of Volokolamsk called his essay against heretics by this same word (*prosvetitel'*). However the same term began to be used even during Peter I's life with reference to him as the creator of secular, Europeanized culture. In this sense the establishment of the new culture which was destroying traditional Orthodoxy was interpreted as the *second baptism* of Russia. Feofan Prokopovič's tragicomedy *Vladimir* is interesting in this connection. The comparison of Peter's reform with the apostolic "enlightenment" of Russia was not only the invention of Prokopovič. In the "*Journal or Daily Record . . . of Peter the Great*" we read: "At that time [1699— Ju. L., B. U.] I founded the Russian Order of the Holy Apostle Andrew for the good reason that the Russian nation received the first elements of the Christian faith from him."[63]

19

In Prokopovič's "tragedocomedy," Vladimir, the enlightener of Rus', figures clearly as Peter I's *alter ego*. The reform by which Christianity is introduced into Rus' ("the enlightenment") was bound to evoke in its audience associations with Peter's reforms. At the same time Peter's opponents from among the Orthodox hierarchy are depicted as pagan sorcerers who try to halt the enlightenment of Russia with the help of devils. There is an exceptionally clear substitution of roles while at the same time the general ideological scenario is retained. It is clear from the direct textual parallels that the priests Žerivol ["Bull-sacrificer"], Piar ["Drinker"] and Kurojad ["Chicken-Eater"] are to be understood as Peter's clerical opponents. In the play when Vladimir announces his wish "to change the law," Žerivol declares that there is no need for this at all:

There is no need for change where nothing
Is at fault. In our laws what defect is there?[64]

Cf. the following quotation from *The Address at the Opening of the Most Holy Governing Synod in the presence of His Imperial Majesty Peter the First* (1721): "But speaking of the accursed ones of our times! They exist and there are many of them who with all-destructive scorn have no shame in rejecting Christian doctrine, sermons and instructions, that is, the only light for our way. To what end, they say, do we need teachers, for what purpose do we need preachers? . . . with us, thank God! all is in order, those that are healthy do not need doctors, but only those that are ill. . . . For what is our world? What is our health? Has it come to such a pass, that anyone, even the most lawless, thinks himself to be honest and more holy than others like one possessed: how healthy we are. . . . This is what has happened, we have been born at a time when the blind lead the blind and the crudest ignoramuses do theology and write laughable dogma."[65]

The advocate of Orthodoxy is identified with the superstitious person who, "like one possessed," "readily believes in women's tales." Rationalism, however, is treated as "true faith," and the sovereign, as the champion of Western enlightenment, takes on the character of Prince Vladimir the equal of Apostles.

3.2. No less indicative is the fact that the generally encountered kind of free-thinking, verging into that practical godlessness which was more often to be found among the Russian gentry than theoretical atheism, often acquires the character of a *change of faith* rather than a rejection of faith. Attention is often concentrated not on the arguments, but on the actual fact of the "receiving" of atheism and the character of the person who has "transmitted" it. It is not something people become convinced of, rather they tag on to it. This brings to mind Fonvizin's well-known record of what Grigorij Teplov said about his dispute with an atheist: "The atheist shouted: 'There is no point in talking about trifles; God does not

20

exist!' I intervened and asked him: 'And who told you that God does not exist!' – 'Petr Petrovič Čebyšev told me yesterday in the Gostinyj dvor,' he replied. 'He found the right place!' I said."[66] Fonvizin himself in conversation with Teplov explained his own method of solving the problem of God's existence as follows: "I begin by considering what sort of people reject God's existence and whether they are worthy of any confidence."[67] That this is a change from one faith to another rather than a transition from a religious outlook to a philosophical view is proved by the fact that the center of attention is put on the question from whom one should obtain the true faith, by whom this conviction is transmitted and – very significantly – whether it is obtained in the correct place.

What historians of culture studying the consciousness of the average Russian gentleman/*dvorjanin*/ of the eighteenth century regard as an external Europeanized gloss under the thin cover of which they discover a pre-Petrine core may be of a quite different character.

Pre-Petrine culture did not expel the world of pagan ideas from the consciousness of the Orthodox Christian. These were preserved in the form of the lowest, demonic, layer of mythology which was acknowledged to be in existence, although it had only a limited and subordinate role. Thus a person *was obliged*, under certain circumstances, to behave in a non-Christian way. Admittedly, Christian patterns of behavior were open and public, whereas pagan ones were secret, hidden and as it were non-existent (e.g. calling on the services of a sorcerer [*koldun*] or witchdoctor [*znachar'*], which was widespread not only among the peasantry, but also among the gentry in the eighteenth century).

The "Age of Enlightenment" did not abolish but inverted this structure. The energetic struggle which was carried on by the secular state and the system of education against the Church monopoly in the sphere of culture was suddenly reinterpreted in the mass upper class consciousness as the regeneration of paganism. The coexistence of two religions persisted, but their relations were reversed: public, official life, "fashionable" ethics and secular patterns of behavior quickly absorbed the reanimated pre-Christian or Eastern features ("pagan" features from the Orthodox point of view – the maintenance of this point of view while the essence of the outlook is changed is significant). Orthodoxy, however, persisted in the "closed," secret part of life – from the chains under the cambric shirts of the men of the Petrine epoch to Potemkin's penances and nocturnal prayers after masquerades and balls.[68] By moving over into deeply intimate, almost secret, spheres, Orthodoxy even gained (it was no accident that it was of influence in childhood and old age).[69]

3.3. The subjective "Europeanization" of life had nothing in common with any real convergence with Western life-style, and at the same time definitely influenced the setting up of anti-Christian forms such as had certainly never been possible in the life of the Christian West.[70] This can be seen in the case, for example, of serf harems, an institution that was quite impossible (in a completely open and public form) in pre-Petrine life, but which became quite normal in the eighteenth century. Serf harems were not a survival from older times—they arose in the eighteenth century, and moreover the master of a harem was generally "enlightened" and a Westernizer, a person struggling against "blind ignorance." Thus in Ja. M. Neverov's *Notes* there is a description of life in P.A. Koškarov's house. He was a landowner and, at the time of writing (the early 1820s), already an old man who had preserved within his household a mode of life that evidently came into being in the 1780s:

. . . Petr Alekseevič had a harem. In fact the life of a woman servant in his house was just like being in a harem. . . . 12-15 young and beautiful girls occupied fully one-half of the house and were intended only to serve Koškarov [in addition to his permanent morganatic wife, a soldier's widow, whom he had not married in church. She was called Natal'ja Ivanovna and had by him a daughter and seven sons. He also had a permanent mistress Feoktista Semenovna, "a woman of middle years, very beautiful, lively and cultured whose mother was in charge of Koškarov's harem," as Neverov remarks. —Ju. L., B. U.] It was these who formed what I have described as the harem. The whole of the manor-house was divided into two halves—one for the men and one for the women. . . . The women's part proper began at the drawing room which was strictly speaking a neutral room because here Koškarov usually sat on one sofa and on another opposite was Natal'ja Ivanovna, and a special place was occupied by Feoktista Semenovna. Here too all the other members of the family and guests usually spent their time and there was also a piano. At the doors of the room leading to the hall there was usually a footman on duty and at the doors opposite leading into Koškarov's bedroom there was a maid on duty. The footman was not allowed to cross the threshold of the bedroom and the maid was not permitted to go into the hall. . . . It was not only the duty footman or any male servant who was forbidden to go through the doorway guarded by the maid on duty, but this prohibition applied to all male members of the family and visitors too. . . . Usually during the evening after supper the maid on duty announced at his command in a loud voice to the duty footman: "The master wishes to sleep," which was a sign for the whole family to disperse to their rooms; Natal'ja Ivanovna took her leave and departed. After her all of us left and the footman would immediately bring a simple wooden bed from the men's half into the drawing room and after putting it down in the middle of the room leave at once. The door from this room to the hall was locked and the girls brought a feather-bed, blanket and other things for Koškarov's bed from the bedroom. Meanwhile he was reciting his evening prayers from the prayer-book, while the girl on duty held a candle up and all the other girls brought their own small beds in and placed them around Koškarov's as all without fail had to sleep in the same room with him except for Matrena Ivanovna

—the head of the harem. . . . Once a week Koškarov went to the bathhouse and all the members of his harem had to go with him. Quite often some of them who were new to this environment, and so had not yet assimilated all its customs, tried to hide themselves out of modesty in the bath-house and were beaten before they came back.[71]

It should be stressed that the harem way of life was regarded as *Europeanized* and in this respect differed from the peasant way of life from which the girls had been torn and which preserved features of pre-Petrine structure. "All the girls without exception were not only literate, but also very cultured and well-read. They had at their disposal a fairly large library consisting of course almost entirely of works of fiction. For every girl the ability to read was obligatory, otherwise she would not have been able to fulfill her duties as a reader for Koškarov, as his partner at whist, etc., and so every new entrant would at once begin learning to read and write." From hearing one of the girls Neverov had in his childhood learned [Puškin's] "The Fountain of Bachčisaraj" by heart and subsequently he kept a copy-book containing the poems of Puškin and Žukovskij." "All of them of course dressed in standard European clothes, not in their own national dress." It is significant that if a girl committed some misdemeanor she would be returned to her family and as punishment "was forbidden to wear the so-called gentry's (European) dress."[72] Thus on entry into the harem she acquired "European" status, but exclusion meant that she reverted to her original "uneducated" (peasant) existence and pre-Petrine clothing.

Of course the identification of the secular ("European") and the pagan (anything non-Christian) was unconscious, and persisted mainly among those who were not well educated and had no direct contact with Europe. However, this milieu was very numerous and had a strong influence on the gentry culture as such. But the unconscious character of these ideas only served to underline their link with deep culture-forming models rather than with the individual level of education. Arakčeev used to perform a libation before breakfast with a cup of coffee at the foot of the bust of Paul I in his garden and ordered that at dinner a place should always be set for the late emperor. He probably had no notion of the pagan rituals which his actions remind us of.[73] Although he deified the the Petersburg emperors he of course had never heard of the Hellenistic idea of the epiphany of the deity in an earthly king. The situation was different: in the dualistic cultural system in Russia there were deep mechanisms which generated both pagan and Christian texts. A blow struck against either part of this dual unity inevitably led to a vigorous and rapid development of the opposite tendency.

The two-level structure of culture proved to be considerably more stable than any of its actual realizations. This was especially clearly shown in the linguistic situation in Russia.

3.4. One of the basic elements of Russian culture in the pre-Petrine epoch was the specific two-level relation between Church Slavonic and the Russian colloquial language. One of the characteristics of the new culture is thought to be the secularization of the linguistic situation: the introduction of the civil alphabet, changes in the structure of the litereary language and so one. "A heavy blow was struck against the medieval fetishism of Church Slavonic by the reform of the alphabet (1708). This clearly indicated that church ideology was no longer predominant."[74]

However, it may be noted that in this case too the two-level structure (the presence within the socium of one language marked as high prestige and one marked as lacking prestige) is preserved, although its elements are also changed. Let us take just one example. In 1694 to commemorate his safe deliverance from shipwreck, Peter I erected a wooden cross fashioned by his own hand in the Pertominsk monastery on the shores of the White Sea. The cross bore the inscription in Dutch that it was made by "Captain Peter."[75]

It is obvious that the inscription on the cross, because of its location alone, should only have been in Church Slavonic and besides, from the point of view of medieval consciousness, the possibility of placing an inscription in a "heretical" language on a cross was emphatically excluded. But this is what Peter I did, demonstrating that in his consciousness Dutch had taken the place of Church Slavonic functionally. Later this place was taken over by German and French.[76]

3.5. The continuity of some aspects of eighteenth-century consciousness in relation to the traditional forms of pre-Petrine social thought was in no way manifested in the opposition between the "Europeanized" surface of life and its "Asiatic" depths, although it was precisely this view of the relation beteeen the old and the new that was often put forward in post-Petrine culture.

> Reading these statutes, instructions and decrees you cannot avoid being impressed by the deep changes in the structure of Russian life, changes which are the result of the benevolent efforts of a solicitous government. It is as if the whole of Russian life is being shifted before your eyes from its foundations and out of the fragments of the old world which has been destroyed there is growing up a new Europeanized Russia. Impressed by this striking picture you then turn to the study of this Europeanized Russia, but making use of documents that recorded the ordinary details of daily life rather than dreams of transformation. And soon no trace remains of your mirage. From the half-jaded pages of these documents, from beneath the facade of the new official jargon you can see old Muscovite Rus' which has safely crossed into the eighteenth century and established itself within the new framework of the Petersburg empire.[77]

It is certainly not for the sake of paradox that we claim that it was this shift brought about by the "Europeanization" (i.e. by what was subjectively felt to be this) that intensified the archaic features of Russian culture. *Mutatis mutandis*, it revealed archaic semiotic models which, although they had also been present in medieval Russian culture as it was in the fourteenth and fifteenth centuries, probably went back to a considerably more ancient stratum. In this respect, contrary to the current superficial view, the eighteenth century was deeply and organically a part of Russian culture itself.

An exceptionally clear demonstration of the connection between post-Petrine eighteenth-century culture and pre-Petrine is provided by the attitude to geographical space in the "new" culture. Although the scientific and realistic conception of the earth's surface had already been formed, as of a space arranged under different latitudes and longitudes, distinguished by the ethnic character of their inhabitants, the conditions of their lives, their natural products and objects of trade, and although the earth was not to be divided into "pagan" or sinful lands and blessed or "holy" ones, residence in which respectively threatens one with destruction or leads to salvation,[78] in the mind of eighteenth-century man, especially the typical member of the Russian gentry, a different view prevailed. Strictly geographic knowledge is in this view something subordinate and technical. In Chapter 43 of the "Preamble" to Tatiščev's *Russian History*, which bore a special heading "General and Russian Geography," Tatiščev declared that "the gentry needs geography,"[79] yet apparently another opinion was more widespread and it was formulated as we know by Prostakova: "This, however, is no science for a gentleman."[80] And yet the medieval kind of attitude which attributed religious and ethical features or general value judgments to geographical space was held on to with exceptional obstinacy.

Not only among the mass of the people, but also among the gentry the idea of the West as a sinful and harmful place persisted. Against this ideological background the notion of the West as a kingdom of enlightenment and the source from which the light of Reason was to come to Russia emerges particularly clearly. Whereas in the medieval mind the holy lands (the East) were the source whence "came the spark of piety even unto the kingdom of Russia,"[81] the eighteenth century began with a clear demonstration that the new enlightener of Russia ought to make a pilgrimage to the West, following Peter I's "Great Embassy." From this point on, a journey to Paris becomes for a Russian gentleman of the eighteenth century a special kind of pilgrimage to a holy place. It is no accident that opponents of Westernization see precisely such journeys as the source of evils. For some people to join in the enlightenment, for others slavish imitation of everything French was achieved by simple movement in space. This is analogous to visiting a holy place during a pilgrimage.[82]

25

Furthermore the West was seen as "new" in relation to "old" Russia. However, here it is essential to note that the "new Russia" being established by Peter was thought of as younger not only in relation to Muscovite Rus', but also in comparison with the Western world (here we have a repetition of Ilarion's schema with the West replacing Byzantium). But whereas in this case "youthfulness" and "new ways" meant association with Western civilization, for archaists such as Griboedov or later the Slavophiles, Russia's "youthful character" was felt to be its spiritual detachment from the West. Griboedov, in his plan for a tragedy about 1812, proposed putting the following words into the mouth of the representative of the West, Napoleon: "Thoughts on this young and original nation and the peculiarities of its dress, buildings, religion and customs. Devoted to its own interest, what would it produce."[83]

3.6. The second half of the eighteenth century developed under the influence of ideas which reveal a parallelism with cultural models from the late Middle Ages in Russia. Again we find an urge to turn away from Culture in the name of Nature. Again there is a decisive break with the past, taking the form of a turning towards the primordial "natural" forms of social existence. This fundamental anti-historicism takes the form of a turn to an artificially constructed Utopia from the past.

This process of "inventing of a memory," the reconstructing of a past Utopia, made some surprising identifications possible. Thus for Radiščev[*] there is no real difference between Classical paganism, Russian paganism and the Christian Orthodox old ways. They all fit into an ideal picture combining the ancient sovereignty of the people and the world of heroes—the people's leaders ("Songs Sung at Competitions in Honor of the Ancient Slavonic Deities"), opponents of tyranny, the Stoics of antiquity (the image of Cato of Utica[**] which runs through the whole of Radiščev's work) or the Christian martyrs (*The Holy Life* [*žitie*] *of Filaret the Gracious*). When he portrayed a contemporary "strong man," F. V. Ušakov,[***] Radiščev is able to combine in him features of Cato and a Christian martyr. (It is no accident that the story was called by him "a holy Life" [*žitie*].)

For the quite different ideological standpoint of Paul I a mixing up together in one Utopian picture of the ideal chivalrous past of Catholicism and Orthodoxy is typical. He freely united detachments of Catholic

---

[*]A. N. Radiščev (1749-1802), best known for his *Journal from Petersburg to Moscow* (1790) for which he was exiled for 10 years to Siberia. Recalled to Petersburg under Alexander I and appointed to the Legislative Commission, he committed suicide in 1802. Many of Ju. M. L.'s writings are devoted to Radiščev, including his *kandidat* dissertation of 1951.

[**]Cato Uticensis, or the Younger, renowned for his integrity and valor, committed suicide rather than fall into the hands of his enemy, Caesar, in 46 BC.

[***]F. V. Usakov (1747-70), Radiscev's friend at Leipzig University, held materialist and sensualist philosophical views.

and Orthodox knights in the Maltese Order which he restored (this is itself interpreted as a restoration of the old ways!). One can hardly imagine a clearer case of historical nihilism parading as a return to the old ways from the subjective point of view.[84]

It is no more surprising to find that some writers regard Slavonic and Scandinavian mythology as identical,[85] but others see them as being sharply opposed.[86] The possibility of *selecting* for yourself the appropriate version of the old ways is highly significant (cf. N. A. L'vov's dispute with Deržavin, L'vov refusing to give up Greek mythology in favor of Scandinavian in his poetry and also preferring Slavonic to it as the "primordial" form of mythology).[87]*

If we also take into account the widespread eschatological spirit (from the social eschatologism of Russian admirers of Mably and Rousseau to the cosmic form in the writings of Bobrov**), the idea that, in total, medieval and eighteenth-century Russian culture at different historical-structural points reveal a typological parallelism, will not seem to be unfounded.

The problem of the search for the primordial sources of national culture, which was under urgent consideration at the end of the eighteenth century, is resolved therefore by means of making various identifications, at times mutually incompatible from the point of view of the previous historical tradition (cf. also on the one hand the somewhat later remarks of Galenkovskij and Gnedič on the primordial identity of the ancient Greek and the Russian national characters, and on the other, Šiškov's opinion that Church Slavonic and Russian written cultures were identical***). However, all these identifications were made against a background of sharp opposition between the national culture as reconstructed and the actual way of life of the gentry, the secular "Frenchified" culture which was felt to be alien, strange and "Western." Further, although this latter was clearly a creation of the eighteenth century, it was considered to be "senile" and the reconstruction which was set in opposition to it was paradoxically thought of as being at the same time both "primordial" and "young," unsullied by civilization. It is quite obvious that the concepts of "youthfulness" and "old age" did not have a real, chronological (historical) sense, but a purely conventional one.

---

*N. A. L'vov (1751-1803), poet, musicologist, man of letters, interested in Slavonic folklore and ancient texts. G. R. Deržavin (1743-1816), foremost poet of the Classical school in Russia.

**S. S. Bobrov (d. 1810), poet noted for his heavy Slavonic style and vivid imagination.

***Ja. A. Galenkovskij (1777-1815), poet, closely associated with Deržavin, member of Šiškov's *Beseda*. N. I. Gnedič (1784-1833), poet, translator of the *Iliad*. A. S. Šiškov (1754-1841), writer and statesman, known especially for his opposition to the Karamzinians and to Sentimentalism in general. Founder of the well-known conservative literary group, *Beseda* (lit. "discussion") of Lovers of Russian Literature. Was particularly interested in the literary tradition of early Russia and in Church Slavonic.

There is no need trying to prove that the eighteenth century in Russian culture was not a straightforward repetition of the medieval cycle—the differences in the very nature of these stages are too deep and only too obvious. Of course there was a real process of Europeanization in eighteenth-century culture. However, it rarely coincided with what the bearers of the culture themselves considered as Europeanization. Likewise, the historical tradition, as we have seen, often became active at the point where a break with tradition was subjectively taken for granted and innovation sometimes took the form of fanatic adherence to artificially constructed "traditions." If we take into account that all this intellectual work depended on the historical experience accumulated by the culture, sometimes in its direct and sometimes in its "inverted" interpretation, then the picture obtained is complex and interesting.

The essence of culture is such that in it what is past does not "pass away," that is, does not disappear as events do in the natural flow of time. By fixing itself in the memory of the culture the past acquires a constant, but at the same time potential, existence. This cultural memory, however, is constructed not only as a storehouse of texts, but also as a kind of generative mechanism. A culture which is united with its past by memory generates not only its own future, but also its own past, and in this sense is a mechanism that counteracts natural time.

A living culture cannot be a mere repetition of the past—it invariably gives birth to structurally and functionally new systems and texts. But it cannot but contain within itself the *memory* of the past. For any culture the interrelation between its potential images of the past and of the future, and the extent to which they interact, is an essential typological characteristic, one that should be taken into account in the comparison of different cultures.

The specific character of Russian culture in the period under consideration, in particular, was that the connection with the past objectively made itself felt most sharply when subjectively there was a predominant orientation towards a total break with it; and on the contrary orientation towards the past was connected with the complete eradication from memory of the real tradition and a tendency to make chimerical constructs of the past.

Translated by N.F.C. Owen

NOTES

1   Lotman & Uspenskij 1971, p. 147. English version, pp. 213-214.
2   We are not dealing here with the vexed question of historical periodization from the point of view of the modern scholar. What is of interest to us are the stages which the bearers of the culture themselves think obvious.
3   Lotman & Uspenskij 1975, p. 173.
4   See, in this connection, Veselovskij 1866, p. 174. According to Veselovskij, "a Byzantine theologian would have thought it blasphemy naively to transfer feudal notions and the *cours d'amour* to the heavenly abode, as is frequently found in Western legends . . . Giacomo [an Italian poet of the thirteenth century] describes heaven as ordered in the feudal manner, the Virgin as a noble lady with her court who gives splendid horses to her admirers."
5   *PVL*, p. 81.
6   Müller 1962, p. 87.
7   Aničkov 1914.
8   Vladimir's idols were situated on a hill above the Dnepr, i.e. up above, while the church of St. Il'ja was located on the Podol, i.e. down below. Later Vladimir made a public demonstration of *casting* the idols down into the Dnepr and founded the Christian church of St. Vasilij (his patron saint) on the hill, "on the hill where the idols of Perun and others had stood." (See *PVL*, p. 81 and p. 56). Whereas the church of St. Il'ja stood "above the Ručaj," the image of Perun was dragged down along the present day Kreščatik and the Podol slope to the Ručaj itself and then into the Dnepr (Aničkov, p. 106).
9   Ždanov 1904, pp. 70-80.
10 Kapterev 1914; see also Priselkov 1918, p. 315.
11 Bodjanskij 1863, p. 31; cf. Nikol'skij 1930, p. 80, n. 2.
12 See Uspenskij 1978.
13 Gerasimov 1910, pp. 3, 56 (*mokošá*, an evil spirit).
14 A.F. Ivanov 1969, p. 267 (*mokos'ja*, a loose woman).
15 Ivanov & Toporov 1965, pp. 90, 150, 190; Toporov 1975, p. 20.
16 Toporov 1975, pp. 19-20; see also, Čičerov 1957, pp. 55-62.
17 "O bor'be" 1865, p. 226.
18 Olearius 1656, Russian version, pp. 128-129.
19 According to the Chronicle, immediately after the acceptance of Christianity by Russia, Vladimir prayed as follows to the Lord: "'. . . Help us against our enemy and, trusting in you and your power, I will defeat his intrigues.' And saying this he commanded churches to be built and placed where the idols had stood," (*PVL*, p.81). Thus the relevant actions are directly linked with the struggle against demonic powers. And in another place the chronicler exclaims in triumph: "Where of old the pagans made sacrifice to the demons on the hills, there now are holy churches with golden roofs and built of stone, and monasteries filled with monks who constantly give glory to God in prayer, vigils, fasts and tears. It is through their prayers that the world survives." (See Šachmatov 1908, p. 264). In the same way former sacred stones, once the object of pagan worship, were sometimes set at the foundation of an Orthodox church. For instance, the stone now situated on the shores of the Pleščeev lake opposite Perejaslavl'-Zalesskij (formerly it stood in the town itself) was taken at the end of the eighteenth century to be used as the foundation stone of the church of the Holy Spirit at Perejaslavl'. A stone female statue found in the Berendeev marsh in the neighborhood of Perejaslavl'-Zalesskij was used to build the church in the

village of Lavrovo. See M.I. Smirnov 1919, p. 8.

20 Nikitina 1928, pp. 311-312. Cf. the songs about Griška Otrep'ev where it is precisely by this feature that Griška is defined as a sorcerer.

21 Efimenko 1877, p. 104. Cf. Vahros 1966, pp. 199-200.

22 Bessonov 1871, p. 29. The word *detjuški* here means *detinki*, "young fellows."

23 See Uspenskij forthcoming.

24 *Voprošenie*, in Popov 1875, p. 79. The manuscript copy quoted is of the second redaction of Feodosij's speech according to the Rumjancev Nomocanon of the sixteenth century and of South Russian composition. The authorship of this work has been disputed. Some scholars attribute it to Feodosij of the Kiev Monastery of the Caves and others to Feodosij the Greek, a writer of the twelfth century.

25 Afanas'ev 1865, p. 250. In the middle of the eighteenth century the Siberian peasant Artemij Sakalov, when arrested on suspicion of apostasy, was found to have in his possession a paper with the text of a spell. In the investigatory proceedings this text is referred to as "Concerning the Jewish heretic Perun" (State Archives of the Tjumen' oblast', Tobol'sk branch, f. 156, p. I, 1761, No. 11, 1.1. We are indebted to N.N. Pokrovskij for this information). In the old Russian legends about the battle with Mamaj, as also in the "Synopsis" by Innokentij Gizel' (where he describes the battle of Kulikovo), Perun appears as a Tatar god, cf. "Then Mamaj seeing his destruction began to call upon worthless gods, Perun, Savat, Iraklij, Gurok and Mahomet who was supposed to be his great helper" (Gizel' 1778, p. 163). See also Šambinago 1906, pp. 67, 118, 160, 187.

26 *PVL*, p. 79; see also Popov 1875, p. 17. This article, introduced into the Chronicle under the year 988, should, taking account of its content, be assigned to a later date.

For a wide number of parallels to the opposition "sky-father" vs. "earth-mother", see Ivanov & Toporov 1965, pp. 101 ff., 207. See also S. Smirnov 1914, pp. 262-263, 266-268. It is curious that these ideas are reflected even in personal names (anthroponymics): see "The monk Selivestr, known as Mother-Earth" in a manuscript of the Rumjancev Collection, No. 154, Folio 375. (See Djuvernua 1894, p. 95).

It is highly significant in this respect that there are frequent prohibitions in the Old Russian books of penance (*epitimejniki*) against men lying prostrate on the ground, or on the belly; in some texts this rule is expounded in greater detail: "If anyone has shouted at his father or mother or has hit them or lain on the ground as if playing with a woman. 15 days penance." See Almazov 1894, p. 151, No. 44, and also pp. 155, 195, 275, 279; S. Smirnov 1914, p. 273, and also appendix, p. 46, No. 15. Cf. in this connection, the use of obscene language (*maternaja rugan'*) as an element of pagan behavior: it is no accident that the Old Russian preacher in his denunciation of the use of bad language says that an obscene word offends the Mother (*mat'*) of God, our second mother who is beloved by everyone, and "the third mother is the earth from which we get our food"; this link between swearing and Mother Earth is clearly conditioned by pre-Christian ideas. In view of what has been said above, the idea found in Old Russian homilies that the use of obscene language is the same as using "Jewish speech" (S. Smirnov 1914, pp. 274, 156) is quite typical.

27 Popov 1875, p. 25. The text quoted is even more indicative in that it is obviously a reinterpretation of the reference to the "Polovtsian clothes" and "horned headgear", which we find in other editions of the work (the story of Petr Gugnivyj); see ibid., p. 26 and also p. 27.

28 Popov 1875, p. 81. This passage has been introduced here into the *Voprošenie* which we have already quoted. It does not occur, however, in other copies of this work and must have been interpolated later.

29 Indeed, in this respect too, various kinds of joke sayings (*pribautki*), which are often constructed as parodic travesties of various texts of the traditional kind, are highly indicative. (Cf. Šejn 1895). In a number of cases of this type the travesty leads more or less organically to the realization of pagan ideas. See for example the following *pribautka* from Vologda:

> This year have come new testaments. A young bagman hastened from the post bringing new testaments. Truth is dead, untruth lives. Falsehood with her crozier has departed. It is written and inscribed from Boris's old man; all without deceit, it is written, not by Roman. Old man Vlas has come, if I such powers were given for this hour and a flock of sheep, I would become their spiritual father, I would give them communion, and drive them in a flock. I would make wheels and ride to heaven. In heaven everything is topsy-turvy: the churches are made of swipes*, the doors of tripes. I grabbed my tripes and tripped into church. Now in the church everything is topsy-turvy: the gods are clay, their pates are wooden; I picked at their pates, ate up the oaten meal.** I began to gather the crumbs and to commemorate Father Yawnmouth [*Pop Zevorot*]. Father Yawnmouth, do not pass by my door, I shall eat you too. (Potanin 1899, Appendix, p. 523). [Translation by Professor R.E.F. Smith].

Traces of paganism ("revived untruth") can be observed here both in the image of the clay idols of gods and in the image of Vlas-Volos, the protector of sheep, etc. We take this opportunity of thanking A.F. Belousov for drawing our attention to this text and also for the evidence quoted in Note 30.

30 This is an account from an anonymous English source, *A Relation concerning the Particulars of the Rebellion lately raised in Muscovy by Stenko Razin* (In the Savoy, printed by Tho. Newcombe, 1671).

> And so he [Razin, Ju.L., B.U.] with his associates, went away to their own Countrey about the River *Don* where he began to act afresh his villainy in Ecclesiastical Matters, driving away many Priests, and hindring Divine Service, and intruding himself into Church affairs. For a pattern of the glorious Ceremonies, which this *Cosack-Pope* introduced, take this, that instead of the usual Ceremonies of Marriage performed by the Priests in *Russia*, he made the contracted couple to goe several times round a Tree dancing, and thus they were married after *Stenko*'s mode. He also cast out blasphemous words against the Savior of the World.

The death sentence which was read to Razin at his place of execution included the following:

> An. 7178 alias 1670. *Thou Villain*, together with thy companions, forgetting the Fear of God, and deserting the Holy Catholick and Apostolick Church, didst, when you were upon the *Don*, speak blasphemous words against our Lord Christ, and prohibit to build Churches and to perform Divine Service in those that were in being; driving away all the Priests, and making such people, as would marry, instead of practising the usual Ceremonies of Marriage, to go round about a Tree. (English text quoted in Man'kov 1968, pp. 95, 103.)

31 Šeremeteva 1928, p. 109; cf. the expression "to be married round a fir tree,

---

* Russian *galašnaja*. B.A.U. & Ju. M.L. comment that this is from *galacha*, "turnip." We prefer the meaning given in Dal', "small beer" or "swipes". (R.E.F.S.)

** Probably a form of *kut'ja* or ritual porridge regularly used in ritual suppers commemorating parents (i.e. ancestor worship) as well as in Christian feasts at peasant level. (R.E.F.S.)

round a bush" [*vencat' vkrug eli, vkrug kusta*], which is used of an unmarried couple; see Dal', I, p. 331. Dal' comments on this expression: "Is this just a joke, or something handed down from paganism?" The romance "The Wedding" [*Svad'ba*] by the Romantic poet A.V. Timofeev* has had a typical fate in this respect. The poet, of whom Senkovskij** said he would be "a second Byron," drew a naive contrast between the Romantic cult of Nature and the Christian wedding ceremony, and apparently without realizing it himself, regenerated a number of ritualistic ideas from paganism. The text, which was set to music by Dargomyžskij, came ultimately to be viewed through the prism of ideas about women's emancipation and of George Sand-ism: it became a favorite song with the progressive intelligentsia of the 1860's and through them passed into the repertoire of the Russian democratic intelligentsia of the end of the nineteenth century and early twentieth century.

32   Stefan of Perm', in his accusation against the *Strigol'niki* (the Shearers) of 1386 mentions that they pray "at crossroads." See Kazakova & Lur'e 1955, p. 240. According to Kozma of Prague, the pagan Slavs used to go to crossroads to conjure up spirits (Kozma of Prague, Russian version, p. 173). Under conditions of the coexistence of Christianity and paganism, crossroads and road junctions were "evil" places where one went to do witchcraft, divinations, and so on.

33   Afanas'ev 1865, Vol. I, p. 143; S. Smirnov 1914, pp. 256, 257, 277-279.

34   Mel'nikov 1910, part II, p. 275.

35   Zelenin 1915, p. 581; Vas. Smirnov 1920, p. 39. Smirnov also notes that the *chlysty* (sectarians) bury their dead *in a marsh* which also coincides with the burial place of evil dead (*založnye*). For details of these and how they were buried in general, see Zelenin 1916, I, Petrograd.

Evidently a similar interpretation could be given to the evidence that the priestless Old Believers "bury their dead . . . near their barns and sheds" (Zelenin 1914, p. 153). It is true that in specialized ethnographical literature there are no references to the burial of the unhallowed dead in such places. In Šolochov's novel *Tichij Don* [*Quiet Flows the Don*], however, there is mention of the burial of an unhallowed man *near the barn* (M. Šolochov, *Tichij Don*, L. 1945, p. 429).

36   Kozma of Prague, Russian version, pp. 107, 173; see also Kotljarevskij 1868, p. 93. Hence the word *roščenie* (*rošča*, a grove) to designate an ancient burial ground. (In this sense the word is retained in the local dialects of Kostroma; see Vas. Smirnov, 1920, p. 36; Bekarevič 1901, pp. 335, 367, 402, 406, 407, 416, 425.)

37   Pečerin 1932, p. 28. Compare the curious evidence that in Russian northern districts tumuli were erected for unhallowed dead, this evidently being a continuation of the pagan tradition of raising burial mounds (Maksimov 1908-1913, VIII, p. 294).

38   In this example it is a question of burial in an ancient (pagan) burial mound. But alongside this some unhallowed dead were covered with *žal'niki* (tumuli), thus continuing the pagan tradition. (Maksimov, op. cit. p. 294.) It is this tradition which probably explains the widespread custom of throwing sticks and other objects over the bodies of such dead (see Zelenin 1916, passim).

39   It should be borne in mind that even as late as the sixteenth century, regular burials of the dead might take place in pagan burial mounds rather than in Christian cemeteries. In the Vodskaja *pjatina* (district) of Novgorod, for instance, as reported in 1534 to the Archbishop of Novgorod, Makarij (the future Metropolitan of Moscow),

_____

*   A.V. Timofeev (1812-1883), writer of Romantic leanings, associated with Senkovskij's *Biblioteka dlja čtenija* journal.

**   O.I. Senkovskij (1800-1858), writer, publisher, orientalist, wrote under pseudonym "Baron Brambeus."

those who kept up the ancient pagan traditions did not go to church or to confession. Instead they summon *arbui* (pagan priests), and "it is said that they place their dead in fields on burial mounds and burial grounds using the services of those same pagan priests. They do not put them in church cemeteries." See Makarij's document sent to the Vodskaja *pjatina* on the eradication of pagan temples and ceremonies in the publication, *Dopolnenija* 1846, p. 28. See also the document of the Bishop of Novgorod, Feodosij, to the Vodskaja *pjatina* of 1548, whose content is analogous, in which the quoted phrase is repeated letter for letter, though in place of *v selech* (in the villages) we find *v lesech* (in the forests), which is probably more likely, op. cit. p. 58. It may be assumed that it was not only among the Finnish population that such traditions persisted.

40 Kirša Danilov 1958, pp. 9, 292.

41 Ibid., pp. 181-182, 409.

42 Ibid., pp. 259-260, 479.

43 *Pamjatniki* 1927, columns 192-193. Cf. the same place in other editions of Avvakum's *Life*, columns 42, 119. Translation from Archpriest Avvakum, *The Life written by himself*, ed. Kenneth N. Brostrom, Ann Arbor, 1979 (Michigan Slavic Publications, 4), pp. 77-78.

44 *Pamjatniki* 1927, column 32; cf. in other editions, col. 111, 186.

45 A particular example of this was that whereas cultures oriented towards "new ways" created an ideal of complex and cultivated behavior, the "old ways" were invariably connected with "natural" behavior that strove towards coarseness as the norm.

46 Lotman 1977.

47 *Pamjatniki* 1927, col. 268.

48 Ibid.

49 Ibid., column 283. Analogously, in Kirša Danilov 1958, in the song, "There over the hills came the Bucharians," nonsense phrases such as "*Vesur, vesur, valachtan-tararach-tarandarufu*" are treated as being at the same time Polish, Hebrew and "Bucharian." These are clearly regarded as being a single "wrong" (i.e. sorcerer's) language; pp. 275, 488-489.

50 Gogol's story "A Terrible Vengeance" [*Strašnaja mest'*] provides us with a striking example of this kind: "Beyond Kiev there appeared an unheard of wonder. All the gentlemen and the *hetmans* assembled and gazed in amazement at this wonder. Suddenly it became possible to see for a long way, to all the ends of the world. Far away the Liman showed blue, beyond it the Black Sea stretched out. Men of experience were able to make out the Crimea, rising like a mountain out of the sea and the marshy Sivač. Galicia was visible *to the left*." (Gogol', *PSS*, Vol. I, p. 275. Our italics, Ju.L., B.U.) If "men of experience" could see from Kiev to the Crimea, then without doubt they were facing south. Western Galicia must have been on their *right*. But the left position was an invariant feature of the West in the Russian medieval mind, not a relative one. And Gogol with his sharp historical and psychological intuition perceived this.

51 See Uspenskij 1977. Of particular significance in this connection is the attitude to the beard, which for many years divided Russia into two mutually antagonistic parts. For the one group, the beard was an essential attribute of Orthodoxy, and even of piety in general, but for the others it became a symbol of "darkness." Just as the Old Believers would not allow shaven people into their churches, the adherents of reform [*novoobrjadcy*] might not permit people with beards to attend their solemn religious ceremonies. Il'ja Bajkov, Alexander I's well-known coachman, had difficulties because of this in gaining access to the Kremlin for the

ceremony of leavetaking from the late Emperor's body (see Šilder 1898, p. 436). In precisely the same way some years later, the artist Al. Ivanov had difficulty in being admitted to the ceremony of consecration of St. Isaac's Cathedral. He thought of himself as an icon painter and so had a beard and wore Russian dress. Count Gur'ev's words to him were: "What! Are you a Russian? I can't possibly let you into the ceremony in this dress and with a beard. If you were French it would be different, but not a Russian!" (Zummer 1925, p. 94). It is extraordinary that at that time it was precisely for a Russian and not for a foreigner that a beard could cause difficulty in entering an Orthodox church!

52   It is essential to note that these processes also went on before the schism, and so to some extent affected the Old Believers too. In this case, however, they did not develop further and did not leave any significant trace.

53   Ioffe 1944-1945.

54   For the dispute about unison, see, for example, Kapterev 1909, pp. 8-9, 84-105. For *chomovoe* and *narečnoe* singing, see Uspenskij 1968, pp. 39-40, 61-65.

55   This may be compared on the one hand with the medieval way of training apprentices, in the course of which the future craftsman had to repeat the complexities and difficulties of his master's path including unproductive efforts, and on the other with a rational course teaching the pupil how to achieve the results of knowledge by the shortest route. In the first case a *path* is taught, in the second, the *result* is what is imparted.

56   Prokopovič 1760, p. 145.

57   Ibid., p. 113.

58   S.M. Solov'ev 1963, p. 553.

59   Kantemir 1956, p. 75. (The italics are ours, Ju. L., B.U.)

60   For the deliberateness and semiotic character of Peter's "blasphemy", see Uspenskij 1977.

61   Petr Alekseev 1818, p. 348.

62   Quoted from Sreznevskij 1893, p. 69. Ivan the Terrible speaks in just these terms in his first letter to Kurbskij where he mentions "the great Tsar Vladimir who brought enlightenment to all Russia by means of Holy Baptism" (*Poslanija*, p. 9).

63   *Žurnal*, p. 7. This explains the addition of the epithet "first-called" to the name of the Order. In the statute of 1720 this tendency was somewhat masked and the Order was represented (in fact quite falsely) as being a continuation of the ancient Scottish Order of St. Andrew. The attempt to present *ex post facto* something that is the fruit of their own creation and in accordance with ancient Russian models as a product of Western influence because this is more prestigious, is extremely characteristic.

64   Prokopovič 1961, p. 178.

65   Prokopovič 1765, pp. 66-67.

66   Fonvizin 1959, p. 103.

67   Ibid., p. 102.

68   In this connection see the fine characterization of Potemkin given by the Prince de Ligne (Lovjagin 1905, pp. 666-667).

69   With reference to the "glimpsing" of pre-Petrine norms and ideas through a Europeanized life-style, Labzina's memoirs are of exceptional interest. See Labzina 1914.

70   In Russia, the West was regarded as anti-Christian and so any "development towards infidel ideas" in the way of life was felt to be Europeanization. Objectively, however, this "Europeanization" was often a further departure from the actual norms of European life.

71   *Zapiski Januarija Michajloviča Neverova (1810-1826 gg)*, quoted in Rusov 1911,

pp. 138-143. Neverov lived as a guest not a servant in Koškarov's household.
72 Ibid., pp. 147-148.
73 Savvaitov 1872, pp. 471-472.
74 Vinogradov 1938, p. 79.
75 Maksimov 1908-1913, X, p. 255, VIII, p. 130, IX, pp. 212-213; Nikitenko 1955, p. 154. Later this cross was moved to the cathedral in Archangel'sk.
76 Lotman & Uspenskij 1975, p. 200.
77 Kizevetter, "Novizna i starina v Rossii XVIII stoletija. Reč' pered magisterskim disputom" in Kizevetter 1912, pp. 268-269.
78 Lotman 1965.
79 Tatiščev 1950, p. 214.
80 Fonvizin 1959, I, p. 163.
81 Poslanija, p. 9.
82 Lotman & Uspenskij 1974, pp. 275-278.
83 Griboedov 1956, p. 343.
84 This makes sense in its own terms. The supporters of the ideas of historical progress and the irreversibility of the forward march of history think historically and study the past as historians. (The emergence of such concepts was one of the basic innovations of post-Petrine culture and, in view of the topic of this article, is not discussed here. It was Karamzin in particular who gave expression to this real, not mythological Europeanization.) The proponents of the "return to the old ways" think in a fundamentally mythological way and see the past as a beautiful legend. For example, M.F. Orlov, while protesting against the monarchic conception of the origin of the Russian state put forward by Karamzin, did not offer any other interpretation of the sources, but demanded rather "a glittering and probable hypothesis" (see M.F. Orlov's letter to P.A. Vjazemskij of July 4, 1818, in LN, Vol. 59, M., 1954).
85 Lotman 1962, pp. 362-374.
86 See letter from N.A. L'vov to G.R. Deržavin of May 24, 1799, in Poèty XVIII veka, II, pp. 246-247.
87 Ibid. For L'vov, the concepts "Russian song" and "Gypsy song" turn out to be synonymous in certain usages (see Artamonova 1933, p. 283).

NEW ASPECTS IN THE STUDY OF EARLY RUSSIAN CULTURE

Ju. M. Lotman, B.A. Uspenskij

The last three decades have seen an exceptionally energetic and intense development of research in the field of early Russian literature and culture. In the pre-war period it was Puškin studies, and to some extent the study of the eighteenth century, that set the standard for literary scholarship and were the testing grounds for new historical and literary ideas; today, however, there is no doubt that priority has passed to the Russian Middle Ages. In bringing this about the Sector for Early Russian Literature at the Academy of Sciences of the USSR (*Puškinskij Dom*) has played a particularly important organizational and scholarly part. It is enough, to give some idea of the work done, to point to the thirty-one volumes of *Trudy Otdela Drevnerusskoj Literatury* (TODRL) [*Works of the Sector of Early Russian Literature*], not to mention a whole series of publications and monographs, many of which have broken fresh ground.

The large number of works of textology, editing, historical and literary research, which have been undertaken, have in fact changed the whole established system of ideas about the culture of early Russia. There is a need now for new works of theoretical interpretation to summarize and generalize the material that has been gathered. One response to this need has been the series of monographs by D.S. Lichačev, the most significant of which, *Poetics of Early Russian Literature* (Lichačev, 1967), is a new and original approach to early Russian literature as an artistic phenomenon. The many works published by Lichačev's pupils have followed in the same lines. There is no need to list them here, though we should like to make special mention of Pančenko's valuable study of the culture of poetry in the seventeenth century. [1]

The latest book by Lichačev and Pančenko, *The "World of Laughter" in Early Russia* (Lichačev and Pančenko 1976) is a landmark for literary studies in the last few years. [2]

The new book, although it contains much new factual material, is not large (200 pp.) and it might seem that in this respect it is outshone by many more extensive works. However it is just this compressed and summarizing quality that brings out the richness of its content.

One of the features of a truly creative work is that, in solving the problems raised by preceding scholarship, it poses new questions, and in this way not only concludes what has been done but also stimulates further research. A truly creative work then must contrast with other lifeless monographs, supposedly giving the last word on their subjects, but which, while summing up what has been done, lead nowhere, like a corridor which comes to a dead end. Of course an author who discovers new problems is always in a more vulnerable position: the newer and more fruitful the problem, the greater the risk of contention.

The book which has prompted this article has precisely these qualities which promise heated and prolonged discussion. Its authors have focussed attention on an exceptionally important, but until now neglected phenomenon of Russian culture; yet they leave it to the reader to think through the numerous and varied implications for scholarship, and the shifts in traditionally held literary and historical ideas, which must follow from the introduction of such questions into the history of culture.

The book is devoted to the investigation of concepts and problems. Its value first and foremost is that it raises questions which until now have lain outside the purview of scholarly research and which, if they did crop up, were treated as isolated phenomena quite apart from the general principles of Russian culture.

In speaking of the creative originality of this research, we have in mind not just the novelty of the conception on which it is founded—in the best works of recent years we have grown accustomed to finding new and sometimes bold ideas. What is new here is something deeper, touching the very nature of how we do research.

Following longstanding tradition, historians equate culture with the sum of all the written documents. Whatever is not directly reflected in them—oral communication, people's behavior in various uncodified situations, gesture, mimicry and everyday ritual—is definitely excluded. Instead of pointing out the obstacles that hinder us from getting this material, the material is declared to be non-existent. Similarly, no one faces the question of how the nature of written texts is itself affected by the fact that they are only a part and not the whole of the culture. Yet we know perfectly well that if we stay within the limits of a text, though we may grasp its internal meaning, we have no chance of determining its essential function in the integral system of the culture, that is, whether it is true or false, sacred or blasphemous, high or low.

Imagine a scholar from the distant future studying any period close to the present, and assume he has only literary sources surviving in the form of books available to him. If he applied the laws of the texts available to him over the whole complexity of the culture, he would inevitably get a picture that is out of focus, or rather, thoroughly distorted. We can be sure that he would not get at the layer which for the actual bearers of the culture is not only obvious, but also deeply significant. And yet this oral, uncodified cultural layer is a key to the written texts, enabling us to decipher their real content.

ITake for instance even that sphere of culture which seems to be most adequately reflected in texts, language. Even here the researcher would be faced with a totally distorted picture: he might naturally assume that people of the period actually spoke as the written documents represent (e.g., in the field of phonetics he would be bound to conclude that *okan'e** was prevalent since it determines the norms of the written language at the present time). The losses and distortions would be all the greater when he tried to reconstruct other, more complex cultural spheres which are founded on a division into domains in principle belonging to written culture and domains in principle excluded from it: the domain of texts on the one hand, and that of behavior and actions on the other; the zone of cultural canons and the zone of permitted anomalies, exceptions to the rules. If we add to this that even the actual sphere of written culture is always hierarchical in respect of value and prestige, and that the place of any text in this hierarchy cannot be established unless one goes outside the world of texts into the extra-textual life surrounding it, then it becomes clear how narrow and inadequate the "world of literary texts" is in relation to the whole "world of culture" in any epoch.

In practice, no researcher can study — for this would simply be impossible — the "world of texts" is isolation, unrelated to extra-textual ideas, everyday common sense, the whole complex of life's associations. However, the researcher of past cultures invariably pursues a simple course in this respect. He sets texts from past historical epochs in *his own* world of accepted ideas, using the latter as a key for deciphering the former. That this procedure is misguided is as obvious as it is widespread. [3]

The originality of the book by Lichačev and Pančenko lies in the fact that their object of research are not texts as such, but texts as part of the culture as a whole, texts indissolubly bound to behavior. And behavior they regard as dependent on a wide context, having its own grammar, stylistics, and genres. In this way culture as such with its literary tradition, speech habits, gestures, and everyday pattern of life, etc. becomes the object of study. Moreover all of this is associated with a wide range of problems to do with world view, thereby forming an integral cultural and ideological universe. A text can only be understood if it is compared extensively with the culture, or more precisely with the behavior of the people contemporary with it; and their behavior can likewise only be made sense of if it is juxtaposed with a large number of texts. The texts provide us with an explanation for the actual behavior of people, even behavior which may seem to us in modern times, from our enlightened point of view, to be strange and morbid, and in this way we are able to make sense of it, see a pattern, a system, the strict ethical code and a very individual kind of beauty. Given such an approach, the world of early

---

* Pronunciation of the unstressed vowel 'o' in the same way as in a stressed position; normally in standard speech it is modified.

Russian culture is no longer something that is alien and remote from the researcher, like something put under a microscope: it becomes a picture that is alive and animated. The investigator ceases to be an outside observer, he enters this world, free of condescension and prejudice, ready to understand its logic, remote though it is from ours. Where traditional literary history failed to find anything worth its attention, he finds complex phenomena of spiritual life in their most popular form.

The subject matter of Lichačev and Pančenko's book is drawn from a broad range of facts from early Russian culture, facts which the authors dub the "world of laughter." Here we find various types of literary parody, the "theater of life," linguistic and behavioral travesties, the penetration of play into medieval man's "serious" behavior. Into the broad frame of this picture the authors inscribe various facts from Russian cultural history, from the behavior of the holy fool* on the square of old Russian towns to the theatricalized forms of the time of the *opričnina*** reform of Ivan the Terrible.

The "World of Laughter" in Early Russia, as we have already said, is a book that evokes in its readers the urge to develop, discuss and sometimes even to dispute the authors' ideas. The last thing it does is to predispose the reader to a dispassionate or disinterested reading.

We think it appropriate therefore to consider some possible further lines of research for those who are in agreement with the authors' basic approach, and who intend to follow the course they have delineated. The first step along this path, it seems, ought to be a preciser definition of the very concept of "world of laughter" or "laughter culture." This concept was brought into scholarly usage by Bachtin[4] and has sparked off a wide response, having at once proved its fruitfulness as a theoretical approach to literary history. The authors' use of this term in a specific sense in their book is not only justified but fruitful, since it enables us to identify and bring together a broad group of cultural phenomena for which previously there was no name and which had not even been noticed. However since Bachtin's weighty ideas have already become established and since the reader will naturally tend to link the term with Bachtin's notions, care should be taken to make a clear distinction between the concept of "laughter culture" as it emerged on the basis of West European material [Bachtin's subject matter] and the specifically Russian phenomena described by Lichačev and Pančenko.[5]

Laughter in the conception of medieval culture developed by Bachtin is an element that lies outside the severe religious and ethical restraints

---

* *Jurodivyj*, "God's fool," simpleton to whom divine powers are ascribed.

** *Opričnina*, Ivan the Terrible's special elite and the lands assigned to them. On the derivation of this word, see below Part III, ch. 1, note 87.

imposed on people's behavior at that time. According to Bachtin, laughter, because of its popular and unruly nature and its general tendency to debunk, abolishes the medieval socio-ethical hierarchy; it is essentially free of religion and of the influence of the state. Laughter lifts medieval man into the world of a popular carnival Utopia, plucking him away from the power of social institutions.

Among the phenomena of Russian culture reviewed by Lichaćev and Panćenko many may indeed be made sense of from the standpoint of this conception of laughter. For example, the authors turn their attention to the fact that in works, defined by V. Adrianova-Peretc as literary documents of democratic satire,[6] "there is mockery of the self or at least of the social group. The authors of medieval and, in particular, of early Russian works more often than not use their own persons to make their readers laugh" (p. 9). This approach makes it possible to modify the established understanding of these documents, since we can see in them a fusion of two essentially different elements: popular satire and carnival laughter. However, also significant for the Russian Middle Ages was a different attitude to many of the objects classified by the authors as laughable. Some "laughter images," active in the system of medieval Russian culture, bear no trace of ambivalence and do not lie outside the bounds of the official medieval ("serious") culture. Russian medieval Orthodox culture is organized around the opposition holiness vs. Satanism. Holiness excludes laughter (cf.: "Christ never laughed"*). However, it has two possible forms: severe ascetic seriousness that rejects the earthly world as temptation, and a pious acceptance of it as God's creation. The second variety, from Archpriest Avvakum's little hen** to Father Zosima in *The Brothers Karamazov*, is linked with inner merriment, expressed in a smile. Thus holiness allows both ascetic severity and a pious smile, but it excludes laughter.

The opposite axiological pole in the ideas of the Russian Middle Ages has a different attitude to laughter. The Devil (and the whole demonic world) is held to possess the features of "holiness inside out" and belongs to the inverted, "left-hand" world. Therefore this world is blasphemous in its very essence, that is, it is not serious. This is a world that guffaws; it is no accident that the Devil may be called the "jester" [šut] in Russian. The kingdom of Satan is the place where sinners groan and gnash their teeth while the devils laugh:

And above them there circles with laughter loud
A black six-winged tiger . . . ***

* A saying from St. John Chrysostom.

** The bird lived and ate with Avvakum's family during their arduous return from exile in Siberia, miraculously providing them in their dire need with two eggs a day.

*** From a Nekrasov poem, "*Vlas.*"

40

Unlike the ambivalent popular carnival laughter, in Bachtin's understanding, the blasphemous belly laugh of the Devil does not shatter the world of medieval ideas: it forms part of that world. The laughing man in Bachtin's conception stood outside the medieval value system—neither on the way to salvation, nor on the path to perdition, he simply lived; whereas the blasphemer with the belly laugh was within this world. While flinging himself into the abyss of perdition and turning his back on God, he did not reject the idea of God. Having crossed over into Satan's camp, he changed his placed in the hierarchy, but he did not deny the fact of its existence.

The external sign of this kind of laughter is that it is not infectious. For those who are not in league with Satan, it is terrifying rather than comical. Prince Dmitrij Ševyrev's writhings while he sang a hymn to Jesus at the stake might cause Ivan the Terrible and his henchmen to laugh aloud, but they hardly seemed funny to the Muscovites who were looking on.

Accordingly, in early Russia it was considered sinful to provoke laughter,[7] and also to laugh excessively, "to laugh till you cry."[8] "Oh, grief to those who are false and full of laughter," exclaims an Old Russian writer,[9] significantly equating these two attributes. If a person laughs, he risks ending up in the sphere of diabolical, sinful, and blasphemous behavior.[10]

Blasphemy has an exceptionally important place in medieval Russian culture. Lichačev and Pančenko are pioneers in their efforts to explicate this phenomenon in historico-cultural terms, and their thoughts on this topic merit the utmost respect. However, it seems that just as Adrianova-Peretc's proposal to interpret blasphemy as an early democratic, anti-feudal form of satire, though it makes some essential aspects of the phenomenon clear, did not cover it fully and was to some extent a simplification, so also to view blasphemy through the prism of Bachtin's conception of laughter, while this does indeed take us further in our understanding of this complex problem, at the same time misplaces the emphasis.

Blasphemy as the "affirmation through negation" of the norms and laws of the medieval world-structure should be distinguished from the heritage of pagan magic (although for the actual bearers of the culture these two things may be identified), which persisted in the actual beliefs of man in early Russia.

Medieval man might make sure of success, safety and good fortune in two ways: on the one hand by prayer or by seeking the protection of the saints and the church, and, on the other, through a system of "black" actions: sorcery, charms, and spells, etc. These two methods complemented and duplicated one another like two mirror-image systems. In this way the system of magic actions would take on the character of a kind of inverted church ceremony or of a "left-hand world." It might even incorporate ritual laughter (as distinct from the ritual seriousness of behavior in church). But it was not funny in the full sense and was not perceived as being comic. A man who sought the help of a sorcerer was not in the least merry. Hence Lichačev's interesting remarks on the inside-out world and its function in the culture of early Russia call for firsthand research in order to distinguish phenomena that are truly humorous from those which, while sharing many features, generally speaking, are not.

It should be stressed that this inside-out character of magic rituals was brought about by subjective and objective causes. On the one hand, from the standpoint of Christian ideas, traditional pagan rituals seemed like "anti-behavior," and merged with anti-Christian behavior in the strict sense of the word. On the other hand, Slavonic paganism, as we know, was very closely involved with the cult of the dead and thus with ideas about the world beyond the grave. And moreover, this other world, even in pre-Christian beliefs, was characterized by being in principle "inverted" in relation to the world this side of the grave, being its mirror-image (cf. the ideas on the switch of right and left, top and bottom, etc.). And so inverted behavior, involving all kinds of such switches, automatically transfers the agent into the sphere of the other world which is controlled by the powers of darkness (which in many cases have come down from the heathen deities).

From this the idea arises of the "inside-out," inverted world as a Satanic one. This is connected with one most remarkable difference between pagan elements in the West European carnival (according to Bachtin) and the Russian ceremonies that are analogous to it. In the West European carnival the formula runs: "if it's funny, it's not to be feared" —since laughter removes a man from the confines of the serious medieval world where he is victim of social and religious "terrors" (prohibitions). In Russia laughter, from the Yuletide and Shrovetide rituals to *Evenings on a Farm near Dikan'ka* by Gogol, is both "funny and scaring." Play does not take a man outside the bounds of the world as such, but allows him to penetrate into its forbidden zones where to pass time seriously would be equivalent to perdition. Therefore it is always play, simultaneously comic and dangerous. For instance, soothsaying at Yuletide, one of the most cheerful moments in the peasant calendar, is at the same time frightening (the evenings from 1st to 5th January in the old calendar are in fact known as "the terrifying evenings" [*strašnye večera*]). It entails playing with the powers of darkness and in many cases is accompanied by a public renunciation of Christianity (soothsayers usually remove their crosses) and there is direct invocation of demons;[11] according to a great deal of evidence. Yuletide soothsaying is characterized by nervous tension, occasionally ending in hysterical outbursts.

Neither blasphemy, which took a "fateful delight . . . in trampling on the cherished sacred objects,"* nor magical laughter, which is connected with the seeking of aid from the "black," inside-out world, belong strictly speaking to "laughter culture," since they totally lack its main element, comicality.

The foregoing compels us to pay special attention to the various instances of liturgical parody. To what extent were such phenomena characteristic for early Russian literary, i.e. written, culture? Can we consider it to be pure chance that all the surviving texts of this type date from no earlier than the seventeenth century (and as a rule, even no earlier than the second half of that century), that is, from a time marked by the intensive Western influence vigorously encouraged by South-Western Russia? If we consider these works outside the perspective of their social effect in the general context of Russian seventeenth-century literature, but from the point of view of their genesis, is it not possible in general to explain the appearance of such texts by the influence, so characteristic for the seventeenth century, of South-Western Russia on Great Russian literary culture? There is no doubt in its turn that the attitude to blasphemy and laughter in South-Western Russia was different from that in Muscovy: as we know, that region was subject to the direct influence of Western literary and cultural tradition, and in the West *parodia sacra* and like phenomena had by no means always a blasphemous significance.[12] Probably it was no accident that the appearance and spread of parodic texts on religious themes, being one way or another connected with the Europeanization of Russian culture, is met with mainly in the relatively educated milieu of school and seminaries (cf. the celebrated "Hymn of praise to a corn cob" [*"Akafist kukuruze"*]). It does in any case seem to be significant that at the end of the seventeenth century, satirical works (not only on religious themes) were generally accepted in Russia as translations from Polish, even if they were of purely Russian origin.[13]

On the other hand, in the oral, non-literary sphere of culture, parody of church ceremony might of course also take place. But if texts of the type of "The Liturgy to the Tavern"[*"Služba kabaku"*] were, to quote Bachtin, "outside the realm of the church and religion," then the analogous behavior during the Yuletide and Midsummer games had first and foremost a blasphemous character and so was significant in religious terms. Blasphemy cannot in principle go outside the framework of the religious universe. It simply acquires within these limits an antithetical value. The parodic Yuletide funeral (with the "priest" in a chasuble made of a bast mat, a clay jug from the wash-stand serving as the censer and instead of the words of the funeral service a choice selection of oaths),[14] with its markedly blasphemous character, belongs to the general plane of magical

---

* From Alexander Blok's poem, "To the Muse."

anti-behavior. In this way precisely the same behavior pattern from a particular time came to fulfil quite a different function and be perceived quite differently in the upper and lower strata of the culture; but this is a consequence of the Europeanization of literary culture which already began in pre-Petrine times and which predetermined Peter's reforms.

* * *

The great merit of the book under review is the authors' attempt to juxtapose literary texts with the behavior they induced in the writer or extempore performer on the one hand, and with that of the audience on the other. Historico-literary and historico-cultural problems are related to problems of historical psychology, behavior patterns in play, and the various forms of behavior associated with the theater and entertainment in the tradition and real life of early Russia. An intricate network of questions directly and deeply relating to many of the mysteries of Russian history arises in the reader's mind.

The conviction has already been expressed many times that one of the weaknesses in our historical scholarship is that insufficient attention has been paid to questions of behavioral psychology, whether it is the general culture of an epoch or the individual aspect of this problem. Consequently the link between the motives for the general social behavior of people or large social groups, and each individual's personal behavior, is missing.

The authors pay considerable attention to the psychology of social behavior in early Russia. The problem of the spectacle and of theatricality in the events and actions of everyday life are of great academic interest. The analysis of play elements in Ivan the Terrible's behavior and of elements of the spectacle in the behavior of the early Russian holy fools is intensely interesting to read, since it enables us to discover the psychological motivation for actions and events which seem "strange" to the positivistically minded historian, but which are of vital importance and entirely "natural" for the people of that time. However, these pages too call for a number of additional comments.

First of all, how far can these behavior patterns be considered laughable? "Laughable behavior," if, we repeat, we are to remain loyal to Bachtin's view, is closely bound up with the carnival. In this respect it has one important feature inherent to it: all kinds of art that are directed towards written culture draw a sharp line between performer and audience. For all the unity of the creative act and the shared experiences associated with it these two groups realize fundamentally opposite patterns of behavior: one group is actively involved, the other looks on. On the other hand all art forms of the folklore type provoke the spectators and audience to join in: to participate in the game or dance, to engage in a shouted exchange with the actors on the stage of the booth, or to point out to them where their enemy is hidden, or where they should themselves hide. One of the present authors has had occasion to point out that it is precisely according to this principle that the popular print [*lubočnaja kartinka*] differs from non-folkloric painting. It is not viewed passively, but is rather "played out or performed" ["*razygryvaetsja*"] by the spectators and unfolds in their perception as does a scenario when it is performed.*

This difference may have a purely functional character. For instance, a folklore performance, when held at a medieval Russian boyar's banquet was often transformed into a non-folklore text, since the boundary between artist and audience already was like a line between two types of behavior. In this respect evidence recorded by one foreign observer [Samuel Collins] is of interest. He was astonished to find that the dancing at the feast was no more than a spectacle and, like any other form of art, was work: the dancer was not having fun, but rather was doing a job, the enjoyment was for the spectators, themselves too important to dance.[15]

In contrast with this we may note, for example, the transition from passive listening to participation in play which is typical of children's reactions. Thus, according to Porošin's account, the Grand duke Paul Petrovič (the future Paul I), when as a child he was looking at engravings of foreign cities as part of his education, would turn the whole activity into a game in the course of which he would run into the engraving and begin to run along the roads and streets depicted in the drawings in front of him.[16] There are many instances when the authors of plays try to involve the spectators as co-participants in popular farces. Leaving aside twentieth century drama (e.g. Pirandello), we might refer to the mayor's outburst in [Gogol's play] *The Government Inspector*: "What are you laughing at? It's yourselves you're laughing at! . . . ," an appeal which was intended to have the effect of abolishing the footlights and addressing the audience directly. It is not surprising that this sort of play subsequently caused difficulties with the censorship which wanted academic spectators, not fellow participants of the stage events.

"Laughter culture" excludes professional or even immobile roles: the speaker and the member of the audience are participants in a shared action, and in its course change places many times. It is precisely here that the deprofessionalizing, levelling and ambivalent nature of that popular laughter which Bachtin wrote about makes itself felt. However those phenomena which Lichačev and Pančenko discuss are much closer, it would seem, to the spectator theater. (We are giving the concept an expanded meaning: gladiatorial combat, bullfighting, and also that typical medieval spectacle, the execution, may all generate emotions somewhat different from those the European of the nineteenth century

---

* Reference to Ju. M. Lotman's "Chudožestvennaja priroda russkich narodnych kartinok" ["The Artistic Nature of the Russian folk picture"] in *Narodnaja Gravjura*, 1976.

was accustomed to associate with the theater; however, the sharp division into active participants and onlookers, and the opposition between them based on types of emotion and behavior, means that these spectacles are theater, rather than carnival [*dejstvo*]). Ivan the Terrible by turns takes up the roles of actor and spectator; accordingly whoever happens to be his partner may watch the Tsar playing or, if he finds himself on the block, he may provide the Tsar with a spectacle (some more complex cases will be considered later). Here we are much nearer to professionalized acting which by its very nature is the antipode of the carnival-style "laughable behavior" in which all may be involved. The division of the country into the *opričnina** and the *zemščina*** puts as it were the finishing touches to the vast divide into active participants and onlookers. A characteristic feature of the theater is that artists and audience experience *different emotions*. Whereas the audience is laughing, the artists perform in such a way as to make the audience do this; they do not themselves laugh, rather they portray laughter. In the carnival situation laughter is meant equally for all the participants, more specifically, it encloses them within the boundaries of the popular Utopian world about which Bachtin was speaking. The situation of the *opričnina* may seem laughable for just one of the partners, if it can be regarded as laughable at all. The holy fool's situation is similarly divided: it implies that the onlooker is located outside this behavior pattern and perceives it as "strange." And whatever is strange is alien, not part of one's own world. It is no accident that in its primary usage "strange" [*strannoe*] meant "foreign" [*inostrannoe*].[17] Anyone whose behavior is strange, whether holy fool, Tsar playing at being a holy fool, or a *skomoroch****, is a wanderer, an outsider, or a foreigner. On this point it is interesting to note the tendency shown by Russian Tsars to play at being a holy fool and at the same to "be foreigners": from the plans of Ivan the Terrible to "become an Englishman" to Peter the Great's disguises. It is significant that Catherine the Great, who was a ruler of foreign origin, made great efforts to play the "Russian," and that Paul I, who already felt himself to be a Russian, took a fancy to being the Grand Master of the Maltese Order, i.e. he wished to play at being what he manifestly was unable to be, a Catholic and a celibate.

In the book under discussion, the *spectacular* side of the holy fool (the fact that his behavior is calculated for its impact on the outside observer) is shown convincingly. It seems to us, however, that it is precisely spectacles of this kind that are in opposition to "*laughter* culture."

* Here the domains assigned to Ivan's elite.

** *Zemščina*, the boyars' domains not included in the *opričnina*.

*** *Skomoroch*—strolling minstrel-cum-clown of medieval Russia.

We must also discuss in general to what extent the types of behavior that interest us may be classified as play, and how far they were linked with elements of magic and pagan behavior that survived with the framework of the everyday practice, not the dogma, of Orthodoxy.

We know that early Russian consciousness assigned to play a clear-cut and comparatively narrow sphere. The world of serious values and, even more so of religious ones was excluded from the sphere of play. The author of "The Supplication of Daniel the Prisoner," who was competent in these matters (Lichačev has convincingly argued that he was involved in the culture of the Russian *skomorochs*), placed on a par the prohibitions against "lying to God" and against "playing with the sublime."[18] Ivan the Terrible, with respect to other people, also drew a sharp distinction between the world of the banquet where one might "while at food play the fool" (i.e. be a joker or play about), and the serious business of war. Play in serious situations was perceived as being blasphemous, "wrong" behavior, i.e. non-Christian, pagan or sorcerous. Someone who behaved in an inverted manner towards other people in serious situations was not perceived as a joker or humorist, but as a magician. For instance, how far can we regard the turning of items of clothing, e.g. a fur coat, inside out as coming within the scope of "laughter culture" (see pp. 20-21)? In fact an inside out fur coat is a characteristic feature of a whole series of utterly serious ceremonies, undoubtedly pagan in origin, associated with agriculture, marriage, and birth.

From what has been said we may also doubt whether the holy fool's behavior should be perceived as play. This behavior was linked with a whole hierarchy of medieval ways of assessing a man's worth. In medieval terms the more "correct" a man's behavior, the greater is the respect he is accorded. Up above the hierarchy of prescriptive rules that determine the norms of correct behavior for men of various estates, there holds sway the general code of behavior for the Christian, whose full implementation is possible only for a man who is marked with the stamp of holiness. From this standpoint normal human behavior is felt to be "incorrect," and the severe code of the "correct" life of the saint is in opposition to it. And so the difference between the saint and the average man is given outward expression in the written lives of the saints, by which in fact the righteous man is to be identified. However, there is yet another highly valued standard by which righteousness is measured, one which does not need any external expression and which moreover, for the outside observer, takes the form of utterly incorrect behavior . By subduing his passions, the saint may realize a pattern of behavior typical of the worst of sinners or act like a magician, "in a contrary fashion." In this case the saint differs from the sinner not by his behavior , but only through the grace that resides in him and which he senses within himself. Only for the spectator who shares this feeling is he distinguishable from a demoniac.

The example from *The Life of Prokopij of Ustjug*, quoted on pp. 133-135 of the book we are discussing, is exceptionally significant. According to his biographer, St. Prokopij would walk "throughout the night to God's holy churches and would pray to the Lord, having nothing else with him but three pokers in his left hand;" these would sometimes point upwards and at other times they hung down. In the former case, there would be an abundance of crops; in the latter case there would be a shortage of grain. [19] Pančenko with good reason attributes the poker to images of pagan origin which had survived in every day magic practices. But it is particularly significant that the three pokers in the hand of Prokopij of Ustjug correlate with the three candles in a prelate's hand during an episcopal blessing. [20] Furthermore, Prokopij carries the pokers in his *left* hand and visits the churches *at night,* not in the day. This behavior comes within a hair's breadth of being a blasphemous parody of a church service and only stops short of this, owing to the circumstance that the concept of parody is in principle not applicable to the idea of the holy fool. *Superficially* the activities of a holy fool may be indistinguishable from magic (sorcerous or pagan) goings on, but in essence they have a totally different content,.

A holy fool may appear to be playing at being Christ only to an external observer to whom it seems that the saint is adopting behavior that is *alien* to him, sinful, ugly and humiliating, in order to humiliate himself, and that he does this, not because it arises from his essential self, but because this behavior is deeply at odds with his true nature. In this view the holy fool really is "play-acting" in that he adopts a pattern of behavior that goes against his essential self. Pančenko has demonstrated effectively that the spectacular element may take hold of the holy fool. Of unusual interest are his observations concerning the differences in a holy fool's behavior when he is on his own and when he is in the company of outside observers. However, we suppose that looked at from the inside, the holy fool's behavior is not "outrageous": it is bound up with a deep anarchic denial of the whole structure of man's social existence and seems natural to him. Infringing the code of decency and normality is the norm for him, not an anomaly. Hence "for him" he is behaving in a serious and unambiguous fashion; he is not play-acting. It may be presumed that the actual behavior of early Russian holy fools fluctuated between these two possibilities depending on whether he was appropriating the point of view of his audience or, on the contrary, making it adopt his own position.

The holy fool's behavior is thoroughly imbued with didactic content. Having personal connections with the Lord, he was, as it were, surrounded by a sacred micro-space, a sort of placenta of holiness; hence behavior becomes possible which *from the external point of view* seems to be blasphemous, but is not so *in essence* (cf. in this connection the striking examples of anti-behavior among the holy fools on pp. 123-125, 133-134 of Lichačev and Pančenko's book). It is his inner holiness that creates the conditions for the antithetically opposed exterior perception: the fact that he is encapsulated in a sacred micro-space endows his behavior with inverted character for the outside observer who is located in the world of sin. In other words the holy fool is in effect forced to behave in an inverted way, his behavior is didactically contrasted with the qualities of this world. The attributes of anti-behavior are switched in this process from the actor to the spectators: the holy fool's behavior converts play into reality, demonstrating the unreal, deceptive nature of the external environment.

Ivan the Terrible's behavior can also be connected with that of the holy fool as Lichačev and Pančenko have shown (pp. 33-34, 41, 99-100, 167-168); it is significant that, as Lichačev has proved elsewhere, the Tsar gave himself the name of Parfenij Urodivyj.*[21] The idea of unlimited despotism, the political conception adopted by Ivan the Terrible, engendered a specific psychological complex. Being convinced of the divine origin of his power, he assumed that just as pious laymen could not pass judgement on a holy fool's actions and had to accept that holiness lay behind his craziness, though without being able to base this conclusion on any rational foundation, so too his subjects ought to submit to his divine authority regardless of the nature of his actions.

The saint's code of behavior, "holiness is based on what is best," linked grace with personal merit. This formula, combined with the idea of the divine origin of power, might well form the basis for autocracy, but contradicted the idea of unlimited despotism in no uncertain terms, since the formula was founded on the idea that the unlimited sovereign was subject to moral and religious restraints. The code of the holy fool, "holiness is based on the worst," made grace independent of personal behavior (outrageousness, humiliation, ineptness in secular affairs only emphasized the boundless mercy of the Most High), and when transferred onto the plane of political behavior at the level of the state, became the basis for despotism, since it sanctioned *any* action by the sovereign. However, as we have said, the disordered, *totally permissive* behavior of the holy fool was only for the external observer. Consequently, if a Tsar or any other petty tyrant played at being a holy fool, he won attention from outside for his own behavior, i.e. his behavior became theatricalized.

Ivan's behavior was that of the holy fool without holiness, not sanctioned from above. Hence he was playing at being a holy fool or parodying one. We must bear in mind that for those of his contemporaries who were witnesses of his activities, this play element might be eliminated; for some, he might well seem like a stereotype from hagiographic literature of a tormentor of saints, or like a tyrant from antiquity, while for others he

* *urodivyi*, "monstrous," cf. *jurodivyj*, "holy fool."

might seem like a wizard who had sold his soul to the Devil and was now living in the topsyturvy world.[22] Both these "readings" switch Ivan's behavior from the plane of play onto that of serious activity.

In many instances, this game takes over the actor himself completely, and he becomes wholly subject to the elemental force of anti-behavior. It is highly characteristic that Ivan's behavior very often comes very close indeed to sacrilege. He not only compelled his *opričniki* to dance in masks like Yuletide mummers; but when Prince Michajlo Repnin preferred death to the sin of putting on a mask, the Tsar ordered him to be executed *in church by the altar during the reading of the gospel:*[23] the theater is turned into real life, and play takes on an almost ritual character. Ivan's adherence, whether intentional or unintentional, to the anti-behavior associated with Yuletide is extremely significant.[24] Thus the despot's masquerade with his *opričniki*—during which they dressed up as monks, and the Tsar himself took the title of Father Superior of the carnival monastery,[25] —to all appearances arises under the influence of the Yuletide games about which the icon painter, Father Grigorij from Vjaz'ma, wrote in his petition to Tsar Aleksej Michajlović in 1651. In it he reported that in Vjaz'ma, "various and disgraceful games take place beginning at Christmas and going on till the Epiphany vespers, during which they take the titles of saints and set up monasteries and are appointed as archimandrites, cellarers and elders."[26] Anti-behavior has its laws and fixed patterns just as correct and normal behavior does. Rejection of the normal code, then, takes already existing forms, and at the same time it adopts the content of these forms. The specifically play element may drift into the background, if not become completely obscured.

* * *

It seems to us, therefore, that the title of Lichačev and Pančenko's book is open to discussion: the authors have brought to light and established as a subject for scholarly analysis some highly important historico-literary and psychological phenomena in Russian culture. However, that these should be defined as "laughable" needs at the very least to be supported by further argument.

We have considered by no means all the interesting aspects of the psychology of culture, which have been raised in this innovative book. The problems the authors have brought up are so vast and intriguing that they will unquestionably continue to be discussed for a long time to come. But it is already quite clear that what they have written is a real achievement, one which future researchers will one way or another have to take into account.

Translated by N.F.C. Owen

NOTES

1 Pančenko 1973.

2 Lichačev and Pančenko 1976. Page references to this work are given in the text.

3 The method of "putting oneself" in the text cannot of course be completely eliminated, and indeed probably should not be. In some instances and within reasonable limits it may even be useful. What is important is to turn it from being an unconscious and almost automatic procedure on the author's part into a *consciously* applied and *controllable* research technique.

4 Bachtin 1965; Bachtin 1975.

5 This last point is especially vital, since we find more and more often that there is a tendency not to develop or interpret Bachtin's ideas, but mechanically to extend them into areas where their very application should be a subject of special investigation. An example is Belkin's *Russian Skomorochs* (Belkin 1975), where at the outset the author, without any serious justification, postulates: "Popular laughter culture was endemic to medieval Russia as a whole to no less a degree than to the medieval West." Further on he even asserts that: "In Russia, to a greater degree and maybe even earlier than in other European countries, humorous forms reached maturity in their ideas, first as a form of defence and subsequently becoming more and more aggressive." (Belkin 1975, pp. 7, 9). From the immediate context it is clear that by the "maturity of ideas" of "laughter culture" Belkin means satire. How can this idea be squared with Bachtin's categorical statement that satire is always univalent and serious? By denying certain phenomena, satire is in principle in opposition to laughter culture which is ambivalent, simultaneously denying and affirming, and which is located outside any of the forms of the serious world. Bachtin's complex and controversial ideas have been oversimplified and made into a handy decoration of scholarship.

6 Adrianova-Peretc 1954; Adrianova-Peretc 1937; Adrianova-Peretc 1936; Adrianova-Peretc 1936a; Adrianova-Peretc 1928.

7 S. Smirnov 1914, appendix (*Materialy dlja istorii drevnerusskoj pokajannoj discipliny*), p. 54 (no. 38), p. 151 (no. 14), p. 125 (no. 114); cf. also p. 212. Cf. *ibid.*, p. 125 (no. 115b) on the penance for playing.

8 *Ibid.*, appendix, p. 62 (no. 16), p. 150 (no. 7); Almazov 1894, pp. 149, 205, 211, 274.

9 "Sbornik poučenij XVII," MS at the Saltykov-Ščedrin Library in Leningrad (Q.I., No. 1307, line 247).

10 Cf. the spell giving protection from wasting disease typically contains references to "bald people and comics" as potential bearers of evil. Efimenko 1878, p. 191.

11 Vas. Smirnov 1927, *passim*; Maksimov 1908-1913, XVII, 1912, pp. 6, 35, 37.

12 Lehmann 1922; Lehmann 1923; Gilman 1974.

13 Works of this kind are accompanied by remarks in the manuscripts such as: "Quoted from Polish sources," "From royal [Polish] sources," and suchlike. See Demkov, 1965, p. 95. Even assuming that these inscriptions are of a defensive character to do with the censorship, they do not lose their significance: the author regards such texts as normal specifically for the Western religious lifestyle.

14 Maksimov 1908-1913, XVII, 1912, pp. 14-15; also, Gusev 1974. Cf. for similar Shrovetide games, Šejn 1898, p. 303; Azadovskij 1924, p. 32.

15 According to S. Maskevič (1611) the Russian boyars laughed at Western dancing, "considering it improper for an honest man to dance. . . . 'An honest man,' they say, 'ought to sit in his place and be amused only at the *jester's*

contortions, he should not himself be the jester for the amusement of others: that is wrong!' " (See *Skazanija*, V, pp. 61-62); cf. Collins 1671, p. 34, Russian version, p. 11: "They are great strangers to Dancing, as esteeming it beneath their Gravity." Cf. Famincyn 1889, pp. 168-169.

16 Porošin 1881, column 482-483.

17 In its turn too "laughter behavior" was sometimes linked with foreign cultural elements, just as it was at times associated with the demonic principle. In one early Russian sermon we read: "It is not meet for a monk to laugh or behave mockingly *like a foreigner*, this applies also to any Orthodox Christian." (S. Smirnov 1914, appendix, p. 176, No. 3).

18 Daniil Zatočnik 1932, p. 79.

19 Prokopij of Ustjug, pp. 57-58. We take this opportunity of correcting a misprint in Lichačev's and Pančenko's book where the pages are wrongly indicated.

20 Cf. in this connection the characteristic proverbial correlation: "candles for God, pokers for the Devil."

21 See Lichačev 1972.

22 Cf. the typical description of Ivan the Terrible by Kurbskij. According to him, the Tsar "to attack the prelate gathers his vicious hordes of Jews, followers of Beelzebub, and the accursed throng of supporters of Caiaphas, with whom he is on good terms like Herod with Pilate, and they come together with the Beast into the great church and sit themselves in the Holy Place." Kurbskij 1914, column 313. The image of Ivan the Terrible is presented as the image of the Beast, the Antichrist, sitting in the Holy Place. This is of course not simply a rhetorical device, but reflects belief in the Satanic nature of the events described.

23 Kurbskij 1914, column 279; S.M. Solov'ev 1960, p. 541.

24 In this connection it is striking that Ivan shows himself to be a connoisseur of the art of the *skomoroch* precisely at the time when this art form was being identified with pagan games, and when the church was leading an active struggle against the *skomorochs* as part of the campaign against paganism. See in particular the activities of the Stoglav Council [1551] which seems moreover to have been convoked by Ivan himself!

25 Polosin 1963, p. 154.

26 The petition of Starec Grigorij in Kapterev 1913, p. 181. The custom of dressing up as a monk at Christmas survived at least occasionally right up to the twentieth century (see Zavojko 1914, p. 138).

ECHOES OF THE NOTION "MOSCOW AS THE THIRD ROME" IN PETER THE GREAT'S IDEOLOGY

Ju.M. Lotman, B.A. Uspenskij

1. A characteristic feature of the ideology of the Petrine epoch* was to envisage that what Russia was experiencing at the beginning of the eighteenth century was a beginning or starting-point. Everything that went before was declared to be as it were non-existent or at least lacking historical reality, a time of ignorance and chaos. In Petrine consciousness pre-Petrine Russia acquired features of entropy. The ideal Russia was thought of as unrelated to what had gone before, while as regards this former Russia it was not its inherent features which were emphasized, but rather that which from the standpoint of the ideal, it lacked.

It should be noted that it was precisely in this nihilistic approach to the past that features of historical continuity were objectively to be found. While erasing the preceding historical tradition the theoretician of the Petrine epoch turned to antiquity as the ideal ancestor of the epoch he was living through. So, for example, the official title of Emperor combined with the appellation "Father of the Fatherland" and "Great" (all three appellations were taken by Peter the Great at the same time – in 1721) clearly points to the Roman tradition and is at the same time evidence of a break with Russian titles.[1] Contemporaries did not notice that to look to Rome as the norm and ideal of state power was itself traditional for Russian culture. For instance, the idea of the consanguinity between the Russian princes and the Roman emperors was an organic element of the political self-consciousness of the sixteenth century. This is also indicated by *The Epistle of Spiridon-Savva* and *The Tale of the Princes of Vladimir* where Rjurik is connected with the descendents of Augustus of Rome's brother, Prus.**[2] This idea indeed formed the basis for many of Ivan the Terrible's declarations. In a letter to King Johannes III of Sweden he wrote: "We are descended from Augustus Caesar but you are belittling us in an ungodly manner."[3] Subsequently, the hereditary link between the

---

*Peter I, the Great, ruled from 1682–1725.

**The *Tale*, written in the 1520's, was a new version of the *Epistle*. Both deal with the genealogy of the Russian Grand Princes of whom Rjurik was the first. The "Prus" of these texts has no historical foundation, but may possibly be the historical Drusus.

Russian monarchs, and Augustus was emphasized at Peter II's* coronation (he was the first Russian ruler to be crowned *Emperor*):

The great sovereigns and Tsars of Russia have their origin in and have been autocrats in Great Russia from the time of the highest and first Grand Prince Rjurik who was descended from Augustus Caesar, the ruler of the world.[4]

The title "Tsar" [*Car'*] and the one that replaced it, "Emperor" [*Imperator*], in fact come from the same source and denote the very same historico-cultural object, but translated into Russian at different cultural periods. Indeed the word "*car'*" derives etymologically from "caesar" (Slavonic: *cesar'*) and is consequently equivalent to Emperor (cf. the German *Kaiser*, "Emperor," which is also derived from the name Caesar, but in a different cultural and historical tradition); when Peter the Great switched from Russian Tsar to Russian Emperor this marked not so much an expansion of power as a reorientation that was cultural.[5] The fact that the titles Tsar and Emperor were perceived not as synonyms but as antonyms of a special kind indicates that there was a conflict between the very languages through which the cultural consciousness of these epochs expressed itself.[6]

Here it is essential to note that in modern times the title of Emperor had belonged only to the head of the Holy Roman Empire (whom the Russians, until Peter became Emperor, had called "Caesar" [*cesar'*]). And so the assumption by the Russian monarch of the imperial title placed him on the same level as the Austrian Emperor:[7] the orientation towards Rome was both direct and also through the Austrian political model.**

2. The idea of "Moscow as the third Rome" was by its very nature dualistic. On the one hand it assumed a connection between the state of Moscow and the highest spiritual and religious values. By making piety the main feature of Moscow's secular power and its basis, this idea emphasized the theocratic aspect of the orientation towards Byzantium. In this variant the idea presupposed separation from the "evil" lands. On the other hand Constantinople was regarded as the second *Rome*, i.e. in the political symbolism connected with this name its imperial essence was emphasized—Byzantium was seen as a *world empire*, the inheritor of Rome's secular power. Hence the idea of "Moscow as the third Rome" brings together two tendencies—the religious and the political. When the second aspect was being considered the connection with the *first Rome* was emphasized, this entailed a suppression of the religious aspect and underlined the secular or "imperial" one. The primary figure in this case is Caesar Augustus, not Constantine. Since it had taken the central

*Peter II (reigned 1727–1730), the grandson of Peter I (Peter the Great).
**The significance of the titles Tsar, Emperor and Caesar is further discussed below, Part III, Chapter 1.

54

place the secular power of the state did not need the blessing of religion, but itself could give religion its blessing. There are hints of this as far back as Ivan the Terrible who wrote to Polubenskij that Christ

> had, by his divine birth, made Augustus Caesar illustrious by deigning to be born during his reign and had in this way brought him glory and extended his kingdom, granting him to rule not only over Rome, but also over the whole world, the Goths, Sarmatians, Italy, all Dalmatia and Anatolia, Macedonia and also Azi [sic], Asia, Syria, Mesopotamia, Egypt and Jerusalem, and even as far as the borders of Persia. [8]

What is characteristic here is that this passage refers to a world-wide, geographically "open" state ideal, rather than one which is closed, and that Rome turns out to be the center of this universal organism, whereas Jerusalem figures only as a remote border province.

And so the dual nature of Constantinople as a political symbol made possible a two-fold interpretation. In the one, piety and priesthood are emphasized, in the other, power and kingship. Jerusalem comes to symbolize the first, and Rome the second. Consequently the ideal for the future development of Moscow as a state could be codified in terms of either set of symbols. It is not surprising that the idea of Moscow as the Third Rome was quite soon being transformed into that of Moscow as the New Jerusalem [9], an idea which does not run counter to the first one but which is regarded as its realization. In the sixteenth century the Russians considered that the old Jerusalem had been "discredited," having been defiled by the infidel Saracens, and so Moscow ought to take the name of Jerusalem (Maxim the Greek specifically argued against this view in his "Homily showing how the holy places remain undefiled even if they are occupied by the pagans for many years").[10] Whereas in its time St. Sophia in Constantinople was the embodiment of the Church for Russians, after 1453 its place was taken by the Church of the Resurrection in Jerusalem. Characteristically, Patriarch Nikon built a New Jerusalem near Moscow with a Church of the Resurrection constructed as an exact replica of the one in Jerusalem. This step was all the more significant in that it provoked the Eastern patriarchs' condemnation and their criticism of Nikon precisely for using the name "New Jerusalem."[11]

In this way the symbol of Byzantium as it were splits into two symbolic images: Constantinople is regarded both as the New Jerusalem, the holy and theocratic city, and as the New Rome, the imperial and political capital of the world. Both these ideas are incorporated in the view of Moscow as a new Constantinople or third Rome, a view which arises after the fall of the Byzantine Empire. The main point here is that the fall of Constantinople to the Turks (1453) coincided approximately with the final overthrow of Tatar rule in Russia (1480); these two events were naturally linked in Russia, being regarded as a shift in the centre of world holiness. At the same time as Islam was victorious over Orthodoxy in Byzantium, in Russia the reverse had taken place, i.e. Orthodoxy was triumphant over Islam.

With the fall of Constantinople the ruler of Moscow became the only independent ruler left in the Orthodox world, except for Georgia which, from the standpoint of Moscow, was more of a legendary kingdom than a real geographical and political entity. In terms of medieval ideology when only the adherents of the true faith were recognized as truly having a right to existence, other peoples, as it were, did not exist; and so the ruler of the state of Moscow was, in these terms, now sovereign of the whole world. In this situation the political and confessional aspects of the doctrine "Moscow as the Third Rome" coalesced in a general theocratic meaning.*

In later times, when other nations came to be recognized as having the right to independent existence whatever their religion, this equilibrium was shattered. Moscow was faced with two choices: to be the New Jerusalem or the New Rome.

3. Peter the Great's contacts with the West created a cultural situation whose main impact was one of novelty. This did not preclude stereotypes from the previous culture having a strong effect on the reformers' own minds. In a number of cases Peter's reforms may be regarded as a series of fundamental renamings within the framework of an already existing cultural code. In many of the ideas on which the system of relations between Peter's government and the West was built we can glimpse the concept of "Moscow as the Third Rome," sometimes to be repudiated, sometimes to be continued though undergoing radical transformations. At certain points this notion influenced actual policy, at others, it took on a purely semiotic character.

A semiotic correlation with the idea of "Moscow as the Third Rome" is unexpectedly to be found in some aspects of the building of St. Petersburg and the transfer there of the capital. There were the two courses: the capital could be the focus of holiness or it could follow the tradition of imperial Rome. Peter chose the latter. This orientation on Rome, leaving Byzantium out of account, naturally gave rise to the question of rivalry with Catholic Rome over the right of the historical succession. This situation in a sense repeated the "dispute over the succession" between Rome and Novgorod as reflected in the *Tale of the White Cowl*.** It should be recalled here that from one point of view, St. Petersburg was regarded as the historical successor to Novgorod.*** This kind of symbolism was reinforced for people of the Petrine epoch, firstly, by suggestions

*See also Part III, Chapter 1, note 70.

**The white cowl was a symbol of the highest ecclesiastical dignity and the authority it had in Novgorod. The emphasis of the *Tale*, written in the fifteenth century, is on the priority of ecclesiastical over secular power.

***Novgorod was the most important city-state in medieval Russia, and lost its independence only with the rise of Muscovy.

that Russia had a historical right to the banks of the Neva as part of the Novgorod *pjatina* (district); secondly, by the link between Novgorod and Petersburg in the fact that they had one and the same patron saint, Alexander Nevskij;* and, thirdly, because Petersburg belonged to the diocese of the Archbishop of Novgorod and Pskov.

In this context the naming of the new capital as the City of St. Peter inevitably had associations both with the glorification of Peter the Great's heavenly protector, and with the notion of Petersburg as the New Rome. This orientation towards Rome can be seen not only in the name of the capital, but also in its coat of arms: as Ju.I. Vilenbachov has shown, the Petersburg coat of arms contains transformed motifs from the arms of the city of Rome (or of the Vatican as the successor to Rome), and this of course could not be accidental. The crossed anchors in the coat of arms of Petersburg correspond to the crossed keys in the Vatican arms. Their position with their flukes pointing upwards clearly betrays their origin, for the keys in the arms of the Pope of Rome also have their key-bits turned upwards. It is precisely by this correspondence that the symbolism of the Petersburg coat of arms is to be decoded. On the one hand, the anchor symbolizes salvation and faith and its use with this meaning is very familiar from Baroque emblems; there is a natural and appropriate association between an anchor and a key. But at the same time the anchor metonymically denotes a fleet: put in place of the Apostle Peter's keys, it indicated how Peter (the Emperor, not the Apostle) intended to open the door of his "paradise." [12] In this way the coat of arms of Petersburg corresponds semantically to the name of the city: the name and the arms are both a verbal and a visual expression of one common idea.

At the same time the heavy emphasis in Petersburg on the cult of the Apostles Peter and Paul acquires a special significance. The cathedral within the fortress of St. Peter and St. Paul is dedicated to them and, according to the original plan, it should have been the center of the city. Surely this is a reflection of the place occupied by St. Peter's in Rome in the semiotics of the city plan.

In view of this, the frequent use, by both Peter and his entourage, of the word "paradise" with reference to Petersburg could have signified not simply praise of the chosen, beloved plot of land but also the holiness of this place. Men'šikov writing to Peter on December 10, 1709 describes Petersburg as the "holy land." [13] The very name "Sankt-Peterburg" [Russian for St. Petersburg] can in fact be interpreted in two possible ways, since the epithet "holy" may apply both to Peter (Apostle or Emperor, see below) and to the *city*. Whereas the German name "Sankt Petersburg" conveys the notion of possession grammatically speaking, and is therefore to be translated as "the city of St. Peter," the name which became accepted in Russia, "Sankt-Peterburg" (which does not contain

---

*Alexander Nevskij, Grand Prince of Novgorod (1220–1263), defeated the Swedes in a famous battle on the ice in 1242. He was later canonized.

the possessive particle -s), obscures this meaning and may be understood as "the holy city of Peter." It is worth noting that the Russian name "Peterburg" in opposition to the German "Petersburg" is constructed according to the Slavonic word-building model, even though it is made up from foreign language components. And finally Petersburg's claim to holiness found expression in the tendency to disparage Moscow's holy places. In this connection we may recall Peter's insistent and demonstrative demand that a theater be built in Moscow actually on Red Square, an act which was felt by his contemporaries to be an outrage against the *holy character of the place* (a theater being an anti-church, the Devil's domain).

The parallels Novgorod–Petersburg, Rome–Petersburg contained the idea of duality which was characteristic for Baroque culture. For example, the figure of the Apostle Peter was sometimes provided with a double in the shape of his brother, the Apostle Andrew. The Apostle Andrew was felt to be more national for Russia since he had visited Eastern Europe and, according to the *Tale of Bygone Years*, had foretold a great future for Russia, had placed a cross on the Kiev Hills and been amazed at the bathhouses in Novgorod. And so he was as it were a "Russian variant" of the Apostle Peter. Hence the clearly expressed cult of the Apostle Andrew in the ideology of the Petrine period: immediately on his return from the Great Embassy* Peter founded the Order of St. Andrew the First-called (the epithet "first-called," which was included in the name of the order, underlined the fact that Andrew had been called by Christ before Peter; this could be understood as the elevation of Russia's patron saint above that of the Pope at Rome). The fleet was given the "flag of St. Andrew." St. Vladimir, equal of the Apostles,** also served as a variant of Peter. At any rate Feofan Prokopovič*** in his tragedy *Vladimir* blatantly endowed the Christianizer of Russia with features of Tsar Peter.

Dualism in Baroque symbolism was combined with an extensive system of substitutions. Thus although regarded not only as the New Rome but also as the New Moscow (the new "reigning city," as it was called by official command), Petersburg was felt to be the New Archangel'sk, since it was a gateway for trade with Europe. However this also had symbolic implications: the protector of Archangel'sk was the Archangel Michael, one of the patron saints of Muscovite Russia. The victory of the City of St. Peter over the town of the Archangel Michael was also interpreted symbolically.

4. What gave Petersburg authenticity in its claim to be the New Rome

*The name given to Peter the Great's eighteen-month tour of Western Europe in 1697–1698.

**i.e. Vladimir I, who in the Orthodox canon is termed "equal of the Apostles" [*ravnoapostol'nyj*].

***Feofan Prokopovič (1681–1736), besides being scholar and writer, was Peter's greatest ecclesiastical administrator and reformer.

was that the principle of holiness was not dominant but subordinate to that of statehood. State service came to mean both serving the Fatherland and at the same time worshipping God, which led to the salvation of the soul. Peter regarded prayer in itself in isolation from "service" as hypocrisy; he felt that the service of the state was the only true form of prayer. Feofan Prokopovič said in a sermon:

> We ask you, rational people, whoever you may be, whether you have slaves or indeed free servants, pray tell us, if you order one of your servants to get you something to drink and he brings you a cap, do you like it? I know what you will say—you will be very annoyed. Well, if you tell him to go to the village to inspect the workmen and he does nothing of the sort, just stands there bowing to you and long-windedly singing your praises, you will find it utterly insufferable... Think then of God. We know that all our doings are guided by his most wise intentions: some are called to serve, others to govern, others to wage war and yet others to be priests and so forth...Hence how very foolish are those who, thinking to please God, set aside their own work and do something else which they should not be doing. Judges, for instance, may be in church singing and doing good works while they neglect their courts which are waiting for them. But, even if it is good in itself, because it is at the wrong time and at variance with God's will, how can it be good and pleasing to God?.. O, how can this prayer be other than sinful![14]

The monk Avraamij had expressed similar ideas already in 1696 in a letter addressed to Peter:

> I think that the Lord God will not ask of Tsars, Grand Dukes, auto-crats and those that serve them long prayers, much bowing, atten-dance at vigils, alms-giving to the poor, the building of churches and monasteries, nor will He require prolonged fasts. Autocrats should work hard rather than spend their time making long prayers and doing much bowing, singing psalms and songs of praise and attending vigils in cells.[15]

Petersburg's holiness lay in its statehood. From this point of view both papal Rome (as distinct from imperial Rome) and Moscow are seen as synonymous symbols for false "hypocritical" holiness. From the stand-point of this deified statehood, traditional Russian Orthodoxy seemed to be suspiciously close to the "papist spirit." This gave rise to a certain sympathy for Protestantism on the part of Peter and Feofan, and made the criticism of Catholic Rome as the inauthentic Rome the more potent. A paradigm of ideas was established in which "papist" Rome and pre-Petrine Moscow were seen as aligned against Petersburg, the true City of St. Peter.

A typical remark of Peter's in this connection was reported by the archpriest of the Moscow Archangel'skij Cathedral, Petr Alekseev, in a letter to the Emperor Paul I: Peter had said that Nikon "had become infected with the Pope's love of power," on which Alekseev commented, "for is it not the arrogance of a Pope, to make the Tsar who has been crowned by God into a groom." [16] The reference here is to the religious ceremony of the "ride on the donkey" which used to take place in Moscow on Palm Sunday when the Patriarch, taking the part of Christ, would ride on a horse which the Tsar led by the bridle. This ceremony was abolished under Peter (the last time it was performed was in 1696). In this way an ancient Russian religious ceremony which had been taken over by the Russians from the Greeks (or more precisely from the church at Jerusalem[17]) came to be directly linked with Catholic Rome.

In the light of what has been said the polemical thrust of the parodic ceremonies of the Assembly of All the Fools* becomes clear. Contrary to established opinion, this parody of the ceremony of the election of a new pope and other Catholic rituals did not lack topicality. The notion expressed by some scholars that these ceremonies only acquired topical interest after the Patriarchate came to be the subject of mockery seems to miss the point. For the people of Peter's entourage mockery directed against Catholic Rome inevitably progressed to the discrediting of the Russian Patriarchate, and the ridiculing of the Patriarch of All Russia merged with the parodying of the power of the Pope at Rome.

5. The city being built by Peter could not do without a central patronal cathedral. A look at the layout of Petersburg shows that the analogy with Rome was definitely present in the minds of the new capital's builders. The Cathedral of St. Peter and St. Paul, which was intended to be the tallest building in Petersburg, was erected in the citadel which, in the original design, was to have been sited at the city center. It is curious to note that with the transfer of the relics of Alexander Nevskij, which Peter organized with the utmost solemnity, the patronal shrines also became associated with Novgorod. In this way the two patronal shrines of Petersburg referred to the Russian and to the universal significance of the new capital. At the same time, behind the "Roman" symbolism of the Cathedral of St. Peter and St. Paul that of Moscow as the Third Rome was clearly discernible. After Peter's death this Cathedral became a kind of replacement for the Archangel'skij Cathedral in Moscow, since it became the burial-vault for the Russian sovereigns.

While the first church in Petersburg (and the *first* public building in the new city) was the Cathedral of St. Peter and St. Paul, founded on the Tsar's saint's day (July 29, 1703), the second was a church dedicated to St. Isaac of Dalmatia which was founded on Peter's birthday, May 30, 1707. It was dedicated to the saint on whose anniversary he had been born in 1672. And so these churches as it were represented a division into two of a single cult, that of the Tsar's heavenly guardians. This only

*Peter's drinking company.

serves to underline the difference between them. On the one hand the religious and cultural significance of the names of the chief Apostles Peter and Paul was incomparably greater than the modest place occupied by Isaac of Dalmatia. While the latter reminded the people of Peter's time above all of the Tsar's birthday, the two Apostles had an independent aureole of religious and cultural significance evoking a whole complex of ideas associated with the universal Church. On the other hand, before Peter's time much more importance was traditionally attached to the celebration of the saint's day than to the celebration of the Tsar's birthday, which had a secular and more private cultural value.[18] In view of all this the church of St. Isaac, although indeed it was a potential rival to the Cathedral of St. Peter and St. Paul as a patronal shrine for the city, was more "European" as distinct from the latter's "Russian and universal" character. This was helped both by the church's location in the "westernized" Admiralty quarter, at that time on the outskirts and occupied by sailors (hence the so-called Marine Streets), who were largely non-Orthodox, and by its connection with the manifestly Protestant tradition of celebrating birthdays, which arose from the absence of any cult of patron saints. It is interesting to note that subsequently, with the shift of the city center to the southern bank of the Neva and in the course of the extensions of the eighteenth and nineteenth centuries, St. Isaac's became the main cathedral of Petersburg, effectively usurping those functions which the Cathedral of St. Peter and St. Paul had been originally intended to perform. Moreover Peter's wooden church dedicated to St. Isaac was rebuilt several times with an ever more pronounced resemblance to St. Peter's in Rome. It is noteworthy that under Nicholas I it was proposed to include in the order of service for the consecration of St. Isaac's a procession around Peter the Great's monument and the singing of anthems to his eternal memory.[19] St. Isaac's has proved to be historically connected with the "imperial" cult of Peter.

The next churches to be built were also more or less directly connected with the glorification of Peter and his deeds. In 1710 the church of the Holy Trinity was erected on the Petersburg side [*Peterburg-skaja storona*]. This was apparently connected with the conventional date of the founding of the city (on Trinity Sunday, May 16, 1703). Later, the church of St. Sampson was built on the Vyborg road. This choice is obviously linked with the panegyrical image of Peter as Samson breaking the lion's jaw, an image which arose after the victory of Poltava (although the church was of course dedicated not to the biblical Samson, but to St. Sampson the hospitaller: this kind of transferred meaning was quite usual for Peter's time). Finally, the fifth church in Petersburg was dedicated to St. Alexander Nevskij and was consecrated in the same year, 1710. And so all the early shrines in Petersburg can be deciphered by means of the symbolism of the Petrine epoch (cf. the motifs of the biblical

Samson, Alexander Nevskij, etc. in the fireworks, emblems and suchlike of Peter's time).

6. The subsequent cult of Peter's personality led to the city of St. Peter being perceived as the city of the Emperor Peter.

This cult had already started in his lifetime and had deep roots in the ideology of the Petrine state in spite of Peter's personal distaste for solemn ritual. Feofan Prokopovič regularly likens the Emperor Peter to the Apostle Peter, playing on the Gospel saying about the Apostle as the rock on which the future building will be founded. He writes: "In our Peter, in whom we first saw a great warrior, then a wise ruler, we now see an Apostle;" he has organized for us and established "all that is good, useful and necessary for temporal and eternal life;" and "everything stands on him as on a sure foundation."[20] In Feofan's speeches the state, and — even at this early stage — Petersburg, correspond to the Gospel image of the Church to come. The panegyrical comparison with the Apostle Peter is already to be found in the school play, *The Play of the Seven Free Sciences* [*Dejstvo o semi nauk*] in which the Tsar is addressed as follows:

You are the stone, designated in Christ our God,
For you have been anointed Tsar and declared Peter by Him
. . . . . .
On that stone, on Peter, the Church was founded,
And by you the Church in Christ was confirmed
As true.[21]

Using the same image, Peter himself in a letter to Apraksin after the victory of Poltava (June 27, 1709) likened this victory to the foundation stone of Petersburg: "The foundation stone for St. Petersburg was ready; now with God's help it is laid."[22] A string of symbols with state significance is created based on the image of the Apostle Peter but now transferred to Peter the Emperor.

This same association of Peter with a stone is realized in the opposition: *wooden* Russia vs. *stone* Petersburg. This opposition was established by a total ban on the erection of stone buildings anywhere at all in Russia except in Petersburg: in 1714 Peter prohibited in his domains "any construction in stone, for any purpose at all, under penalty of the destruction of the whole estate and exile." Hence in effect not only the image of Petersburg as a capital built of stone is created, but also that of a wooden Russia as its antipode. Petersburg is thought of as being the future of Russia, but along with this there is formed not only an image of the future, but also of its past. This Utopian image of Russia which Petersburg embodies is clearly expressed in Feofan Prokopovič's words:

The Roman Emperor Augustus when he was dying felt it to be the highest praise to say of himself: *I found* a Rome *built of bricks and leave behind one of marble.* But to say this of our Most Noble

Monarch would be no praise at all. It has to be said that he found a Russia made of wood and created one made of gold.[23]

When he speaks of a "golden Russia" Feofan has in mind primarily Petersburg which he contrasts with "wooden Russia;" here what is important for us is also the association between Petersburg and Rome, Peter and Augustus. At another point Feofan addresses himself to Peter: "The whole of Russia is your statue, transformed by your superb craftsmanship."[24] The stone comes to symbolise Russia and Petersburg as its embodiment, and Peter is presented as the creator-demiurge, the sculptor who has transformed it.

As a result of this way of thinking, Petersburg as the creation of Peter is naturally linked with his name and personality, and the name of the city is itself perceived in these terms. This is demonstrated in a particularly graphic way by the naming of Petersburg as "Petrograd" and also "Petropol'." In general the name "Sankt-Peterburg," or "Peterburg" as its abbreviation, is translated as either the "City of St. Peter" [*Grad Svjatogo Petra*] or as "Petrograd"/"Petropol'." In the first case the reference to the Apostle Peter is preserved, in the second it is obscured and accordingly the name "Petrograd"/"Petropol'" is associated with the Emperor rather than the Apostle. The tradition for this interpretation apparently goes back to the time of Peter. Feofan Prokopovič already links "reigning Petropol'" explicitly with the Emperor's name, thereby emphasizing that in the Emperor Peter we "can already see the Apostle as well."[25] This kind of association between Petersburg and Peter the Great can be found also in texts of the end of the eighteenth and the beginning of the nineteenth centuries, for example an epigram on Paul I:

No crowned head are you in Peter's glorious city
But a barbarian, a corporal at the changing of the guard.[26]

See also Batjuškov's lines in "The Crossing of the Rhine":*

From the Volga, the Don and the Dnieper,
From the city of our Peter.[27]

Puškin uses the forms "Petrograd" ("Above overcast Petrograd. . .") and "city of Peter": ("Show forth your beauty, city of Peter. . .")** as synonyms; in both instances it is the city of the Emperor Peter he has in mind. Thus the image of the Emperor gradually displaced that of the Apostle as patron of the city. The Emperor Peter begins to be ascribed not only the historical qualities of founder and builder, but also mythological traits of protector and defender.[28]

---

*K.N. Batjuškov (1787–1855) wrote his historical elegy "The Crossing of the Rhine" in 1814.
**Phrases from Puškin's narrative poem *The Bronze Horseman*.

63

7. On the level of ideas, Petersburg was seen in relation to three temporal models. As the "new Holland," a true embodiment of the ideal of a "proper state," Petersburg became part of European real, historical time. This idea is apparent from the speeches of Peter and his collaborators, where emphasis was laid on the rapidity of the new city's growth and on the present moment in time. However, association with the notion of "Moscow as the Third Rome" could also set Petersburg in a mythological time-model. In this sense Petersburg was, on the one hand, from the moment of its founding, treated as an *eternal* city; this being a reflection of the belief that, as the new and true "Third Rome," there could be no fourth. On the other hand, this same mythology admitted the possibility of an opposite interpretation. Opponents of reform who considered the true Third Rome to be Moscow and who denied the possibility of a fourth, declared that Petersburg did not exist at all, that it had only an apparent existence, "it was dreamt up" and would pass away like a dream.

All three points of view have been reflected in the corresponding cultural models of Petersburg. The first occurs in the introduction to Puškin's *The Bronze Horseman* ("A hundred years have passed, and the young city. . .has arisen"). The second was given special treatment in conjunction with the idea of Petersburg's historical youthfulness: to refer to Rome as the "eternal city" evoked the idea of its uninterrupted existence through many past centuries, whereas Petersburg's claim to "eternity" refers to the "eternity of the future." The third point of view is reflected in a wide range of texts of "Petersburg" literature (especially Gogol, Dostoevskij and the Symbolists).* [29]

Translated by N.F.C. Owen

* "Petersburg literature" would include for instance Gogol's stories *The Nose* and *The Nevsky Prospect* which are set in Petersburg and where the boundary between reality and fantasy is blurred; Dostoevskij in *Notes from the Underground* referred to Petersburg as the "most abstract and contrived city in the world," and his novel *Crime and Punishment* among many other of his writings is set there. Of the Symbolists, most significant is Andrej Belyj's novel *Peterburg* (1913–1916), and many of Blok's lyrics are set in the city (for instance "The Unknown Woman" ["*Neznakomka*"] 1906), which once again is the setting where dream and reality merge.

NOTES

1   On medals struck in honor of Catherine's coronation in 1724, Peter is depicted "in Roman dress standing under a canopy" (see Barsov 1883, p. 155). The Roman dress is clearly associated with the title of Emperor.
2   Dmitrieva 1955, pp. 162, 175, 188-9; cf. also pp. 197, 208; see also Gol'dberg 1976; Dmitrieva 1976.
3   *Poslanija* 1951, p. 158.
4   Barsov 1883, p. 111. Feofan Prokopovič also wrote about this connection, see Moiseeva 1980, p. 33. It is also significant that Augustus's cup is referred to along with Monomach's cap in the introduction to the coronation ceremony of Ivan the Terrible and of Fedor Ivanovič (see Dmitrieva 1955, pp. 183-4, 194).
5   In this sense the opposition between *cesar'* and *kesar'* in the Old Slavonic redaction of John xix. 15 is highly characteristic. Cf., for example, the Suprasliensis MS: "We have no king [*cěsarě*] but Caesar [*kesara*]" (see Sever'janov 1904, p. 435); the Marianus Gospel has *čsrě/kesara* (Jagič 1883, p. 393); the *Izbornik* of 1073, *cěsarja/kesarja* (Sreznevskij 1893-1912, III, col. 1461); the twelfth-century Mstislav Gospel, *cesarja/kesarja* (Karskij 1962, p. 19). In the later redaction, instead of *cesarja*, there is *carja*. Accordingly the opposition *cesar'* (or *car'*) and *kesar'* emerges as one between Byzantine and Roman supreme power. It is no accident that before declaring himself Emperor, Peter declared Romodanovskij (his double so to speak; on this, see below, "Tsar and Pretender," § 6), to be *knjaz'-kesar'*. Both *imperator* and *kesar'* indicate an orientation specifically to Rome.
    The initial synonymity of the words *imperator* and *cesar'* was reflected in the titles of members of the Imperial family. When Peter took the title of Emperor the question arose as to how his wife, the Tsarina, and daughters, the Tsarevnas, should be addressed. There were no corresponding words in the Russian language. The Senate and Synod in conference in the Synod Chamber in Moscow on December 23, 1721 decided that the Tsar's wife should be called "*Imperatrica* or *Cesareva,*" and the daughters, *Cesarevna*. (It is curious to note that these forms are morphological Polonisms). Peter confirmed this decision, but replaced *Cesareva* by "*Imperatrica, ee Cesarevino veličestvo*" [Empress, her Caesarean majesty]. In the Manifesto this was supported by reference to the "Orthodox Greek Emperors" (S.M. Solov'ev 1963, IX, p. 538). Berchgol'c (1902-3, II, p. 55) provides evidence that the Tsarevnas began to be called *cesarevna*. Meanwhile, however, the daughters of Ivan Alekseevič* continued to be called Tsarevnas and his wife (Praskov'ja Fedorovna), Tsarina. Later the term *cesarevic* came to signify the heir to the throne exclusively. In the Decree on the Imperial family issued by the Emperor Paul on April 5, 1797, it was stated that this title was to be restricted "to the heir to the throne who had been publicly declared to be such" (§ 31, cf. also the note to § 30). In the Act on the Succession published the same day, Paul appointed as his heir his eldest son, Alexander, who thereupon became known as *cesarevič*. But on October 28 of the same year, a Manifesto was issued according to which this same title of *cesarevič* was given to Paul's second son, the Grand duke Constantine Pavlovič, "as a reward and for his greater distinction." Unlike Alexander who bore this title until his accession, Constantine Pavlovič retained it for life. An indication of the instability and novelty of the title *Imperatrica* is provided by the case of Trediakovskij's poem "Song" which was composed in Hamburg in 1730 on the occasion of Anne's coronation: the sovereign is addressed as *imperatriks* and this fact attracted the attention of the Privy Chancellery. The poet had to provide an explanation for what he had done, but

*Ivan V, Peter's half-brother.

65

significantly, when Trediakovskij cited the Latin form the matter was dropped, the explanation being acknowledged as adequate (see Mel'nikov 1879).

6   Peter's taking of the title of Emperor provoked protest among conservative elements of the population. Since Rome was regarded as the kingdom of the Antichrist, the Old Believers saw in this confirmation of the fact that Peter was Antichrist. And so the founder of the Old Believer sect of the *stranniki* ["wanderers"], Evfimij, declared in 1784: "Peter declined the title of Tsar, preferring that of Emperor after the fashion of Rome"; from this he drew the conclusion that Peter's nature was Satanic (Kel'siev 1860-2, IV, p. 253). In 1885, LM. Ermakov, an Old Believer of the Fedoseevskij sect, testified:

> I do not recognize Alexander Nikolaevič as Emperor, but as Tsar. F or the title of Emperor was ... taken by Peter the Great from the impious and Satanic Pope of Rome. The title of Emperor means Perun, Titan or the Devil. (ibid. I, p. 220)

7   It is not surprising that Vienna reacted negatively to this step; see Florovskij 1972 for the reaction of the Viennese court. A corresponding sense of the word *cesar'* was reflected in the use of the term *cesarcy* ["Caesarites"] for Austrian subjects (Dal' 1880-2, IV, p. 574).

8   *Poslanija* 1951, p. 200.

9   Efimov 1912.

10   Maksim Grek 1859-62, II, pp. 292-3.

11   Gibbenet 1882-4, II, pp. 196-7, 367.

12   Private communication from Ju. I. Vilenbachov to the authors.

13   Peter 1887-1977, IX, p. 1356.

14   Prokopovič 1765, pp. 7-8.

15   Baklanova 1951, pp. 151-2; Volkov 1973, p. 317.

16   Alekseev 1863, Col. 698-9.

17   Nikol'skij 1885, pp. 46-7.

18   Cf. the information provided in Kotošichin concerning the celebration of the birthdays of the Tsar, Tsarina and their children in pre-Petrine Russia (Kotošichin 1906, pp. 18, 76; idem 1980, pp. 32-33, 114-5).

19   Filaret 1885-88, IV, pp. 332-3.

20   Prokopovič 1765, p. 157.

21   *P'esy škol'nych teatrov* 1974, pp. 158-9.

22   Peter 1887-1977, XI, 1, p. 231, No. 3259.

23   Prokopovič 1760, p. 113.

24   Idem, 1765, p. 164.

25   Ibid., pp. 151, 157.

26   Gukovskij and Orlov 1933, p. 54.

27   Batjuškov 1936, "Perechod čerez Rejn."

28   Whereas originally the replacement of the form "Petersburg" by "Petrograd" was felt to be connected with the reinterpretation of the city of the Apostle Peter as that of the Emperor Peter, later this renaming acquired a different interpretation: it came to be regarded as a rejection of foreign names, in this case substitution of a Russian for a German one. This interpretation can already be found in the second half of the nineteenth century. See, for example, this epigram of the 1880's concerning the Slavophile tendencies of Petersburg scholars of German origin:

> Moscow, be silent!
> Here Petersburg has become Petrograd.

Here Gil'ferding, Frejgang and Miller
Are dealing with matters Slavonic. (Veresaev 1929, p. 15)

In the twentieth century, for rather different reasons, Academician Ol'denburg became known as Academician Ol'dengrad (see letters from G.A. Il'inskij to M.G. Popruženko of 1928 in, Kostadinova, Florova, Dimitrova 1968, pp. 135, 138, 139.) The official renaming of Petersburg as Petrograd in 1914 is based on this play of words.

29 The young Mandel'štam disputed this sort of treatment of Petersburg by the Symbolists. In the volume significantly named *Kamen'* [*Stone*] (see above for the symbolism of the stone in relation to Peter and Petersburg), it is the imperial image of the city and its *style Empire* that are emphasized:

"And on the Neva there are the embassies of half the world . . . "

In the light of our discussion, one can understand Mandel'štam's later switch from stone to wood:

"And now it is not of stone,
But of wood I sing."

In this way the symbolism of the Middle Ages which had persisted through the centuries had its effect on the ideas and artistic consciousness of poets.

67

PART TWO

THE DECEMBRIST IN EVERYDAY LIFE: EVERYDAY BEHAVIOR AS A HISTORICAL–PSYCHOLOGICAL CATEGORY

Ju. M. Lotman

The laws of history are not realized automatically. The complex and contradictory movement of history entails the intersection and the conflict of processes in which man is a passive agent and of others in which his activity appears in the most direct and immediate form. To understand the latter (which are sometimes defined as the subjective aspect of the historical process) it is necessary to examine not only the socio-historical premises of a given situation, but also the specific features of the agent himself—the individual. If we are to study history from the point of view of the actions of people, we cannot dispense with examination of the psychological premises of their behavior. However, this psychological aspect also operates on several levels. It is certain that some features of people's behavior and their reactions to external situations are peculiar to man. This is the level which interests the psychologist, who, when he approaches historical material, does so only in order to discover within it illustrations of psychological laws as such.

However, this general psychological stratum, which is acted on by exceptionally complex socio-historical processes, provides the basis for specific forms of historical and social behavior, epochal and social types of reaction, as well as general conceptions as to which actions may be considered correct or incorrect, permitted or forbidden, valuable or worthless. Regulators of behavior emerge, such as shame, fear or honor. The individual's consciousness is, as it were, plugged into complex ethical, religious, aesthetic, practical and other semiotic norms, on which is constituted the psychology of group behavior.

However, group behavior as such does not exist in reality. Just as the norms of language are realized and at the same time inevitably broken in thousands of individual utterances, so group behavior is formed from innumerable enactments and violations of it within the system of individual behavior of the numerous members of a collective. But even the "incorrect" behavior which breaks the norms of a given social group is by no means accidental. There were distinct differences between violations of the generally accepted norms of behavior, the eccentricities and even the "outrages" of the individual of the pre- and post-Petrine era, depending on whether they were committed by nobleman or merchant, peasant or monk (quite apart from the existence of "national"varieties of norm violation which were common to everyone). Moreover, the norm and its violations cannot be set in opposition like inert facts. There is a constant interchange between them. There emerge rules for the violation of rules and anomalies which are necessary to norms. The real behavior of the individual will fluctuate between these poles. In this respect, different types of culture will dictate subjective orientation towards the norm (in which "correct" behavior, life conducted "in accordance with custom," "like other people," "as laid down" etc., is highly valued) or, on the other hand, violation of the norm (a striving for originality and the unusual, eccentricity, the behavior of a holy fool and a devaluation of the norm by the ambivalent combination of extremes).

People's behavior is always heterogeneous. This must not be forgotten. Appealing abstractions such as "Romantic behavior" or "the psychological type of the young Russian nobleman of the early nineteenth century" will always be extremely notional constructions. Moreover, any normalization of psycho-social stereotypes entails the existence of variants by age ("the childish," "the youthful" etc.; "absurd is the empty-headed old man, absurd is the staid youth"*), sex and other categories.

The psyche of each individual presents such a complex, multi-level structure, with such heterogeneous personal regulating factors, that the emergence of two identical individuals may be excluded as a practical possibility.

However, while taking account of the richness of individual psychological variants and the multiplicity of possible forms of behavior, we must not forget that, so far as society is concerned, by no means all the actions of the individual exist in practical terms, but only those which possess social significance in the given system of culture. Thus society, in interpreting the behavior of the individual personality, simplifies and typifies it in accordance with its social codes. At the same time, the individual personality, as it were, completes its self-organization by assimilating this viewpoint of society, and thus becoming "more typical" not only to the observer, but also from the position of the subject itself.

In analyzing the structure of people's behavior in any historical era and in creating constructions on this basis, we shall constantly, therefore, have to consider the connection of these behavior-structures with numerous variants, as well as the complex dialectical interweaving of the regular and the accidental, without which it is impossible to understand the mechanisms of social psychology.

So then, was the everyday behavior of the Decembrist peculiar to him in a way that distinguished him not only from reactionaries and "repressors," but also from the mass of the liberal, educated gentry of the time? Study of the materials of that age allows us to answer that

*Lines from Puškin's poem "To Kaverin" (1817).

72

question positively. We ourselves even sense this directly, as the cultural successors of previous historical development. Thus, without consulting the commentaries, we feel that Čackij is a Decembrist.* However, Čackij is not shown to us at a meeting of "the most secret society"; we see him in everyday surroundings, in a Moscow mansion. Several phrases in Čackij's monologues, which characterize him as an enemy of serfdom and ignorance, are of course relevant to our interpretation of him, but no less significant is his manner of conduct and speech. It is precisely for his *behavior* in the Famusovs' house, for his refusal to adopt the set type of everyday behavior:

> At one's patrons' to yawn at the ceiling,
> To appear, simply to keep silent, to shuffle, to dine,
> To offer a chair, to pass a handkerchief . . . . .

—that he is accurately defined by Famusov as "a dangerous man." Numerous documents reflect the various aspects of the everyday behavior of the nobleman revolutionary,** making it possible for us to talk about the Decembrist not only as the bearer of a particular political programme, but also as a specific cultural-historical and psychological type.

It must not be forgotten that the individual in his behavior does not realize any one single programme of action, but constantly makes a choice, by actualizing one strategy out of an extensive set of possibilities. It is by no means the case that every individual Decembrist conducted himself as a Decembrist in his real everyday behavior: he sometimes acted like a nobleman, an officer (more specifically, like a guardsman, a hussar or a staff theorist), an aristocrat, a man, a Russian, a European, a young man and so on.

However, there existed within this complex set of possibilities a certain special kind of behavior, a particular type of speech, action and reaction, which was specific to the member of a secret society. It is the nature of this special behavior which will be of most immediate interest to us. We do not intend to describe those manifestations of this behavior which coincide with the general outline of the enlightened Russian noblemen of the early nineteenth century. Rather, we shall attempt to indicate only those specific features which the Decembrist movement cast on the behavior of those whom we call nobleman revolutionaries.

Naturally, each of the Decembrists was a living person and in a certain sense behaved in a unique manner: in everyday life Ryleev was unlike Pestel', while Orlov did not resemble either Nikolaj Turgenev or

---

*Čackij is the central character of the satirical comedy *Gore ot uma (Woe from Wit)* written 1822-1824 by A.S. Griboedov (1795-1829). In Russian literary criticism Čackij is usually held to be an example of a Decembrist. Famusov and Repetilov are also characters in this play.
**The Russian term is *dvorjanskij revoljucioner.*

Čaadaev.* However, this consideration is no basis on which to doubt the legitimacy of the task we have set ourselves. After all, the fact that people's behavior is individual does not detract from the validity of studying such problems as "the psychology of the adolescent" (or of individuals of any other age), "the psychology of women" (or of men) or, finally, "the psychology of man." We must supplement our view of history as a field where social and general historical laws are manifest by an examination of history as the result of *the activity of people*. Failure to study the historical-psychological mechanisms of human acts will inevitably leave us in the grip of extremely schematic conceptions. Moreover, the very fact that the laws of history do not realize themselves directly, but through the medium of the psychological mechanisms of the individual, is in itself a most important mechanism of history: for it absolves history from the fatal predictability of its processes. Were this not so, the entire historical process would be completely redundant.

The Decembrists were first and foremost people of action. This was demonstrated not only by their socio-political emphasis on the practical reformation of the political life of Russia, but also by the personal experience of most of them as military officers. They were men who had come of age in the era of the Napoleonic wars and who valued bravery, energy, enterprise, firmness and determination no less than the ability to compose a manifesto or conduct a theoretical dispute. As a rule (and there were, of course, exceptions such as Nikolaj Turgenev), political doctrines interested them not so much *per se*, but as criteria for the assessment and selection of specific courses of action. This orientation towards activity may be sensed in the facetious words of Lunin,** to the effect that Pestel' proposed "first to write an Encyclopedia, and then to tackle the Revolution."[1] Even those members of the secret societies who were more accustomed to staff duties emphasized that "orderliness and good form"

*K.F. Ryleev (1795-1826), poet and member of the Northern Society; P.I. Pestel' (1793-1826), founder and director of the Southern Society. Both these were among the five Decembrists executed (the others being S.I. Murav'ev-Apostol, M.P. Bestužev-Rjumin and P.G. Kachovskoj). General Count M.F. Orlov (1788-1842), founder member of the Union of Welfare, exiled for his part in the rebellion. (On the Orlov brothers, see below, ch. 6.) N.I. Turgenev (1789-1871), member of the Northern Society, left Russia in 1824 but condemned to indefinite penal servitude. P.Ja. Čaadaev (1794-1856) was briefly associated with the Northern Society in 1821; after his conversion to mystical Christianity he wrote his *Philosophical Letters* which had an enduring influence on nineteenth century Russian thought. On his resignation from government service, see below, pp. 88-93.
**M.S. Lunin (1787-1845), a member of both the Northern and Southern Societies. He was sentenced to 20 years' hard labor.

74

were necessary for "the most successful action" (in the words of S. Trub-eckoj*).[2]

Therefore, as the limits of the present study do not allow us to examine the entire complex of problems to do with the historical-psychological characteristics of the Decembrist movement, we will concentrate on one aspect, namely the *behavior* of the Decembrist, his actions, and not the internal world of his emotions.

At this point we must make another reservation. The Decembrists were noblemen revolutionaries: their behavior was the behavior of members of the Russian gentry and in its essential features corresponded to the norms laid down between the period of Peter the Great and the Napoleonic War of 1812. Even when denying class-based forms of behavior, struggling against them and refuting them in theoretical treatises, the Decembrists remained organically bound to them in their own everyday practices. It is impossible to understand and describe the behavior of the Decembrist without broaching a greater problem, that of the behavior of the Russian nobleman between 1810 and 1825. But ours is not so broad a task: we therefore exclude from examination everything that was common between the active life of the Decembrist and that of the young Russian nobleman of his time.

The significance of the Decembrists in the history of the life of Russian society is not limited to those aspects of their activity which have until now attracted most of the attention of scholars: the development of their socio-political programmes and conceptions, their thoughts on the tactics of revolutionary struggle, their participation in literary polemics and their artistic and critical creativity. To these questions (and the many others which are examined in the scholarly literature) must be added one other, which has been neglected until now: the Decembrists demonstrated significant creative energy in the development of a special type of Russian man, one which was clearly distinct in behavior from anything known to earlier times. In this sense they acted as genuine innovators. This specific behavior, on the part of a significant group of young people who found themselves by reason of their talents, characters, origins, personal and family connections and professional considerations, at the centre of social attention, exercised a significant influence on a whole generation of Russians (although the majority of Decembrists did not, and could not for reasons of age, occupy high state posts, a significant proportion of them belonged to that circle which might expect to rise to such posts in the future). They thus acted as a kind of school of civic feeling. The ideo-

*Prince S. Trubeckoj (1790-1860), founder-member in 1816 of the first secret society, the Union of Salvation.

logical-political tendency to revolution among the gentry also produced specific features of human character, a special type of behavior. The aim of the present work is to characterize some of the chief indicators of this behavior.

It is difficult to point to any other period of Russian life in which the spoken word, in the form of conversations, friendly debates, casual exchanges, preaching and angry tirades, played such a role. From the moment of the birth of the movement, which Puškin neatly defined as "friendly arguments" "between the Lafite and the Cliquot," to their tragic appearances before the Investigating Commission, the Decembrists were remarkable for their "loquaciousness," their striving to embody their thoughts and feelings in words. Puškin was justified in describing a meeting of the Union of Welfare* thus:

> Famed for their cutting rhetoric,
> The members of this family gathered . . . . . .
> [*Eugene Onegin*, X, 14]

This feature gave rise to the criticism, from the point of view of later norms and conceptions, that the Decembrists were mere phrasemongers, who substituted words for actions. Such a view tended to be expressed not only by the "nihilists" of the 1860's, but also by close contemporaries, even those who shared many of the Decembrists' ideas. It is from a Decembrist position, as M.V. Nečkina has shown,** that Čackij accuses Repetilov of bombast and phrasemongering. But he himself is not spared the same reproach, directed at him by Puškin:

> Everything he says is very clever. But to whom is he saying all this? To Famusov? To Skalozub? To little old Moscow ladies at a ball? To Molčalin? This is unforgiveable. The first sign of a clever man is to know at once who you're dealing with . . .[3]

In 1826, Vjazemskij,*** arguing that to accuse the Decembrists of regicide was invalid, was to stress that regicide is an action, a deed. And the conspirators, in his opinion, had made no attempt to move from word to deed. He defined their behavior as "murderous chatter" (*"bavardage atroce"*)[4] and resolutely rejected the case for condemning them as if they had translated their words into actions. His words contain not

---

*The Union of Welfare (*Sojuz blagodenstvija*), secret revolutionary organization between 1818 and 1821.
**See Nečkina 1947.
***Prince P.A. Vjazemskij (1792-1878), poet, leading member of "Arzamas" and close friend of Puškin.

only a juridical defence of victims of injustice, but also indications that, in his opinion, the "chatter" of the conspirators far outweighed the significance of any "action" on their part. Other examples of such a view of the Decembrists can easily be found.

However, it would be a definite error, and a consequence of applying to the Decembrists' era norms derived from other historical periods, to regard the particular significance of the "cutting rhetoric" as merely a weakness on the part of the Decembrists and thereby to judge them by the same measure as that which Černyševskij* applied to Turgenev's** heroes. We see our task here not as a largely meaningless "condemnation" or "justification" of those involved, men whose names now belong to history, but as an attempt to explain this particular feature.

It was not only the "loquaciousness" of the Decembrists which drew the attention of their contemporaries. They also emphasized the sharpness and directness of their opinions, the categorical nature of their verdicts and their tendency, "improper" from the point of view of society norms, to call things by name, avoiding the conventional euphemisms of society formulas. Remarkable too was the Decembrists' constant determination to express their opinions plainly, without observing either the established ritual or the hierarchy of speech behavior in society. Nikolaj Turgenev was renowned for this kind of abruptness and deliberate disregard of "speech manners." Their studied disregard of "drawing room" norms and the "tactlessness" of their speech behavior were described as "Spartan" or "Roman" in circles close to the Decembrists, and contrasted with "French" behavior which was viewed negatively.

Themes which were forbidden in society conversation, or which were introduced only euphemistically (for example, questions of landowners' power, bureaucratic protectionism, etc.) became the subject of open discussion. The behavior of the educated, Europeanized society of the nobility of the Alexandrine era was fundamentally dualistic. In the sphere of ideas and of "ideological speech" the norms were those of the European culture which derived from the Enlightenment of the eighteenth century. However, the sphere of practical behavior, which had to do with the customs, the practice and the real-life conditions of the landowner economy, and with the real circumstances of service employment, fell outside the area of "ideological" interpretation, from the point of view of which the practical sphere "did not really exist." Naturally, in verbal activity the practical sphere was associated with the oral, conversational medium and was only minimally reflected in texts of elevated cultural value. The result was a hierarchy of behaviors, constructed on the principle of rising cultural value (which coincided with a growth in semioticity). Marked off within this hierarchy was the lowest, purely practical stratum, which

*N.G. Černyševskij (1828-1889), radical critic of the 1860's.
**I.S. Turgenev (1818-1883), the novelist.

77

from the point of view of the theorizing consciousness "did not really exist."

It was just this pluralism of behavior, the possibility of selecting styles of behavior according to situation, and the duality which lay in the differentiation between the practical and the ideological, which characterized the *progressive* Russian of the early nineteenth century. This also distinguished him from the nobleman revolutionary. This question is of the utmost relevance: for while it is quite easy to differentiate Skotinin's* type of behavior from Ryleev's, there is significantly more of importance in the contrast between Ryleev and Del'vig** or between Nikolaj Turgenev and his brother Aleksandr.***

By their behavior, the Decembrists rejected the hierarchy and stylistic variety of the act. Above all, they effaced the distinction between oral and written language: the elevated regularity of system, the use of political terminology and the syntactical finality of the written language was transferred to oral practice. Famusov had reason to say that Čackij "talks as he writes." In this instance, this is not just a saying: Čackij's speech differs distinctly from that of the other characters in its literary quality. He talks as he writes, in that he sees the world in its ideological, rather than real-life manifestations.

At the same time, purely practical behavior not only became the object of interpretation in the terms and concepts of the ideological-philosophical sphere, it also took on a sign function, passing from the category of unvalued actions into that group of acts which may be interpreted positively or negatively, as "noble" and "elevated," or "vile," "boorish" (in Nikolaj Turgenev's terminology) or "mean."[5]

Let us take one particularly telling example. Puškin recorded a characteristic conversation:

> Del'vig once invited Ryleev to visit the brothels with him. "I am married," replied Ryleev. "So what," said Del'vig, "does that mean you can't have lunch in a restaurant just because you have a kitchen at home?"[6]

The conversation between Del'vig and Ryleev recorded by Puškin is of interest not so much for its reconstruction of the actual biographical features of their behavior (both were living people, whose actions might be regulated by numerous factors, producing an incalculable number of variants at the level of real-life acts), as for an understanding of their attitude to the very principle of behavior. We are dealing with a confrontation between the "playful" and the "serious" attitude to life.

---

*A "country bumpkin" character who prefers pigs to people in *The Minor*, a classic comedy by D.I. Fonvizin (1745-1792).
**A.A. Del'vig (1798-1831), poet and a friend of Puškin.
***A.I. Turgenev (1784-1845), man of letters.

Ryleev is a man of serious behavior. In real life, as at the level of elevated ideological constructions, this approach entails a particular single norm of correct actions for every significant situation. Del'vig, like the members of "Arzamas"* or the members of the "The Green Lamp,"** practiced playful behavior, ambivalent in its essence: the situation of the game is transferred into real life, and this allows the conventional replacement of "correct" behavior by its opposite to be considered permissible in certain situations.

The Decembrists cultivated seriousness as a norm of behavior. It was characteristic for Zavališin*** to emphasize that he "was always serious" and that even in childhood he "had never played games."[7] The Decembrists were just as negative in their attitude to the culture of wordplay as a form of speech behavior. In the exchange of remarks just quoted, the two men are in fact talking in different languages: Del'vig has no intention of taking Ryleev's words seriously as a declaration of moral principles,—what interests him is his witticism, his *mot*. Ryleev, on the other hand, cannot enjoy a paradox when ethical truths are at issue. Every statement he makes is a program.

Milonov**** gave particularly precise expression to the antithesis between play and the sense of civic duty in his epistle to Žukovskij,† in which he demonstrated the extent to which this division, which ran through the works of the progressive younger writers, was consciously held:

> . . . we shall remain each with his own —
> You with your nonsense, and I with my Parnassian sting;
> Call yourself Schiller, while I call myself Juvenal;
> Posterity will judge us, and not your friends,
> But Bludov,†† it seems, is no judge between us.[8]

Here we have a full paradigm of oppositions: between nonsense (wordplay, the self-referential joke) and satire, elevated, civic-minded and serious; between Schiller (here, in his capacity as author of the ballads translated by Žukovskij; cf. Kjuchel'beker's††† contemptuous reference to Schiller as the author of ballads and as a model for Žukovskij,

---

*"Arzamas," Petersburg literary circle of 1815-1818.

**"The Green Lamp" (*Zelenaja lampa*), Petersburg literary-political circle of 1819-1820 strongly influenced by the Union of Welfare.

***D.I. Zavališin (1804-1892). See below, Ch. 5, pp. 180 ff.

****M.V. Milonov (1792-1821), minor poet.

†V.A. Žukovskij (1783-1852), leading poet of early Russian Romanticism.

††D.N. Bludov (1785-1864), one of the founders of "Arzamas"; Minister of Internal Affairs 1832-1838.

†††V.K. Kjuchel'beker (1797-1846), poet and friend of Puškin, condemned to death for his part in the Decembrist rebellion, though the sentence was commuted to penal servitude.

"the immature Schiller," in his article "On the trends of our poetry ..."),[9] whose name is linked with the fantasy of ballad stories, and Juvenal, who is viewed as the citizen-poet; between the judgment of the literary elite, the opinion of a closed circle (Polevoj described the irritation aroused by the Karamzinists' propensity to refer to the opinions of "famous friends" outside their camp)[10] and the opinion of posterity. In order fully to grasp the sense of the antithesis outlined by Milonov, we should recall how close it is to Puškin's criticism of Žukovskij in the early 1820's, including the attack on Bludov (see his letter to Žukovskij, dated between the 20th and 29th of April 1825).

From Del'vig's position, the visit to the brothels comes into the sphere of real-life behavior, which does not correlate at all to ideological behavior. That he could be one thing in poetry and another in life he did not see as duality, nor did it cast any shadow on his character as a whole. Ryleev's behaviour, on the other hand, is whole in principle, and such an act would have been equivalent for him to a theoretical admission of man's right to amorality. What for Del'vig had no significance (was not a sign), for Ryleev was full of ideological content. Thus, the difference between the freedom-lover Del'vig and the revolutionary Ryleev stands out not only at the level of ideas or theoretical conceptions, but also in the nature of their everyday behavior. Karamzinism established a variety of behaviors and their alternation as a norm of the poetic attitude to life. Karamzin wrote:

Is it not natural for the sensitive soul to change?
It is soft as wax, as clear as a mirror ...
... Such a soul cannot appear as a unity to you.[11]

By contrast, for Romanticism it was the unity of behavior, the independence of acts from circumstances that was considered poetic.
"Alone,—he was everywhere, cold and unchanging ...," Lermontov wrote of Napoleon.[12] "Be yourself," Bestužev wrote to Puškin.[13] The priest Myslovskij described Pestel's behavior at his trial in the following terms: "He was everywhere and always equal to himself. Nothing could shake his firmness."[14]
Moreover, the Romantic ideal of the unity of behavior did not contradict the Classicist conception of heroism; for it coincided with the principle of "the unity of action." In this respect, Karamzinian "Proteanism" was closer to the realist concept of a multiplicity of levels. In a well-known comment, Puškin contrasted the homogeneity of the behavior of Molière's heroes to the life-like heterogeneity of Shakespeare's creations:

The characters created by Shakespeare are not, as in Molière, types of a certain passion or a certain vice; rather, they are living beings, replete with many passions and vices. Circumstances unfold before the audience their various and many-faceted personalities.[15]

80

When, in the transition from his observations of life to the poetic text which he creates, the artist of Classicism or Romanticism consciously selects a particular single level, because he considers it alone worthy of literary representation, then a transformation is effected in the reverse transition, from the reader's apprehension of the text to the reader's behavior. The reader, taking the text to be a programme for his everyday behavior, assumes that particular aspects of real-life activity are completely absent from the ideal. What the text passes over in silence should be excluded from real behavior. Thus, for example, a rejection of the genre of love elegy in poetry could be interpreted as a demand for the rejection of love in life. We should note the general "literariness" of the behavior of the Romantics, their constant attempts to regard *all* acts as significant.

On the one hand, this leads to an increase in the role of *gesture* in everyday behavior. Gesture is action or an act which has not so much a practical intent as a relationship to some meaning. Gesture is always a sign and a symbol. Therefore, *any* action on the stage, including those which pretend to be completely free of any scenic purpose, is a gesture; its significance lies in the author's intention.

From this point of view, the everyday behavior of the Decembrist appeared theatrical to the contemporary observer, behavior calculated to affect the spectator. It should clearly be understood, however, that "theatricality" of behavior in no way implies insincerity or any other negative characteristics. It is simply an indication of the fact that the behavior has acquired a certain sense beyond that of real life, that it has become a subject of attention, in which value is attached not to the acts themselves, but to their symbolic meaning.

On the other hand, the usual correlations of word and deed change places in the everyday behavior of the Decembrist.

In the normal speech behavior of the time the relationship between acts and utterances was constructed according to the following scheme:

expression   ————————→   content

word   ————————→   deed

When designating an action, the word had a tendency towards different kinds of shifts, euphemistic, periphrastic or metaphorical in nature. On the one hand, this gave rise to the everyday language of society with its "she availed herself of a handkerchief" on the lower social level and its French terms for "Russian" actions on the higher level. The genetic and typological connection of this language to Karamzinism was clearly perceived by contemporaries, who accused both the literary language of the Karamzinists and society language of affectedness. This tendency to weaken or "loosen" the bond between the word and its designate, a tendency characteristic of society language, was to rouse Leo Tolstoj to a lasting campaign to expose the hypocrisy of society talk.

On the other hand, the same principle of the "ennoblement" of low-grade activity inspired bureaucratic language with its "lamb in paper" (the term for a bribe), and its euphemistic "I am obliged to make a deposition," in the sense of "you'll have to increase the amount," and with its specific meanings for the verbs "give" and "take." Consider the chorus of the clerks in Kapnist's* *Slander (Jabeda)*:

> Take, there's no great art to it;
> Take whatever you can.
> What have we been given hands for,
> If not in order to take?[16]

Commenting on these lines, Vjazemskij wrote:

> Here there is no need for further explanations: it's obvious what kind of taking is being discussed. In the same way, the verb "to drink" is equivalent to the verb "to get drunk" ... Another official said that when he had to sign service records and to enter in the appropriate columns the words "worthy" and "capable," he often felt like adding: "Capable of any dirty trick, worthy of any amount of contempt."[17]

Hence at times the transformation of the practical language of the office into a secret language, reminiscent of a priestly language for the initiate. The visitor was required not only to carry out certain actions (giving a bribe), but also to solve the riddles of which the clerks' speech consisted. This, for instance, is the basis of the conversation between Varravin and Muromskij in Suchovo-Kobylin's** *The Affair*. Čechov also provides a model of this kind of office language:

> "I say, old man, give us half a marvel and twenty four nuisances."
> The waiter soon brought on a tray half a bottle of vodka and several plates with various hors d'oeuvres.
> "Well now, my friend," Počatkin said to him, "give us a portion of the grand master of gossip and slander with mashed potatoes."[18]

The linguistic behaviour of the Decembrists was highly specific. We have already noted that one of its characteristic features was their tendency to call by their name those things which, although occurring in the sphere of everyday behavior, were taboo in language. However, this naming was of a special kind and did not entail the rehabilitation of low, vulgar or even simply everyday vocabulary. One attribute of the Decembrist's consciousness was the radical polarization of moral and political values: any act could find itself categorized as "boorish," "base," "tyrannical,"

---

*V.V. Kapnist (1758-1823), dramatist and poet; *Slander* was written in 1793.
**A.V. Suchovo-Kobylin (1817-1903), dramatist and academician. The play *The Affair (Delo)* was part of his trilogy of plays about bureaucratic life.

or "liberal," "enlightened" or "heroic." There were no neutral or insignificant acts; that such acts might exist was not even considered.

Acts which existed beyond verbal designation, as well as those which were designated euphemistically or metaphorically, were given unambiguous verbal labels. The set of these designations was relatively limited and coincided with the ethical-political lexicon of Decembrism. The first result of this was that everyday behavior ceased to be simply everyday: it acquired an elevated ethical-political meaning. Secondly, there was a reversal in the usual correlations between the planes of expression and content, as they apply to behavior: it is no longer the word which designates the deed, but the deed which designates the word:

At this point, it is important to emphasize that it is not the thought, the evaluation of the act, which becomes content, but the word itself, and specifically the word spoken aloud: the Decembrist was not satisfied with negatively evaluating to himself some manifestation of the "past age." He openly and publicly called things by their proper names, "made a racket" at balls and in society, because it was precisely in this naming activity that he saw the liberation of man and the beginnings of the transformation of society. For this reason, straightforwardness, a certain naiveté and the capacity to adopt what were, from society's point of view, absurd positions, all of these features were just as much part of the Decembrists' behavior as their cutting wit, their pride and even their haughtiness. But it absolutely excluded compliance, the play of values and any capacity to "follow the tone" such as that of Molčalin,* or even the style of Petr Stepanovič Verchovenskij.**

It may seem that this characteristic is applicable not to the Decembrist in general, but to the Decembrist of the period of the Union of Welfare, when "oratory at balls" was the done thing. As is well known, the emphasis was transferred to conspiratorial behavior in the later tactical evolution of the secret societies. The new tactics replaced the society propagandist with the conspirator.

However, it should be noted that this change in the tactics of the struggle did not lead to a fundamental shift in the style of behavior: the fact that he had become a plotter and a conspirator did not mean that the Decembrist began to behave in the salon "like everyone else." No conspiratorial aims could force him to behave like Molčalin. While he no longer expressed his attitude in a blazing tirade, but with a contemptuous

*The servile secretary in Griboedev's *Woe from Wit*.
**Verchovenskij is the leader of a revolutionary cell in Dostoevskij's novel *The Devils*.

83

word or a grimace, he remained a "Carbonari"* in his everyday behavior.
When D.I. Zavališin reached Petersburg after a voyage round the
world in 1824, his conduct in the sphere of everyday behavior, by
refusing to avail himself of a letter of recommendation to Arakčeev,**
was such that the latter remarked to Baten'kov: "So that's Zavališin!
Well, Gavrilo Stepanovič, listen to me:he must be either an extremely
proud man, just like his father, or a liberal."[19] What is characteristic
here is Arakčeev's view that a "proud man" and a "liberal" will behave
in an identical manner. It is also interesting that, although Zavališin had
not yet entered the political scene, his behavior served to unmask him.
However, it did not occur to any of the Decembrists to accuse him of this,
even though they were no longer the enthusiastic propagandists of the
Union of Welfare era, but conspirators who were preparing for decisive actions. By contrast, if Zavališin had shown a capacity for putting on
appearances and gone to pay his respects to Arakčeev, his behavior
would probably have aroused condemnation, and he himself would not
have been trusted. It is characteristic that the intimacy of Baten'kov
and Arakčeev was disapproved of by the conspirators.

There is another revealing example. In 1824 Katenin*** expressed
his disapproval of Ćackij's character precisely because of those features
of "the propagandist at the ball" in which Nečkina rightly detected a
reflection of the tactical devices of the Union of Welfare:

This Ćackij is the main character. The author has drawn him *con
amore* and, in the author's opinion, Ćackij possesses all virtues and
commits no sin; in my opinion, however, he talks a lot, criticizes
everything and makes inopportune speeches.[20]

However, only a few months before this remark (and we have no reason
to believe that there had been any development in his views during that
intervening period) Katenin attempted to persuade his friend Bachtin to
participate openly, without the use of pseudonyms, in literary polemics.
To this end, he formulated in very direct terms the demand that one's
convictions should be openly demonstrated not only in words, but in
one's entire behavior:

One's duty now is to stand up for oneself and for what is right, to speak
the truth without hesitation, to praise boldly the good and to expose
the bad, not only in books, but also *in one's acts*, to repeat what has
been said to them, to repeat it without fail, so that the knaves cannot
pretend they haven't heard, to force them to drop their masks,
to come out for a duel and, when they come out, to beat them

*The Carbonari were members of secret political societies in Italy in the early
nineteenth century. In *Woe from Wit*, Famusov calls Ćackij a carbonari.
**A.A. Arakčeev (1769-1834), most powerful figure of the reactionary years
of Alexander I's reign.
***P.A. Katenin (1792-1853), poet, translator, dramatist and critic.

half to death.[21]

It does not matter that what Katenin understood by "what is right" was the propaganda of his own literary programme and his own services to literature. If a man could express his personality in *such* words, then these very expressions must in substance have already become the password of a generation.

The fact that it was everyday behavior which in a whole series of instances enabled the young liberals to distinguish what was "their own" from that of the "repressors" is a special characteristic of gentry culture, which created an extremely complex and extensive system of behavior signs. However, it was in this respect too that the specific features which identified the Decembrist as a nobleman *revolutionary* were revealed. Indeed, everyday behavior became one of the criteria for selection of candidates for the society. It was on this basis that the chivalry specific to the Decembrists emerged, a quality which, on the one hand, determined the moral fascination which the Decembrist tradition holds in Russian culture, but which, on the other hand, served them ill in the tragic conditions of their trial and unexpectedly proved to be a source of instability: they were not psychologically prepared for action in the conditions of legalized baseness.

The hierarchy of the significant elements of behavior is composed of the sequence: gesture – act – behavior - text. The latter should be understood as a completed chain of meaningful acts that runs between intention and result. In the real-life behavior of people, a complex activity governed by numerous factors, behavior texts may remain incomplete, be transformed into new ones, or intersect with parallel texts. But at the level of the individual's ideal interpretation of his behavior they always form completed, meaningful plots. Were it not so, purposeful activity would be impossible. Thus, at the level of intention, a specific programme of behavior corresponds to each behavior-text at the level of acts. The relations between these categories may be extremely complex and will also depend ultimately on the type of culture at issue. The two categories may be closely related, in which case activity and the interpretation of it strive to "speak a common language," or they may consciously (or unconsciously) diverge. To the second instance beongs the romantic "disjuncture between dream and reality" (as in Gogol): for example, the divergence between the "behavior-texts" and the dreams (the behavior programmes) of the artist Piskarev in Gogol's story *Nevskij Prospekt*; or the way in which Chlestakov's [in Gogol's play *The Government Inspector*] blarney supplements his wretched behavior by inventing alluring programmes which are presented as reality;

or the reminiscences of General Ivolgin [in Dostoevskij's novel *The Idiot*]. The memoirs of D.I. Zavališin are a tragic variant on this. Prince Myškin, however, did not expose or mock General Ivolgin, as Gogol did his hero; instead, he took the general's reminiscences as *"acts performed in intention."* To the general's high-flown blarney about his influence on Napoleon, Myškin says: "You did a good action, . . . for in the midst of his angry feelings you insinuated a kind thought into his heart" [*The Idiot*, trans. Eva M. Martin, Everyman, p. 482].[22] Zavališin's memoirs as well deserve just such an attitude on our part.

The day-to-day behavior of the Decembrist cannot be understood without an examination not only of gestures and acts, but also of the individual and completed units of a higher order, those of behavior-texts.

Just as the gestures and acts of the nobleman revolutionary had meaning for himself and for those around him, in that their significance was expressed in the *word*, so any series of acts would become a text (acquire significance) if it could be illuminated by association with a literary plot. The death of Caesar, the heroism of Cato; the preaching and stance of a denunciatory prophet, Tyrtaeus, Ossian or Bajan* singing to the warriors on the eve of battle (the latter story was invented by Narežnyj**); Hector leaving for battle and saying farewell to Andromache,—these were the plots which gave meaning to particular chains of everyday acts.

Such an approach entailed "enlarging" one's entire behavior, allocating to one's real-life acquaintances the masks of literary types and idealizing the place and space of the action (real space being interpreted through literary space). Thus, in Puškin's epistle to F. Glinka,*** Petersburg is Athens, and Glinka himself Aristides. This is not only the result of the transformation in Puškin's verses of a real-life situation into a literary one, but the active functioning of the opposite process: in the life situation it was what could be related to a literary subject which became significant (and, consequently, noticeable to the participants). Thus, Katenin in 1821 describes himself to his friend N.I. Bachtin as one who has been exiled "not far from Siberia."[23] However, the province of Kostroma, to which Katenin had been exiled, was closer to both Moscow and Petersburg than Siberia, as Katenin and his correspondent knew perfectly well. This geographical absurdity is explained by the fact that by that time Siberia had already become a literary subject and part of the oral mythology of Russian culture as a place of exile; it was associated in this respect with scores of historic names (Ryleev was to transport his hero Vojnarovskij to Siberia, just as Puškin was to transport himself there in his "Imagined conversation with Alexander I"). Kostroma, on the other

*Legendary bards of the Spartans, Gaels, and Russians respectively.
**V.T. Narežnyj (1780-1825), prolific novelist.
***F.N. Glinka (1786-1880), poet and one of the leaders of the Union of Welfare.

hand, had no associations in this respect. Consequently, just as Athens stands for Petersburg, Kostroma stands for Siberia, i.e. exile. The relationship between the different types of art and the individual's behavior varies. While realism justifies itself by claiming that this is how people behave in reality, and Classicism holds that this is how people should act in an ideal world, Romanticism prescribes forms of behavior, including everyday behavior, to the reader. Given the apparent similarity between the second and third of these principles, the difference between them is extremely relevant: the ideal behavior of Classicism's hero is realized within the ideal space of the literary text. Only an exceptional individual, who has risen to the heights of the ideal, could attempt to transfer this behavior into life. However, for the majority of readers and observers the behavior of literary characters is an elevated ideal, intended to ennoble their practical behavior, but not to be put into practice.

In this respect, Romantic behavior is more accessible, as it contains not only literary virtues, but also literary vices. For example, egoism, an exaggerated demonstration of which formed part of the norm of "everyday Byronism":

Lord Byron by a successful whim
Shrouded in despondent Romanticism
Hopeless egoism.

The very fact that the literary hero of Romanticism was a contemporary made it easier to approach the text as a programme for the actual future behavior of the reader. The heroes of Byron and Puškin in his Romantic period, of Marlinskij* and Lermontov,** gave rise to a whole phalanx of imitators among the young officers and government servants, who adopted the gestures, the expressions and the manners of these literary characters. If a realist work of art imitates reality, in the case of Romanticism, reality itself hastens to imitate literature. It is characteristic of realism that a particular type of behavior emerges in life and then starts to appear on the pages of literary texts (Turgenev, for example, was renowned for his ability to detect in life itself the emergence of new norms of consciousness and behavior). In a Romantic work of art the new type of personal behavior emerges on the pages of a text and is transferred from there to life.

The behavior of the Decembrist was marked by the stamp of Romanticism: their acts and behavior-texts were determined by literary plots, by model literary situations such as "the parting of Hector and

---

*A.A. Bestužev (1797-1837), exiled after the Decembrist revolt, popular novelist who wrote under the pseudonym of A. Marlinskij.
**M.Ju. Lermontov (1814-1841), Russia's greatest Romantic poet and author of the enormously influential novel, *A Hero of our Time.*

Andromache," "the oath of the Horatii" etc., or by names which in them-selves suggested literary subjects. In this sense, Puškin's exclamation,— "Here is Caesar—so where is Brutus?"—was easily deciphered as the pro-gramme of a future act.

Indeed, it is only by reference to literary models that we can deciph-er many of the actions carried out by people of that era, actions which are puzzling when seen from any other point of view. Thus, for example, both contemporaries and later historians have been bewildered by Čaa-daev's action in retiring at the very height of a successful career, after his meeting with the Tsar in Troppau in 1820. As we know, Čaadaev was adjutant to Adjutant-General Vasil'čikov, the commander of the Guards corps. Following the mutiny in the Semenovskij regiment,* he volunteered to take the report on the disturbance to Alexander I, who was at the Congress of Troppau. His contemporaries viewed this as a desire on Čaa-daev's part to advance himself at the expense of the misfortune of his friends and erstwhile regimental comrades (Čaadaev had served in the Semenovskij regiment in 1812).

If such an action on the part of Čaadaev, who was known for his noble sentiments, seemed inexplicable, his unexpected retirement soon after his interview with the Emperor threw everyone into confusion. Čaadaev himself explained his action thus in a letter to his aunt A.M. Ščerbatova on 2 January 1821:

> This time, dear aunt, I am writing to you to tell you positively that I have resigned . . . My request caused a real sensation among some people. At first they refused to believe that I was making a serious request. Later, they had to believe it, but they still cannot under-stand how I could determine upon this at the moment when I was to receive what I seemed to desire, what the whole world desires and what it is considered most flattering for a young man of my rank to receive . . . The fact is that I was indeed about to be appointed aide-de-camp on the return of the Emperor, at least, according to Vasil'čikov. I found it more amusing to scorn this favour than to accept it. It amused me to demonstrate my contempt for those peo-ple who despise everyone else.[24]

A. Lebedev thinks that in this letter Čaadaev was trying to "reassure his aunt,"[25] who was supposedly extremely interested in the court successes of her nephew. This seems very doubtful[26] : it was not nec-essary to explain to the sister of the well-known *frondeur* Prince M. Ščerbatov the contempt of an aristocrat for court careerism. If Čaadaev had retired and settled in Moscow as a powerful nobleman, a rebellious member of the English Club, then his behavior would not have seemed puzzling to his contemporaries, or reprehensible to his aunt. But the fact

---

*This mutiny in 1820 in one of the crack regiments, and the severity of its suppression, alerted the public to Alexander's reversion to more reactionary policies.

is that his commitment to the service was well-known. It was known that he had blatantly sought a private meeting with the Tsar to advance his career, that he had gone against the opinion of society and aroused the jealousy and hatred of those comrades in the service whom he had "overtaken" in seniority. (It should be remembered that the system of promotions by length of service was an unwritten, but strictly observed rule of progress up through the ranks. To circumvent this system was to contradict the code of comradeship and was taken among officers to be a violation of the rules of honor.) It is precisely the combination of his obvious interest in his prominent and rapidly advancing career and his voluntary retirement *before* his efforts were due to be brilliantly rewarded that constitutes the enigma of Čaadaev's action. [27]

Ju.N. Tynjanov considers that during the meeting in Troppau Čaadaev attempted to explain to the Emperor the link between the "Semenovskij events" and serfdom, and to persuade Alexander towards the path of reform. In Tynjanov's view, Čaadaev's ideas found no sympathy with the Tsar, and this brought about the rift between them: "The unpleasantness of meeting the Tsar and reporting to him were too obvious." Later, Tynjanov describes this meeting as a "catastrophe." [28] Lebedev shares this hypothesis. [29]

Although Tynjanov's deduction is more convincing than the other explanations offered so far, it has its weak point: the rift between Čaadaev and the Emperor did not follow the meeting and report in Troppau immediately. On the contrary, the significant service promotion which was to result from the meeting, and the fact that after his promotion Čaadaev would have found himself in the retinue of the Emperor, i.e. would have been brought closer to him, testifies to the fact that the conversation between the Emperor and Čaadaev was not the reason for the rift and the coolness between them. It is difficult to interpret Čaadaev's report in Troppau as a career catastrophe. Čaadaev's "fall" evidently began later: the Tsar was no doubt unpleasantly surprised by Čaadaev's unexpected request of retirement, and his irritation was later increased by Čaadaev's letter to his aunt, mentioned above, which would have been intercepted in the post. Although Čaadaev's words about his contempt for people who despise everyone else were aimed at his superior, Vasil'čikov, the Emperor could well have taken them as applying to himself. Indeed, the entire tone of the letter must have appeared intolerable to him. Obviously, this was the basis of the comments, "extremely unfavorable" to Čaadaev, about which Prince Volkonskij wrote to Vasil'čikov on 4 February 1821, and as a result of which Alexander I arranged to retire Čaadaev without promoting him to the next rank. It was at this time that the Emperor "was pleased to comment on this officer in extremely unfavorable terms," as Grand duke Constantine Pavlovič later reported to Nicholas I.

Thus, Čaadaev's retirement cannot be viewed as the result of a conflict with the Emperor, as the conflict itself was the result of the retirement. It is our opinion that reference to certain literary subjects may illuminate the enigmatic behaviour of Čaadaev.

Herzen* dedicated his article "The Emperor Alexander I and V.N. Karazin" to N.A. Serno-Solov'evič,**, calling him "our last Marquis of Posa."*** This is evidence that Posa was, for Herzen, a definite type even within Russian life; and it seems to us that a comparison with the story of Schiller's play may well illuminate a great deal in this puzzling episode of Čaadaev's biography. First of all, Čaadaev's familiarity with Schiller's tragedy is beyond doubt: Karamzin, on a visit to Berlin in 1789, saw *Don Carlos* on the stage and wrote a brief, but very sympathetic comment on it in his *Letters of a Russian Traveller*, in which he singled out the role of the Marquis of Posa. At Moscow University, which Čaadaev entered in 1808, there was in those years a real cult of Schiller.[30] Both Čaadaev's university professor, A.F. Merzljakov, and his close friend Nikolaj Turgenev went through a period of intense adulation of Schiller. Another friend of Čaadaev's, Griboedov, freely quoted from the famous monologue of the Marquis of Posa in his sketch for a tragedy entitled *Rodamist and Zenobija*. Speaking of the participation of a republican "in an autocratic empire," he wrote: "Dangerous to the government and a burden to himself, for he was *a citizen of another time*."[31]

These emphasized words are a rephrasing of Posa's self-characterization: "I am a citizen of a future time" (*Don Carlos*, Act III, Scene 9).

The suggestion that Čaadaev wanted by his behavior to act out a variant of "the Russian Marquis of Posa" (just as, in conversations with Puškin, he took on the role of "the Russian Brutus" and "the Russian Pericles") sheds light on the "enigmatic" aspects of his behavior. Above all, it allows us to dispute Lebedev's assertion that in 1820 Čaadaev counted on government liberalism: "As is well known, hopes for the 'good intentions' of the Tsar were generally very pronounced among the Decembrists and the pro-Decembrist nobility of the time."[32] There is an inaccuracy in this statement: one should be very wary of talking about any constant attitude on the part of the Decembrists towards Alexander I, without reference to exact dates and concrete statements. It is known that by 1820 almost no one in practice believed the Tsar's promises. But there is a more important factor: according to M.A. Cjavlovskij's most persuasive proposition,[33] supported by other authoritative scholars, Čaadaev had discussed plans for regicide with Puškin before his visit to Troppau. It is difficult to reconcile this fact with the

---

*Alexander Herzen (1812-1870), liberal socialist.

**N.A. Serno-Solov'evič (1834-1866), revolutionary democrat and publicist, exiled to Siberia in 1864.

***The aristocratic hero of republican sympathies in Schiller's *Don Carlos*.

assertion that it was faith in the Tsar's "good intentions" which prompted him to ride to the Congress.

Schiller's Philip is not a liberal Tsar. He is a tyrant. It is to a despot, not a "benefactor on the throne" that Schiller's Posa addresses his homily. The suspicious two-faced tyrant relies on the ruthless Alba, who may well have recalled Arakčeev.[34] But it is the tyrant who needs a friend, for he is always alone. The first words of Posa to Philip are about his loneliness. It is these words which strike Schiller's despot.

Contemporaries, at least those who, like Čaadaev, were able to talk to Karamzin, knew how Alexander suffered from loneliness in the vacuum created around him by the system of political autocracy and by his own suspicious character. Contemporaries also knew that, like Schiller's Philip, Alexander I deeply despised people and suffered acutely from this contempt. Alexander was not above exclaiming aloud: "People are swine! ... Oh, the scoundrels! That's who surrounds us, unhappy rulers!"[35]

Čaadaev selected his time brilliantly: choosing a moment when the Tsar could not fail to be experiencing the strongest anxiety,[36] he came to tell him of the sufferings of the Russian people, just as Posa told Philip of the sorrows of Flanders. If we imagine Alexander, shaken by the rebellion in the first guards regiment, exclaiming in the words of Philip:

Now I need a man. Oh, Lord,
You have given me much, give me now
A man![37]

—then the words: "Sire, give us freedom of thought!"—spring spontaneously to mind. One may well picture Čaadaev several times on his way to Troppau recalling Posa's monologue.

But Posa's freedom-loving speech could persuade Philip only on the one condition that the monarch trusted the personal incorruptibility of his friend. It was no accident that the Marquis of Posa refused all rewards and had no desire to serve the king. Any reward would turn him from a disinterested friend of the truth into a hireling of autocracy.

To obtain an audience with the Tsar and to recite one's credo to him was only half the task: then it was necessary to demonstrate personal incorruptibility by refusing rewards. The words of Posa, "*Ich kann nicht Fürstendiener sein*" (Act III, Sc. 3), literally became Čaadaev's program. Accordingly, he refused the post of aide-de-camp. There was, therefore, no contradiction between the desire for a conversation with the Emperor and the request for retirement: they were the links in a single design.

What was Alexander I's attitude to this? Above all, did he understand the meaning of Čaadaev's behavior? For an answer to this question it is worth recalling the episode, apocryphal perhaps, but in this instance extremely characteristic, which Herzen has preserved for us:

> In the first years of Alexander I's reign . . . the Emperor Alexander I held literary soirées . . . On one of these occasions the reading lasted a long time; a new tragedy by Schiller was being read. The reader came to the end and stopped. The Tsar was silent, his head lowered. Perhaps he was thinking of his own destiny, which resembled that of Don Carlos too closely, perhaps that of Philip himself. There was complete silence for several minutes. The first to break it was Prince Aleksandr Nikolaevič Golicyn; bending his head to the ear of Count Viktor Pavlovič Kočubej, he said in a half-whisper audible to everyone:
> —We have our own Marquis of Posa![38]

Golicyn was thinking of V.N. Karazin.* However, what is of importance to us is not the evidence of Alexander I's interest in Schiller's tragedy, but something else; according to Herzen, Golicyn's naming of Karazin as Posa was a cunning device of court intrigue, aimed at "bringing down" a rival. Golicyn knew that the Emperor would not tolerate any pretender to the role of moral instructor.

Alexander I was a despot, but not one of Schillerian persuasion: kindly by nature, a gentleman by upbringing, he was a Russian autocrat, and consequently a man who could not forego any of his real-life prerogatives. He badly needed a friend, an absolutely incorruptible friend. It is known that even a trace of suspicion about his "personal views" would thrust a current favourite out of the category of friends into the despised status of courtier. The Schillerian tyrant was captivated by incorruptibility combined with nobility of opinion and personal independence; Alexander's friend had to combine incorruptibility with so deep a personal devotion that it was akin to servility. It is known that the Emperor tolerated Arakčeev's refusal to accept a decorative order and his insolent return of the decorations which Alexander in a special rescript had ordered his friend to wear. In demonstrating the honesty of his absolute devotion, Arakčeev had refused to carry out the royal will, and in reply to the insistent requests of the Emperor he had agreed to accept only a portrait of the Tsar, —not as a reward from the Emperor, but as a gift from a friend.

However, sincere love of the Emperor had only to be combined with independence of opinion (what was important was not the political nature of the ideas, but their independence) for the friendship to come to an end. Such is the story of Alexander's cooling towards the politically conservative Karamzin, a man who was personally very fond of the Emperor and, being absolutely incorruptible, never asked anything

---

*V.N. Karazin (1773-1842), romantic idealist, who won the ear of Alexander in the first years of his reign.

for himself.[39] Still less could Alexander tolerate a gesture of independence from Čaadaev, a man with whom his acquaintanceship had only just begun. The gesture which finally drew Philip's heart to the Marquis of Posa just as irrevocably turned the Tsar away from Čaadaev. Čaadaev was not destined to become the Russian Posa, any more than the Russian Brutus or Pericles.

In this example we see how the real-life behavior of an individual of the Decembrist circle takes the form of an encoded text, and a literary plot is the code which enables us to penetrate its hidden meaning.

Let us take another example. We all know the heroic deeds of the Decembrists' wives* and the truly historical significance their action had for the spiritual history of Russian society. However, the straightforward sincerity of the act's content in no way conflicts with the laws of its expression; similarly, even the most ardent exhortation is subject to the same grammatical rules as those which apply to any expression in that language. The action of the Decembrists' wives was an act of protest and a challenge. But in its expression it inevitably rested on a particular psychological stereotype. Behavior also has its norms and rules, always bearing in mind, of course, that the more complicated the semiotic system, the more complex becomes the relationship between control and freedom within its limits. Did there exist in Russian gentry society *before the action of the Decembrists' wives* any behavioral precedents which could have given form to their sacrifice? Yes, such forms did exist.

First of all, it should be noted that to follow one's exiled husband to Siberia was a traditional behavior norm in the customs of the Russian common people: the transport parties would be accompanied by strings of carts which conveyed the families of the exiles into voluntary banishment. This was not regarded as a heroic action, or even as an individually chosen form of behavior: it was the norm. Moreover, in pre-Petrine life the same norm applied to the family of an exiled nobleman (if there were no punitive arrangements made for his wife and children). Thus, when Radiščev's sister-in-law, Elizaveta Vasil'evna Rubanovskaja, followed him to Siberia, she was enacting a form of behavior proper to the common people (or one that was fundamentally Russian, pre-Petrine). How little she considered she was acting heroically may be judged from the fact that she took with her only Radiščev's younger children, leaving the older ones to complete their education. And the general attitude to her action was quite different from that of 1826: no one thought to restrain her or dissuade her, her contemporaries did not seem to notice this great sacrifice. The entire episode remained within the Radiščev family's affairs and did not receive any public airing. Radiščev's parents were even shocked by the fact that, despite not being married to Radiščev, Elizaveta Vasil'evna followed him to Siberia and there, despite their kin-

---

*In following their exiled husbands to Siberia.

ship, became his wife. Radiščev's blind father refused for this reason to give his blessing to his son when he returned from Siberia, although by that time Elizaveta Vasil'evna herself had died, unable to survive the rigors of exile. The act of heroism she had committed was not understood or valued as such by her contemporaries.

There was one further existent norm of behavior which may have prompted the Decembrist wives to their decision. They were mainly officers' wives. The Russian army of the eighteenth and early nineteenth centuries still retained the old custom, already forbidden to the soldiery, but still practised by officers, particularly those of age and seniority, of taking their families with them in the army transports. Thus, for instance, Kutuzov's staff at Austerlitz included his daughter Elizaveta Michajlovna Tisenhausen (the future E.M. Chitrovo) who was the wife of his favorite adjutant Ferdinand Tisenhausen (the "Fedja" of Kutuzov's letters). After the battle, when the bodies of the dead had been exchanged, she placed her husband's corpse on a cart and, the army having taken different roads towards the east, she conveyed it alone to Revel', for burial in the cathedral. She was then twenty-one. General N.N. Raevskij also used to take his family on campaigns. Later, in conversation with Batjuškov, denying that his sons had participated in the battle of Daškovka, he said: "My youngest son (he was just a child then) was collecting berries in the wood, when a bullet went through his trousers."[40] Thus, the fact of a wife's following her husband into exile or on a dangerous, difficult campaign was not unheard of in the life of the Russian noblewoman. But one other condition was required for an act of this sort to become *a political deed*. Let us recall a passage from the *Notes* of N.V. Basargin, whom P.E. Ščegolev describes as a typical Decembrist:[41]

> I remember that I happened once to read to my wife a recently published poem by Ryleev, entitled *Vojnarovskij*, and in doing so I began to think about my own future. "What are you thinking about?" she asked me. "Perhaps exile awaits me too," I said. "Well, what of it, I'll come with you, to comfort you and share your fate. Exile cannot part us, so what is there to think about?[42]

Basargina (née Princess Meščerskaja) did not succeed in carrying out her intention: she died suddenly in August 1825 and thus did not live to see her husband's arrest.

However, the point is not Basargina's personal fate, but the fact that Ryleev's poem placed the action of a woman in following her husband into exile on the same level as other manifestations of civic virtue. Ryleev's "meditation" *Natalija Dolgorukova* and his narrative poem *Vojnarovskij* (1825) created a stereotype for the behavior of a heroine:

> I have forgotten my native town,
> Riches, honor and fame,

94

In order to share with him the cold in Siberia
And to experience the vicissitudes of fate.[43]

(Natalija Dolgorukova)

Suddenly I see: a woman comes,
Covered by a wretched coat,
And struggling with a bundle of firewood,
Worn down by work and care.
I go to her, and what? . . . I recognize
In this unhappy one, in frost and driving snow,
My young cossack lass,
My beautiful beloved! . . .
Learning of my fate.
She from her native land
Had come to find me in exile.
Oh wanderer! It was hard for her
Not to share my suffering with me.[44]

(Vojnarovskij)

The biography of Natalija Dolgorukova had been the subject of literary treatment before Ryleev's meditation, in the story by S.N. Glinka, *A model of wifely love and fidelity, or The sufferings and virtues of Natalija Borisovna Dolgorukova, daughter of Fieldmarshal B.P. Šeremet'ev* (1815). However, to Glinka this subject was an example of wifely fidelity which contrasted with the behavior of "fashionable women." Ryleev placed her story among "the life histories of the great men of Russia." [45] He thereby created an entirely new code for the decipherment of women's behavior. It was literature, together with the religious norms which entered the national-ethical consciousness of Russian women, which gave the Russian noblewoman of the early nineteenth century a program of behavior which was consciously thought of as heroic. At the same time, the author of the "meditations" also sees in them a program of activity, models of heroic behavior which ought to bear directly on the actions of his reader.

It may be supposed that it was precisely the "meditation" *Natalija Dolgorukova* which exerted a direct influence on Marija Volkonskaja. Both her contemporaries, including her father General N.N. Raevskij, and scholars, have remarked that she could not have had profound personal feelings for her husband,* whom she had not known at all before their marriage and with whom she had spent only three months out of the year which passed between their marriage and his arrest. Marija Nikolaevna's father bitterly repeated her declarations "that her husband was unbearable to her," adding that he would not have objected to her journey to Siberia if he had been convinced that "her wife's heart drew her to her husband."[46]

However, these circumstances which bewildered her relatives, as well

*Prince S.G. Volkonskij (1788-1865), member of the Southern Society.

as many subsequent scholars, only intensified Marija Nikolaevna's own heroic ideals and her need to go to Siberia. She must have remembered that only three days elapsed between the marriage of Natalija Šeremet'eva to Prince I.A. Dolgorukov and his arrest. It was after this that Dolgorukova's life of heroism began. In Ryleev's words, her husband "had been given to her, like an apparition, for an instant." Volkonskaja's father, N.N. Raevskij, was correct in his feeling that it was not love, but a conscious striving for heroism, that moved his daughter. "She was not following her feelings in going to her husband, but the influence of the Volkonskij women, who, by praising her heroism, assured her that she was a heroine."[47]

N.N. Raevskij was wrong in only one respect: the "Volkonskij women" were quite innocent. Volkonskij's mother, the lady-in-waiting Marija Fedorovna, was quite cold in her attitude towards her daughter-in-law and showed complete indifference to the fate of her son: "My mother-in-law questioned me about her son and among other things said that she could not bring herself to visit him, as the meeting would kill her. Then on the next day she left with the Dowager Empress for Moscow, where preparations for the coronation were already beginning."[48] Marija Nikolaevna did not meet her husband's sister, the Princess Sof'ja Volkonskaja, at all. The "guilty" parties were Russian literature, which had created the concept of a women's equivalent to a citizen's heroic behavior, and the moral norms of the Decembrist circle, which demanded a direct transferral of the behavior of literary heroes into life.

Also characteristic in this respect was the Decembrists' total inability to cope with their interrogation and trial; in this tragic situation of behavior they had no witnesses to whom they could address heroic acts, counting on their understanding, and there were no literary models, since death without monologues, in the vacuum of military-bureaucratic life, had not yet become a topic for the art of that time. What emerged in these conditions were other norms and stereotypes of behavior, ones which had lain in the background, but which were perfectly familiar to all the Decembrists: the duty of an officer to his seniors in calling and rank, the obligations of the oath, the honor of a nobleman. These norms burst into the behavior of the revolutionary, causing an erratic movement between one of these norms and another in the accomplishment of real actions. Not all of them could, like Pestel', adopt posterity as interlocutor and hold a dialogue with it, without regard for the eavesdropping of the Investigating Commission, thereby mercilessly destroying himself and his friends.

It is revealing that the theme of the closed trial without witnesses and tactics of struggle with the judicial process became very prominent in the literature *after* 1826, from Griboedov's *Rodamist and Zenobija* to Poležaev and Lermontov. The humorous reference in Nekrasov's narrative poem *The Trial* (*Sud*, 1867) nevertheless demonstrates clearly that in Žukovskij's poem *The Trial in the Dungeon* (*Sud v podzemel'e*) the readers of the 1830s were interested not in the fate of the nun who was a victim of the Inquisition, but in something else: they imagined themselves to be in the situation of "the trial in the dungeon."*

The powerful effect of language on behavior and of sign systems on day-to-day life, described above, is particularly clear in those aspects of everyday life which in their nature are most removed from social semiosis. One of these spheres is leisure.

In its social and psychophysiological functions leisure has to be constructed as a direct opposite to the normal structure of life. Only thus will it be capable of fulfilling the function of a psychophysiological changeover and release of tension. In a society with a complex system of social semiotics leisure will inevitably be concerned with what is direct, natural and non-semiotic. Thus, in urban-type civilizations leisure invariably entails exodus to "the bosom of nature." For the Russian nobleman of the nineteenth century, and in its second half for the bureaucrat as well, the strict regulation of life by the norms of society decorum and the hierarchy of ranks, whether class-based or bureaucratic, meant that leisure came to be associated with participation in the life of the actors' community or the gypsies' encampments. Among merchant circles, the strict "orderliness" of normal existence had its contrast in the drinking bout, which knew no limits. The need to change social masks is particularly evident in the fact that, if in everyday life a member of a collective belonged to the category of the oppressed, then when he was on a "bout" he had to play the part of a devil-may-care; whereas, if in ordinary life he was endowed with high authority within the given collective, his role in the mirror world of the holiday would often entail playing at being one of the downtrodden.

The usual distinguishing feature of the holiday is its marked differentiation from the remaining "non-holiday" world. Its space is demarcated: a holiday often demands another place (either one that is more imposing in the case of a festival, a ceremonial hall or a cathedral; or one that is less so, — a picnic area or some hideaway). Holiday time is also specified (as for calendar holidays or evening and night time, when during the working week people are supposed to be sleeping).

The holiday in the life of the early nineteenth-century gentry was

---

*The hero of Nekrasov's humorous tale receives a summons to appear before an open court on a charge of offending the censorship laws in one of his books. He recalls how as a youth he shuddered at reading Žukovskij's ballad about the underground trial at the time of the Inquisition.

a somewhat complex and heterogeneous phenomenon. On the one hand, especially in the provinces and rural areas, it was still closely associated with peasant calendar rituals; on the other hand, the young, post-Petrine gentry culture, which had existed for not more than a hundred years, did not yet suffer from the entrenched ritualization of normal, non-holiday life. On the contrary, there was evidence that at times there wasn't enough order to everyday life. One result was that the ball (like the army parade) became at times a place at which the level of ritualization was not lowered, but heightened. Leisure consisted not in the removal of restraints on behavior, but in the replacement of diverse unritualized activity by a strictly limited number of types of purely formal and ritualized behavior: dances, whist, "the orderly harmony of oligarchical conversations," in Puškin's words.

The world of young military men was quite different. From the time of Paul I there had been established in the army (particularly in the Guards) the cruel regime of depersonalizing discipline, which reached its height on the parade ground. A contemporary of the Decembrists, Timotheus von Bock, wrote to Alexander I: "The parade is a triumph of nonentity, and every fighting soldier who won one's respect on the day of battle becomes a mannequin at the parade, while the Emperor seems like a god who alone thinks and controls." [49]

Where everyday existence was represented by the drill and the parade, leisure naturally took on the form of riotous drinking or orgies. In this sense, the latter were a quite legitimate element in the "normal" behavior of young military men. We might even say that at a certain age and within certain limits such activities were an obligatory element in the "proper" behavior of an officer; though we must, of course, take into account the quantitative and qualitative differences not only as regards the antithesis between the Guards and the army as a whole, but also as regards the different kinds of troops and even the regiments, which had their own obligatory traditions.

However, the early nineteenth century saw the emergence against this background of a special type of debauchery which even then was viewed not as a norm of army leisure, but as a variant of free-thinking. The element of free thought showed itself here in a unique kind of everyday romanticism, which consisted in an attempt to eliminate *all* restraints and to act in a completely uncurbed manner. The typical model for such behavior was a victory over some leading practitioner of this type of wild behaviour. The point of the action was to accomplish something unheard-of, surpassing the person whom no one had yet been able to overcome. Puškin characterized this type of behaviour with great accuracy in Sil'vio's* monologue:

*In Puškin's story, *The Shot*.

98

I served in the *** hussar regiment. You know my character: I am accustomed to take first place, but from the time I was young it was a passion within me. In our time riotous conduct was in fashion and I was foremost among all the young rakes in the army. We prided ourselves on getting drunk: I out-drank the famous B[urcov], celebrated by D[enis] D[avydov].50

The expression "out-drank" identifies that element of competition and the passion to be first which was the characteristic feature of the riotous behavior fashionable at the end of the second decade of the nineteenth century, a kind of behavior which was already on the borderline of transition into "everyday free-thinking."

Let us take a typical example. The literature on Lunin includes an episode told by N.A. Belogolovyj from the words of I.D. Jakuškin:

Lunin was a guards officer and was stationed one summer with his regiment near Peterhof. It was a hot summer and both officers and soldiers greatly enjoyed bathing in the gulf in their free time. The commanding general, a German, then unexpectedly forbade any further bathing, under threat of severe punishment, on the grounds that this bathing was taking place near the main road and thus offended decency. Lunin found out when the general would be passing along the road and, several minutes before, entered the water in full uniform, in his shako, regimental dress and jack-boots. The general could see even from a distance the strange sight of an officer floundering about in the water and when the general drew level, Lunin quickly jumped to his feet and there in the water drew himself up and gave a respectful salute. The perplexed general called the officer over and recognized Lunin, the favourite of the Grand dukes and one of the outstanding guards officers. In amazement he asked Lunin: "What are you doing?" "I am bathing," replied Lunin, "but so as not to disobey your excellency's command, I am endeavouring to do so in the most decent manner."51

N.A. Belogolovyj quite rightly interpreted this event as a demonstration of the "unbridledness . . . of the protests." However, the point of Lunin's action will not be entirely clear until we compare it with other evidence which historians have overlooked. The memoirs of Prince Zubov's dwarf Ivan Jakubovskij contain a story about Valerian Zubov's natural son, the cadet Koročarov of the uhlan guards regiment:

What do you think happened to him! They were stationed in Strel'nja. Several officers went off to bathe and he went with them, but their chief, the Grand duke Constantine Pavlovič, who was taking a walk along the beach, came up to where they were bathing. They all took fright and jumped out of their boat into the water, except for Koročarov, who stood up straight, as naked as the day he was born, and cried out: "Your good health, your highness!" The Grand duke took a great liking to him from then on and declared: "He will make a brave officer."52

Both episodes come from the same time.

So the story may be reconstructed in the following form: a cadet from the Guards uhlans, without losing his head, acted with spirit. His action evidently prompted both the admiration of the guards and the instruction forbidding bathing. Lunin, as "the foremost rake in the army," was bound to surpass Koročarov's action (not the least factor in this must have been his desire to uphold the honour of the Horse-Guards by "outdoing" the uhlans). The value of riotous behavior consists in *crossing the limit* that no one else has yet crossed. Tolstoj caught this aspect when he described the drinking-bouts of Pierre and Dolochov [in *War and Peace*].

Another sign of the transformation of riotous behavior into oppositional activity was the tendency to see it not as a recreation which complemented service life, but as its antithesis. The world of riotous behavior became an independent sphere and involvement in it *excluded* service life. In this sense it began to be associated, on the one hand, with the world of private life and, on the other, with poetry, both of which, even in the eighteenth century, had already come to function as antipodes to service life.

This process was continued by a link-up between riotous behavior, which before belonged wholly to the sphere of purely practical everyday behavior, and theoretical ideological ideas. This link-up entailed, on the one hand, the transformation of riotous, drinking-bout behavior into a kind of socially significant behavior and, on the other hand, the ritualization of such behavior, which at times made the friendly drinking session resemble a travesty of the liturgy or a parody of a masonic meeting.

In his evaluation of passion, of man's impulse towards happiness and joy, and of the attempt to find a specific place for these feelings in the system of ideas and concepts, the thinker of the early nineteenth century was faced with the need to choose one of two concepts, each of which was seen at the time to be associated with certain trends in progressive thought.

The tradition which derived from the philosophers of the eighteenth century was based on the view that the right to happiness was integral to man's nature, and that the general good of all entailed the maximum good for each individual. From this point of view, the man striving for happiness is realizing the prescriptions of Nature and Morality. Any call for the renunciation of happiness was viewed as a doctrine which served despotism. And by contrast, the ethic of hedonism adopted by the materialists of the eighteenth century was viewed at the same time as a manifestation of the love of freedom. Passion was interpreted as the equivalent of the impulse towards liberty. Only the man who is filled with passions, who longs for happiness and is open to love and joy cannot be a slave.

From this point of view, the ideal of freedom could have two manifestations of equal value: a citizen full of hatred for despotism, or a passionate woman, filled with a longing for happiness. It was these two images of freedom-loving which Puškin juxtaposed in his poem of 1817:

> ... in my fatherland
> Where is the true mind, where will we find genius?
> Where is the citizen with a soul that is noble,
> Elevated and ardently free?
> Where is the woman —with beauty that is not cold,
> But ardent, captivating, alive?53

So, adherence to the love of freedom was thought of as a festival, while the feast and even the orgy had features of the ideal of liberty made manifest.

However, there was also another variety of freedom-loving morality. This was based on that complex conglomerate of leading ethical ideas which was connected with the re-examination of the philosophical heritage of the materialists of the eighteenth century and which derived from extremely contradictory sources—from Rousseau in the interpretation of Robespierre to Schiller. This was the ideal of political stoicism, of Roman virtue, of heroic asceticism. Love and happiness were banished from this world as egotistical, demeaning feelings which were unworthy of the citizen. Here the ideal was not "the woman ... with beauty ardent, captivating, alive," but shades of stern Brutus and Martha, Mayor of Novgorod* ("the Cato of her republic," in the words of Karamzin). The goddess of love was banished for the sake of the muse of "liberality":

> Run, hide from view,
> Feeble queen of Cythera!
> Where are you, where are you, threat of tsars,
> Proud songstress of freedom?54

In the light of these ideas riotous behavior acquired a directly opposite significance. The only common factor was that in both instances it was regarded as *possessing significance*. It was transposed from the area of routine behavior to the sphere of semiotic activity. This difference is an essential one. The area of routine behavior is distinguished by the fact that the individual does not select it for himself, but receives it from society, from the age or his psychophysiological constitution as something to which there is no alternative. Semiotic behavior is always the result of a choice and, consequently, entails the free activity of the subject of the behavior and his selection of the language in which he

*The historical Marfa Boreckaja was the central character of Karamzin's historical tale *Martha the Mayor, or The Subjugation of Novgorod [Marfa-posadnica, ili Pokorenie Novagoroda*, 1803]; Martha led the resistance to Ivan III's encroachment on Novgorod's traditional rights.

relates to society. Particularly interesting are those instances in which non-semiotic behavior becomes semiotic in the perception of a casual observer, as, for example, a foreigner, who involuntarily complements it with his own capacity to act differently in such situations.

The question which interests us here directly involves our evaluation of such important phenomena of Russian social life of the 1820's as "The Green Lamp," "Arzamas" and "The Society of Loud Laughter."* The history of the study of "The Green Lamp" is the most revealing in this respect.

Rumours of orgies reportedly held at "The Green Lamp" circulated among the younger generation of Puškin's contemporaries; and indeed Puškin himself knew the situation of the 1810s to the early 1820s only by hearsay. These rumours entered early biographical literature and established the tradition, which goes back to the writings of P.I. Bartenev and P.V. Annenkov, according to which "The Green Lamp" was an apolitical society, a scene of orgies. In an article written in 1907, P.E. Ščegolev took issue with this tradition and raised the question of a connection between this society and the Union of Welfare.[55] The publication by B.L. Modzalevskij of part of the archive of "The Green Lamp" gave documentary support to this speculation,[56] and this has enabled several scholars[57] to attempt to prove this hypothesis. The problem is treated in just this way in M.V. Nečkina's work.[58] Finally, this point of view on "The Green Lamp" was put forward in extreme detail and with typical critical acumen by B.V. Tomaševskij in his book *Puškin*, where the relevant section occupies more than forty pages of text. There are no grounds for re-examining these propositions.

But it is precisely the fullness of treatment and the wealth of detail with which the view of "The Green Lamp" as a branch of the Union of Welfare has been discussed which makes this approach somewhat one-sided. Let us leave aside legends and gossip, and consider only the cycle of Puškin's poems and the letters which he addressed to members of the society. We shall notice at once that they have something in common, something which, moreover, connects them with the verses of Ja. Tolstoj,** whom B.V. Tomaševskij with some justification considers to have been "the court poet of 'The Green Lamp.'"[59] This common feature

*"The Society of Loud Laughter" was founded in 1816 in Moscow by M.A. Dmitriev (nephew of the poet I.I. Dmitriev). At first, like "The Green Lamp" it was a friendly literary circle. The chairman was M.A. Dmitriev and the members included: S.E. Raič, A.O. Kornilovič, P. Novikov, A.R. Kurbatov, M.A. Volkov, D.A. Pančalidzev. In 1818 Dmitriev left Moscow and Fedor Šachovskoj, the future Decembrist, became chairman. The society became a literary political group, like "Arzamas." In December 1819 Šachovskoj left Moscow and the society evidently ceased to exist. (Note from B.A. Uspenskij)

**Ja.N. Tolstoj (1791-1867). Officer, member of "The Green Lamp"; later in the secret police.

consists in the combination of an obvious and unambiguous love of free-dom with a cult of joy, sensual love, blasphemy and a certain defiant libertinage. It is no accident that the reader encounters so often in these texts rows of dots,* the very presence of which would be impossible in works addressed to N. Turgenev, Čaadaev or F. Glinka. Tomaševskij quotes an excerpt from Puškin's epistle to F.F. Jur'ev and compares it with Ryleev's dedication to *Vojnarovskij*. Tomaševskij writes:

> The word "hope" had a civic sense. Puškin wrote to one of the participants of "The Green Lamp," F.F. Jur'ev:
> "Greetings, dashing knights
> Of love, freedom and wine!
> For us, young allies,
> The lamp of hope is lit."
> The significance of the word "hope" in its civic sense is evident from the dedication to Ryleev's *Vojnarovskij*:
> "And again in the heavenly heights
> The star of hope has shone out." [60]

However, while emphasizing the similarity of imagery between these texts, we must not forget that in Puškin's case the quoted verse was follow-ed by lines which would be quite impossible for Ryleev but which are very characteristic of the entire cycle under consideration:

Greetings, youth and happiness,
Table-goblet and bordello,
Where with loud laughter sensuality
Leads us drunkards to the bed. [61]

If it is considered that the *entire* point of "The Green Lamp" is ex-pressed in its role of a branch of the Union of Welfare, then how are we to connect verses like these — which are far from being unique — with the order in *The Green Book* (of the Union) that "the dissemination of the rules of morality and virtue is the very aim of the Union," and that mem-bers are charged as a duty "in all speeches to exalt virtue, to deprecate vice and to show contempt for weakness"? Let us recall N. Turgenev's disgusted attitude to "banquets" as an occupation worthy only of "boors": "In Moscow there is a bottomless pit of sensual enjoyments. They eat, they drink, they sleep, they play cards — all this at the expense of peas-ants burdened with work" [62] (the note is dated 1821, the year of the publication of Baratynskij's *Banquets [Piry]*).
    The first scholars to study "The Green Lamp" emphasized its orgiast-ic character and denied it any political significance. Modern scholars, however, have discovered the depth of the real political interests of the members of the society and have simply rejected any difference between

---

*In Soviet scholarly editions obscenities are regularly omitted.

103

"The Green Lamp" and the moral atmosphere of the Union of Welfare. Nečkina remains completely silent on this aspect of the question. Tomaševskij found a way out by distinguishing between the serious sessions of "The Green Lamp" which entirely corresponded to the spirit of the Union of Welfare and those evenings at the home of Nikita Vsevoložskij, which did not lack a degree of licence. "It is time to distinguish between the Vsevoložskij evenings and the sessions of 'The Green Lamp,'" he wrote.[63] However, on the next line Tomaševskij significantly modifies this assertion by adding that "for Puškin, of course, the evenings at Vsevoložskij's house were as inseparable as the meetings of 'Arzamas' and the traditional goose suppers were from each other." It remains unclear why there is a need to differentiate between things which Puškin considered indistinguishable. Is it also necessary in the case of "Arzamas" to distinguish between "serious" meetings and "frivolous" suppers? It is doubtful whether any such task could ever be carried out.

"The Green Lamp" was undoubtedly a freedom-loving literary association, and not a gathering of debauchees. There is no longer any need to break a lance over this question.[64] It is no less evident that the Union of Welfare tried to exert influence on it; the participation in "The Green Lamp" of F. Glinka and S. Trubeckoj leaves no room for doubt on this account. But does this mean that it was simply a branch of the Union and that there was no difference between these two organizations?

The difference lay not in the ideals and the emphases of their programmes, but in the type of behavior.

The Masons called their lodge meetings "work-sessions." For the member of the Union of Welfare his activity as a participant in the society was also "work" or, to put it more solemnly, service. Puščin* said as much to Puškin: "I am not the only one who has entered this new service of the fatherland."[65] The dominant mood of the political conspirator is serious and solemn. For the member of "The Green Lamp" love of freedom was coloured in tones of merriment, while the ideals of liberty were to be realized by transforming life into an unending holiday. Grossman correctly noted in his description of the Puškin of that period: "He looked on political struggle not as denial and sacrifice, but as a joy and a festival."[66]

However, a festival of this kind is associated with the fact that life, overflowing its bounds, mocks prohibitions. Wild behavior (cf. the "dashing knights") distinguishes the ideals of "The Green Lamp" from the harmonious hedonism of Batjuškov (and the measured jollity of the members of "Arzamas") and resembles rather the "hussar spirit" of Denis

*I.I. Puščin (1798-1859), friend of Puškin, was condemned to indefinite penal servitude.

104

Davydov* and the student pranks of Jazykov.**

Their infringement of the Karamzinian cult of "decorum" shows in the speech behavior of members of the society. Naturally, it is not a matter of using unprintable words: in this respect, "The Lamp" would be no different from any army carousing. The conviction on the part of some scholars who believe that young officers and poets, when drinking or even just getting excited, kept to the vocabulary of the Russian Academic Dictionary and who seek to prove that the notorious greetings of the Kalmyk*** must simply have been evidence of a lack of wit, is rather comic. This conviction is born from the hypnosis with written sources which characterizes contemporary historical thought. A document is equated with reality, and the language of the document with the language of life. The question is one of the *mixture* of the language of elevated political and philosophical thought, of refined poetic imagery, with the vocabulary of the street. This creates a special, markedly familiar style, typical of Puškin's letters to the members of "The Green Lamp." This language, rich in unexpected juxtapositions and stylistic combinations, became a kind of password, a means of recognition. The existence of a linguistic password, of a strongly marked circle jargon, is a characteristic feature of both "The Lamp" and "Arzamas." It was this existence of a "special" language that Puškin identified when he transported himself in thought from his exile to "The Green Lamp":

Again I hear, true poets,
Your enchanted language ... [67]

Speech behavior was bound to possess a corresponding form of everyday behavior, based on the same mixture of elements. As early as 1817, Puškin, addressing Kaverin (the hussar atmosphere was then paving the way for the atmosphere of "The Lamp"), wrote that:

... one may live amicably
With verses, with cards, with Plato and with a glass,
So that under a light covering of lively pranks
One may conceal a lofty mind and heart. [68]

Let us recall that the moralist and preacher Čackij reacted sharply against just such a combination (for the attitude of the Decembrists to cards, see below):

When I am busy — I hide from pleasures,
When I wish to play the fool — I play the fool,

*D.V. Davydov (1784-1839), war hero and poet.
**N.M. Jazykov (1803-1846/47), poet and friend of Puškin.
***The Kalmyk in question was a servant who officiated at the evenings organized by N.V. Vsevoložskij for members of "The Green Lamp."

105

But to mix these two trades
There is a host of those willing, but I am not of their number.

Familiarity, elevated into a cult, led to a unique ritualization of every-day life. But this was a ritualization "inside out," one which is reminiscent of the clowning rituals of the carnival. Hence the characteristic blasphemous usages: the "Maid" (*La Pucelle*) of Voltaire for the Virgin Mary; the irreligious paganism of "the Holy Bible of the Graces." An assignation with a "Laïs"* could be referred to directly, with a blatant disregard for the language taboos of society:

> When again we'll sit all four
> With ... [whore] and wine and chibouk-pipes,—[69]

—and translated into the language of blasphemous ritual:

> Spent a pious night
> With a young nun of Cythera.[70]

This may be compared with the carnivalization of masonic ritual in "Arzamas." The anti-ritual spirit of the clowning ritual is evident in both cases. But if the "liberalist" did not take his pleasure in the same way as Molčalin did, equally the leisure activity of the Russian "carbonari" (i.e. Čackij) differed from the amusements of the former.

Everyday behavior, no less acutely than formal entry into a secret society, separated the nobleman revolutionary not only from people "of the past century," but also from the wide circle of *frondeurs,* free-thinkers and "liberalists." The fact that such markedly different behavior ("There is in you no end of these peculiarities," says Sofija to Čackij) in effect contradicted the idea of conspiracy did not embarrass the young conspirators. It is indicative that it was not the Decembrist Nikolaj Turgenev, but his cautious elder brother who had to persuade their younger brother, Sergej Ivanovič, who was passionately attracted by the Decembrists' norms and ideals, not to let his views show in everyday life. Nikolaj Ivanovič, however, taught his brother the opposite: "We are not adopting liberal rules in order to please the boors. They cannot like us. And we shall always despise them."[71]

The "terrible look and biting tone," to use Sofija's words about Čackij, were hardly conducive to carefree joking as distinct from denunciatory satire. The Decembrists were not jokers. When they entered the company of carnivalized merriment of the young liberalists the Decembrists destroyed the very basis of these organizations by trying to direct their members to "elevated" and "serious" activities. It is difficult to imagine what F. Glinka did at the meetings of "The Green Lamp," even more so at the Vsevoložskij suppers. However, we are well aware of the

---

*Laïs, a legendary Greek courtesan, was the polite term for prostitute.

106

turnabout which took place in "Arzamas" with the arrival of the Decembrists. The speeches of N. Turgenev and, even more so, of M. Orlov were "ardent" and "practical," but they can hardly be described as full of carefree wit. Orlov realised this himself:

Can the hand which is accustomed to bear the heavy steel sword of battle take up the flimsy armament of Apollo, and is it right for the voice which has grown hoarse from shouting loud, unending commands to talk in the divine language of inspiration, or the subtle tones of the joke? [72]

Similarly, the speeches of the Decembrists at the "Society of Loud Laughter" were far from humorous. One of them is described as follows in the memoirs of M.A. Dmitriev:

Šachovskoj invited to the second meeting two visitors (not members) —Fonvizin and Murav'ev ... During the meeting the guests lit pipes, then went into the next room and whispered together for some reason. When they came back, they started saying that such work was too serious and so on, they started to give advice. Šachovskoj blushed and the members took offence. [73]

There was no "loud laughter."

By effacing the division of everyday life into the spheres of work and leisure which dominated gentry society, the "liberalists" wished to make all life into a holiday, but the conspirators wished to make it "service."

All forms of society entertainment—dances, cards, flirtations—are severely condemned by the Decembrists as signs of spiritual emptiness. In a letter to Jakuškin, for instance, M.I. Murav'ev-Apostol* unambiguously connected the passion for cards with the general decline in public-spiritedness in the conditions of reaction: "After the war of 1814 the passion for gaming, it seemed to me, had disappeared among people. To what should we ascribe the return to this despicable pursuit?"— he asked, [74] obviously not admitting any symbiosis between "cards" and "Plato."

As a "base" pursuit, card-playing is equated with dancing. Both were excluded from the evenings at which "the cream of intelligent youth" gathered. There were no "cards or dancing"[75] at the evenings held by I.P. Liprandi. Griboedov, wishing to emphasise the gulf between Čackij and those surrounding him, concluded his hero's monologue with the stage direction: "He looks round, everyone is waltzing with the greatest enthusiasm. The old men have wandered off to the card tables." Nikolaj Turgenev's letter to his brother Sergej is very characteristic. Nikolaj expresses his amazement that in France, a country which lives

---

*A founder-member (with his brother Sergej, who was executed in 1826) of the Union of Salvation in 1816.

an intense political life, people can waste their time dancing:

> I hear that you go dancing. Count Golovin's daughter wrote to him that she had been dancing with you. And so I learnt with some surprise that they still dance in France! *Une écossaise constitution-nelle indépendante, ou une contredanse monarchique ou une danse contremonarchique?*[*76]

The fact that the issue lies not in a simple lack of interest in dancing, but in the choice of a type of behaviour of which the rejection of dancing is merely a *sign* is borne out by the way in which in 1818-1819 (a time when, under the influence of the Decembrists' behavior, "seriousness" came into fashion and spread to a wider circle of society than the immediate circle of the members of the secret societies) young people went to balls *in order not to dance*. The words of Puškin's *Novel in Letters* are well-known from anthologies: "Your perceptive and important arguments belong to the year 1818. At that time the fashion was for strict rules and political economy. We would appear at balls and not remove our swords (any officer intending to dance would unfasten his sword and hand it to the doorman before entering the ballroom. – Ju.L.) – we felt it improper to dance, and we had no time for the ladies."[77] Cf. the remark of the old princess in *Woe from Wit*: "Dancers have become terribly rare."

The ideal of "feasts" was demonstratively opposed by the "Russian luncheons" given by Ryleev. These occasions, Spartan in spirit and emphatically Russian in the choice of dishes,

> were always held between about one o'clock and three o'clock in the middle of the day and were usually attended by numerous writers and members of our Society. The luncheon invariably consisted of a carafe of purified Russian wine, several heads of sour cabbage and rye bread. Don't you find such a Spartan luncheon strange?

It "fitted in with Ryleev's constant inclination–to put the stamp of Russianism on his life."[78] M. Bestužev is far from being ironical when he describes writers, "walking to and fro with cigars, nibbling at cabbage leaves,"[79] and criticizing Žukovskij's murky Romanticism. However, this is a typical combination: the cigar was an automatic habit, indicating the profound Europeanization of real-life conduct, while the cabbage was an ideologically loaded sign. M. Bestužev sees no contradiction in this: the cigar is on a different level from the cabbage, and therefore is remarkable only to the outside observer, i.e., us.

In contrast to the young man who divided his time between balls and drinking sessions among friends was the anchorite who spent his time in his study. The enthusiasm for work in one's study gripped even the

---

*"A constitutional, independent *écossaise*, or a monarchist 'counterdance,' or a counter-monarchist dance?"

young officers, who by this time were more reminiscent of young scholars than licentious army men. N. Murav'ev, Pestel', Jakuškin, Zavališin, Baten'kov and dozens of other young people of their circle spent their time studying, listening to private lectures, or copying out books and journals and avoided the company of ladies:

> ... the fashionable circle is now quite out of fashion.
> You know, my dear, we are all now at liberty.
> We do not go into society, we do not know our ladies.
> We have left them to the mercy of old men,
> To the pleasant favorites of the eighteenth century.
> (Puškin, "Say, by what chance . . . ," 1821)

> Professors!! – our kinsfolk studied with them,
> And left! now to the apothecary's, to be apprentices,
> They run from women . . .
> (Griboedov)

D.I. Zavališin, who at the age of sixteen was appointed teacher of astronomy and higher mathematics to the Naval College from which he had just graduated brilliantly, and who at the age of eighteen left on a scientific world voyage, complained that in Petersburg there were

> endless guests, endless card-playing and fuss of social life . . . I hardly have a spare moment for my beloved practical and academic pursuits.[80]

The non-noble intellectual at the turn of the century, conscious of the gulf between theory and reality, might adopt an evasive position:

> . . . Wear a mask in society,
> But be a philosopher, locked in your study.[81]

The reclusive life of the Decembrist was accompanied by open, unambiguous expression of contempt for the usual pastimes of the nobleman. A special point in *The Green Book* prescribed:

> Time is not to be wasted in the sham pleasures of high society, but leisure after the fulfilment of duties is to be devoted to useful pursuits or conversations with right-thinking people.[82]

The type of the hussar-cum-wise man, recluse and scholar such as Čaadaev becomes possible:

> . . . I shall see the study,
> Where you are always a wise man, and sometimes a dreamer
> And an impassive observer of the empty-headed crowd.
> (Puškin, "To Čaadaev," 1821)

Puškin and Čaadaev passed their time by *reading* together (" . . . I strolled [83] with Kaverin/ Cursed Russia with Molostvov/ Read with my

Čaadaev"). Puškin provides an exact description of the range of these opposite moods manifest in everyday behavior: feasting, "daring conversations," reading. This not only aroused the suspicions of the government, but also irritated those for whom debauchery and independence remained synonymous:

> It's all Jomini and Jomini!*
> But about vodka—not a word![84]

However, it would be quite mistaken to imagine the member of the secret societies as a stay-at-home solitary. The characteristics mentioned above signify only a rejection of the old forms of association in everyday life. Moreover, the notion of "combined efforts" becomes the leading idea of the Decembrists and permeates not only their theoretical conceptions, but also their everyday behavior. In many instances it precedes the idea of political conspiracy and psychologically eases the first steps on the path of conspiracy. D.I. Zavališin recalled:

> When I was at college as a pupil (Zavališin spent the years 1816 to 1819 at college; he entered the Northern Society in 1824. – Ju.L.), I not only observed attentively all the defects, disorders and abuses, but always brought them into discussion with those of my comrades who were serious, in order to elucidate their causes by our combined efforts and to think of means to remove them.[85]

The cult of brotherhood, based on the unity of spiritual ideals and the exaltation of friendship were extremely characteristic of the Decembrist, often at the expense of other connections. Ryleev, who was ardent in friendship according to the dispassionate recollections of his hired serf attendant Agap Ivanov, "appeared frigid towards his family, and didn't like them to disturb him at his work."[86]

Puškin's words about the Decembrists—"Brothers, friends, comrades" —accurately describe the hierarchy of intimacy in relations between members of the Decembrist camp. And if the circle of "brothers" had a tendency to narrow towards the conspiratorial, at the other extreme stood the "comrades"—a concept which was easily broadened to "youth" or "enlightened people." However, even this extremely broad concept became to the Decembrists part of the even broader cultural "we," as against "they." "From us, from young people," says Čackij. "The senior positions (in the fleet,—Ju.L.) were occupied at that time by insignificant people (especially the English) or dishonourable ones, which became particularly obvious by comparison with the talent, education and undoubted sense

---

*General A.A. Jomini (1779-1869), a Swiss in the Tsar's service, was a leading theoretician of war. This couplet, from Davydov's *Song of an old Hussar (Pesnja starogo gusara)* contrasts the older generation who drank and fought, and the younger who only theorize.

of honor of *our generation*," wrote Zavǎlisin.[87]

We must bear in mind that not only did the world of politics penetrate the fabric of personal, individual relationships, but that the Decembrists were also characterized by the opposite tendency: everyday, family and individual ties penetrated the network of political organizations. If later stages of the social movement were to be characterized by the breaking up of friendship, love and long-standing attachments for considerations of ideology and politics, then the Decembrists were marked out by the fact that the political organization itself took the form of direct human contacts, friendship and attachment to the person, not just to his convictions. The fact that all the participants in political life were involved in established extra-political ties of some sort,—that they were relations, members of the same regiment, comrades at educational institutions, had participated in the same battles or were simply social acquaintances,—and that these ties encompassed the whole circle from the Tsar and the Grand dukes, who might be met or engaged in conversation at balls or when out walking, right down to the young conspirator,—this feature laid a special stamp on the whole picture of the age.

In no other Russian political movement do we encounter such a quantity of kinship ties. Quite apart from the interconnections in the Murav'ev-Lunin circle, or around the house of the Raevskijs (M. Orlov and S. Volkonskij were married to daughters of General N.N. Raevskij, while V.L. Davydov—a cousin of the poet—who was among those condemned in category I to perpetual hard labor, was a half-brother to the general), it is enough to mention the four Bestužev brothers, the Vadkovskij brothers, the Bobriščev-Puškin brothers, the Bodisko brothers, the Borisov brothers, the Kjuchel'beker brothers and so on. If we take into account connections in shared attributes, first-cousin and second-cousin relationship, the possession of neighboring estates (which involved shared childhood memories, often as close a bond as actual kinship), the picture which emerges is one which will not be found in the subsequent history of the liberation movement in Russia.

It is no less significant that relations of kinship and friendship—ties based on clubs, balls, society activities or regiments, even wartime acquaintanceships—linked the Decembrists not only to their friends, but also to their opponents. However, this contradiction did not eliminate either set of connections.

In this respect, the fate of the brothers Michail and Aleksej Orlov is important, even if it is by no means unique. We may recall the example of M.N. Murav'ev, who moved from being a participant in the Union of Salvation and one of the authors of the rules of the Union of Welfare, to become the cruel suppressor of the Polish uprising. However, the indeterminacy which society connections and friendship lent to the personal relations of political enemies is more clearly seen in the examples

111

of ordinary men. During the day of 14 December 1825 the aide-de-camp N.D. Durnovo was on the square beside Nikolaj Pavlovič.* Late that night it was Durnovo who was sent to arrest Ryleev and he fulfilled his commission. By that time he already enjoyed the complete trust of the new Emperor, who during the day had given him the dangerous mission (which remained unfulfilled) of negotiating with the mutinous *carré* of the Decembrists on Senate Square.** In a short time. N.D. Durnovo was transporting M. Orlov to the fortress.

The issue would appear to be quite clear: we have to do with a reactionary follower of the Emperor, who from the point of view of the Decembrists, is an enemy. But let us take a closer look at this man. [88]

N.D. Durnovo was born in 1792. In 1810 he entered the cavalry college. In 1811 he was promoted to retinue lieutenant and was attached to the staff commander, Prince Volkonskij. At this point Durnovo entered a secret society until recently known only from the mention of it in the memoirs of N.N. Murav'ev:

Also members of the society (apart from cavalryman Ramburg, – Ju.L.) were the officers Durnovo, Aleksandr Ščerbinin, Vil'deman and Dellingsgauzen; although I had heard of the existence of this society, I didn't know its aims in detail because its members, who gathered at Durnovo's, kept them secret from their comrades. [89]

Until now this was the only evidence we had. Durnovo's diary adds new details. On 25 January 1812, Durnovo noted in his diary:

A year has passed since the foundation of our society, called "Knighthood" (*Chevalerie*). After dinner at Demidov's I left at 9 o'clock for our meeting, which took place at the Recluse's (*Solitaire*). It continued until 3 o'clock in the morning. This meeting was chaired by four of the original knights. [90]

From this note we learn for the first time the exact date of the foundation of the society, its name, which curiously recalls the "Russian Knights" of Mamonov and Orlov, and some aspects of its internal ritual. From a note dated 25 January 1813, it is obvious that the society had written rules:

Today it is two years since our K(nighthood) was formed. I alone of the brothers am in Petersburg, all the other enlightened (*illustres*) members are on the battlefields, whither I too intend to return. On this evening, however, there was no meeting, as is provided for

*I.e. Nicholas I.

**The Decembrists' troops were drawn up in the traditional square-sided battle formation of the *carré*. At one point, Durnovo was requested by Nicholas to negotiate with the Decembrists but, when he approached their ranks, they threatened to bayonet him and he was forced to run back. See: Nečkina 1955, Vol. II, pp.272, 280.

On the eve of the war with France in 1812 Durnovo arrived in Vil'no and here came into close contact with the brothers Murav'ev, who invited him to take quarters in their home. He became particularly close to Aleksandr and Nikolaj. Soon their circle was joined by Michail Orlov, with whom Durnovo was already acquainted as a friend from their joint service in Petersburg with Prince Volkonskij, and also S. Volkonskij and Kološin. Together with Orlov, he attacked Aleksandr Murav'ev's mysticism, and this gave rise to bitter arguments. Meetings, walks and conversations with Aleksandr Murav'ev and Orlov fill every page of the diary. Let us take the entries for 21 and 22 June alone:

> Orlov returned with General Balăsov. They had been to conferences with Napoleon. The Tsar had spent more than an hour in conversation with Orlov. They say he is very pleased with the behavior of the latter in the enemy army. He replied very sharply to Marshal Davout, who had tried to taunt him with his words.

On 22 June:

> What we foresaw has happened,—my comrade Orlov, adjutant to Prince Volkonskij and a lieutenant of the cavalry regiment, has been appointed aide-de-camp. He deserves this honour in all respects.92

In the retinue of Volkonskij, following the Emperor, Durnovo and Orlov together left the army and set off for Moscow.

Durnovo's links with Decembrist circles evidently did not cease in the future. At least, in his diary, which in general gives a detailed record of the external aspects of life, but clearly avoids all the dangerous moments (for example, there is no information about the "Knighthood," apart from that quoted, although the society clearly held meetings; conversations are often mentioned, but their content is never revealed), we suddenly encounter an entry such as that dated 20 June 1817:

> I was strolling peacefully in my garden, when a courier from Zakrevskij called for me. I thought it was going to be about a journey to distant parts of Russia, but then was pleasantly surprised to discover that the Emperor had ordered me to keep order during the movement of troops from the gate to the Winter Palace.93

To the above may be added the fact that after 14 December Durnovo apparently declined the imperial favours which were generously bestowed on all those who had been near the Emperor on the fateful day. Having been an aide-de-camp to Alexander I as early as 1815,94 and after having received a series of Russian, Prussian, Austrian and Swedish decorations in the campaigns of 1813-1814 (Alexander I said of him: "Durnovo is a brave officer"), under Nicholas I he occupied the modest position of director of the chancellery of the controller of the General Staff. But apparently he felt uncomfortable: in 1828 he requested transfer to the active serving army (and in transfer was promoted to major-general) and was killed in the storming of Šumla.*[95]

After all this, is it surprising that Durnovo and Orlov, whom fate had led to opposite poles in 1825, met not as political enemies but, if not as friends, as close acquaintances and engaged in amicable conversation all the way to the Peter-Paul fortress?

This peculiarity also had its influence on the behavior of the Decembrists during their trial. The revolutionary of later times was not personally acquainted with those against whom he was fighting, and saw them as political forces, not as people. This to a large extent made possible his uncompromising hatred. However, even in the members of the Investigating Commission, the Decembrist could not help seeing people who were familiar to him from his service life or his society and club contacts. They were either his acquaintances or his superiors. He may have felt contempt for their senile lack of understanding, their careerism or their servility, but he could not see them as "tyrants" or despots worthy of the denunciations of a Tacitus. Since it was impossible to appeal to their political emotions, the arrested Decembrists were thrown off balance.

Although the poetry of the Decembrists has been largely overshadowed by the work of their brilliant contemporaries (Žukovskij, Griboedov and Puškin) and though their political conceptions were already obsolete by the time of Belinskij and Herzen [in the 1840s], it is by their creation of a *type of man* completely new to Russia that their contribution to Russian culture is unsurpassed. So close did they come to an approximation of the norm and the ideal that their contribution is comparable to that of Puškin to Russian poetry.

The whole profile of the Decembrist was inseparable from a sense of personal dignity. This feeling was based on an exceptionally developed sense of honor and on the belief of each of them that he was a great man. One is even struck by the naiveté with which Zavališin wrote about those of his fellow-students who, in their ambition for rank, gave up serious theoretical studies "and thus became, almost without exception, ordinary people." [96]

This attitude meant that *every* act had to be seen to be significant, to deserve the memory of posterity and the attention of historians, and to be of the utmost value. Hence, on the one hand, the degree of aestheticism or theatricality of their everyday behavior (cf. the scene of Ryleev's

*Šumla was a Bulgarian town prominent in the Russo-Turkish wars.

explanation with his mother, as described by N. Bestužev),[97] and, on the other hand, their belief in the significance of any act, a belief which, consequently, set high demands on the norms of everyday behavior. The sense of the political significance of *all* of one's behavior came to be replaced, when they were in Siberia, years when historicism became the predominant theory, by a sense of historical significance. "Lunin lives for history,"—Sutgof* wrote to Muchanov.** Lunin, comparing himself with the grandee Novosil'cev,*** wrote on the news of the latter's death: "What a difference in our fates! For the one—the scaffold and history, for the other—the chairman's seat in the Council and an entry in the government almanach." It is curious that in this note real fate—the scaffold, chairmanship of the Council—is the expression of a complex sign which was what Lunin thought human life to be (life has meaning). The content of the sign is represented by the presence or absence of spiritual values, which in their turn are symbolized in a particular text: an entry in history or an entry in the almanach.

The comparison of Decembrist behavior with poetry is not merely a matter of the beauties of style, but has a serious basis. From the unconscious medium of language poetry constructs a conscious text which possesses a more complex secondary meaning, and in which everything becomes significant, even those elements which, within the system of language itself, are purely formal.

The Decembrists constructed from the unconscious medium of the everyday behavior of the Russian nobleman at the turn of the century a conscious system of ideologically significant everyday behavior, as finalized as a text and endowed with supreme value.

Let us take just one example of the purely artistic attitude to the material of behavior. An individual may alter his hairstyle, his gait, his posture, etc. within his external appearance. These elements of behavior, then, which are the result of choice, are easily weighted with meanings ("an unkempt hairstyle," "an artist's hairstyle," "a hairstyle à l'empéreur," etc.). However, there are no alternatives to the features of one's face or one's build. The writer may endow his hero with physical features in the forms which suit him and make them bear important meanings, but we in everyday life normally semioticize not the face, but its expression, not the build, but the way people hold themselves. Of course, these constant elements of external appearance we also interpret as specific signals—dependent, however, on their being included in complex paralinguistic systems. All the more interesting are those instances when

*A.N. Sutgof (1801-1872), Decembrist. Sentenced to death, but sentence commuted to 20 years' imprisonment.
**P.A. Muchanov (1799-1854) was a member of the Union of Welfare. Sentenced to 12 years hard labour.
***N.N. Novosil'cev (1768-1838), a leading statesman. Noted for his cruelty in his administration of Poland after 1813.

a naturally given external appearance is treated as a sign. Here, man approaches himself as a communication, the meaning of which he himself has still to decode (i.e. to learn from his external appearance his own predestination in history, in the destiny of mankind, etc.). Consider the comment of the priest Myslovskij, who befriended Pestel' in the fortress:

> He was more than 33 years old, of medium height, with a pale pleasant face which had striking features or physiognomy; he was quick, decisive and extremely eloquent; a profound mathematician and a superb military tactician: in his gestures, his movement, his height and even his facial appearance he very much resembled Napoleon. And it was this resemblance to a great man, a resemblance unanimously confirmed by all who knew Pestel', that was the reason for all his mad ideas and his crimes.[98]

In the reminiscences of V. Olenina we find the following: "Sergej Mur(av'ev)-Apostol was a no less remarkable personality (than Nikita Murav'ev,—Ju.L.) and had moreover an unusual resemblance to Napoleon I, which probably affected his imagination considerably."[99]

One has only to compare these characteristics with the external appearance which Puškin gave to Hermann* to see a general artistic principle at work. However, Puškin applies this principle to the construction of an artistic text and to an invented hero, while Pestel' and S. Murav'ev-Apostol apply it to their own real-life biographies. This attitude to one's own behavior as something consciously created according to the laws and models of ideal texts did not, however, lead to the aestheticization of the category of behavior in the spirit, for example, of the "life-creation" of the Russian Symbolists of the twentieth century. To the Decembrists, behavior, like art, was not an aim in itself, but a means, an external expression of the lofty spiritual content of the text of life or the text of art.

Although one cannot help noticing the connection between the every-day behavior of the Decembrists and the principles of the Romantic world-view, it must be borne in mind that the high signification (the showiness, the theatricality, the literariness) of their day-to-day behavior did not turn into stilted speeches and extended declamations, but, on the contrary, was strikingly combined with simplicity and sincerity. According to the description given by V. Olenina, who knew many of the Decembrists from childhood, "the Murav'evs in Russia were just like the family of the Gracchi," but she also remarked that Nikita Murav'ev "was shy in a nervous, sickly manner."[100] Taking the entire range of characters, from the childish simplicity and shyness of Ryleev to the refined simplic-

*Hermann is the "Napoleonic" hero of Puškin's story, *The Queen of Spades* (Pikovaja dama).

ity of Čaadaev's aristocratic ideals, we will be convinced that the Decembrist ideal of everyday behavior was not characterized by cheap theatricality.

The reason for this may be found, on the one hand, in the fact that, as distinct from behavior like Bazarov's,* the Decembrist ideal of everyday behavior was constructed not as a denial of the norms of everyday etiquette established by culture, but as an assimilation and a reworking of these norms. This was a behavior oriented not towards Nature, but towards Culture. On the other hand, this behavior remained in its fundamentals an attribute of the nobility. It depended on a good upbringing. And the truly good upbringing of the cultured section of the Russian nobility meant simplicity in social relations and an absence of that uptightness and sense of social inferiority which was the psychological basis for the ungracious manners of the non-noble intelligentsia like Bazarov. This also serves to explain the apparently surprising ease with which the exiled Decembrists could communicate with the common people, a facility which had already been lost by the time of Dostoevskij and the Petraševskij circle. N.A. Belogolovyj, who had the opportunity of observing the exiled Decembrists over a prolonged period with the sharp eye of a child from a non-noble background, remarked on this feature:

> Old Volkonskij, who was then more than 60 years old, had the reputation in Irkutsk of being a great eccentric. When he arrived in Siberia, he somehow broke off all connections with his brilliant, illustrious past, turned into a busy, practical gentleman, lived simply, formed friendships with peasants ... The townspeople who knew him were quite shocked when, passing through the bazaar on their way from mass on Sunday, they saw the prince, perching on the edge of a peasant cart piled up with sacks of corn, having a lively conversation with the peasants crowded round him and breakfasting there with them on a crust of black rye bread. ... Again, it was most often peasants who were the prince's guests, and his floors always showed the marks of dirty boots. Volkonskij used to appear in his wife's salon stained with tar or with pieces of hay on his clothing, his full beard sprayed with the aromatics of the farmyard or similar salon perfumes. In general in society he was an eccentric phenomenon, although he was highly educated, spoke French like a native, strongly accenting his r's, was very kind and always affectionate and gentle with us children. [101]

This ability to be "oneself" without pretence, organically and naturally, in a society salon, with peasants in a bazaar and with children, is the special cultural feature of the everyday behavior of the Decembrist; it is this ability which resembles the poetry of Puškin and which remains one of the supreme manifestations of Russian culture.

What we have said enables us to touch on one further problem. The

*The Nihilist hero of Turgenev's novel, *Fathers and Sons [Otcy i Deti]*.

question of the Decembrist tradition in Russian culture is most often examined on the purely ideological plane. However, there is also a "human" aspect to this question—the tradition of a specific type of behavior, a type of social psychology. Thus, for example, if the question of the role of the Decembrist ideological tradition in relation to Tolstoj appears a complex one and in need of reconsideration, then the direct human continuity between Tolstoj and the Decembrists, the tradition of the historical-psychological type in the entire complex of cultural behavior, is obvious. It is revealing that Tolstoj himself, talking about the Decembrists, distinguished between their ideas and their personalities. The diary of T.L. Tolstaja-Suchotina contains an extremely interesting note on this subject:

> Repin is continually asking papa to give him a subject . . .Yesterday papa said that he had thought of a subject, but it did not quite satisfy him. It was the moment when they led the Decembrists out to the gallows. The young Bestužev-Rjumin was much taken with Murav'ev-Apostol—*more with his personality than with his ideas*,— and walked all the way alone with him and only before his execution did he weaken and start weeping, then Murav'ev embraced him, and they went together to the gallows.[102]

Tolstoj's treatment is very interesting: his thoughts are constantly drawn to the men of 14 December, but in the first place to the men themselves, who were closer and dearer to him than the ideas of Decembrism.

Within the behavior of the individual, as within any form of human activity, it is possible to distinguish layers of "poetry" and of "prose."[103] Thus, for the Emperor Paul and his sons the poetry of army existence lay in the parade, while its prose was in the action of battle.

> The Emperor Nicholas, convinced that beauty was a sign of strength, strove for unquestioning obedience and uniformity . . . in his strikingly disciplined and well-trained troops,

wrote A. Fet in his memoirs.[104]

For Denis Davydov poetry was associated not simply with battle, but with irregularity, "*the organized disorder* of the armed peasants."

> This calling, filled with poetry, demands a romantic imagination and a passion for adventure; it is not satisfied with dry, prosaic bravery. —It is a stanza from Byron!—Let him who fears not *death*, but fears *responsibility*, remain under the eyes of his superiors.[105]

One is struck by the unreserved transferral of poetic categories to the forms of military activity.

The demarcation of the "poetic" and the "prosaic" in the behavior and actions of people is generally characteristic of the age which interests us. Thus, Vjazemskij criticized Puškin for making Aleko* travel around

*The hero of Puškin's narrative poem *The Gypsies (Cygany)* (written 1824).

118

with a bear and suggested robbery as a direct contrast to this prosaic occupation, – "better suggest that he be a speculator and gypsy horse-dealer. Although it is not completely innocent, this trade does possess some daring and consequently some poetry." [106]   The domain of poetry is in real life the world of "daring."

In the age of Puškin and Vjazemskij the individual moved freely to and fro between the area of prose and that of poetry in his everyday behavior. In this context, just as in literature only poetry was "esteemed," so the prosaic aspect of behavior was disregarded, as it were, in the assessment of a man. It was as if this side of things did not exist.

The Decembrists brought coherence to the individual's behavior, not by rehabilitating life's prose, but by passing life through the filters of heroic texts and thus simply eliminating whatever was not suitable to be inscribed on the tablets of history. Prosaic responsibility to one's superiors was replaced by responsibility to history, and the fear of death by the poetry of honor and liberty. "We breathe liberty," declared Ryleev on the square on 14 December. The transferral of liberty from the sphere of ideas and theories into "breath," into life, is the essence and the significance of the everyday behavior of the Decembrist.

Translated by C.R. Pike

NOTES

1   *Vosstanie*, IV, 1927, p. 179.
2   Ibid., I, 1925, p. 23.
3   A letter to A. Bestužev before the end of January 1825. Included in Puškin, *PSS*, Vol. 13, p. 138.
4   Lotman 1960, p. 134.
5   In N. Turgenev's political vocabulary "boor" [Russ, *cham*] stood for "reactionary," "serf-owner" and "enemy of enlightenment." See also, for example, statements such as: "Darkness and boorishness are everywhere and have taken over everything" – in a letter to his brother Sergej of 10 May 1817 from Petersburg (N.I. Turgenev, 1936, p. 222).
6   Puškin, *PSS* Vol. 12, p. 159.
7   Zavališin 1908, p. 10.
8   *Poèty 1790-1810*, 1971, p. 537.
9   V. Kjuchel'bcker, "O napravlenii našej poezii, osobenno liričeskoj, v poslednee desjatiletie." (Quoted according to *Dekabristy* 1951, p. 552).
10   "The words *illustrious friends* or simply *illustrious* had a special significance in the conventional language of the time" (Polevoj 1934, p. 153).
11   Karamzin 1966, pp. 242-243.
12   Lermontov 1954, Vol. II, p. 183.
13   Puškin, *PSS*, Vol. 13, p. 142.
14   Myslovskij 1905, p. 39.
15   Puškin, *PSS*, Vol. 12, p. 159.
16   Kapnist 1960, Vol. I, p. 358.

17 Vjazemskij 1929, p. 105.
18 Čechov 1960-1963, Vol. 7, p. 506.
19 Zavališin 1908, p. 86.
20 Katenin 1911, p. 77.
21 Ibid., p. 31 (My italics, – Ju.L.).
22 Dostoevskij, *PSS*, Vol. 8, p. 417 (My italics, – Ju.L.).
23 Katenin 1911, p. 22.
24 Čaadaev 1913-1914, Vol. I, pp. 3-4 (The original is in French).
25 Lebedev 1965, p. 54.
26 Unfortunately, A. Lebedev's most interesting book is not free from arbitrary treatment of documents and a certain modernization.
27 M. Žicharev, a relation of Čaadaev's, later recalled: "Vasil'čikov sent ... Čaadaev with the report to the Tsar, although Čaadaev was the youngest adjutant and the oldest should have gone." And later: "On his return (Čaadaev's, – Ju.L.) to Petersburg, he was the target, almost throughout the guards college, of a widespread, immediate outburst of displeasure towards him because he had taken on the trip to Troppau and the report to the Tsar about the 'Semenovskij affair.' He was told that not only should he not have gone, he should not have suggested himself for the trip, but should have tried to avoid it in any way possible." And further: "That instead of refusing to undertake the journey, he sought after it and achieved it is also beyond doubt so far as I am concerned. In this unfortunate incident he yielded to the inherent weakness of excessive vanity; I do not think it was so much the aide-de-camp's insignia which glistened on his epaulettes in his imagination when he left Petersburg, so much as the enchantment of a personal meeting, a brief conversation and close acquaintanceship with the Emperor" (M. Žicharev 1871, p. 203). Of course, Žicharev did not have access to Čaadaev's private thoughts, but he knew a great deal, better than his contemporaries, and his words deserve attention.
28 Tynjanov 1946, pp. 168-171.
29 Lebedev 1965, pp. 68-69.
30 See: Harder 1968; Lotman 1958/1959; Lotman 1958.
31 Griboedov, *PSS*, Vol. I, p. 256.
32 Certainly, it is said at this point that Čaadaev "may well have relied too much on the good intentions of the Emperor." In this instance, the author sees the aim of the conversation as being intended "finally and irrevocably to clarify the real intentions and plans of Alexander I" (Lebedev 1965, pp. 67-69). The latter comment is impossible to understand: why should a conversation with Čaadaev have produced such clarity when it was not achieved in the scores of conversations which the Tsar had with various individuals or in his many pronouncements?
33 Cjavlovskij 1962, pp. 28-58.
34 The image of Alba, stained by the blood of Flanders, acquired special meaning after the bloody suppression of the Čuguevskij rebellion. On the Čuguevskij rebellion, see Cjavlovskij 1962, p. 33 ff.
35 Šilder 1897, p. 48.
36 Vjazemskij wrote at this time: "I cannot think without horror and despair of the Tsar's loneliness at such an important moment. Who will respond to his voice? Irritated self-regard, a disastrous counsellor or insignificant lackeys, or something even worse than that" (see Lotman 1960, p. 78).
37 *Don Carlos*, Act III, sc. 1.
38 Herzen 1954-1964, Vol. XVI, pp. 38-39. The reading apparently took place in 1803, when Schiller sent *Don Carlos* through Wolzogen to Marija Fedorovna (wife of Paul I and mother of Alexander I) in Petersburg. Wolzogen acknowledged receipt on 27 September 1803. See: Schiller 1862, p. 125; Harder 1968, pp. 15-16.
39 In this respect, the example of Karamzin is particularly notable. The Tsar's

cooling towards him began in 1811 with the presentation in Tver' of "A Memoir on Ancient and New Russia." A second and more crucial episode occurred in 1819, when Karamzin read "The opinion of a Russian citizen" to the Tsar. Later, he recorded what he had said to Alexander on this occasion: "Sire, you have too much self-regard ... I fear nothing. We are all equal before God. What I said to you, I would have said to your father... Sire, I despise those who are liberalists for a day, I prize only that freedom which no tyrant can deprive me of ... I no longer ask for your blessing. Perhaps this is the last time I shall speak to you." (Karamzin 1862, p. 9. The original is in French.). In this instance, the criticism came from positions which were more conservative than those adopted by the Tsar. This makes it particularly obvious that it was not the progressive or reactionary nature of ideas, but the independence of opinion which the Tsar detested. In these circumstances, the activity of any Russian pretender to the role of the Marquis was doomed in advance. After Alexander's death Karamzin again emphasized his love for the deceased Tsar in a note addressed to posterity ("I loved him sincerely and affectionately, sometimes I got indignant and angry at the monarch, but I continued to love the man"), but he had to admit that his mission as an adviser at the throne had been a complete failure: "I was always sincere and he was always patient, unassuming and inexplicably pleasant to me; he did not demand my advice, but he would listen to it, although for the most part he did not follow it, so that now, in mourning his passing along with the rest of Russia, I cannot comfort myself with the thought of the ten years of kindness and trust shown to me by such a great ruler, because the kindness and the trust brought no benefit to my beloved Fatherland" (ibid., pp. 11-12).

40 Batjuškov 1934, p. 373.
41 Basargin 1917, p. XI.
42 Ibid., p. 35.
43 Ryleev 1971, p. 168.
44 Ibid., p. 214.
45 Bazanov 1964, p. 267.
46 Geršenzon 1923, p. 70.
47 Ibid.
48 Volkonskaja 1914, p. 57.
49 Predtečenskij 1951, p. 198.
50 Puškin, PSS, Vol. 8, bk. I, p. 69.
51 Belogolovyj 1898, p. 70.
52 Jakubovskij 1968, p. 68. Koročarov, with the rank of cavalry captain, possessing three crosses and having been put forward for a George Cross, was fatally wounded in the taking of Paris during a bold attack on the Polish uhlans.
53 "The inexperienced lover of foreign lands ... " Puškin, PSS, Vol. 2, bk. I, p. 43.
54 "Liberty: an Ode" (1817). Ibid., p. 45.
55 See Ščegolev 1912 (the chapter entitled "The Green Lamp"); see also Ščegolev 1931.
56 Modzalevskij 1928.
57 See: Ryleev 1934 (commentary); Bazanov 1949.
58 Nečkina 1955, pp. 239-246.
59 Tomaševskij 1956, p. 212.
60 Ibid., p. 197.
61 "To Jur'ev"(1819). Puškin, PSS, Vol. 2, bk. I, p. 95.
62 N.I. Turgenev 1921, p. 259.
63 Tomaševskij 1956, p. 206.
64 At the same time, it is impossible to agree either with P.V. Annenkov, who

wrote that the investigation of the Decembrists revealed "the innocent, i.e. orgiastic nature of 'The Green Lamp'" (Annenkov 1874, p. 63), or with B.V. Tomaševskij, who put forward the suggestion that "the rumors about orgies may have been circulated in order to discourage . . . curiosity and to draw attention away in a false direction" (Tomaševskij 1956, p. 206). At the beginning of the century the police prosecuted immorality no less than free-thinking. Annenkov unconsciously transferred to the Alexandrine era the morals of "the dark seven years." As far as the assertion of B.V. Tomaševskij is concerned, that "the meetings of a conspiratorial society could not take place on the days of the landlord's weekly guest-nights," which, in the opinion of the scholar, is an argument in favour of the division between "evenings" and "meetings," then one cannot help remembering "the secret gatherings// On Thursdays. A most secret union . . . " of Repetilov. A conspiracy of 1819-1820 was quite far removed from what was entailed in this concept by 1824.

65 Puščin 1956, p. 81.
66 Grossman 1958, p. 143.
67 "From a letter to Ja.N. Tolstoj" (1822). Puškin, *PSS*, Vol. 2, bk. I, p. 264.
68 Ibid., Vol. 1, p. 238.
69 "27 May 1819." Ibid., Vol. 2, bk. I, p. 77.
70 "To Ščerbinin" (1819). Ibid., p. 87.
71 N.I. Turgenev 1936, p. 208.
72 Arzamas 1933, p. 206.
73 Grumm-Gržimajlo and Sorokin 1963, p. 148.
74 Murav'ev-Apostol 1922, p. 85.
75 *Russkij archiv*, 1866, bk. 7, col. 1255.
76 N.I. Turgenev 1936, p. 280. Extremely interesting evidence of the negative attitude towards dancing as an occupation incompatible with "the Roman virtues," on the one hand, and simultaneously of the belief that everyday behavior ought to be constructed on the basis of texts which describe "heroic" behavior, on the other hand, is found in the memoirs of V. Olenina which describe an episode from Nikita Murav'ev's childhood: "At a children's party at the Deržavins' Ekaterina Fedorovna (the mother of N. Murav'ev, –Ju.L.) noticed that little Nikita was not dancing, so she went up to encourage him to do so. He asked her quietly: *'Maman, est-ce qu'Aristide et Caton ont dansé?'* (Mama, did Aristides and Cato dance?). His mother answered: *'Il faut supposer qu'oui, à votre âge'* (We must suppose that at your age they did). He immediately got up and went to dance" (Olenina 1938, p. 484).
77 Puškin, *PSS*, Vol. 8, bk. I, p. 55.
78 Bestuževye 1951, p. 53.
79 Ibid., p. 54.
80 Zavališin 1908, p. 39.
81 Slovcov 1971, p. 209.
82 Pypin 1908, p. 567.
83 On the semantics of the verb "to go strolling" [Russ. *guljat'*] there is an indicative passage in V.F. Raevskij's diary where he records a conversation with the Grand duke Constantine Pavlovič. In reply to Raevskij's request to be allowed to go for a walk Constantine said: "No, major, that is absolutely impossible! There will be plenty of time for strolling when you are discharged." However, it became clear later that they had misunderstood each other: "Yes! Yes! – the Cesarevič responded. – You want to take a walk in the fresh air for your health, but I thought you wanted to go strolling, that is to go drinking. That's another matter" (Raevskij 1956, pp. 100-101). Constantine considered the drinking bout a norm of military behavior (it was no accident that Puškin called him a "romantic"), which was forbidden only

to an arrested man. For the "spartan" Raevskij, however, the verb could only mean to go for a walk.

84 Davydov 1962, p. 102.
85 Zavališin 1908, p. 41.
86 Ryleev 1954, p. 254.
87 Zavališin 1908, p. 39 (My italics, –Ju.L.).
88 The basic source for judgments about N.D. Durnovo is his extensive diary, Durnovo 1914 and Durnovo 1939 (see the pages devoted directly to the uprising of 14 December 1825). However, the published section is only an insignificant part of an enormous diary which occupies several volumes and is written in French (GBL).
89 Murav'ev 1885, p. 25; cf: Černov 1960, pp. 24-25; Lotman 1963, pp. 15-17.
90 GBL, f.95 (Durnovo), No.9533, 1.19. (An excerpt from a Russian typed copy, apparently prepared for the *Vestnik obščestva revnitelej istorii*–CGALI, f.1337, op.1, ed. chr.71).
91 GBL, f.95, No.9536, 1.7 ob.
92 Ibid., 1.56.
93 Ibid., No.3540, 1.10.
94 In the information included in the publication of the manuscript section of the USSR Lenin Library, Durnovo is named as aide-de-camp to Nicholas I, but this is obviously a mistake (see Durnovo 1939, p. 8).
95 See *Russkij invalid*, 1828, No.304, from 4 December.
96 Zavališin 1908, p. 46.
97 Bestuževye 1951, pp. 9-11.
98 Myslovskij 1905, p. 39.
99 Olenina 1938, p. 485.
100 Ibid., pp. 486 and 485.
101 Belogolovyj 1898, pp. 32-33.
102 Tolstaja-Suchotina 1973, p. 194 (My italics, –Ju.L.).
103 Cf. Galard 1974.
104 Fet 1890, p. IV.
105 Davydov 1822, pp. 26 and 83.
106 Quoted from Zelinskij 1887, p. 68.

"AGREEMENT" AND "SELF-GIVING"
AS ARCHETYPAL MODELS OF CULTURE

Ju.M. Lotman

If we analyze the most archaic socio-cultural models we may identify two in particular which have a special interest in the light of their subsequent transformations in the history of culture. With some degree of conventionality we will call one of them magical, and the other religious. The magical system of relationships is characterized by the following: 1) *Reciprocity*. The agents who are involved in these relationships are both active (e.g. the magician performs certain actions, and *in response to these* the force invoked performs certain others). One-sided actions do not occur in the system of magic, because if a magician should, from ignorance, perform actions that are incorrect and therefore incapable of invoking the power concerned and causing it to be active, then these words and gestures are not recognized as actions within the system of magic. 2) *Compulsion*. This means that certain actions by the one party inevitably entail obligatory and precisely predictable actions by the other. In the sphere of magic many texts have been established which bear witness to the fact that the magician forces the supernatural power to appear and to function against its will, even though he (the magician) has less power at his disposal. The performance of certain definite actions by the one party compels specific actions in response by the other. Hence power is, as it were, evenly distributed. The supernatural forces have power over the magician, but so does he over them. 3) *Equivalence*. The relationships between the two parties are like an exchange of equivalent values and may be compared to an exchange of conventional signs. 4) *Agreement*. The two parties involved enter into a special sort of agreement. This may be given external expression (the conclusion of a contract, oath-taking, the observance of conditions, and suchlike) or it may be implicit. However, the existence of an agreement also implies that it may be broken, just as in the conventional, semiotic nature of the exchange there lies the possibility of deception and misinformation.[1] Hence inevitably there follows the possibility of various interpretations of the · agreement, each party seeking to put into the express formulations of the agreement a content to suit his own purposes.

A religious act has as its basis an unconditional act of self-giving, rather than an exchange. One party surrenders itself to the other without making any conditions at all, and moreover, the receiving party is acknowledged to be the bearer of supreme power.[2] Relationships of this type

Feast of the Pious and Impious. Detail of a Russian woodcut.

125

have the following characteristics: 1) *One-sidedness*. The relationships are unidirectional: the one who yields himself up counts on receiving protection, but between his action and the response there is no necessary connection, absence of reward cannot be grounds for a break in relations. 2) From this there follows a *lack of compulsion* in the relationship: the one party gives away everything, but the other may give or not: he may reject a worthy donor and reward an unworthy person (who takes no part in the system of relations or who breaks it). The actions of the deity are by definition unpredictable for the first party. It is for this reason that what, from the human standpoint, looks like inexplicable arbitrariness is a feature of his actions. 3) *The relationships are not equivalent*. They preclude the psychology of exchange and there can be no thought of any conditionality or conventionality as regards the basic values. And so in this case the means of communication are not signs but symbols whose nature precludes the possibility of expression being alienated from content, and consequently also the possibility of deception or interpretation. 4) Consequently relationships of this type take the form of an *unconditional gift* rather than an agreement.

It must be emphasized that we are dealing with a model of the cultural psychology of such relationships: actual world religions have never been able to dispense with some element of magical psychology. For example, while they have abandoned any thought of a *quid pro quo* exchange in the relations between man and God within the bounds of earthly life, they have in many instances incorporated the idea of recompense beyond the grave by setting up a system of compulsory (i.e. unambiguously conditioned and hence just) relations between life in this world and life in the next.

The official church of the Roman Empire in its last centuries, behind the façade of which there were hidden highly secret cults of a religious character, was magical. The system of sacrificing to the gods provided the basis for treaty relations with them, and the official worship of the Emperor took the form of a convention with the state. Precisely because of these magical features, the Romans' "religion" did not contradict either their sophisticated ideas about law, which were rooted deep in their cultural psychology, or the whole structure of the highly developed legal basis for the state. Christianity for the Roman was a deeply anti-state element since it was a religion in the precise sense of the word and consequently took no account of the formal-juridical and conventional-legal consciousness. Abandonment of this form of consciousness was, for a man steeped in Roman culture, a denial of the very idea of statehood.

Russia's pagan cults evidently had a shamanistic, i.e. magical, character. The fact that the introduction of Christianity coincided with the rise of the Kievan state had a series of vital consequences in the area we are discussing. The ensuing coexistence of two faiths gave rise to two opposite models of social relations. The relationships between the prince and his personal troops, which needed to be formally clarified, tended towards the agreement-principle. This model most adequately reflected the emergent system of feudal relationships, which were founded on patronage and vassaldom, as well as the whole structure of mutual rights and obligations, and the exchange of etiquette signs, on which the ideological framework of chivalric society rested. The traditions of Russian pagan magic here entered organically into the new order which emerged from the European synthesis between the tribal institutions of barbarian peoples and the Roman juridical tradition; for the Roman tradition had remained firmly rooted in the old towns of the Empire, where the communes maintained their own rights, a complex system of legal relationships held sway and there was an abundance of lawyers.

However, in the West the sense of agreement, though having its remote origin in magic, had the authority of the Roman secular tradition and held a position equal to the authority of religion; in Russia, on the other hand, it was felt to be pagan in character. This affected the way society evaluated it. It is significant that in the Western tradition an agreement as such was ethically neutral. It could be drawn up with the Devil (for example, St. Theophilus who sold his soul to the Devil, and later redeemed it by his repentance), but one might also make agreements with the forces of holiness and goodness. In *The Little Flowers of St. Francis*, for instance, there is the well-known tale of the agreement between Francis of Assisi and the savage wolf of Gubbio. Having accused the wolf of behaving "like a villain and the worst of murderers," devouring not only animals, but also of trying to attack people who are made in the likeness of God, Francis concluded: "Brother wolf, I want to establish peace between you and them [i.e. the inhabitants of the province of Gubbio, Ju.L.]." Francis offered the wolf an exchange of equivalent values: the wolf was to refrain from its villainy, while on their part the inhabitants of Gubbio were to give up trying to hunt it and were to supply the wolf with food. "'Do you promise this?' And the wolf, inclining its head, indicated that it did." [3] The agreement was concluded and was observed by both parties until the wolf's death.

No such texts are to be found either in Russian folk tradition or in medieval Russian literature. An agreement may only be made with a Satanic power or its pagan counterpart (e.g. the agreement between the peasant and the bear*). This first of all casts an emotional light on the agreement as such: it lacks the aura of cultural value. In the knightly

---

*This evidently refers to the folktale, "The Peasant, the Bear and the Fox" in which the peasant makes an agreement with a bear to sow turnips and then cheats him.

lifestyle of the West where relations with God and the saints could be modelled on the pattern "suzerain – vassal" and subjected to a conventional ritual of the same type as initiation to knighthood and the service of the lady, the agreement, the ritual that seals it, the gesture, the parchment and the seals, are surrounded by an aura of holiness and are endowed with the authority of the highest values. In early Russia, an agreement was regarded as a purely human affair (human as opposed to divine). The fact that kissing the cross was introduced in cases where it was necessary to ratify an agreement is evidence indeed that without this unconditional, extra-contractual, divine authority it was insufficiently guaranteed. Secondly, if an agreement was made with one of the powers of darkness, to observe it was sinful and to break it led to salvation. It is in dealing with such forces that the fact that communication through verbal signs is based on convention and that this enables words to be used for deception, is made apparent.* The possibility of variously interpreting a word (casuistry) was likewise understood as the wish to deceive rather than an attempt at explaining its true meaning (cf. in Dostoevskij: "A lawyer's a corrupt conscience")**. Another example is the episode from the folk tale "The Dragon and the Gipsy." [4] The dragon and the gipsy agreed to a whistling competition:

> The dragon whistled and immediately the leaves fell off all the trees. "You whistle well, my friend, but you cannot outdo me," said the gipsy. "First blindfold your eyes, or else as soon as I whistle they will pop out of your head!" The dragon took him at his word and blindfolded his eyes with a kerchief. "Come on, whistle!" he said. The gipsy took a cudgel, and how it whistled against the dragon's head. . .

This play on words which exposes the conventional nature of the sign, and turns an agreement into a deception, is permissible in dealings with the Devil, a dragon, or a bear, but was unthinkable in dealing with God and the world of holiness. Daniel the Prisoner's saying is well known***:

*Lotman makes a distinction here and below between the *sign* (of which the most common example is the word in natural language) and the *symbol*. The sign is "arbitrary," "conventional," "non-motivated" in that there is no logical or natural reason why, for instance, the English sound "tree" should evoke the same mental image as the Russian sound "*derevo*" or the French "*arbre*": the connection between the expression (signifier) and the content (signified) of these words is a matter of human convention. A symbol, on the other hand has some obvious connection between expression and content; a crown symbolizes royal power, or in the example which Lotman cites from Saussure below, the scales symbolize justice.

**Russian: *Ablakat – prodažnaja sovest'*, where *ablakat* in the speech of a peasant or other representative of folk wisdom is a corruption of the normal Russian word for lawyer, *advokat*.

***The Supplication of Daniel the Prisoner* is a thirteenth century work of unknown authorship.

"Lies, he said, are for the world, not for God: you cannot lie to Him, nor play with the sublime." Note that "to lie" [*solgati*] and "to play" [*igrati*] are equated.

The usual way of breaking a contract with one of the forces of evil is by repentance (cf. *The Tale of Savva Grudcyn**). The "apocrypha" of Adam** is a more complex variant. There is one text (A.N. Pypin says that it was extracted from an Old Believer manuscript but does not give any information about it), according to which Adam made an agreement with the Devil in return for the cure of Eve and Cain:

> And the Devil said: "For this you must give a written undertaking as follows: 'Living I belong to God, but dead to you.'" [5]

However, it is not surprising to find that in a text which was clearly more widespread Adam consciously outwits the Devil when he makes the agreement with him. After his expulsion from paradise Adam yoked his ox and began ploughing the land.

> And the Devil came: "I will not let you work the land since it is mine, whereas the heavens and paradise belong to God [. . .] Write down a declaration that you are mine, then work my land." Adam said: "Whoever the land belongs to so do I and my children."

Later the author explains that Adam managed by his cunning to outwit the Devil; for he knew that the earth belonged to Satan temporarily, that Christ would at some future time appear in flesh ("that the Lord would come down to earth and be born of a virgin") and would redeem the earth and its inhabitants from the Devil with his own blood.[6]

In the West European tradition an agreement is neutral – it may be good or bad; while in its specifically chivalric form, with its cult of the sign, keeping one's *word* becomes a matter of honor. There are numerous stories of knights who keep their word to Satan (cf. the inversion in the legend of Don Juan: although he breaks all the obligations of religion and morals, he keeps his word to the statue of the commander). In the Russian tradition an agreement acquires its binding power from the holy object by which its maintenance is guaranteed. Without this holy authority from the non-conventional power of faith, it has no "force." Therefore a word given to Satan (or his earthly deputies) *must* be broken.

Because of this the system of relationships that became established in medieval society, a system of mutual obligations between the supreme power and the feudal lords, came very early to be viewed in a negative light. Thus Daniel the Prisoner assured his prince that his councillors

---

*The hero of this seventeenth-century tale ends up in a monastery.

**"Apocrypha" – writing on a religious subject that was not recognized by the Church.

were crafty servants and would bring their sovereign to grief, and he contrasts them with an ideal of loyalty; he himself would not be ashamed to be compared with a dog. "Or you may say, oh prince: you have lied like a dog. But princes and noblemen love a good dog." Service based on contract is bad service. Even Peter the Great would write angrily to Prince Boris Šeremet'ev whom he suspected of secret sympathy for the ancient rights of the nobles: "It is as if a servant who sees his lord drowning does not want to save him until he has checked that it is written in his contract that he should pull him out of the water."[7] We may compare this remark with a letter from Kurbatov to Peter: "I wish to serve you truly, my sovereign, without any pretence, as I serve God."[8] Service "by contract" is suspect, but service "as to God" is genuine. This comparison between the sovereign and God is not accidental, for it has deep roots. The centralized form of government was modelled much more directly on the pattern of religious relations than in the West. The isomorphic model was outlined in *Domostroj**: God in His universe, the Tsar in his kingdom, the father in the family; this reflected three levels of unconditional personal commitment and matched the religious system of relations on other levels. The notion of "service to the sovereign," which developed under these circumstances, took for granted the absence of conditions between the parties. From the one side total and unconditional self-commitment was assumed and from the other favour. The concept of "service" derived genetically from the psychology of the bondsmen of the prince's lands. As the role of this bureaucracy which was personally dependent on the prince expanded and turned into a state bureaucracy, parallel with the increasing role of the prince's hired soldiery, the mentality of the prince's court became that of the servants of the state. Religious feelings were transferred to the sovereign, state service [*služba*] was tranformed into religious service [*služenie*]. Merit 'was determined by favor. "If it were not for your favor, where would I be?" wrote Vasilij Grjaznoj to Ivan the Terrible (Grjaznoj was an *opričnik*** and belonged to a noble family). Relations between the Grand prince and his allodial vassals had a contractual character, but for his soldiery his authority was godlike ("You, o Sovereign, are like God").

The clash between these two types of psychology can be traced over the whole period of the Russian Middle Ages. Further, whereas the psychology of exchange and contract cultivates the sign, ritual and etiquette, the state-religious position is oriented towards both the symbol and practical action. Such a paradoxical combination should not surprise us. Chivalric culture was oriented towards the sign. In order to acquire cultural value in this system a thing had to become a sign, i.e. it had to

*Sixteenth-century set of rules of family life.
**See above, p. 39.

130

be cleansed as much as possible of its practical, non-semiotic function. Hence for a feudal lord in early Russia, "honor" would be connected with obtaining a rich portion of the booty of war or a large hand-out from his suzerain. However, once so obtained, the laws of honor required that it should be used in such a way that its material worth was belittled as far as possible, thereby stressing its value as a sign: "They began to make bridges across the marshes and muddy places using their coats, their mantles, their sheepskin jackets and all their highly adorned Polovtsian clothing."[9] A model of knightly behavior is to be found in the Russian redaction of the epic poem about Digenis Akritas, *Devgenievo dejanie* [*The Exploit of Digenis*] (translated in the eleventh to twelfth centuries).* The hero Digenis decided to win as his wife "Stratigos's beautiful daughter," whose suitors her father and brothers always killed. When he reached Stratigos's court he found the girl was alone, her father and brothers being away. Digenis could easily have taken his beloved away with him, but he ordered her to stay at home and to inform her father of her pending abduction. Stratigos refused to believe her. Meanwhile Digenis burst through the gates and having ridden into the courtyard, "began shouting loudly for Stratigos and his strong sons *to come out and see their sister being taken away*" (the italics are mine, Ju. L.). However, even now Stratigos refused to believe that someone had appeared bold enough to challenge him to a fight. Digenis, after waiting for three hours in vain, took his bride away. But this success gave him no joy, in fact it saddened him: "Great shame have I suffered."[10] Finally he did manage to pick a fight in which he defeated his bride's father and brothers and took them prisoner. He then released them, let his bride return home, again came to pay court to her, and at last obtained his bride "with great honor." Everything here, the bride, the battle and the wedding, is turned into a sign of chivalric honor and has no value in itself but only in terms of the meaning attributed to it. The bride is not valued for herself, but only for the difficulty in obtaining her. A battle is prized not because of the victory itself, but principally because the victory has been won according to certain rules, and secondly because the conditions have been as difficult as possible. Defeat and disaster while attempting the impossible are more highly valued than victory and its attendant practical advantages, when these have been come by through calculation and practical flair or the usual military efforts. Effect was more highly valued than effectiveness. Igor' Svjatoslavovič's hopeless venture with his small band in attempting "to seek out the city of T'mutarakan" inspires the author of the *Lay of Igor's Campaign*** more than the modest, but highly effective operations of the united forces of

---

*Russian translation of a Byzantine epic.
**Twelfth-century Russian epic.

131

the Russian princes in 1183–1184. The singer of *The Song of Roland** expresses the same psychology. The sign-aspect of behavior causes emphasis to be placed on the element of play: the object of an action is not so much its practical result as correctness in the use of the language of behavior. Thus in West European chivalry the tournament became the equivalent of the battle. In Russia, hunting took over the function of the tournament in the life of the feudal lord. It became a special form of play on which the semiotic values of the chivalric war code were focused. It is no accident that Vladimir Monomach enumerated his hunting expeditions along with his military exploits as matters of equal pride.**

The opposite kind of behavior excludes conventionality. One of its basic features is its tendency to reject play and the relativity of semiotic means and to identify the non-conventional with truth. Non-conventionality in the social meaning of behavior shows itself in two ways: for those at the top of society there is a trend towards symbolism in behavior and in the whole semiotic system, but for those at the bottom the tendency is towards the zero level of semioticity, behavior being transposed into the purely practical sphere.

Saussure noted the difference between the conventional sign and the non-conventional symbol, a distinction now used in semiotics:

> A feature of the symbol is that it is never entirely arbitrary; it is not empty, there is a rudiment of a natural connection between the signifier and the signifed. The symbol for justice, the scales, could not be replaced with just anything, for example by a chariot.[11]

Power from the point of view of the symbolic consciousness of medieval Russia is endowed with the traits of holiness and truth. Its value is absolute. It is the image of celestial power and embodies in itself eternal truth. The rituals it surrounds itself with are like those of the heavenly order. Before it the individual is not a party to a contract, but comparable with a drop of water flowing into the sea. When he submits himself he demands nothing in return, beyond the right to do this. Peter Šafirov*** for instance, advocating a military diversion aimed at kidnapping Charles XII [of Sweden] from Turkish territory, wrote as follows to Peter the Great from Istanbul after the battle of Poltava: "But even if they do find out that the Russians have done this, all that will happen is that I will suffer here."[12] Many other similar cases could be quoted. The point to notice is that the bearer of "conventional" psychology, when faced with the need to sacrifice his life, regarded death

---

*Twelfth-century French epic.

**In his *Instruction* of c. 1117.

***Of humble origin, Šafirov rose quickly in Peter's service and was the first Russian to be given the title of baron.

as an *act of exchange* of life for glory. "If a man is killed on the field of battle, what reason is there for surprise?" said Daniel Galickij to his soldiers. "Others die *ingloriously* at home, whereas these *have died gloriously*."[13] From the opposite point of view, there can be no thought of an exchange of values, rather a poetic sense of self-sacrifice and anonymous death. The reward is the merging of the self in the absolute and from the absolute nothing can be expected in return. Dracula* does not promise his soldiers glory, nor does he link death in battle with the idea of just recompense;[14] he simply expects them to die at his orders and without any conditions: "Whoever wishes to give thought to death, let him not come to battle at my side."[15]

Because this sort of social mentality extended the sense of religion to statehood, it required society in effect to hand over all semiosis to the Tsar who became a symbolic figure, a sort of living icon.[16] The behavior of other members of society was allotted zero semiotic value. All that was required of them was practical activity. (It is of interest that practical activity continued to be regarded as of very little value. For this reason Ivan the Terrible could describe his colleagues as *stradniki* [labourers]: it was as if they were demoted to a level occupied in early feudal society only by serfs who had no part at all in the semiotics of society). Practical service with real results was what was required of the subject. If subjects were concerned with their work and lives as social signs, this was regarded as "laziness," "trickery" or even "treason." The changed attitude to hunting is indicative: it ceased being an affair of honor and became a form of amusement that was considered shameful because it diverted people from the business of government. (The sovereign did retain the right to hunt, but only as a diversion.) Already in *The Tale of the Battle on the P'jana*, the negligent army commanders' passion for hunting is contrasted with military service to the sovereign: "They hunt, organize pleasure for themselves, thinking they are at home." [17] Later, Ivan wrote in similar terms to Vasilij Grjaznoj: "You should not have slept as if you were out hunting. You thought you were out with your dogs hunting hares and so the Crimeans succeeded in trapping you."[18] Grjaznoj had had no objection to being described as a *stradnik* (agreeing with the Tsar he had written: "You, my sovereign, are like God: you make great things from small ones"); but he took offence at this latest reprimand and wrote to Ivan that he had been wounded and mutilated in battle in his sovereign's service, not while hunting.

The Baroque period brought far-reaching changes in the whole system of culture. However, this new state in social psychology and the semiotics of culture was a transformation of what had gone before, not a total break

---

*The *Tale of Dracula* was translated from the German in the mid-sixteenth century.

with it. On the surface of the culture and way of life, the most striking change was in the official ideology. The state-religious model did not vanish but underwent interesting transformations. Axiologically, its top and bottom had changed places. Practical activity was elevated from the bottom to the highest place in the hierarchy of values. Life was "de-symbolized" and the prestige of practical work heightened. This was accompanied by a demonstrative display of contempt for--and indeed public mockery of--the symbols of the previous period. The poetry of craftsmanship, of useful skills, of actions which are neither signs nor symbols, but are of value in themselves, largely contributed to the spirit of the Petrine reforms and of Lomonosov's scientific activities.* Osip Mandel'štam saw this spirit as the essence of the eighteenth century:

> I am constantly drawn to citations from the naive and wise eighteenth century; here I am reminded of the lines from Lomonosov's famous "Epistle on Glass:"
> They think improperly about things, Shuvalov,
> Who value Glass less than Minerals.
> Whence this pathos, the elevated pathos of utilitarianism, whence this inner warmth which stimulates poetic meditation on the fate of the industrial crafts? What a striking contrast to the brilliant, cold indifference of nineteenth century scientific thought! [19]

Of Peter the Great's manner of behavior, Lomonosov wrote that he,

Born for the sceptre, stretched forth his hands to work.

The ideal of the worker-Tsar was many times repeated, from Simeon Polockij's poem "Doing" ["Delati"] in his collection The Many-Flowered Garden [Vertograd mnogocvetnyj],** to Puškin's poem "Stanzas." *** However, the inverted system, as well as differing from its initial form, also had some similarity with it. Petrine statehood was not the embodiment of a symbol, since in itself it represented the final truth and, having no higher authority than itself, was neither the representative nor the image of anything else. But like the pre-Petrine centralized state, it did demand of its subjects their *faith* in it and their total merging with it. A person surrendered his self to it. A secular religion of statehood came into being and " practical activity" soon ceased to be part of extra-semiotic empirical experience.

*M.V. Lomonosov (1711–1765), scientist, poet and polymath who fixed the standards of the literary language. His "Epistle on Glass" of 1752 is dedicated to Count I.I. Šuvalov.
**Simeon Polockij (1629–1680), poet and theologian.
***Puškin's poem "Stansy" (V nadežde slavy i dobra. ., 1826) contains the lines: "Now scholar, now hero, / Now seaman, now carpenter, / His eager spirit embracing all pursuits, / He was a tireless worker on the throne."

There was a radical change in the relative importance of the semiotics of agreement in the general structure of the culture of the period. Having been almost totally destroyed along with the whole cultural heritage of the early Russian Middle Ages, the notion of agreement found powerful support in Western cultural influence.

In Feofan Prokopovič's speeches and those of other supporters of Peter's policies, the political ideas of Puffendorf and Hugo Grotius,* curiously refracted through the Russian tradition, were further developed. The authority of the Tsar is seen as divinely given and justified by reference to St. Paul (Epistle to the Ephesians, vi. 5).** However, it is affirmed at the same time that in assuming power the Tsar enters into an implicit contract that binds him to rule for the good of his subjects. The Tsar ceased to be a symbol, and thereby became obliged to serve his subjects *practically*, as they were to serve him:

> If all rank is derived from God, . . .that same is most necessary to us and pleasing to God, his own high rank demands that I should have mine, you yours and likewise for everyone. If you are Tsar you should rule, making sure that there is no unhappiness among the people, that the government is just and that the fatherland is secure from enemies. If you are a senator, attend to your duties likewise Moreover you should speak in a simple way, weigh everything up carefully, that your calling requires of you, and do your duty vigorously?[20]

The system of national honors and ranks, introduced in the eighteenth century, which contended with the principle of unconditional and innate nobility based on blood, was also founded on the notion of exchange of merit for signs. The principle of equivalence in this exchange, although it was infringed in practice, was in theory to have been rigorously observed. To this end there were elaborate statutes and a system of promotion through the ranks based on a strict succession according to length of service. The fact that someone who had been passed over for reward might, in accordance with the customs and laws of the time, draw attention to himself and demand his due, by listing his rights, proves that in the consciousness of the time this was no extra-legal favor, but an exchange of obligations between the government and its public servants, which was well-regulated and subject to rules.

The contractual spirit which permeated eighteenth-century culture caused people to rethink (or, at least, to rephrase) their attitude to traditional institutions. Thus it is typical that although everyone knew that

---

*Hugo Grotius (1583–1645), Dutch jurist; Samuel, Baron von Puffendorf (1632–1680), writer on jurisprudence who followed and extended Grotius's system. Peter the Great ordered a Russian translation of Puffendorf's *De officiis hominis* in 1724.

**"Slaves obey your earthly masters with fear and trembling, single-mindedly, as serving Christ."

Russia was an autocracy and that to acknowledge this was part of official ideology (in particular, in the official use of titles), as well, of course, of practical government, it was considered a breach of good taste to acknowledge it as a fact. Catherine the Great argued in her "Instruction" [*Nakaz*] that Russia was a monarchy and not an autocracy, i.e. that it was governed by law, not by arbitrary rule. Alexander I would repeatedly stress that autocracy was an unfortunate necessity which he personally did not favor. For him, as for Karamzin, autocracy may have been a fact, but it was not an ideal. This attitude was particularly marked in considerations about the rights of the nobility. As early as 1730, Kantemir,* in his second satire ' On Nobility" ["*O blagorodstve*"] saw the nobles' privileges as an advance payment on the merits of their forefathers, which had to be worked off by personal service to the state. This idea was taken up by writers such as Sumarokov** and converted into the theory of the exchange of personal services for honors obtained through one's ancestors' merits. The nobleman who failed to perform these personal services was no better than a cheat, taking and giving nothing in return:

> The title to nobility flows in our blood from generation to generation.
> But let us ask why nobility is thus bestowed.
> If my grandfather's life was to the benefit of society,
> For himself he earned payment, for me an advance:
> And I, receiving this advance through another's merit,
> Should not let his noble deeds end with him. . .
> For encouragement I have taken a decent advance,
> Is it right that I should have plenty without myself doing work? [21]

An opposite process was at work against this background. At the same time as the tendency to rationalize the semiotic exchange, and to switch its center of gravity on to its content, there existed a counterflow, the urge towards an irrational emphasis on the sign system as such. Convention, ritual, and the arbitrariness of the sign were stressed; and thus the closed culture of the nobility, as part of its rapid development, cultivated etiquette and the theatricalization of their life-style. A semiotics of corporate honor became established and duels became more frequent as a ritual procedure for the satisfaction of offended honor.

The culture of the dandy that emerged was based on play with the conventional link between the content of signs and their expression. There arose a need for dictionaries to explain the meanings of conventional forms of expression, and in particular the language of courtly love.

---

*Prince Antioch Kantemir (1708–1744), writer, best known for his nine satires which were not published until 1762.
**A.P. Sumarokov (1718–1777), poet and playwright.

For instance Dreux du Radier's *Lexicon of Love*, which was adapted to Russian usage by A.V. Chrapovickij, was constructed on the lines of a normal dictionary (the word, phraseological example, and the dictionary entry). For example:

DISQUIET. *I am suffering mortal disquiet.* This means: "I am obeying the accepted rules and am presenting a seemly aspect to my ardor."

TO TALK. If a beautiful woman should say pleasantly: *You are talking nonsense*, this means: "Although I do want a lover, I am afraid of your tendency to be indiscreet" [. . .] *Remember whom you are talking to*, or *I do not understand this*, and other such expressions have the same meaning.

TORMENT. *I am enduring intolerable torment* usually means: "I am pretending to be in love, and as you often go to the theater you think that people are not in love unless they suffer torment. To please you I have to summon up these passionate words. . ." [22] .

Metatexts such as these are needed to understand the language of beauty spots:

A velvet beauty spot. . .on the temple indicates *ill-health*, a taffeta one on the left side of the forehead stands for *pride*, below one of the lower eye-lashes it denotes *tears*, on the upper lip a *kiss*, on the lower one, *inclination*, and so on. . .The key to this code, like that of a minister [minister here means ambassador or diplomat, Ju. L.] is not fixed; words are arbitrarily selected and changed for security reasons. [23]

Languages of flowers and of fans evolved. The popularity of masquerades brought an element of relativity even into what one would have thought were natural oppositions: the men dressed up as women, and the women as men. [24] It should be recalled that the popular consciousness continued to regard unmotivated signs as coming from the Devil. This is demonstrated by the attitude, widespread in moralistic literature, that associated the semiotic relativism of the dandy culture with atheism and moral relativism.

It would be a mistake, though, to look at the dandy culture of the eighteenth century from the same angle as its critics and to regard it only as an ugly social anomaly. For it was from the depths of that culture that consciousness of the autonomy of the sign came into being, the consciousness which was to be an important stimulus for the formation of the personality-based culture of the Romantic era. Trediakovskij* in his *Voyage to the Island of Love* [1730] represents the source of this

*V.K. Trediakovskij (1703–1769), poet, translator and literary theorist. His *Voyage to the Island of Love* [*Ezda v ostrov ljubvi*] was a translation of a French seventeenth-century allegorical novel by Paul Tallemant.

culture in Russia and Karamzin,* in his capacity of author of *Letters of a Russian Traveller* [1791–1792] brings down the curtain on it: this fact obliges us to see in it more than just a sequence of caricatures ranging from Korsakov in Puškin's *The Negro of Peter the Great* to Sljunjaj in Krylov's *Trumf*.**

The tension of social conflict at the end of the eighteenth century brought about further shifts in the structure of the languages of culture. The close bond between the world of signs and the social structure of society discredited the sign as such in the eyes of the Enlightenment thinkers of the eighteenth century. Following Voltaire, they subjected "age-old prejudices" (Puškin's phrase***) to thorough-going criticism, which in practice meant a review of the whole store of semiotic concepts accumulated over the centuries. Rousseau, exposing the falsity of the world of civilization, identified as its original principle the conventionality of the connection between expression and content in the word. The contrast he posited between the word on the one hand, and intonation, gesture and facial expressions on the other in fact amounted to an antithesis between the unmotivated and the motivated sign. However, while striving to free himself from the tyranny of the sign, Rousseau built up his social ideal on the basis of the social contract, i.e. on the idea of an exchange of equivalent values between people; but this ideal is not possible if the conventionality of signs is eradicated. Though rejecting social semiotics, Rousseau wanted to retain its results.

Masonic ideology evolved at the opposite pole. The Masons were opponents of the contractual theory of society. Against it they advocated the idea of self-surrender to some absolute principle (e.g. their order, ideal humanity, God) and of the merging of the self within it without thought of recompense. But though subjectively oriented in the Middle Ages, they remained men of the eighteenth century. Their emblems were not medieval symbols but a conventional secret language for the initiated, lying closer on the semiotic scale to the language of beauty spots than to the symbolism of the Middle Ages.

Both these attempts to escape from linguistic conventionality ended in failure. The eighteenth century concluded with two extravagant

---

*N.M. Karamzin (1766–1826), enormously influential as the proponent of Sentimentalism in Russia and in the last two decades of his life as historian of the Russian state. His important *Letters of a Russian Traveller* which introduced the Russian reader to Western views and taste were first mostly published in 1791–1792 but were added to and revised until 1801.

**Korsakov and Sljunjaj are both fops: the former, according to Puškin's story (1828) at the court of Peter the Great, and the latter in the play properly called *Podščipa* ["Pincher"], written in 1800, by A.I. Krylov (1769–1844) who is best known as the writer of fables.

***Eugene Onegin, Chapter Two, stanza xvi.

masquerades: a "Roman" one in revolutionary Paris and a knightly one at the court of Paul I.

Our discussion does not cover the nineteenth century. We may note, however, that early in the new century the idea of "self-surrender" and the rejection of culture based on the conventionality of the sign came once more to the fore. On the one hand there was the archaic idea of the providential mission of the autocracy, fanatically propagated by Nicholas I, and on the other, the ideal that inspired the progressive section of society: that of self-surrender to the objective, absolute values of freedom, history, the people or "the general good."

Translated by N.F.C. Owen

NOTES

1   See Reichler 1979.
2   It is indeed power rather than grace that we mean, since the religious worship of evil forces is also possible.
3   Quoted from St. Francis 1903, pp. 58–62.
4   Afanas'ev 1936–1939, No. 149; Afanas'ev 1897, No. 86.
5   Tichonravov 1863, Vol. I, p. 16.
6   Ibid. p. 4.
7   Peter 1887–1977, Vol. III, p. 265.
8   S.M. Solov'ev 1959–1966, book IV, col. 5.
9   Slovo 1952, p. 11.
10 Kuz'min 1962, p. 149.
11 Saussure 1962, p. 101. In the Russian translation this remark sounds less categorical: "It is a feature of the symbol that *it is always not completely arbitrary.*" (Cf. the French original: "Le symbole a pour caractère *de n'être jamais tout à fait arbitraire.*") For a discussion of the difference between sign and symbol, see Todorov 1972, pp. 275–286; idem, 1977, pp. 9–11 ff.
12 S.M. Solov'ev 1959–1966, book IV, col. 42.
13 PSRL Vol. II. 2nd edition, 1908, p. 822. (My italics, Ju. L.)
14 Cf. "Death on the field of battle is usually known as 'judgement'" in Meščerskij 1958, p. 85.
15 Dracula 1964, p. 127.
16 It was the nature of the authority of royal power as a symbol rather than a sign that precluded any possibility of play behavior for the Tsar. It is for this reason that play elements in Ivan the Terrible's behavior were perceived both subjectively and objectively as Satanism.
17 PSRL Vol IV, issue 1, 1919, p. 307.
18 *Poslanija* 1951, p. 193.
19 "The nineteenth century," Mandel'štam 1928, p. 62. [Also in Mandel'štam 1964–1981, Vol. 2, pp. 319–320. English translation from Mandelstam 1979, p. 139].
20 Feofan 1961, p. 98.
21 Sumarokov 1935, p. 203.
22 Dreux du Radier 1779, pp. 9, 18, 42. [Translations from the Russian text.]

23 Ljubov' 1798, pp. 134 – 135.

24 Cf. this remark by Catherine the Great: "A most amusing idea occurred to me.
We must hold a ball at the Hermitage. . .We must tell the ladies to come simply
attired and without paniers and without headdresses. . .In the ballroom there will
be four booths with clothing and masks on one side, and four booths with clothes
and masks on the other; one side for the men, the other for the women. . .The
booths with the men's clothes will have the sign 'Clothing for Ladies' and the
booths with women's clothing will have the sign 'For Gentlemen'." Catherine 1901 –
1907, Vol. XII, p. 659. [French in the original.]

THE THEATER AND THEATRICALITY AS COMPONENTS
OF EARLY NINETEENTH-CENTURY CULTURE

Jurij M. Lotman

In memoriam P. G. Bogatyrev

In *The Folk Theater of the Czechs and Slovaks*, P. G. Bogatyrev
wrote:

> One of the major and basic theatrical characteristics of any theatri-
> cal event is transformation. The actor exchanges his own personal
> appearance, dress, voice, and even the psychological traits of his
> character for the appearance, dress, voice, and personality of the
> character he is acting in the play.[1]

It is not only in the case of the actor that transformation occurs; in the
process of becoming theatrical the world as a whole is reconstructed
according to the laws of theatrical space in which things become the
signs of things.

In his writings, Bogatyrev several times examined the processes
by which the extra-theatrical world influences the theatrical world and
vice versa. His attention was constantly attracted to the theatricalization
and ritualization of certain aspects of the extra-theatrical world and to
the situation in which the theater becomes a model of behavior in real
life. The present writer had these things in mind in dedicating this article
to the memory of Petr Grigor'evič Bogatyrev.

Although, objectively speaking, art always reflects the phenomena
of life in one way or another as it translates them into its own language,
the conscious attitude of the author and the audience in this respect can
be of three kinds.

Firstly, art and extra-artistic reality may be regarded as domains
between which the difference is so great and unbridgeable in principle
that even comparison between them is excluded. Thus, for example, up
to the last war there was preserved in the Catherine Palace at Carskoe
Selo a portrait of Empress Elizabeth by Caravaque[2] in which the face
executed like a portrait was combined with the totally naked body of
a Venus. For the artistic consciousness of later epochs, a canvas of this
kind must have seemed improper, or even insulting, no less, when account

was taken of the status of the person depicted. Observers of the eighteenth century, however, looked at the picture in a different way. It could not have entered their heads to see in this naked female body a representation of the real body of Empress Elizabeth. They would see in the picture a combination of texts having two different degrees of conventionality: the face belonged to portraiture and therefore related to specific external reality as an iconic depiction of it, while the body was ascribed to the norms of allegorical painting, which worked in terms of emblems; the latter were symbols of objects and not representations of them. Just as the face of Catherine the Great and the eagle at her feet in Levickij's well-known picture assert different degrees of conventionality (the face represents a face, but the eagle represents power), so the face and body in the portrait of Empress Elizabeth were correlated in different ways with the world of extra-artistic reality.

Thus, where the fine arts or the theater (as in ballet, for example) work with signs that are known to be conventional, and the relation between representation and content is determined not by similarity but by historical convention, there is no possibility of these two dimensions getting "mixed up," and an insuperable barrier is set up between canvas and observer, stage and auditorium. Artistic and extra-artistic spaces are divided by so clear-cut a boundary that they can only interrelate and not interpenetrate.

In the second of these three attitudes, the domain of art is regarded as the area of models and programs. Active influence is directed out of the realm of art into the area of extra-artistic reality. Life selects art as a model and strives to "imitate" it.

In the third case, life is seen as the area of modelling activity: it creates examples which are imitated by art. If in the second case art supplies forms for people's behavior in life, then in the third case the forms of behavior in life determine behavior on the stage.

In full awareness of the conditional nature of this account, we may compare the first instance with Classicism, the second with Romanticism, and the third with Realism.

Historians of literature and art often speak of the "Classicism" or "Neoclassicism" of early nineteenth-century Russian culture. B. V. Tomaševskij spoke of the *Empire* style as a renaissance of Classicism in the literature and architecture of the early nineteenth century.[3] L. Ja. Ginzburg writes:

> The Karamzinians, of course, are not Classicists in terms of the content and form of their art, but they are Classicists in respect of their historical function, the role it was their lot to play in the literature of the 1810s, into which they brought a spirit of system and organization, the norms of "good taste" and logical discipline. To carry out

142

these tasks they needed (in a mild form, of course) the well-ordered stylistic hierarchy of Classicism.[4]

Students of culture have pointed to a new wave of enthusiasm for antiquity.[5] They customarily cite a well-known passage from the memoirs of F. F. Vigel':

> What the new Brutuses* and Timoleons* ultimately wanted was to recreate this exemplary antiquity of theirs in their own surroundings. . . . Everywhere there appeared alabaster vases with mythological scenes in relief, censers and side-tables shaped like tripods, curule armchairs, long couches whose arms rested on eagles, griffins or sphinxes.[6] The enthusiasm for Classicism was so strong in Russia that all artists working in this direction had great success among their contemporaries. Martos** and Count F. Tolstoj** form the boundaries within which the Russian *Empire* style is encompassed.[7]

In his memoirs, Sergej Glinka interestingly compared the cult of antiquity during the 1800s on the one hand with civic-mindedness and love of liberty, and on the other with the cult of military glory, which in the first years of the new century took the form of Bonapartism (the national interests of Russia and France had not yet come into conflict; see, for example, the Bonapartism of Pierre and Andrej Bolkonskij at the beginning of *War and Peace*). Glinka writes:

> The voice of the virtues of ancient Rome, the voice of the Cincinnatuses*** and Catos,**** echoed loudly in the passionate young hearts of the cadets. . . . Ancient Rome became my idol too. I didn't know under what government I was living, but I did know that liberty was the soul of the Romans.

*Lucius Junius Brutus expelled the Tarquins from Rome and became first consul; Timoleon of Corinth drove the tyrants from Sicily and established a democratic form of government there.
**I. P. Martos (1745-1835), sculptor, author among other things of the "Minin and Požarskij" group in Red Square, Count Fedor Petrovič Tolstoj (1783-1873), another well-known sculptor of the period.
***Lucius Quintius Cincinnatus was a model of old Roman frugality and integrity. He was called from the plough in 460 BC to assume the dictatorship and save Rome from the Aequians. Sixteen days after the victory he modestly withdrew again to his farm.
****There were two famous Catos of ancient Rome: Marcus Portius Cato (Cato Major) who was renowned for his frugal and simple life, distinguished himself in the Second Punic Wars and was elected censor in 184 BC. All his life he stood for the old Roman virtues against the tide of luxury that was sweeping Rome at that period; Cato Major's great grandson, M. P. Cato Uticensis continued the lofty and abstemious principles of his great grandfather. His suicide in 46 BC, rather than fall into the hands of Caesar, was a popular literary topic in Europe in the eighteenth century.

And further on: "Anyone who had been familiar with the heroes of Greece and Rome since their early days was at that time a Bonapartist."[8] This "military Classicism" determined, for example the treatment of the Russian *Empire* style in architecture in the early nineteenth century:

> Monuments, pediments and the cornices of buildings are decorated with figures *à la grecque*, lions' faces, helmets, shields, spears and swords. The attributes of war appear even on the walls of churches.[9]

The turn towards Classicism is even more noticeable in Western European culture. In France, where Classicism went beyond the framework of the culture of a particular epoch and acquired the significance of a national tradition, this tendency was essentially never broken, but only changed its coloration in the transition from Revolution to Empire. But Germany too, when it had outlived the *Sturm und Drang* rejection of Classical cultural forms, turned back to them in the work of the later Schiller and Goethe.

Thus it might seem that the tradition of Classicism either continued without a break (France) or was restored in a comparatively unchanged form (Russia, Germany). This conclusion would be mistaken indeed.

In a number of studies it has already been pointed out that "Neoclassicism" was, irrespective of its declarations, essentially disguised Romanticism (see G. A. Gukovskij's writings, for example). For the particular purposes of this article there is no need for us to go into this question fully. We will dwell on just one aspect of it.

Despite the frequent similarity in structure between Classicist and Neoclassicist texts if looked at immanently, there is a marked transformation in the pragmatic aspect of such texts, as well as in the attitude of the audience to them and the formula of their correspondence with extra-textual reality.

As I have already remarked, Classicism divided art off from life with an insuperable barrier. This led to the spectator understanding, even as he was being enraptured by the heroes of the theater, that their place was on the stage, and that he could not imitate them in life without risking seeming ludicrous. Heroism was dominant on the stage, and decorum in life. The laws of each of these things were strict and rigorous for artistic as for real spaces. We may recall Heinrich Heine's joke that a modern Cato, before committing suicide, would sniff the knife to see if it smelled of herrings. The idea of the witticism lies in confusing the mutually exclusive spheres of heroism and decorum.

When, in 1770, at the height of his clash with Saltykov, the commander-in-chief of Moscow, Sumarokov wrote his emotional letter to Catherine, the Empress sharply drew his attention to the "impropriety" of bringing the norms of theatical monologue into life. "For me it will always be more pleasant," she wrote to the dramatist, "to see the presentation of the passions in your dramas than to read about them in letters."

And many years later, Grand duke Constantine, who had been brought up in the same tradition, wrote to his tutor Laharpe:

> No-one in the world more than I fears and hates actions done for effect, actions whose effect is calculated in advance, or actions that are dramatic and full of enthusiasm.[10]

At the beginning of the nineteenth century, however, the dividing line between art and the everyday behavior of the audience was expunged. The theater invaded life and actively restructured everyday behavior. The monologue comes into the letter and the diary into everyday speech. What shortly before had seemed pompous and comic, since it was ascribed only to the domain of theatrical space, became the norm of everyday speech and everyday behavior. The people of the Revolution behave in life as upon a stage. When Gilbert Romme is sentenced to the guillotine and stabs himself, then plucks the knife from the wound and gives it to his friend, he is repeating a feat of classical heroism that was known to people of his epoch through its many reflections in the theater, in poetry, and in the fine arts.[11] Art becomes a model that life imitates.

Examples of how people of the late eighteenth and early nineteenth centuries constructed their personal behavior, their everyday speech, and in the last analysis their destiny in life, according to literary and theatrical models are very numerous. Anyone who has studied the history of non-literary texts of that time knows how abruptly their style changes as it comes closer to norms that have been evolved in the purely literary sphere.

We will cite just one example, from the memoirs of Sergej Glinka that have already been quoted, one that is of interest because of its double encoding—the norms of Classical heroism, drawn from literary texts, become a model for the real behavior of people drawn into the practical everyday situations of Russian life in the 1790s. But this behavior is offered to us in verbal paraphrase. The narrator could interpret the content of his narration from various points of view; he could speak of his hero as a bearer of the virtues of yore (and the antithesis of the "fops" and fashionable cynics), as an eccentric or even a madman, or in any other kind of way. But he goes into the mode of "Classical antiquity" and makes the narrator's point of view accord with the position of the person he is talking about.

> We had our own Catos, we had imitators of the valiant ancient Greeks, we had our Philopoemens.* We had our Cato in Guinet, who after being a cadet became a training officer and teacher of mathematics. If he had been in Regulus'** place, he would probably have found

---

*Philopoemen of Megalopolis, renowned Greek general, d. BC 183.
**Marcus Atilius Regulus, Roman commander and consul, when captured by the Carthaginians sacrificed his life to ensure that Rome continued the war (BC 250). Famous for his frugal, agricultural life.

himself sending a request from the army's encampment to the Senate of Rome for permission to plough and till his cornfield. He had nothing besides his salary, but he had a brother whom he valued above all price. Their mutual love seemed to have brought Castor and Pollux to life. But *they* were heroes of fable. In the domain of historical brotherly love, Guinet was the equal of Cato the Elder, who in reply to the question, "Who is your best friend?" stated: "My brother, my brother, and my brother." The brother of our officer-Cato was serving in Kronstadt, and he fell seriously ill. The news of his brother's illness struck our Cato-Guinet hard.

The Epiphany frosts were at their most savage. The Gulf was stilled under its icy mantle. There wasn't a sledge to be hired, but he had a soul that moved his legs, and a heart, and Guinet set off on foot, wearing just his long boots and even without stockings. Could he have got warm boots and money from someone? But what did it mean to ask? —To get into debt. The ancient Roman endured and did not ask. In just over a day and a half, Guinet crossed the Gulf, reached his brother, embraced him, and returned to the college by his appointed day on duty. Even though signs of fever had appeared, even though people tried to persuade him to take a rest, and offered to stand his guard for him, he replied: "I will not betray my duty." He stood his guard and then took to his bed, and in delirium from a cruel fever he kept seeing his brother, talking to him, and with his name on his lips he drew his last breath.

Further on:

> When he was in military college, Kulnev, a hero of 1812, followed in the footsteps of Fabricius* and Epaminondas.** Like Epaminondas of Thebes, he loved his mother and shared his salary with her, and like Philopoemen he was simple in dress and behavior . . . . Bringing Epaminondas and Philopoemen back to life in his person, and with a soul akin to that of Fabricius, Kulnev prized his poverty and called it "the greatness of ancient Rome." When his fellow officers angled for invitations to dinner with him, he would say: "There's cabbage soup and gruel, but bring your own spoon." He carried a Plutarch with him always; he took his rest on his modest cape with the *Lives* in his hand, took it with him when he inspected the sentries, and from it he imbibed the sentiment that found greatness in the bare necessities of life and in poverty.[12]

This "Roman" poetry of poverty, which lent theatrical grandeur to material want, was later to be characteristic of the younger Decembrists (Fedor Glinka, for example), but it was decidedly alien to the non-noble intellectuals of the following generation. The way Sergej Glinka

---

*Caius Fabricius Luscinus, popular figure of early Roman history, model of frugality and integrity. **Epaminondas of Thebes, general and statesman, distinguished by his moral uprightness (d. 362 BC).

deals with Kulnev's behavior is also interesting because other contemporaries "decoded" his actions in a different way, seeing them as "eccentricities," for example, in the style of Suvorov. Compare Denis Davydov's well-known lines:

> Relate the feats of the mustachioed hero,
> O Muse, tell how Kulnev made war,
> Wandering through the snows in shirtsleeves,
> Appearing in battle in a Finnish cap.
> May the world hear
> Of Kulnev's antics, and the thunder of his victories.[13]

Marx discussed the social causes of this "antique masquerade" in *The Eighteenth Brumaire of Louis Bonaparte*. However, "Roman pomp," as Belinskij termed it, was part of a wider movement whose center was literary Romanticism, a movement which transformed artistic texts into programs for behavior in life. Puškin's Silvio* imitated not the heroes of antiquity but the characters of Byron and Marlinskij; the principle, though –of the imitation of literature–was identical. It is interesting that the heroes of Gogol, Tolstoj, or Dostoevskij, that is, of texts which themselves imitate life, aroused no imitation among their readers.

A special role in the culture of the early nineteenth century on a pan-European scale was played by the theater. This is all the more indicative because during that period the role of the theater is in no degree proportional to the place of the drama in the general system of literary texts. The epoch as a whole was theatricalized. Specific forms of staginess move out from the theatrical stage and take command of life. First and foremost this applies to the culture of Napoleon's France. When Russian travelers got to Paris after Tilsit, they were struck by the ritualization and pomp of the court at the Tuileries, which was far removed from the calculated simplicity of court life at St. Petersburg under Alexander I. (People of the older generation, accustomed to the splendor of Catherine's court, saw this as a manifestation of the Emperor's miserliness). A detailed description of the impression made by Parisian court ritual on Russian travelers was given by Count E. F. Komarovskij in his memoirs:

A very large number of people had been summoned to the palace: the entire diplomatic corps, all the principals, the military, the civilian, and the courtiers made the court magnificent in the highest degree. There were several marshals in their capes and full uniform, each with his baton in his hand, which gave things even more splendor. The court attire was red, with silver embroidery on the breast and cuffs. In the center of this court, glittering with gold and silver, Napoleon in the plain uniform of an officer of the *chasseurs* made the greatest possible contrast.... Nothing was more majestic and at the same time

*Chief character of Puškin's story *The Shot*.

147

more warlike than the sight, on every step of the grand staircase of the Tuileries, of a grenadier of the Imperial Guard, standing on either side in their bearskins, looking courageous and martial, adorned with medals and chevrons.

There follows a description of the ritual surrounding the presentations to the Empress Josephine and the princesses:

When the parties for cards had been made up, both sides of the doors were opened, and all the men and women had to go individually to make their bow—this was the term used—to the Empress and the two Queens, of Spain and of Holland, and to the Princess Borghese, who responded with a slight bow. During this time, Napoleon was standing in the same room and seemingly making an inspection. . . . For the ladies, this ceremony was extremely burdensome, for they had to maneuver without turning round, using only their feet to push away the extremely long trains of their dresses. The Empress's table was on its own on the transverse wall of the room, and the other three on the lengthwise one. Because of this it was necessary to make three bows as one went directly up to the Empress's table; and then, turning a little to the right, to make a bow to each of the Queens and the Princess as one went sideways from one to the other, and then proceed backwards towards the doors.[14]

Madame de Genlis gave an interesting explanation of the theatricality of court life under Napoleon:

After the fall of the monarchy, they set up etiquette and court rules in accordance with what they had observed while passing through and laying waste other kingdoms, the titles of Highness, Excellency and Chamberlain became just as common as in Germany and Italy. . . . In the Tuileries one could see a strange mixture of foreign systems of etiquette. Court ceremonial was further expanded by the addition of a good deal that came from theatrical custom. There was one witty fellow of the time who observed that the ceremonial of presentation at court was a precise imitation of the presentation of Aeneas to the Queen of Carthage in the opera *Dido*. It is well known that a certain famous actor was frequently approached for advice concerning the costumes created for ceremonial occasions.[15]

However, it was not Court etiquette that was the fundamental area where the aesthetic and theatrical element penetrated into extra-artistic life; this area was that of warfare.

The Napoleonic period brought into military activities, apart from the features essential to it, an indubitable element of the aesthetic. Only when we take this into account can we understand why writers of the following generation, such as Mérimée, Stendhal, and Tolstoj, needed to expend so much creative energy in order to de-aestheticize war, to tear away from it the veil of theatrical enchantment. War in the general cultural system of the Napoleonic epoch was a stupendous spectator show (not only and not entirely this, of course). The contrast between the court at the Tuileries and the general staff decked out on the battlefield in theatrically extravagant uniforms, on the one hand, and the Emperor on the other, dressed in everyday "working" uniform, immediately excluded Napoleon from theatricalized space and made it clear who were the actors and who the director in this enormous play. Let us recall that the conditions and norms of war during those years meant that by no means every empty space was suitable as a "military space." The most suitable was considered to be a gigantic natural amphitheatre like Austerlitz or the fields of Borodino. The commanders-in-chief, disposed on the heights, were in the position both of directors and audience. Feofan Prokopovič had earlier pointed out that there could be "spectator" positions and "actor" positions in battle as in the theatre, when he spoke of the personal participation of Peter the Great in the battle of Poltava and his bullet-pierced hat: "He stands not on one side, as in a theater, but is himself in the action of this great tragedy."[16]

"This great tragedy," the one played out on the fields of Europe, was an active formant of the psychology of people in the early nineteenth century; in particular it accustomed them to see themselves as the dramatis personae of history, it "magnified" them in their own eyes, accustomed them to a consciousness of their own greatness, and this could not but affect their political self-awareness later on. It is indicative that even Denis Davydov, wanting to define the essence of partisan war, made a comparison that emphasizes the aesthetic perception of "minor warfare": "This calling, filled with poetry, demands a romantic imagination, a passion for adventure; it is not satisfied with dry, prosaic bravery. It's a stanza by Byron!"[17]

It is true that Denis Davydov demonstratively rejected the "Classical" interpretation of the war of 1812 (which was characteristic of the Russian *Empire* style, as in the well-known bas-reliefs by Count Fedor Tolstoj, for example),[18] and did not construct his personal behavior according to Roman models. His exemplar was not the Russian nobleman conducting himself like Cato or Aristides,* but the Russian nobleman whose behavior imitated a man of the common people:

> I discovered from experience that in a War of the People one must not only speak the language of the lower orders, but also be like them in manners and clothes too. I donned a peasant's kaftan, let my beard grow and instead of my Order of St. Anne I hung an icon of St. Nicholas round my neck, and started talking with them in popular language.[19]

This may be compared with Ryleev's idea of dressing in "a Russian

---

*Aristides, the Just, famous Athenian general, d. 468 BC.

kaftan" before going out on to the Senate Square on 14 December. Just as with the Slavophiles later, the very fact of transformation was significant, since Ryleev, of course, did not think that he could be taken for a man of the people in this costume. Not for nothing did Nikolaj Bestužev call this plan a "masquerade."[20]

The aesthetic, game-playing essence of this kind of behavior lies in the fact that when he became a Cato, a Brutus, a Požarskij, a Demon or a Melmoth, * and started behaving in accordance with the part he had assumed, the Russian nobleman never stopped being simultaneously a Russian nobleman of his time, no more and no less. This duality in behavior, which was so characteristic of an entire generation, and which was sharply manifested in Jakubovič,** for example, evoked much censure, by no means all of which was fair, on the part of the men of Dobroljubov's and Bazarov's generation.***

One graphic manifestation of "theatricality" in everyday behavior was the heightened sense of the entr'acte. It should be noted that the sense of theatricality as a change in the degrees of conventionality in behavior was especially characteristic of the culture of the eighteenth and early nineteenth centuries, with its custom of combining tragedy, comedy and ballet in one evening's performance, where "one and the same performer declaimed in the tragedy, made jokes in the vaudeville, sang in the opera and posed in the pantomine."[21] In order to understand to the full how acutely the sense of transformation was experienced, one should remember that the theater-lover of the time usually knew the actor or actress as a person and liked popping backstage during the interval. It should also be recalled that among an actor's skills a high value was placed precisely on the art of transformation, and this made makeup an obligatory element in the theater. What was valued in an actor was his ability to renounce his own system of behavior and switch into the conventionally traditional behavior prescribed for the given type of character. The assessment of two actors made by a seasoned theater-lover like S. T. Aksakov is highly indicative:

> The most interesting play after *The Two Figaros* was a little comedy called *The Two Crispins*, which was acted along with some other piece. The two Crispins were played by the famous and noble rivals

---

*Prince Požarskij, together with Minin, drove the Poles from Moscow in 1613 and thus put an end to the Time of Troubles. The Demon, outcast from Paradise, is the hero of a narrative poem of that name by Lermontov. *Melmoth the Wanderer*, by Maturin (1820), one of the most famous of Gothic novels. Melmoth sells his soul to the devil in return for a prolonged life.

**A. I. Jakubovič, a colorful figure in Decembrist circles. While holding the confidence of the Tsar he went out among the mutineers on 14 December 1825 urging them not to give in.

***N. A. Dobroljubov (1836-61), radical critic who propounded socialist and utilitarian views. Bazarov is the Nihilist hero of Turgenev's novel *Fathers and Sons* .

F. F. Kokoškin and A. M. Puškin; the latter, like Kokoškin, had translated one of Molière's comedies, *Tartuffe*, also adapting it to Russian manners. Lovers of theatrical art long remembered this "war of the actors." One of them had to conquer and one be defeated; but the public was divided into two equal halves, each half considering and proclaiming its hero the victor. Those who esteemed Puškin said that he was much better than Kokoškin since he was adroit, lively, amiable, unpretentious, and natural in the highest degree. All this is true, and in this respect Kokoškin bore no comparison with Puškin. But Kokoškin's admirers said that for better or worse he was playing Crispin, while Puškin played Puškin, and this was absolutely true as well, and from it one ought to conclude that both actors were unsatisfactory as Crispin. Crispin is a well-known character on the French stage, one that has been played and is to this day played (if it is played at all) according to tradition; this is how Kokoškin played it, but I think unsuccessfully, because of a lack of naturalness and animation. Puškin definitely played himself, or, at the very least, he played a modern Artful Dodger; he didn't even put on the famous costume that Crispin always appears in; in short, there wasn't a ghost of Crispin in it.[22]

The change in the type of stage behavior, which sharpened the sense of conventionality, and the problem of the interval and the footlights as boundaries of the theatrical space on the boards and in time, are organically linked with each other.

In the everyday behavior of the Russian gentleman of the end of the eighteenth and early nineteenth centuries it is characteristic both for a certain type of behavior to be bound to a particular "stage area" and for there to be an inclination towards the "entr'acte," the intermission during which the semiotic value of behavior is reduced to a minimum. In order to appreciate these characteristics to the full, it is enough to recall the behavior of the 'Nihilist' of the 1860s, for whom the ideals were "be true to oneself," be immutable in one's social image, and follow the same norms in both family and social, "historical" and personal life. The demand for "sincerity" implied a withdrawal from a markedly semiotic system of behavior and at the same time eliminated the necessity for having intervals during which "one was oneself for a while."

The everyday life of the gentry at the end of the eighteenth century and the beginning of the nineteenth was based not only on a hierarchy of behavior patterns created by the hierarchical nature of the political order of the post-Petrine state, organized as it was by the Table of Ranks, but also as a set of possible alternatives ("service/retirement," "life in the capital/life on the country estate," "Petersburg/Moscow," "military service/civil service," "the Guards/the army," and so on), each of which entailed a particular type of behavior. One and the same person behaved differently in Petersburg and in Moscow, in his regiment and on his

151

estate, in the company of ladies and in that of men, on campaign differently from when in barracks, at a ball differently from what Puškin called "the hour of bachelor revels." Furthermore, as opposed to the everyday life of the peasant, in which individual behavior altered in accordance with the calendar and the cycle of rural work, and in which the type of behavior consequently depended not on individual choice,[23] but was therefore openly social and without individual character, the lifestyle of the gentry afforded an ever-present possibility of choosing one's type of behavior. At the same time, however, if the peasant had no physical possiblity of practising "non-peasant" behavior, then for a gentleman, "non-gentlemanly" behavior was excluded by the norms of honor, custom, state discipline and the habits of the caste. The infrangibility of these norms was not automatic, but in each separate case it was an act of conscious choice and the free manifestation of will. However, "gentlemanly behavior" as a system not only permitted, but even assumed certain departures from the norm, departures which are structurally isomorphous with the intervals in plays. The gentleman's urge to take part in a different existence for short periods—the life of the stage, the gypsy encampment, the folk revels (compare, in bourgeois life, the analogous function of the picnic, going out "into the bosom of nature," accompanied by a marked simplification of social ritual; in the twentieth century sport sometimes plays a similar role, especially hiking)—this urge engendered intermissions in normative behavior and its replacement by conduct that functioned as socially non-normative. However, this non-normative quality was only functional within the limits of the given system. Outside it, the self-same behavior appeared to be highly normative. This is evident if only because the types of such infringements were strictly classified in accordance with the age and place of the person in the social hierarchy. Society distinguished clearly between "correct" (permissible) and "incorrect" (impermissible) departures from the norm.

One interesting indication of the theatricalization of everyday life are the amateur theatricals and domestic theaters that were widespread in the life of the gentry at the beginning of the nineteenth century; like participation in the professional theater, they were regarded as a departure from the world of the conventional and insincere life of the beau-monde into a world of genuine feelings and directness, that is, as a *diminution* of the level of semioticity in behavior.[24]

Noteworthy too is the constant striving to interpret the laws of the life of gentry society through the prism of the most highly conventional forms of theatrical play—the masquerade, the puppet show, and the folk farce (*balagan*), something we meet with constantly in literature of the late eighteenth and early nineteenth centuries.[25]

We have already noted that in examining the spectator culture of the early part of the century, the military actions of massed troops cannot be overlooked, just as one cannot exclude the circus from the spectator culture of Rome or the bullfight from that of Spain. Of course, in all these cases the fact that in the course of the spectacle real blood is spilled does not cancel out the principle of aestheticization, but is a condition of it. In the long chain of transitions that divides the boards of the theatre from the knightly tournament or professional boxing, the horrific and the beautiful fall into interrelationships specific to each gradation. At the extreme ends of the chain they exchange places; in the tragedy, what is beautiful is perceived as terrible, while in a real battle perceived aesthetically, what is terrible is perceived as beautiful.

However, the army during the period of Paul I and Alexander I provided another form, one which was perceived as the antipode and complete opposite of battle: this was the parade. The parade, of course, to immeasurably greater degree than the battle was directed towards the spectator. In one respect it was precisely here that there ran a line dividing the military men of the time into two camps. In the one were those who regarded the army as an organism destined for making war, while in the other were those who regarded its highest destiny as the parade. Naturally, in the first case the practical function was pushed into the limelight, while in the second it was pushed back to the very furthest plane. However, if the aesthetic function was present in the first case only as a barely perceptible tinge that modified the coloration of the picture but not its outlines, then in the second, it came bursting forward, pushing aside all practical considerations.

Behind the orientation of the army towards battle or parade there stood two different military doctrines, both of them pedagogical and theoretical, and in the last analysis, both philosophical as well.[26] That they are socio-political opposites is obvious, just as is the tendency of the one towards Classical culture and the other towards Romantic culture. From another point of view, one of them was perceived as "Prussian" and the other as nationally Russian. At the juncture of all these oppositions there arose a profound difference in the way these two basic aspects of the contemporary army were experienced aesthetically.

Participation in war was a crucial element in the biography of an entire generation of young men in Europe, an element without which the character of the Decembrist as he was in life is impossible, and which had a substantial influence on the type of personality. Battle was realized as a kind of organization (it was determined by the general disposition of the army, but the placing and role of the individual participant were determined by the role assigned to his unit, and by the nature of the duties laid upon him in accordance with his rank and obligations), and yet war opened up a significant amount of freedom for personal initiative. The organization of battle, which brought together people who were extremely different in terms of their place in the social hierarchy, and simplified the forms of intercourse between them, in one respect abolished that social hierarchy and was perceived as a simplification of it. Where, apart from the field of Austerlitz, could a young officer see the Emperor weeping? Besides this, during battle the atoms of the social structure were much freer in their orbits than in social life, repressed as it was by a bureaucratic system of law and order. The "fortune" that made it possible to bypass the middle steps of the social hierarchy, leaping from the bottom directly to the summit, the same "fortune" that in the eighteenth century was associated with the Empress's bed, in the early nineteenth summoned up in people's imagination the image of Bonaparte at Toulon or on the bridge at Arcole (cf. Prince Andrej's "my Toulon" in *War and Peace*). It was not just the means, but the ends that changed; the ambitious man of the eighteenth century was an adventurer, dreaming of personal advancement, while the ambitious man of the early nineteenth also dreamed of a place on the pages of history. Court life in the Alexandrine period knew almost none of those vertiginous rises and falls which, so characteristic of Catherine's reign, were taken by Paul to the level of caricature. It was only war, in unfettering the initiative of hundreds of junior officers, that taught them to regard themselves not as the blind executants of another man's will, but as people into whose hands the fate of the fatherland and the lives of thousands of men had been committed. Participation in the war against Napoleon and the activation of civic self-awareness brought together a wartime spirit of enterprise and the political love of liberty. Puškin laid stress on the connection between liberalism and the military past of a generation

> Who, gaining their liberty at fifteen years of age,
> In three wars got used to powder and the field, no more.[27]

The parade was the direct opposite; it strictly regulated the conduct of each man, making him a silent cog in an enormous machine. It left no room at all for variation in the behavior of the individual. On the other hand, initiative was transferred to the center, to the personality of the parade commander. From the time of Paul I this was the Emperor. Timotheus von Bock wrote:

> Why does the Emperor love parades so passionately? Why does that very man we knew in the army as a luckless diplomat turn during peacetime into a fervent soldier who drops everything as soon as he hears a drum beat? It's because the parade is a triumph of a non-entity, and every fighting soldier who won one's respect on the day of the battle becomes a mannequin at the parade, while the Emperor seems like a god who thinks and controls.[28]

If battle was associated in the minds of contemporaries with the Romantic tragedy, the parade was clearly oriented towards the corps-de-ballet. Nicholas I's balletomania is symptomatic. Alexander I was indifferent to drama and opera; above all kinds of spectacle he preferred the parade, in which he kept the part of producer for himself and used his thousands-strong army as an enormous ballet company. Drill was a science and art at the same time, and considerations of beauty or "order" were always the highest criterion, something to which all Paul's sons sacrificed their soldiers' health, their own popularity in army circles, and the army's fighting efficiency. Of course, it would be idle to see in this permanent inclination nothing more than a manifestation of the strange personal qualities of Paul and his sons; the parade became an aestheticized model of the ideal military organization and of the ideal state organization as well. It was a grandiose performance that every single day reaffirmed the principle of autocracy.

We should not, however, lose sight of the fact that although drill mania was met by almost unanimous condemnation among the fighting officer corps (documentary evidence of this is abundant and eloquent), the art of drill formed part of an expert knowledge of the secrets of military service, and no military man could ignore it. Pestel' was a connoisseur of parade formations, and the Decembrist Lunin earned the favor of Grand duke Constantine, who was a fanatical advocate of drill, not only by his chivalry and insane bravery, but also through his subtle knowledge of the mysteries of drill procedures. The aesthetic of the parade could not have been completely alien to any professional military man, and even from Puškin, in *The Bronze Horseman*, it evoked lines about its "monotonous glamour" [*krasivost'*] (which did not prevent Puškin from being conscious of the connection between monotony and slavery; cf. "Monotonous as the song of slaves").* The parade aesthetic and the ballet aesthetic had a deep common root—the serf-owning structure of Russian life.

Between the situation "Napoleon on the battlefield" and the situation "Paul on parade," despite all their obvious differences, there is still a substantial similarity. It resides in the fact that what is going on is divided into two spectacles. On the one hand, the spectacle is made up of a mass (in battle or on parade) and the audience is represented by one man. On the other, this man is actually himself a spectacle for the mass, which in this case plays the part of audience. This would appear to be the end of the similarity. Let us examine both sides of this double spectacle.

If we get away from the idea of Napoleon and Paul not just as spectators but as participants, the nature of whose actions is different in principle, and examine them as audience alone, then we cannot help uncovering a difference in principle in their attitudes to the spectacle. Paul watches a spectacle that has an "iron scenario" (Eisenstein's phrase); every detail is worked out in advance. The beautiful is equivalent to carrying out the rules, and a departure from the norms, even the slightest, is perceived as

*Line from *The Gypsies*.

something aesthetically ugly and punishable through disciplinary procedures. The highest criterion of beauty is "order," that is, the capacity to make different people move uniformly according to rules worked out in advance. Order and beauty in movement interests the connoisseur here more than the plot. The question of how things will end has only secondary significance in both ballet and parade. The audience for a battle is comparable with the audience for a tragedy whose plot is unfamiliar to them; no matter how much the majesty of the spectacle enraptures them, their interest in the outcome outweighs it.

The spectacle differs even more when seen from the position of the mass. Napoleon acts out before the eyes of his soldiers, of an amazed Europe, and of posterity a play called "Man Struggles with Destiny," "The Triumph of Genius over Fate." Connected with this was the emphatically human image of the main character (his simple costume, the role of "the common soldier") and the inhuman enormity of the obstacles standing in his way. Through his conduct and his destiny (determined in large part by the historical role he chose for himself), Napoleon anticipated the themes and plots of an entire branch of Romantic literature. In future, genius could be interpreted as a theme in different ways—from demon to one or another historical personage—and the obstacles in his path could also be labelled in different ways—God, feudal Europe, the backward crowd, etc. The schema, however, was fixed. Of course, it was not Napoleon who invented it; he had picked out his role from that same literature. But having embodied it in the play of his own life, he gave the part back to literature with the same boosted power that a transformer adds to the electrical impulses it receives.

Paul played a different role. When he commanded a parade in his crown and imperial mantle (commanding a detachment of troops during Catherine the Great's reign was thought of as the job of a corporal, not an emperor; the Tsar's regalia was used only in exceptional, formal circumstances, and even on these occasions Catherine was keen to replace the crown with a sign standing for it, a scaled-down bejewelled ornament shaped like a crown)—when Paul commanded a parade, he was trying to show Russia the spectacle of God. Lomonosov's metaphorical expression about Peter the Great, "He was thy God, thy God, O Russia!," Paul tried to embody in this extravagant and terrifying spectacle. In this sense it is absolutely no accident that in Marin's parody of Lomonosov's *Ode, Taken from Job*, Paul took the place of God.

Alexander I didn't like the theater and shunned opulent ceremonies. The modesty of his personal life often gave cause for accusations of miserliness. The young Emperor's way of approaching people was charming in its simplicity and directness. It seemed as if he was his father's antipode made flesh, and that the beginning of his reign should have marked the end of the epoch of theatricality.

However, the further we go into the significance of the policies and the personality of Alexander I, the more often—and even with a certain astonishment—we pause before the profound continuity between father and son. Alexander did not avoid play-acting and transformations; on the contrary, he loved changing masks, at some times extracting practical advantage from his ability to play different roles, and at others abandoning himself to the pure artistry of the change of persona, apparently taking pleasure in misleading the people he was talking to, who took this play-acting for reality. We will give just one example.

In mid-March 1812, for a number of reasons, Alexander decided to remove Speranskij from state service. It is not the political and public aspects of this incident that are of interest for us at the moment (they have been well explained in the scholarly literature), but the nature of the sovereign's personal conduct in these circumstances. On the morning of 17 March the Emperor called in the Director of the Chancery of the Ministry of Police, Jakov de Sanglen [Jacques de Sanglin], who was one of the mainsprings of the intrigue against Speranskij, and said, with apparent regret: "No matter how painful it is for me, it is necessary to take my leave of Speranskij. It is essential to remove him from Petersburg." That same evening Speranskij was summoned to the palace and had an audience with the Emperor, after which he was sent off into exile. When he received de Sanglen on the morning of 18 March, Alexander told him: "I raised Speranskij up, brought him close to me, had unlimited trust in him, and have been obliged to exile him. I wept! . . . What scoundrels people are! The very ones who only yesterday were soliciting smiles from him today congratulate me and rejoice in his banishment." The sovereign picked up a book from his desk, angrily threw it back down, and declared with indignation: "O, villains! This is who surrounds us, we unfortunate sovereigns!"[29]

The same day the Emperor received A. N. Golicyn, whom he considered to be his personal friend and in whom he had unlimited trust, and spoke his mind in the same spirit. Seeing extreme gloom on the Tsar's face, Prince Golicyn enquired after his health, and received the reply: "If you had had your hand cut off, you would certainly cry out and complain that you were in pain; well, last night they took Speranskij away, and he was my right hand!"[30] And he was *weeping*. He also wept when he was saying farewell to Speranskij. However, we now know for a fact that nobody cut off Alexander's right hand; taking advantage of a few stupid and pointless denunciations, Alexander had by degrees personally laid the grounds for the entire intrigue. When Speranskij nearly spoiled the dramatic removal that the Emperor had devised by submitting his own resignation, Alexander not only considered it necessary to decline his request, but raised his already doomed victim even higher.[31] But another scene is even more amazing. While all this was being played out,

Professor G.-F. Parrot, Rector of the University of Dorpat, by chance happened to be in Petersburg. A man distinguished by a rare nobility of spirit, Parrot was one of a very limited circle of people who were trusted by the suspicious Alexander. It was precisely because he was not in waiting or a courtier, rarely saw Alexander and never made any petitions to him, that he had a basis for considering himself the personal friend and confidant of the Emperor. On 16 March in the evening, he was summoned to the palace. Parrot writes:

> The Emperor described Speranskij's ingratitude with an anger I had never seen in him, and with enough feeling to call forth tears. When he had set out the proofs he had received of this treachery, he said to me: "I have decided to have him shot tomorrow, and it is because I want to know your opinion of this that I have invited you to see me."[32]

Parrot besought the Emperor to give him time to think. On the morning of 18 March in a special letter he attempted to alleviate Speranskij's fate. The Emperor gave him a gracious reply, and Parrot set off for Dorpat, convinced that he had saved Speranskij. It is obvious, however, that Alexander had no intention of having Speranskij shot, and when he thanked Parrot for his letter and seemed to be graciously attending to his arguments, Speranskij's fate had already been sealed, and he was even then on his way into exile.

Šilder relates this episode not without a certain element of perplexity —a feeling that students of Alexander's personality are almost never without—and sums up:

> In the correspondence of de Sanglen with M. P. Pogodin there occurs the following curious reference to Parrot by Alexander: "These learned men see everything crooked and never hit the mark and have little acquaintance with life, even though he's a man of the world." From his side, Pogodin adds: "Parrot was misled, as was everyone else." When he wrote these lines, our historian did not fully suspect what a great truth he had uttered, since he had no inkling of the deliberate comedy that was played out on 16 March by the main character in this truly Shakespearian drama taken from modern Russian history.[33]

Not for nothing do theatrical terms come to the historian's mind here. There is only one point on which we may disagree with him; Alexander was not playing out a "Shakespearian drama"—this was a continuous "one-man show." A subtle element of calculation shines through the Emperor's every transformation, but it is impossible to be rid of the idea that the ability itself to change masks provided him, besides everything else, with a profound "disinterested" satisfaction. Napoleon showed profound insight when he dubbed him "the Talma of the North."

Alexander's "theater" was closely connected with his style of tackling political problems. He made no distinction in principle between the interests of the State and his own personal ones, and he systematically transformed political relations into personal ones (in this sense, irrespective of the mildness of his personality, Alexander consistently supported the despotic system and was the true son of his father). In the sphere of foreign policy this engendered a style of personal diplomacy which Alexander was able to impose on the courts of Europe, enabling the Emperor of Russia to carry off a series of diplomatic coups. In domestic policy it was a matter of counting on personal devotion to the monarch, something that in the early nineteenth century looked hopelessly archaic and brought about the eventual collapse of Alexander's entire domestic policy.

Alexander's "play-acting" went beyond the style of the epoch; Romanticism demanded a consistent mask which would as it were become part of the individual's personality and form a model for his behavior. This style of constructing the personality was perceived as majestic. Alexander's "Proteanism" was perceived by contemporaries as "craftiness," an absence of sincerity. The verb "to dupe" occurs frequently in assessments of the Tsar, even by his inner circle. Changing his masks so as to "captivate" everyone, Alexander alienated everyone. One of the most talented actors of the age, he was its least successful.

There are epochs when art intrudes imperiously upon everyday life, making its day-to-day course aesthetic in the process. Such were the Renaissance, the ages of Baroque and Romanticism, the art of the early twentieth century. This incursion has many consequences. The flare-ups in creative talent that occur at these times are evidently connected with it. It was not only the theater, of course, that made a powerful impact on the penetration of art into life in the age that interests us here; no less a part was played by sculpture, and, more especially, by poetry. Only against the background of the powerful incursion of poetry into the life of the Russian nobility of the early nineteenth century can the colossal phenomenon of Puškin be understood and explained. However, this question goes beyond the limits of this article.

It is essential to look at one other side of the problem. The everyday course of life and the literary reflection of it give the individual different degrees of freedom in self-preservation. Man is frozen into ordinary everyday life like Dante's sinner into the ice of Caina. He loses his freedom of movement and ceases to be the initiator of his own conduct. The people of the eighteenth century still lived to a significant degree by force of custom. The supra-individual flow of everyday life automatically determined the conduct of the individual. And although the adventurism that in the eighteenth century was unprecedently widespread opened for the most active people of the age a way beyond the bounds of day-to-day life's routine, this was, on the one hand, a course that was unique in principle, and on the other, one that was openly and demonstratively immoral; and it was a course of personal assertion in life that yet did not undermine the foundations of life. The hero of the picaresque novel didn't destroy the life around him; all his energy, all his ability to burst his way out of the iron bands of social constriction, were directed towards no more than fitting back into these bands, but in a manner more advantageous and pleasant for himself. Objectively speaking, his activity did not break down the established order of life, but rather confirmed it.

It is precisely because theatrical life differs from everyday existence that the view of life as performance offered people new possibilities for behavior. Everyday life compared with theatrical life seemed to be immobile; events and happenings in it either did not take place at all, or were rare exceptions to the norm. Hundreds of people could live their lives through without experiencing a single "event." Powered by the law of custom, the day-to-day life of the average Russian gentleman of the eighteenth century was "plot-less." Theatrical life appeared as a chain of events. A man was not a passive participant in the impersonally flowing course of time, for, liberated from everyday life, he existed as a historical person, himself choosing his type of behavior, making an active impact on the world around him, and either going under or winning through.

Viewing real life as a performance not only offered a person the possibility of choosing his type of individual behavior, but also filled it with the expectation that things were going to happen. Eventfulness, that is, the possibility that unexpected phenomena and turns of events would happen, became the norm. It was precisely the awareness that any political turn of events was possible that shaped the sense of life that young people had in the early nineteenth century. The revolutionary consciousness of the younger generation of the nobility had many sources. Psychologically it was prepared in part by the habit of looking at life "theatrically." It was precisely the model of theatrical behavior that, by turning a person into a character in a play, liberated him from the automatic sway of group behavior and of custom. A little time would pass, and the literariness and theatricality of the real life imitators of Marlinskij's or Schiller's heroes would itself become a group norm that hindered the individual expression of the personality. The man of the 1840s to 1860s would be seeking to find himself by rejecting literariness. This does not do away with the fact that the early nineteenth century, a period that ran its course under the sign of the incursion of art—and first and foremost the theater—into Russian life, will for ever remain a significant epoch in the history of Russian culture.

Translated by G. S. Smith

NOTES

1 Bogatyrev 1940. Quotation from the Russian translation in Bogatyrev 1971, p. 14.
2 I would like to take this opportunity to thank V. M. Glinka for valuable advice.
3 See Batjuškov 1936, pp. 28-29; Tomaševskij 1960, p. 107.
4 Ginzburg 1964, pp. 18-19.
5 Kazoknieks 1968, p. 73.
6 Vigel' 1928, I, pp. 177-79.
7 Grabar' V; Vrangel' n.d., p. 171.
8 Glinka 1895, pp. 61-63, 194.
9 Grabar' op. cit., p. 171.
10 Sb. RIO, V, 1870, p. 66.
11 Cf. Radiščev's lines:
       Behold, Arria boldly plunges
       The sharp steel into her breast;
       Take it, my kind Paetus,
       No, it doesn't hurt. . .
    [Arria, when her husband, ordered to commit suicide by the Emperor Claudius, hesitated to do so, plunged the knife into herself, then handed it to her husband. Radiščev took the story from Tacitus.]
12 Glinka 1895, pp. 61-63. As an example of the active influence of a "Classical" model upon the real behavior of people of the time, the duel between Černov and Novosil'cev may be indicative. The terms of the duel themselves were abnormal, and had a stern, almost Roman tinge of civic awareness and duty, in that Novosil'cev had to fight to the death using pistols with the brothers of his fiancée from the youngest up, and if he succeeded in killing them all, he had to take on the father too, an old man. This was not reminiscent of the duel in upper-class society, whose victim was usually
       . . . a young friend,
       Who with an immodest glance or reply,
       Or some other kind of trifle
       Insulted you over a bottle or two.
    It is very likely that contemporaries would have called to mind the contest between the Horatii and the Curiatii. The parallel was the more palpable in that in Livy's History too, the patriot-brothers, fighting against the enemies of Rome, had to kill the fiancé of their sister. The Černovs' sister committed suicide, just as Lucretia did.
13 Davydov 1962, p. 64.
14 Komarovskij 1914, pp. 159-64.
15 Genlis 1818, I, pp. 18-19. This dictionary doesn't justify its orotund title; factual information is frequently replaced by vulgar moralistic lucubrations. The "certain famous actor" is Talma.
16 Feofan 1760, I, p. 158.
17 Davydov 1822, p. 88.
18 Cf. his assertion that "Matters of argument between states are not now decided by the contest between the Horatii and the Curiatii," ibid. p. 46.

19   Davydov 1962, p. 320.
20   Bestuževy 1951, p. 36.
21   Grossman 1926, p. 6.
22   Aksakov 1955-56, III, pp. 47-48. The actor Sosnickij was famous for his skill
      in transformations. In 1814, while still a young actor, he astonished the
      audience by playing eight different parts in one comedy. One example of the
      crude incursion of theatricality into the sphere of non-theatrical everyday
      life is the appearance, at a non-costume ball in Petersburg in the early 1820s,
      of Kokoškin and the Klejnmichel family, dressed up as Georgian peasants,
      falling at the feet of Arakčeev, and thanking him for their fortunate life.
      There are, however, other examples, which demonstrate a subtle sense of
      stage convention and theatrical semiotics, to be cited: it is only, for instance,
      in conditions where theatrical culture is in a high state of development as a
      special sign system that a spectacle could occur whose piquancy consists in
      a man being transformed into a sign for his own self. S. T. Aksakov recalls
      an intermezzo given by the actors and theater-goers of Moscow on D. V.
      Golicyn's birthday: "The special thing about this intermezzo was that certain
      people acted themselves; A. A. Bašilov played Bašilov, B. K. Danzas played
      Danzas, Pisarev played Pisarev, Ščepkin played Ščepkin, and Verstovskij
      played Verstovskij after first pretending to be Reutov, the retired chorister."
      (Aksakov 1955-56, IV, pp. 125-26.) Between this case and A. M. Puškins's
      "playing himself" there is a difference in principle, in that Puškin was acting
      himself involuntarily, since he was unable to cast his own behavior aside.
      As a result, the semiotic behavior (the role) was reduced to the level of the
      ordinary. At the evening in honor of Golicyn, the actors *acted* themselves,
      that is, they raised their ordinary behavior to the level of a sign of their
      personality.
23   Cf. "When it's raining outside, you've *got to* stay at home, when it's a fine
      spell you've *got to* go and scythe and mow, etc. *Not responsible* for anything,
      thinking up nothing for himself, a man lives only *in obedience*, and this state
      of obedience that occupies every minute and every second, turned into labor
      every minute of the day, is what forms his life." (G. I. Uspenskij 1956,
      p. 120; Uspenskij's italics.) This assertion by Uspenskij, based on the careful
      observation of Russian life over many years, cannot be taken without sub-
      stantial corrections, however. On the one hand, the transforming effect on
      the material of Uspenskij's own views in the early 1880s is here clearly ap-
      parent. On the other, Uspenskij's observations relate to peasant life after
      it had gone through a profound historical transformation. The structure of
      Russian peasant life was established basically in the pre-Petrine period. On
      the one hand, the abundance of ritualized holidays, and on the other, the
      persistent ritualization of everyday life and even of labor, which was a result
      of the necessity of transmitting from one generation to another the most
      sensible habits of work movement, led to a broad transformation of behavior
      in life that was in accordance with the laws of the drama. That severe uniform-
      ity in behavior, whose causes Uspenskij dis.erned in "the sway of the soil"
      and which he was inclined to poeticize (even though he did connect them,
      percipiently, with poverty and the grim struggle for a crust of bread), was by
      no means an ancient feature of folk life; it was a result, first, of a century and
      a half of serfdom, and secondly, of impoverishment after the Emancipation
      [1861]. As a result, the life of the people was made primitive (one of the
      results of this destructive process was the disappearance of folklore, which
      began precisely during the post-Reform era).
      If in peasant life as presented in folklore the alternative to labor was the
      holiday, with its own highly ritualized forms of behavior, then for the kind

of everyday life that Uspenskij observed there were no alternatives. Consequently, the holiday meant not adopting *a different kind of* behavior, but
non-behavior. Hence the replacement, in holiday behavior, of a subjective
orientation towards "decency" by an orientation towards "lack of decency "
that has been noted by all observers of peasant life of those years, one that
was accompanied on the one hand by a rise in the use of alcoholic drinks, and
on the other by a change in the function of "drunken" conduct; in becoming
the only alternative to being fettered by the conditions of life, it acquires
at one and the same time the features of complete freedom and complete
absence of decency.

24   Cf. what was said about actors by the well-known theater buff Pisarev, preserved for us through S. T. Aksakov's memory: "It's with this kind of people
I want to live and die, with actors, people filled with a love of art and who
loved me as a man of talent! Catch me pining away with boredom in the
drawing rooms of your high-society decent people! Catch me dying with
weariness as I listen to the banalities and encounter the ignorant understanding
of the artist by your no doubt worthy people! O no, I remain your humble
servant! My feet will tread nowhere except the theater, the homes of my
friends, and the lowly apartments of actors and actresses, who are better,
kinder, more honest, and simply more frank than your genteel ladies of
goodwill" (Aksakov 1955-56, III, p. 89). Cf. in A. N. Ostrovskij's play
The Forest the remark that the comedians are artists while their audience
are not noble, but comedians. [This reference is presumably to the parting
remark of the strolling player Neščastlivcev to his wealthy hostess Gurmyž-
skaja: "Comedians? No, we are artists, noble artists. You are the comedians!"]

25   There is a passage in Krylov's *Correspondence between Shades* that belongs
to the very earliest comparisons between high society and the masquerade:
"I know not whether they dress themselves up in this manner so as to present
themselves in their real aspect as befits the way their spirits are inclined,
perhaps corresponding with the disgraceful aspect they have taken upon
themselves; or whether they like being unrecognizable and always looking
different from their real selves. If this observation is just, then one could say
. . . that this world is nothing other than a capacious building into which
a great multitude of masked people have been gathered, a large part of them
bearing in their hearts, beneath their surface persona, deceit, malevolence
and perfidy." (Krylov 1945, pp. 60-61.)

26   See Prokofev 1953; Nečkina 1947, pp. 248-82; Lotman 1958.

27   From Puškin's fragment, "Skaži, kakoj sud'boj. . .," Puškin *PSS*, VII, pp. 246,
367.

28   Predtečenskij 1951, p. 189. Baron von Bock had an unhappy history. Declared insane after he had written a daring letter to Alexander I in 1818 he
spent ten years in solitary confinement in the Schlusselberg fortress. Released
by Nicholas I he shot himself soon afterwards on his estate in what is now
Estonia.

29   Šilder 1897, pp. 38, 48. Cf. also *Russkij Archiv* 1871, p. 1131.

30   Šilder op. cit., p. 49.

31   All the threads were concentrated in the Emperor's hands to such an extent
that even the most active participants in the intrigue against Speranskij, Ja.
de Sanglen (mentioned earlier) and Adjutant-General A. D. Balašov, who were
both among the people closest to the Emperor, and who were dispatched to
Speranskij's house in order to arrest him when he got back from the palace
after his audience with the Tsar, confessed to each other with melancholy
incomprehension that they were not sure whether they would end up arresting
Speranskij or whether he would receive the Emperor's warrant to arrest them.

163

In conditions such as these it is obvious that Alexander was not yielding to pressure from anyone, but pretending to do so while in fact firmly sticking to the course he had chosen, and all the time, as always, playing it sly, changing his masks, and preparing the next set of scapegoats.

32 Šilder op. cit., pp. 38-39.
33 Šilder op. cit., p. 368.

THE STAGE AND PAINTING AS CODE MECHANISMS FOR CULTURAL BEHAVIOR IN THE EARLY NINETEENTH CENTURY

Ju. M. Lotman

At the battle of Austerlitz a seventeen-year old cornet of the fourth cavalry squadron, Count Pavel Suchtelen, was wounded by a sabre thrust in the head, and by a splinter from a cannon-ball in the right leg. He was taken prisoner, and, among the throng of Russian officers was noticed by Napoleon, who, riding past, spoke scathingly of the youthfulness of the prisoner. Suchtelen took Napoleon aback by answering him with the famous lines from *Le Cid:*

> *Je suis jeune, il est vrai, mais aux âmes bien nées*
> *La valeur n'attend point le nombre des années.*[1]
> [I am young, it is true, but in well-born souls
> Valor does not wait for the count of years.]

Napoleon ordered a picture of this theme to be painted for the Tuileries Palace.

This episode shows, with classic precision, the triad "stage — life — canvas": the young Suchtelen encodes his behavior with the norms of the theater, while Napoleon unerringly singles out from a real life situation a subject for a painting.

In the preceding article (Part Two, Chapter 3) we dwelt on the interrelation between the stage and the real, everyday behavior of people in the early years of the nineteenth century. Now it remains to introduce a third component — painting.

In the period with which we are concerned, the connection between these kinds of artistic text was significantly more obvious and intimate than might appear to a reader of our times. What painting and theater had in common was manifest above all in the clear tendency of theatrical productions to use purely pictorial methods of artistic modelling: i.e. the tendency on the part of the theatrical text of a performance not to portray an uninterrupted (non-discrete) flow, imitating the passage of time in the outside world, but to present a distinct articulation of the spectacle into separate, synchronically arranged, fixed "cross-sections," each of which, like a picture, was given a scenic frame, and was itself arranged according to the strict rules of composition for figures on a painted canvas.

Only given the functional connection between painting and theater could a phenomenon such as the Jusupovs' theater at Archangel'skoe (near Moscow) come into being. For this theatre Gonzago painted his remarkable sets which have been preserved to this day.* These sets are works of the highest pictorial art, with an exceptionally rich and complex play of artistic spatial areas (all representing fantastic architectural motifs). However the aspect that is most interesting is their functional role in the performance: they were not the background for the actions of live actors, but themselves were the spectacle. The performance consisted in changing the sets before the eyes of the spectators, with the aid of a system of machines, to the accompaniment of specially composed music. This changing of the pictures was the spectacle.

According to this kind of text perception what was common to the theater and to painting was foregrounded while the differential factor between them—movement—became a variable element of a lower level; this explains the popularity of performances such as *tableaux vivants* where the action consisted in a composed arrangement of motionless actors in the frame of the stage. As in painting, movement was portrayed by the dynamic poses of motionless figures. However, though immobility could be perceived as a portrayal of movement as is the case with sculpture as well as painting (i.e. the dynamic pose *signified* movement), and though on the level of scenic expression the feature movement/immobility was not relevant, because of the importance of such categories as the frame which closes off the space, and colour, it was not possible to identify the stage with grouped sculpture. The recommendations were to minimize the three-dimensional quality of the stage action; and the motionless actor was identified not with a statue, which would appear to be more "lifelike" but with a figure in a painting. This shows that we have to do not with some kind of natural resemblance, but with a particular type of artistic code. It is indicative that Goethe in his *Rules for Actors* (1803) which he dictated to Wolf and Gruener and which were subsequently revised and published by Eckermann, prescribed that "the stage must be regarded as a picture without figures, in which the latter are replaced by the actors."[2] The natural corollary of this was the striving to make the scene look flat:

> [The actor] must not step out on to the proscenium. This is a most disadvantageous position for an actor, for the figure stands out from that space within which he, together with the sets and the other

*Pietro Gonzago (1751-1831) was responsible for the decorations of the private theater of the Prince Jusupovs at their mansion at Archangel'skoe.

players, constitutes a unity.[3]

Following the rules of the time for the disposition of figures on a canvas, Goethe forbade the actors to place themselves "too close to the wings."[4] The likening of the stage to a picture gave rise to the special genre of *tableaux vivants*. (Let us recall that for Karamzin, on his own admission, a real landscape became an aesthetic fact when it was perceived through the prism of a literary transformation, whereas for the young Puškin this function was performed by the landscapes depicted in theatrical sets with the actors grouped in front of them — "everywhere before me moving pictures"*). Once this perception of the stage had become systematically developed, a further development became possible: theatrical plots, which required live actors to imitate pictures. Then came the animated representation of pseudo-pictures. On 14 December 1821, for instance, at the benefit performance for Asenkova, Šachovskoj** presented on the Petersburg stage the one-act play, *Live Pictures, or things are bad with us, but good everywhere else.* "Upstage there were shown several *tableaux vivants* in various forms, and downstage several portraits."[5] The theme of Šachovskoj's vaudeville was to mock the pseudo-connoisseurs who were shown condemning the works of a Russian painter and contrasting them with foreign works at an exhibition to which they had been invited by a rich patron. Once all the canvases had been subjected to critical abuse, it turned out that they were not paintings but live pictures, and that the portrait of the patron was the patron himself. In a spectacle like this it was the movement of the actors on the stage which was the anomaly that made the audience gasp.[6]

These extreme manifestations of the identification of the theater with painting are, however, interesting in the first place because they graphically reveal the norm for the perception of the theater in cultural systems of the early nineteenth century. The spectacle was broken up into a sequence of relatively motionless "pictures." Discreteness and stasis were the rule for the stage modelling of uninterrupted dynamic reality. This was no coincidence. Remember that Goethe, in the above quoted work (the writer ascribed great significance to these conversations, calling them the "grammar" or "elements," by analogy with Euclid, of the theater), prescribed that characters playing important roles should be less mobile on stage than those in secondary roles. For instance, he indicated that in the stage positioning,

the most respected characters always stand on the right side . . .

---

* *Vezde peredo mnoj podvižnye kartiny*, lines from the poem "The Countryside" [*Derevnja*] of 1819. Here Puškin describes the natural landscape as if it were the "moving sets" of a theatre.
**Prince A.A. Šachovskoj (1777-1846), dramatist and impresario.

167

The person standing on the right must therefore insist on his privi-
lege and not let himself be pushed into the wings, and *without changing his position* [my italics, Ju.L.] he must make a sign with his
left hand to whoever impinges on him.[7]

The point of this position will be clear only if we bear in mind that Goethe
adopted the stage conventions of that time, according to which only the
actor positioned on the left could move, while the one on the right had
to be motionless. Particularly noteworthy is par. 19 in the chapter "Posings
and Groupings on the Stage": here Goethe affirms that the laws of pictorial disposition and expressive poses are in general applicable only to
"superior" characters:

> Obviously these rules must principally obtain when noble and dig-
> nified characters are represented. But there are characters with op-
> posite functions, for example, the peasant or the fool.[8]

This attempt to link the actor's performance with a fixed set of significant poses and gestures and to reduce the art of the producer to the
composition of figures, was as a result much more apparent in tragedy
than in comedy. From this point of view, life outside the theater was at
the opposite pole from tragedy, and comedy occupied the middle ground
between them.

A natural consequence of the similarity between theater and painting described above was the creation of a relatively stable system of facial
expressions, poses, and gestures which formed a tendency to create a
"grammar of stage art," which is clearly perceptible both in the theoretical works and the practical, instructional works for the stage of that
time.[9] Highly indicative is the role of illustrations of gestures and poses
in the theatrical manuals of the time. The drawing becomes a metatext
in relation to the theatrical performance. The sketches in the work of the
film director Eisenstein have a comparable function: in his early period
when the montage of figures in a frame, and the montage of frames in
relation to each other, was Eisenstein's chief concern, the sketch would
most often resemble a plan; but when later Eisentein's chief device became
the gesture and pose of the actor before the lens, the shots being then
mounted in complex arrangements, then the significance of the sketch
as a metatext for instructing the performer was sharply increased, and
indeed the sketch came to resemble the instructional sketches in theatrical art of the eighteenth century.

The distinction in behavioral style between "high" and "low"
characters on the stage corresponded to a particular conception of everyday human behavior: in the sphere of non-artistic reality human behavior was divided into two levels—the significant or semiotic, and the
non-significant. The first was conceived as a set of poses and gestures,
that is, it included discreteness and stasis; a historical action was indis-

solubly linked to gesture and pose. The second had no significance and was not subject to regulation; no principle of repetition could be discerned. Gesture was not a sign and therefore was not to be noticed. The first type of behavior tended towards ritual. It attracted art into its compass and actively worked upon it. It would be a mistake to think that the art of the age of Classicism was not concerned with the representation of people's everyday behavior (though this is how it seemed when the integrated world-picture of that time broke up and was replaced by another); but it regarded the "high" ritualized behavior, and not the behavior of "peasants and fools," to use Goethe's expression, as real and lifelike; and in its turn "high" behavior drew on superior models which art offered for its norms.

In the pre-Romantic period these dividing lines shifted: at first it was the private life of ordinary people which began to be accepted as historical, and pose and gesture, which had formerly been a property of descriptions and representations of the official spheres of reality, were introduced into it. Thus in the genre pictures of Greuze* there are more poses and gestures than in the genre paintings of previous periods, while Radiščev introduced an antique statue-like quality into the scene [in *A Journey from St. Petersburg to Moscow*] where Anjuta's mother milks the cow (in the chapter called "Edrovo"). [10] Subsequently, as we have already mentioned in the preceding article [Part Two, Chapter Three], semiotic behavior invaded spheres of everyday life, making it, too, theatrical. [11]

Underlying this was the division of everyday behavior into two "styles": one was constructed on the basis of a stable sign-system of poses and gestures, while the other was marked only by an elementary ordering of gestures within the limits of the general para-linguistic laws of the linguo-cultural system in question. In the first style there was a tendency towards discreteness, and immobility within each discrete unit (i.e. the tendency to form "pictures"); the second was distinguished by fluidity and mobility, and could only with difficulty be broken into units. Beyond this division we can easily discover a more profound difference: the self-consciousness of the age identified the idea of significant, "high," or "historic" behavior with behavior of the first style. A "historic action" was also associated with gesture and pose, as a "historic phrase" was with an aphoristic form. The following story is a good example: on 9 September 1830 Puškin informed Pletnev of the death of his uncle, V.L. Puškin.** He wrote:

Poor uncle Vasilij! Do you know what his last words were? I had

*Jean-Baptiste Greuze (1725-1805), French painter of sentimental subjects.
**Vasilij L'vovič Puškin (1770-1830), minor poet and man of letters, the favorite relative of his famous nephew.

gone to him, and found him unconscious; when he regained consciousness he recognized me, wept for a moment, and then having
been silent for a while, said "How boring Katenin's articles are!"
And not another word. How about that? That's what it means to die
an honorable warrior, on your shield, *le cri de guerre à la bouche*
[a war cry on your lips] ! [12]

A somewhat different version was given by Prince P.A. Vjazemskij:

> Four hours before he died, V.L. Puškin, seeing that I had picked up
> the *Literary Gazette* which was lying on the table, said to me, gasp-
> ing for breath and in a dying voice, "How boring Katenin is!" Katenin
> wrote long articles in that paper at the time. *"Allons-nous en"* [Let
> us go], Alexander Puškin said to me then, *"il faut laisser mourir mon
> oncle avec un mot historique!"* [We must let my uncle die with a
> historic quip!] [13]

In order that Vasilij L'vovič's words and conduct should be historic,
they had to be (i) the last words of a dying man and connected with a
unique, statistically isolated and at the same time most important, culmin-
ating point in his life; (ii) perceived as an aphorism; (iii) associated with
a gesture-code or pose, approved as historic. In this case, for instance,
the conduct of Vasilij L'vovič was identified with the pose of a dying
warrior, on his shield, with a battle cry on his lips. It is interesting to
recall that the death of Vasilij L'vovič evoked another legend: quoting
one of the dying poet's close acquaintances, P.V. Annenkov recounts
that Vasilij L'vovič

> got out of bed, struggled over to the bookcases of his huge library
> where the books were in three rows one behind the other, took
> down Béranger* and with this burden walked across to the divan
> in the room. Here he began to turn over the pages of his favorite
> poet, gave a heavy sigh, and died over the French original. [14]

In this case everyday behavior again becomes historic insofar as
through gesture and pose it is allied with a legend, albeit a different
one,—the legend of Anacreon, the lighthearted poet choking on a grape-
pip, but lightheartedly facing his passage to eternity.

There are cases where the opposite process is at work: in the mar-
gin of Batjuškov's elegy "The Dying Tasso,"** for instance, Puškin wrote:
"This is the dying V.[asilij] L.[vovič] and not Torquato." [15] Here we
must mention that for Puškin the very contrast between the two types
of conduct was already losing its point (although the contrast between
on the one hand the heroic Peter of *Poltava*, where he resembles the mo-

---

*Pierre Jean Béranger (1780-1857), French poet of radical and free-thinking
views.

**K.N. Batjuškov's elegy written in 1817 must have already sounded dated
by 1830. Torquato Tasso (1544-1595) was one of Batjuškov's favorite writers.

saics of Lomonosov, and the statue of Peter in *The Bronze Horseman*,* and, on the other, the non-discrete flow of human life, is related to the above mentioned tradition).

What we have said explains not only the pictorial quality of the theater, but also the theatricality of pictures in the eighteenth century. Scenes created by artists look like a representation of theater rather than of life. At a time when the cultural code of the eighteenth century had been forgotten, this gave rise to the conviction that the artists of those times did not represent reality, or were not interested in it. This is unquestionably a mistake. The point here is not only that for a rationalist of the Cartesian school the world of ideas was more real than the current forms of everyday life; it is also, as we saw in the Suchtelen example, that in order for a fact of life to be recognized as a subject for a painting it had first to be modelled in theatrical forms.

The facts we have adduced show convincingly that the "theatricalization" of painting was not a quality exclusive to Classicism: it is equally a property of pre-Romanticism and Romanticism. Thus in 1802 the pre-Romantic Karamzin, suggesting subjects for pictures from Russian history, deliberately set them out as scenes. Speaking of picturesque episodes from the reign of Princess Olga,** Karamzin remarked: "It remains for the artist . . . to choose any of ten possible *scenes* [*predstavlenij*, Karamzin's italics]."[16] The fact that the painting was regarded as a historical episode seen through the prism of a "scene" is further confirmed when the pictorial text is associated not only with a series of poses, but also with certain words which Karamzin placed in the mouths of the characters of the projected pictures: "The Prince, having said: 'Let our bones lie here, for the dead feel no shame,' bares his sword. What a moment for a painter!"[17]

The two-way encoding of theater and painting produced one of the dominant codes of the time, a code which, though it existed alongside others, nevertheless turned out to be the most important one at a certain stage of gentry culture. It influenced poetry, as has already often been remarked, and the general ideological and aesthetic principles on which poetry was based. However, having in some respects broken with Deržavin's traditions,*** the poetry of the Russian *style Empire* turns out to

*In the narrative poem *Poltava* (1828) Puškin describes Peter the Great as follows: " . . . His eyes/ Are shining. His countenance is terrible./ His movements are swift. He is superb,/ Like divine wrath/ He comes . . . " In *The Bronze Horseman* (1833) Peter is represented by his statue, the bronze horseman of the title, which comes to life.

**Olga ruled Kiev from 945 to c. 962 after the death of her husband Prince Igor. She was later canonized.

***G.R. Deržavin (1743-1816), the greatest of Russian eighteenth-century poets. The Deržavin tradition would have been associated with the writing of odes.

171

have been more linked with sculpture than with painting. Etkind has noted that while the initial thought of Puškin's ode "Freedom" [1817]

> is expressed in the form of a complete multi-figure composition; the poet, wreathed and with a lyre, drives away from himself the goddess of love and summons another goddess . . . in Batjuškov his allegorical groups are *sculptured*.[18]

A.M. Kukulevič has made a similar observation in relation to the poetics of Gnedič*:

> Gnedič's idyll was far removed from the topical aesthetic problems facing Russian poetry at the beginning of the [eighteen] twenties: the problem of how to show the inner world of the hero, his spiritual experiences and attitude to life, etc.; on the contrary, [his work] was intimately related to the aesthetic principles of representational art, to the principles of painting and sculpture, in terms of Winckelmann's neo-Classicism. The realistic tendencies of "Homeric style" . . . are organically linked with these principles. Not for nothing did Gnedič, characterizing the style of the Homeric epics, emphasize precisely the plastic side of his poetics: Homer does not describe an object, but as it were places it before our eyes; we see it. [19]

However, this had an even more marked influence on the processes of interconnection between art and the behavior of people at that time. On the one hand there was the influence, which we noted in the preceding article (Part Two, Chapter 3), on everyday life at that time of the theatrical/painting code; on the other, the authors of memoirs, jottings and written testimony on which the historian draws, selected from the words and actions in their own memory only what lent itself to theatricalization, usually intensifying these characteristics even more when translating their memories into the written text. This has a direct bearing on the position of the scholar who is trying to reconstruct non-textual reality from texts.

In such cases the historian finds particularly valuable the curious "bilingual" texts like the conversations of General N.N. Raevskij** as recorded by Batjuškov, who was at that time his adjutant:

> We were in Alsace . . . The campaign of 1812 was the subject of conversation.
> "They made a Roman of me, dear Batjuškov," he said to me. "Of Miloradovič they made a great man, of Vitgenstejn—a savior

---

*N.I. Gnedič (1784-1833), poet and translator of the *Iliad*. His idyll "The Fishermen" [*Rybaki*] was written in 1822.
**General N.N. Raevskij (1771-1829) who was later to befriend Puškin during his southern exile.

of the Fatherland, of Kutuzov * a Fabius.** I am not a Roman, but then these gentlemen were not big shots either...They said of me that I offered my children as sacrifice at the battle of Daškovka."

"I remember," I answered, "In Petersburg they lauded you to the skies."

"For what I did not do; while for what I truly merited praise, they praised Miloradovič and Osterman. Such is glory, such are the fruits of labor!"

"But forgive me, your Excellency, was it not you who took your children by the hand, and with the flag went to the bridge, saying, 'Forward, lads! I and my children will blaze a path of glory for you,' or something like that?"

Raevskij laughed. "I never talk in that florid style, as you yourself know. Certainly I was in front. The soldiers were wavering and I was encouraging them. There were adjutants and orderlies with me. On the left all were killed or wounded; they were firing case-shot at me. But my children were not there at that moment. My younger son was gathering berries in the woods (he was then a mere child) and a bullet went through his trousers; that's all, the whole anecdote was made up in Petersburg. Your friend [Žukovskij] put it into verse, the engravers, journalists and fiction writers used it as they liked, and they make a Roman out of me. *Et voilà comme on écrit l'histoire!* [That's how history is written!]"[20]

However it would be rash to take a bilingual code like this as evidence that in order to reconstruct the original events the "Roman" (more properly, "theatrical") coloring has to be removed on the grounds that it belongs not to the real behavior of private individuals, but to the text describing this behavior. The fact is that the legend which was disavowed by Raevskij himself was in no way foreign to his real behavior and obviously did not arise accidentally; and similarly, Raevskij's declaration that he did not express himself "in florid style " should not be taken too much at face value. For firstly, the code which influences the text afffects behavior also. Secondly, it is quite possible to imagine that in conversing with Batjuškov, Raevskij was transcoding his own real behavior into another system—that of "the soldier general," the simple-hearted hero and daredevil. Indeed the same Batjuškov recounts another episode of which he was an eye-witness, not from the words of Raevskij, but from his own impressions. During the battle of Leipzig Raevskij was with the grenadiers at the centre of the fighting.

---

*Count M.A. Miloradovič (1771-1825), Count P.Ch. Vitgenstejn (1768-1842) were both generals in the 1812 campaign of which Kutuzov (M.M. Goleniščev-Kutuzov, Prince of Smolensk, 1745-1813) was commander in chief. Miloradovič was to be a victim of the Decembrist mutiny.

**Quintus Fabius "Cunctator" (d. 203 B.C.), Roman General who perfected the art of delaying tactics in the war against Hannibal.

On both left and right all was in disarray. Only the grenadiers were still standing. Raevskij was in the line, gloomy and silent. Things were not going too well. I saw the dissatisfaction on his face, but not a trace of anxiety. In danger he was a true hero, he was wonderful. His eyes burned like coals, and the noble bearing of his figure became majestic.

Suddenly he was wounded by a bullet in the middle of the chest. They galloped off to get a physician. "One decided to brave the bullets, another turned back." Turning to Batjuškov, the wounded Raevskij declaimed:

> *Je n'ai plus rien du sang qui m'a donné la vie.*
> *Ce sang c'est épuisé, versé pour la patrie.*
> [I have no more life-giving blood.
> This blood is spent, shed for my country.]

And this was spoken with unusual animation. His torn shirt, the stream of blood, the physician bandaging the wound, the officers who were fussing around their badly wounded general, perhaps the best in the whole army, the ceaseless firing and the smoke of the guns, the importance of the moment: in a word, all the circumstances lent interest to this quotation.[21]

The above quotation once more shows how rash it would be to attribute the theatricality of behavior only to description and to believe absolutely in Raevskij's incapacity to express himself "in florid style."

Cultural behavior requires a description of itself, and such a description enters into the make-up of culture, claiming its own reality, and regulating the most varied cultural mechanisms. From what we have said we may conclude, in the first place, that the system of codes which forms the regulator of the culture tends towards unity, that this is attained by dividing into hierarchies the encoding mechanism of several dominant systems, each having a claim to universality; on the basis of such systems the structure of a culture's self-description is formed, and this, being the most highly organized and simplified model of the culture in question, cannot in theory correspond to the complexity and structurally multi-faceted nature of the real organism of culture. The self-description becomes, however, not only a fact of self-knowledge, but also an active regulator, intruding into the make-up of the culture and heightening the degree of its orderliness by way of the artificial unification of its different mechanisms.

In the second place, this unification can never go far enough, inasmuch as culture is like a living organism of a self-regulating type. The possibility of choice at different levels, the intersection of different types of organizations, and the free "play" among them,—these are some of the minimum number of essential cultural mechanisms. In the example of General Raevskij, for instance, it is important that he could behave in the sphere of real conduct both like a tragic hero, "a Roman," and like "a soldier-general." The legend was created when Raevskij embodied the second form of behavior, while his contemporaries placed him in the first system, as was the case with the episode on the bridge at Daškovka. However, both codes belonged to what lay within the confines of the really possible.

The fact that we are faced with two codes, and not one coded form of behavior and one uncoded, purely practical form of behavior (if that is indeed possible) is testified to in the famous verses of Deržavin's "The Bull-Finch" ["*Snegir*'"], where in the description of Suvorov* the odd lines are written in one code, and the even ones in another, and it is the very clash of these two codes which generates the semantic effect:

He who, ardent in the face of the host,
Will ride some old nag and eat dry crusts
In winter's rage and burning heat, with tempered sword,
Will sleep on straw and watch till dawn.

Here two contrasted types of behavior enter into a structural opposition and turn out at some higher level to be mutually equivalent, a fact which essentially changes the essence of each of them and makes it specific precisely to that system of cultural behavior.

Translated by Judith Armstrong

NOTES

1 Corneille 1963, p. 126.
2 Goethe 1803. Quoted from Mokul'skij 1955, p. 1029. Cf. the memoirs of the actor Genast the Younger who wrote that when at a rehearsal a techician thrust his head out from the wings, Goethe instantly thundered, "Mr. Genast, remove that inappropriate head from the front right-hand exit. It is encroaching upon the frame of my picture." (Mokul'skij 1955, p. 1037). [All translations have been made from the Russian texts].
3 Ibid. p. 1029.
4 Ibid.
5 Arapov 1861, p. 310. Šachovskoj's play, *Živye kartiny, ili naše durno, čužoe chorošo* put to theatrical effect a well known anecdote of the time. Cf. the poem by V.L. Puškin, "To Prince P.A. Vjazemskij" (1815):

Then they turned their gaze to the work of the artist.
"The portrait," they all decided, "is worth nothing:
A real freak, an Aesop, a long nose, a brow with horns!
It is the duty of the owner to consign it to the flames!"
"My duty is not to take any notice of such experts,"
(O marvel! The picture answered) /
"Before you, gentlemen, am I, and not a portrait."
(*Poèty 1790-1810*, 1971, p. 680)

*Count A.V. Suvorov (1730-1800), the greatest general of his period. Deržavin's poem (1800) was written as a tribute to Suvorov on his death.

175

6   For the significance of the opposition "mobile/immobile" see the important work by Roman Jakobson (Jakobson 1975).

7   Goethe 1803, Mokul'skij 1955, p. 1026. The right and left hand disposition is another link between the stage and a picture: "right" designates the right side in relation to the actor when facing the audience, and vice versa.

8   Ibid. p. 1029.

9   See Boguslawski 1965; Riccoboni and Schroder 1821; Engel 1804, Vol. I; Le Breun 1718.

10   "I compared this noble mother with her sleeves rolled up over the dough or over her milking pail near the cow with urban mothers," Radiščev 1958, p. 138; Radiščev PSS, Vol. I, p. 308.

11   One can speak of a certain theatricalization of private life in particular instances even in the eighteenth century, but at that time it was a phenomenon of quite another order, namely the result of the influence of fairground puppet shows. A clear example of this is the organization of the everyday life of Vasilij Vasil'evič Golovin, as described in Kazanskij 1847, pp. 60-63. See below, Part Two, Chapter 7. It is evident, however, that theatricalization of this type has no tendency to divide everyday activity into immobile "pictures," or to fix poses and expressions.

12   Puškin PSS, Vol. XIV, p. 112.

13   Vjazemskij 1854, p. 11. P. Bartenev offers another version: "Contemporaries have told us that having heard these words from the dying Vasilij L'vovič, Puškin went on tiptoe to the door and whispered to the foregathered relatives and friends: 'Gentlemen, let us go, let those be his last words.' " (Russkij Archiv, 1860, p. 1369)

14   Annenkov 1874, p. 18.

15   Puškin PSS, Vol. XII, p. 283.

16   Karamzin 1964, Vol. II, p. 191. ("On the occurrences and the characters in Russian history that could be subjects for the arts").

17   Ibid. p. 192.

18   Etkind 1970, pp. 141-142.

19   Kukulevič 1939, pp. 314-315.

20   Batjuškov 1934, pp. 372-373.

21   Ibid. pp. 373-375.

GOGOL'S CHLESTAKOV:
THE PRAGMATICS OF A LITERARY CHARACTER

Ju.M. Lotman

Gogol considered Chlestakov* to be the central character of his comedy. S.T. Aksakov** wrote in his memoirs: "Gogol always complained to me that he couldn't find an actor able to play this part and for that reason the play lost its meaning, and should be called *The Mayor* rather than *The Government Inspector*." [1] According to Aksakov, Gogol "deeply regretted the fact that *the leading role* (italics mine, Ju. L.), that of Chlestakov, is badly played both in Petersburg and in Moscow, and for that reason the play loses its meaning completely [. . .]. On his return from Petersburg he suggested staging *The Government Inspector* in a private house; he himself wanted to play the part of Chlestakov." [2] This last circumstance is significant, for in that amateur performance the assignation of parts, made by the author himself, had a special meaning. Thus the postal censor Tomaševskij, according to Gogol's plan, was to play "the part of the post-master." [3]

There were, however, some grounds for transferring the main emphasis onto the Mayor's role; such an understanding of the play was dictated by the idea that its basic meaning is the unmasking of the world of the bureaucrats. From this point of view Chlestakov indeed becomes a character of secondary rank—an auxiliary character, on whom the anecdotal plot hangs. The basis for this interpretation had been laid by Belinskij, who saw the idea of this work to be that "a spectre, a phantom, or, better still, the shadow of the fear felt by a guilty conscience, had to mete out punishment to the man of spectres." [4] "Many consider Chlestakov the hero of the comedy, its main character. This is wrong. Chlestakov does not appear in this comedy in his own persona, but purely by accident, in passing [. . .]. The hero of the comedy is the mayor, as the representative of the world of spectres." [5] This article [*"Woe from Wit"*] was written at the end of 1839, but by April 1842 Belinskij wrote to Gogol, "I understand why you consider Chlestakov the hero of your comedy and I understand that he is indeed its hero." [6]

This new approach was not, however, elaborated as significantly as

*Chlestakov is the impecunious impostor who wreaks havoc in the lives of the small-town bureaucrats in Gogol's play, *The Government Inspector* (1836).
**S.T. Aksakov (1791–1859), best known for his memoirs of his childhood.

the view presented in the earlier article "*Woe from Wit*"; the latter inter-pretation indeed became the basis for the traditional perception of *The Government Inspector* by Russian literary criticism and the nineteenth century public.

Chlestakov's character remains a problem, although a number of profound remarks by twentieth century scholars and critics, as well as theatrical interpretations, ranging from those of M. Čechov to I. Il'inskij,* have done much to clarify this essentially enigmatic figure, defined by Gogol as "a phantasmagoric person."[7]

Every literary work can be simultaneously examined from two points of view: as a separate artistic world, possessing its own immanent organi-zation, and as a more general phenomenon, part of a particular culture, of a structural unity of a higher order.

The artistic world created by the author models, in a specific way, the world of extra-textual reality. However, this extra-textual reality is in itself a structurally complex whole. What is beyond the text is by no means beyond semiotics. The man, observed by Gogol, was part of a complex system of norms and rules. Life itself was, to a large degree, realized as a hierarchy of social norms: the Europeanized, post-Petrine state system of the bureaucratic type, the semiotics of rank and official gradations, the rules of behavior, determining one's activity as a nobleman, a merchant, a government bureaucrat or an officer, an inhabitant of St. Petersburg or of the provinces, all these created an exceptionally ramified system, where the deeply-embedded, centuries-old types of psyche and types of activity showed through the more temporary or quite momentary ones.

In that sense reality itself appears as a kind of stage, which imposes a certain type of role on everyone. The more mediocre, more ordinary the person, the closer his individual behavior approaches the social scenario.

Thus the recreation of life on stage is like a theater within a theater, a reduplication of social semiotics in theatrical semiotics. This inevitably caused Gogol's theatre to gravitate towards comicality and puppetry, for playlike representation of reality can arouse serious feelings in the audience, but the playlike representation of playlike representation nearly always transports us into the sphere of laughter.

Therefore it is appropriate to begin the examination of the essence of Chlestakov with the analysis of the real norms of behavior, which made "Chlestakovism" a fact of Russian life both before and outside the Gogolian text.

One of the basic characteristics of Russian culture in the post-Petrine period was a peculiar world-duality: the ideal way of life had in principle

---

*M.A. Čechov (1891–1955), nephew of the writer, and I.V. Il'inskij (b. 1901), both renowned for their playing of Chlestakov.

not to coincide with reality. The relations between the world of texts and the real world could oscillate along a very broad gamut, from notions of an ideal, exalted norm and the violations of it in the sphere of base reality, to conscious governmental demagogy, expressing itself in the creation of laws not destined for implementation (*Nakaz*) and of legislative bodies, which were not to deal with real legislation (the Commission whose task was to draft the new code).* For all the profound differences that existed between the activity of the theoreticians of the period of Classicism and the political practice of "the Empire of façades and stage sets," they shared one trait that made for very deep unity: from the moment when a cultured person of that period picked up a book, went to the theater or found himself at court, he was simultaneously present in two, as it were coexisting, but nowhere intersecting worlds – the ideal and the real. From the point of view of the ideologist of Classicism, solely the world of ideas and theoretical conceptions was endowed with reality; at court, in conversations about politics and during theatralized festivities, which demonstrated that "Astraea's Golden Age"** had already come to Russia, the rules of the game prescribed that one must consider the desired as existing, and reality as nonexistent. However, this was precisely the world of play. The sphere that was mostly allocated to this world of play was the one where, in reality, life manifested itself most powerfully: the sphere of social practice, of everyday life, namely the whole sphere of official 'façade' life. Here any reminder of the real situation was an unforgivable violation of the rules of the game. However, alongside there went on the bureaucratic life of the government employees, the life of service and state-matters. Here realism was recommended, practical people and not dreamers were needed. The Empress herself, passing from the theater to her study, or putting aside the letter she was writing to a philosopher in Europe, or the *Nakaz*, in order to make a decision on current matters of internal or external policy, immediately became a businesslike, practical woman. Theater and life had not become inter-mixed as was to happen later under Paul I. A man of the Potemkin*** generation and status was still able to combine 'dreaminess' with prac-ticality (the more so because Catherine the Great, who in the affairs of state always remained pragmatic and businesslike, valued in her 'amiable friend' that fancy and imagination which her own dry nature lacked, and allowed him to be 'a dreamer' in politics):

*Reference to Catherine the Great's Instruction [*Nakaz*] of 1766 which summoned the Legislative Commission into existence.
**Astraea, star maiden of the Golden Age in Greek mythology, goddess of justice in Roman mythology. The poet Deržavin, for instance, used to address Catherine as Astraea.
***Prince G.A. Potemkin (1739 – 1791), most influential of Catherine's lovers.

My thought turns round in chimeras:
Either I abduct the prisoners from the Persians,
Or I turn my arrows towards the Turks,
Or having dreamt that I am the Sultan,
I frighten the whole world with my glance,
Or suddenly, tempted by a gown,
I rush off to my tailor for a tunic... [8]

But for people of the following generations there arose a situation in which one had to choose between practical activity that was alien to ideals, or ideal activity which unfolded outside practical life. One had either to renounce one's "reveries" or live out one's life in imagination, substituting words, poetry, "activity" in dreams or conversations for real actions. The word began to occupy a hypertrophied place in culture. This stimulated the development of creative imagination in artistically gifted people, and of what A.E. Izmajlov* called "a great talent for lies" in mediocrities, though these distinctions could be blurred. Karamzin wrote:

What is a poet? a skilful liar... [9]

But the propensity to lie is connected psychologically with a certain age: the passage from childhood to adolescence, the period when the development of the imagination coincides with a dissatisfaction with reality. When mendacity becomes a trait not of individual but of historical psychology, it activates infantile characteristics in the adult, group or generation. We shall illustrate this phenomenon with an example, striking in its extremity, that of D.I. Zavališin's life.

D.I. Zavališin was an exceptionally colorful figure. M.K. Azadovskij characterized him as follows: he was "an outstanding public figure, very well educated, with a great zest for social problems, but, together with all these, an extremely vainglorious man with an abnormally developed feeling of self-importance, in whose character existed indubitable traits of the adventurer." [10] A full account of Zavališin's role cannot be undertaken in the present article, particularly as his actual political make-up and his place in the Decembrist movement, according to Azadovskij who is authoritative on the subject, "remain totally obscure." [11] Here we are concerned not so much with Zavališin's political as with his psychological make-up, in which we can glimpse some of the general qualities that are of more interest to us than his individual psychology. Among the Decembrists Zavališin was a loner. Even N.A. Bestužev, who was best disposed towards him, wrote: "You have to become closer acquainted with Dmitr[ij] Irinarch[ovič] to stop liking him." [12] Of course it was

---

*A.E. Izmajlov (1779 – 1831), writer of fables.

not his outstanding talents, memory and erudition that made him stand out among his associates in the political struggle and his fellow-exiles in Siberia; there were more outstanding figures there than Zavališin. And exaggerated ambition and even adventurousness were traits that could be found in other members of the Decembrist movement. Something else made him totally unlike the rest: D.I. Zavališin was a very mendacious person. He continued to lie and deceive all his life: he lied to Alexander I, presenting himself as an ardent supporter of the Holy Alliance and a fighter for monarchic authority; he lied to Ryleev and the Northern Society, presenting himself as the emissary of a powerful international secret society; he lied to the Beljaevs and to Arbuzov, whom he had admitted into a nonexistent society and had fooled with allusions to his part in the preparations for an attempt on the life of the Tsar, to be made during festivities in Peterhof; later, when the festivities passed off peacefully Zavališin told them that he was almost compelled to flee abroad and even alleged that he had made an agreement with a certain skipper but that after a while all this changed because "a man was found who needs no goading." [13] Still later he deceived the officials who conducted his investigation, presenting his activity as an attempt to uncover the existence of a secret society, an attempt ostensibly halted only by the unexpected death of Alexander I. After the collapse of this version he tried to present himself as Ryleev's victim and without hesitation blamed the latter for everything, including some of his own verses. It is his memoirs, however, which in this respect are the summit; they are among the most interesting phenomena of this type of literature.

Zavališin's lies were neither simple nor trivial. First of all, they were not only disinterested, but, as a rule, entailed very grave, and in the final count, even very tragic consequences for Zavališin himself. Besides, these lies invariably displayed the same tendency: both his plans and his ambitious claims were incommensurable even with the most rosy-colored realistic estimates. Thus, at the age of eighteen, holding the rank of midshipman, he wanted to become the head of a universal order of knights, and considered acquaintanceship with Alexander I, to whom he had addressed himself with this aim in mind, merely as the first and self-evident step. At the age of twenty, when recalled during a round-the-world voyage in order to go to Petersburg, he suggested the government should create an empire in the Pacific, with its center in California, which would become a vassal state of Russia (whose head of course was to be Zavališin himself), and at the same time he was preparing to lead Russia's underground political movement. Naturally, the chasm dividing his universal plans and his modest post as a junior naval officer, though his career had begun brilliantly and though he stood out among the rest thanks to his exceptional talents, was nevertheless striking. Still, Zavališin was a man of the Decembrist generation, i.e., a man of action. The round-the-world voyage, the meeting with the Emperor, who was astounded by his eloquence, the close relations with Ryleev—all these were *actions*. But he was born too late by about ten years: he did not take part in the war of 1812; as for his age, rank, real possibilities, political experience and political importance—these could only gain him a second-rate position, were he to pursue a career in the state apparatus or were he to engage in political struggle. But this did not suit him at all. Life was not giving him sufficient scope and he used to correct it systematically in his imagination. A fantasy born in his passionate and uncontrollable mind would at once become a reality, and he was quite sincere when, writing to Nicholas I, he called himself a man 'devoted to the service of Truth.'[14]

Zavališin wrote his memoirs in old age, when his life, begun so brilliantly, was nearing its close, having deceived all his expectations. And then he writes a narrative, rich in information about the Decembrist movement (his memory was amazing), but in it he is describing not the real life of the memoirist, distorted and full of mistakes, but that brilliant life which he *could have had*. He recreates his life as an artist. Everything was different from reality: his birth was accompanied by lucky omens, in the military school (*korpus*) he was called "a small man, but a great miracle," during an exam he was told to his face that "he has nothing to learn from our teachers." [15] He was the "first pupil in the whole school." [16] In Sweden (Zavališin was fourteen at the time), "Bernadotte took a great liking to me, used to have me sit by his side while playing chess with our ambassador." [17]

> That I was extremely successful in everything, to that effect too many witnesses and too many testimonies exist. Here I wish to draw attention to that circumstance which had influence on my participation in the political movement, namely that long before I took part in it I was already what is called a reformer in all the spheres and in my service activity, where I had the occasion to act. [18]

In this manner Zavališin presents his years in the military school. Then begins his round-the-world voyage under the command of Lazarev. During the period of preparation for the cruise, as almost all the other officers were still on leave. . .

> I immediately went to Kronstadt and we began to work, only the two of us, myself and the senior lieutenant. So Lazarev entrusted me with one mission after another. I was entrusted with everything that had to do with the Admiralty, while the senior lieutenant was to occupy himself only with work relating to the frigate, but even here I used to help him. I was charged with the reorganization of artillery according to a new arrangement which later served as a model for the whole fleet; I was also entrusted with the building of rowing boats.

Zavališin maintains that he was entrusted the the posts of "director of chancellery, regimental aide-de-camp, treasurer and permanent inspector of all the parts of the ship's maintenance: provisions, quartermaster, skipper, artillery and navigation units." Such abundance of missions "amazed everyone" and "Lazarev received an official inquiry." In his reply he explained that

> as I, according to general opinion, was one of the navy's brightest hopes, and that already at present they had become used to regard me as a person in charge in the future, for that reason he saw it as his duty, for the good of the service, to acquaint me with all the areas of management.[19]

Naturally, it was Zavališin and not Lazarev who, in fact, headed the expedition on the *Krejser* (*Cruiser*), which has become one of the most famous round-the-world cruises accomplished by a Russian ship. When Zavališin was recalled, everything went to rack and ruin.

Thereafter follows a new series of triumphs: Zavališin organizes special works during the flood in Petersburg [December 1824], senior officers carry out his orders without a murmur seeing their own impotence and his talent for organization; the Emperor thanks him; his suggestions and his projects arouse general admiration. Mordvinov* was amazed,

> as he himself put it, by my outstanding knowledge in this matter and at my far-sighted foresight concerning colonies. . .Meanwhile the head directorate of the R[ussian]–A[merican] company had been waiting impatiently, for some time already, to establish direct relations with me.[20]

The secret society Zavališin came across in St. Petersburg in his memory becomes transformed into a kind of underground parliament, with permanently working committees, noisy and crowded general meetings, where his voice rang out loudest:

> though there were many who praised my talents as a speaker, my eloquence and particularly, as many said, my invincible logic and dialectics, on the whole I was not too fond of these crowded and noisy gatherings, where many people went only in order "to listen to Zavališin." I preferred small meetings, or as they used to be called "committees," where special questions were debated.[21]

One has to keep in mind that Zavališin was neither a member of the Northern nor of any other Decembrist society and even if this network of "meetings" and "committees," about which he writes, did indeed exist, he would never have had free access to their sessions. Ryleev even "advised [. . .] being on one's guard in Zavališin's company" for "he himself, as he confessed, was prejudiced against him."[22]

---

*Admiral N.S. Mordvinov (1754–1845), Minister of the Navy from 1802.

Relations between Ryleev and Zavališin were hostile; Ryleev and A. Bestužev suspected that Zavališin was fooling them with his stories about "The Order of Restoration" (as was exactly the case), while his correspondence with the Emperor inspired misgivings. It is impossible to say how the following, enigmatic episode of Zavališin's biography was connected with these circumstances: having written his usual letter to Alexander I, Zavališin had then left Petersburg to go to Moscow, where the news of the Emperor's death reached him. From Moscow he set off for Kazan' and Simbirsk, where he was arrested on his estate by a state courier sent from Petersburg. In his memoirs the whole affair acquires a totally different character, imbued with adventure and excitement: Ryleev and Zavališin struggle for the leadership of the Northern Society; the majority of rank and file members support Zavališin, and Ryleev decides to remove him from Petersburg. With that aim in mind Zavališin is sent on a mission to inspect the activities of secret society members on the spot. He discovers that the Moscow group has broken up, but in Simbirsk, where in some unexplained manner, members of "his" section happen to be, everything goes well. Their activity is so energetic, his arrival is awaited with such impatience that he is met by "members of the society. . .who waited. . .for him already at the city gates." Although it is well known that in Simbirsk there weren't any members of secret societies whatsoever, still, what we have here is in no way a mere vulgar lie. Apparently someone (probably one of his relatives) did meet Zavališin, in order to warn him that an officer, with a warrant for his arrest, was already waiting in Simbirsk. But Zavališin's imagination transformed reality in the same way Don Quixote's fantasy turned shepherds into knights.

Using Zavališin's memoirs presents a difficulty in that they contain a great number of facts, some unique. However, every time Zavališin recollects some quite real situation, he, like a film director dissatisfied with his pieces of reel, demands a "retake" and creates a different variant of the plot. It is as if he were taking revenge on life. Zavališin's memoirs tell us about the confrontations that took place, but not how these were resolved.

Zavališin is a man of a transitional period. One of the most characteristic traits of the "state" created by Peter the Great was the lack of all regularity in the actual course of state life. Just as the *Statute on the Succession to the Throne* of February 5, 1722 did away with automatic succession and, by unleashing vainglorious ambitions, triggered off a series of palace revolutions, so the abolition of Precedence (*mestničestvo*) in 1682 and the government's subsequent fight against appointments to governmental posts according to "birth"[23], sharply changed the psychology of the service class. The *Table of Ranks** put a new order in place of the old, and, by linking advancement in the state service with merit, provided some scope for initiative and ambition. However, the *Table of Ranks* was never the only law of promotion through the ranks of service. Side by side with its norms, which demanded that everyone ought to go through the drudgery of serving ("gentry children [. . .] should be promoted from the very bottom"[24]), there existed a different regulator – "chance," which promised a quick rise from the lowest rank to the highest, bypassing all norms and rules. In *War and Peace*, Tolstoj put forward, with extraordinary clarity, the idea that it is not a question of a system of violations and anomalies, but of two permanent mechanisms, opposed and united simultaneously, whose interaction created the real conditions of service facing the Russian nobleman of the eighteenth to early nineteenth century.

> At that moment Boris clearly realized that [. . .] besides the subordination and discipline prescribed in the military code, which he and the others knew in the regiment, there was another, more important, subordination, which made this tight-laced, purple-faced general wait respectfully while Captain Prince Andrej for his own pleasure chose to chat with Lieutenant Drubeckoj [. . .] He felt now that merely by having been recommended to Prince Andrej he had already risen above the general who at the front had the power to annihilate him, a Lieutenant of the Guards.[25]

Service came to resemble a card-game: one could play solid and peaceful commercial games—*l'hombre* or Boston, and advance in the service aided by "moderation and thoroughness," but one could choose the road of hazard (the term "chance" [*slučaj*] used in relation to career is simply a translation of the card-term "hazard" [*azart*], French— *hasard*), once again balancing risk and ambition: whether "to play for small stakes," to put full simple stakes or to double the stakes, striving to break the bank. Favoritism, whose beginnings date back to Peter's time ("instances of non-nobles rising to the highest posts in the state were rare and, as a rule, were the result of Peter's patronage," writes Professor K.A. Safronenko[26]; it should be remembered that the peculiar "democratism" of service promotion in Peter's times was inseparable from favoritism), under Catherine II took the form of a special organism inside the state and the economy. Ja.L. Barskov wrote as follows:

> Favoritism presents a curious page of court as well as of economic life; it is one of the most important factors which contributed to the creation of great fortunes in the Russian aristocratic milieu of the

---

*A hierarchy of fourteen grades established by Peter the Great in 1722 which covered all government employees and court officials as well as naval and military officers.

185

eighteenth century. Fortunes made by the favorites themselves, or with their assistance, considerably surpassed the ancient estates of the hereditary gentry. Tens and even hundreds of years were needed in order to create a large-scale estate of several thousand acres or to amass a capital of several hundred thousands roubles, to say nothing of millions, while a favorite, even one as insignificant as Zavadovskij, became a millionaire in two years. It is true to say that the enormous fortunes, which were come by easily, used to be quickly spent and many a favorite died without leaving any descendants; but still the most famous rich of the second half of the eighteenth century or the first half of the nineteenth owed their fortunes to favoritism. [27]

It seemed to contemporaries that the development of favoritism was connected with the personal idiosyncrasies of the Empress; but the reign of Paul I proved the opposite: the desire to carry "regularity" to some fantastic limits was accompanied not by the abolition of favoritism, but by just as extreme a development of it as earlier. Paul's love for order and his aversion to luxury, his personal abstinence when compared to that of Catherine, changed nothing, because the root of this phenomenon was in the principle of unlimited autocratic power itself and not in the characteristics peculiar to its bearers.

Favoritism, coupled with the general European process of shattering the foundations of feudal monarchies, and the rising power of money and personal initiative, resulted in a monstrous growth of adventurism and opened seemingly unlimited possibilities for personal ambition.

However, at the end of the eighteenth century the psychology of ambition had to undergo considerable changes. Alongside the idea of self-affirmation and changing one's personal status in an unchanging world (this was the goal of the hero of the picaresque novel), there emerged the ideal of activity directed at changing the world. First examples from antiquity, then the experience of the French Revolution were perceived as paradigms of historical behavior, which, when emulated, allowed anyone to earn the right to a few lines, a page or a chapter in history. Finally, the fate of Napoleon Bonaparte became as it were a symbol for the unlimited power man wielded over his own destiny. The expression "We all strive to become Napoleons'* was no hyperbole: thousands of junior officers in all the armies of Europe asked themselves whether the hand of fate was not pointing to them. Faith in one's own predestination, the notion that the world was filled with great men, constituted a feature of mass psychology of young noblemen at the beginning of the nineteenth century. Puškin's words:

Aren't there two or three great men
Among my own friends? (*Ezerskij*, Puškin PSS, V, 102)

*Line from Puškin's *Eugene Onegin.*

186

in 1832 sounded ironically; but at the beginning of the 1820's these words would have been taken quite seriously. People spotted a resemblance between Pestel' and Murav'ev-Apostol on the one hand, and Napoleon on the other.[28] What is important is not whether such a resemblance indeed existed, but that it was sought. For hadn't Plutarch taught how to recognize the essence of one's contemporaries by discovering in them a likeness to historical figures, even if this likeness was only external and accidental?

No matter how different the selfish ambition of an eighteenth century adventurer and the self-sacrificing love of glory of a "liberal" from the beginning of the nineteenth would appear, they shared one common trait—the ambitious impulses were inseparable from *activity*, and were realized in *deeds*. Zavališin was one of the youngest figures of this generation (he was born in the summer of 1804). He was one of those, who, though "he visited this world in its fateful moments," yet "rose too late and on the way was overtaken by Rome's night," as Tjutčev* wrote in 1830. He came too late not only to take part in the Napoleonic wars but even too late to join a secret society. His ambitious dreams were realized not in practical actions but in imaginary feats. Hypertrophy of imagination served to compensate for a failed life.

And yet it would be a profound fallacy not to notice that Zavališin and Chlestakov belong to different epochs and that their psychologies, for all the apparent similarity, stand rather in opposition to one another. The difference between Chlestakov's lying, Repetilov's** lying or the self-deceit of Zavališin is very great indeed. Zavališin is filled with very great respect, even tender love, for his own person. His lying consists in attributing to himself circumstances and actions, words and situations, different from those that really occurred; ones in which his "I" could have displayed itself with the brilliance and the genius, which, he was convinced, constituted the essence of his personality. Transforming the world with the power of his fancy, he transforms his environment, because he is dissatisfied with it, but in this imaginary world he remains himself, i.e. Dmitrij Irinarchovič Zavališin. Repetilov does not glorify himself, but on the contrary excuses himself; yet, in the grip of self-condemnation, while hyperbolizing his personality traits, he remains himself. If he says that he "kept a ballet-dancer! not one; but three at the same time," then it is plausible to assume that he had some kind of a little backstage affair. When he characterizes himself as follows:

I rejected everything: laws! conscience! faith!—

then probably some drawing-room free-thinking is implied.

*F.I. Tjutčev (1803–1873), poet. Lines from his poem "Cicero."
**The bombastic, witless, clubroom orator from Griboedov's play *Woe from Wit*.

187

Chlestakov is a different kettle of fish altogether. The basis of his lying is infinite contempt for his own person. The act of lying makes him drunk, precisely because in his imaginary world he is able *to cease being himself*, he can get rid of himself and become *another*, he can change the first person singular for the third, because Chlestakov himself has this profound conviction that only that "he" and not this "I" can be truly interesting. This lends to Chlestakov's boasting an unhealthy shade of self-assertion. He praises himself to the skies because secretly he is full of self-contempt. This split, which in Dostoevskij's *The Double* was to become an object of special scrutiny, and which is completely alien to the man of the Decembrist epoch, is already found in Chlestakov: "I go to the department for two minutes only, just to say: Do that this way, do this that way and there the copying clerk, such a rat he is, starts scribbling tr. . . tr. . . tr. . . with his pen" [*The Government Inspector*, Act III, sc. 6].[29] In this amazing passage Chlestakov, who has soared into the world of lying, invites the company to laugh at the real Chlestakov, for the "copying clerk, such a rat" is *none other than himself*, in his actual Petersburgian-departmental existence.

It is highly significant that Gogol took great pains to find the most lethal, most repulsion-loaded formulations for his hero's own self-characterization. At first (in the so-called "second redaction" [Act III, sc. 6]) Chlestakov in Chlestakov's own eyes looks thus:

Well, I come at this sort of time [. . .] I see that in the hotel some such young man, as is usually called (waves his hand) ugh, ugh, is waiting! with a kind of beak, the devil-may-care sort of beak. As soon as he enters I say to myself, you're a fine kind of gander, you are (IV, p. 292).*

Compare in his "Characters and Costumes: Remarks for the Actors," where Gogol writes about Chlestakov: "He is one of these people, whom in government departments they call empty-headed" (IV, p. 9). Then in the first published redaction [Act II, sc. 5] appears this "copying clerk," who "this very minute scribbles with his pen: tr. . . tr. . . tr. . ., all this so very quickly" (IV, p. 412). But Gogol was looking for sharper words of self-evaluation and in the final redaction he introduced "such a rat!" The liar of the 1820's was striving to escape from the conditions of his life, Chlestakov strives to escape from himself. In that respect it is interesting to note how demonstratively Gogol draws the contrast between on the one hand Chlestakov's poverty of imagination on all the occasions when he (i.e. Chlestakov) attempts to invent a fantastic transformation in the external conditions of his life (it is still the same soup, though "it came by boat from Paris " and it is served at the table in a pan; it is still the same watermelon, though it "cost 700 roubles"), and on the other, the diversity of personae he would have like to be transformed

* References in this form are to Gogol *PSS*.

188

into. These include a famous writer, a man of the world, a back-stage *habitué*, a departmental director, the commander-in-chief and even the Turkish ambassador and Dibič-Zabalkanskij. With all the poverty of imagination of "a departmental rat " manifesting itself in the way he conceives the essence of each of the above roles,[30] the difference here is very substantial: in the fantastic world the environment remains the same as in the real everyday life of the bureaucrat, while the quantitative aspect acquires monstrous proportions (see in this respect the use of numerals: 700 roubles for a watermelon, 100 roubles for a bottle of rum, Chlestakov pays 800 roubles for his "little flat," which is fantastic only as regards its price, but otherwise seems to be quite normal for the average office worker, "three such nice rooms" [Act III, sc. 6, second redaction variant], IV, p. 294) but the roles Chlestakov chooses are based on a different principle. First of all, they have to be exotic in the extreme; existence has to be at *a maximal remove* from Chlestakov's real life, and, secondly, in their kind, these parts have to be of the highest status; thus if a writer is chosen, then he is the friend of Puškin; if a military man, then he must be commander-in-chief. In this Chlestakov resembles not only Popriščin,* who transforms himself into the king (the highest degree) of Spain (exotic), but also the devil from *The Brothers Karamazov*, who dreams of being transformed into a merchant's wife weighing 250 pounds and lighting a candle in the church "with a pure heart." If the hero of *The Double*, like Gogol's characters, sees his ideal other existence in what is incompatibly different on a rising scale of social values, then Ivan Karamazov's devil constructs his on a descending scale.

The desire to get rid of one's self compels this type of character to divide the world into *their own* space which is devoid of social values, and a highly rated *other* space. All they strive for in life is to live in that *other* space. The tightly closed door and the attempts of Gogol's characters to catch a glimpse of what is happening behind it, become a symbol of these strivings. Popriščin jots down:

> I would like to see at close quarters how these gentlemen live; all these quibbles and court jokes, what they are; what they are doing in their own circle. . .I would like to catch a glimpse of the drawing-room whose open door you sometimes see, and beyond the drawing-room yet another room [*Diary of a Madman* (November 11)], (III, p. 199).

Bobčinskij says, "All I want is just one tiny peep through the crack of the door, don't you know, to see how the young man acts" [*The Government Inspector*, Act I, sc. 6] (IV, p. 22). Gogol emphasized this moment by a vaudeville action, as if apprehensive that the audience was not going to

---

*The madman in Gogol's *The Diary of a Madman* (1835).

appreciate it properly: "At this minute the door falls down and Bobčinskij, who was eavesdropping on the other side, is pushed together with it onto the stage" [Act II, sc. 10] (IV, p. 38). This passion for peeping is linked psychologically with the conviction that one's own life is grey and dull, and is akin to the desire to see "beautiful life" on stage, in a book, or on the screen.

These traits come through particularly vividly in the scene of Chlestakov's drunkenness. The use of alcoholic beverages (or other means for the chemical regulation of individual behavior) is too vast a subject, and is related to problems which are at once too general and too ancient, to be tackled here, even superficially. However, one could note that, from the point of view of types of "festive" or "ritual" behavior, two orientations are possible. (These would correspond to types of culture: the one oriented towards the use of extremely weak alcoholic beverages—as an example one can cite the ancient norm of wine diluted with water and the notion that undiluted grape wine as a beverage is unacceptable within the sphere of culture—and the other towards extremely strong beverages; accordingly, in the first instance there is an orientation towards relaxed consumption, towards *the process* of drinking, in the second type orientation is towards *the result*, towards the effect of drink on the consciousness.) [31]

The one orientation will aim at strengthening the individual's qualities, at the liberation of the personality from all that interferes with being oneself; hence it implies an emphasis on memory of oneself, such as one is in a "non-festive" situation. Only those individual qualities, which, due to the counter-action of the world around us could not be developed, suddenly become released. As in the process of fantasizing *à la* Zavališin the reality of the outside world suddenly loses its rigidity, it begins to yield to fantasy's deforming action. Life releases its grip on man and he, intoxicated, realizes his hitherto suppressed possibilities, i.e., he becomes more himself than when he is sober.

The second orientation implies a change within the personality itself; consequently, oblivion, and the necessity to kill the memory of one's former (usual) condition and of the essence of one's personality, become the basic purpose of chemical behavior regulation. The trait that distinguishes Chlestakov is his short memory (this, in particular, is the cause of his inability to make complicated calculations of self-interest and selfishness and endows him with the qualities of "frankness and simplicity," which, as Gogol reminded the actors, were the basic traits of his personality); at the moment of his inebriation this lack of memory is transformed into the incapacity of preserving the unity of his personality; it breaks down into separate moments, none of which preserves the memory of its predecessor. It is as if Chlestakov is born anew every minute.

Any kind of conservatism or traditionalism is alien to him, as he is devoid of memory. Moreover, constant change constitutes his natural state. This is the law governing his behavior, both when he makes a declaration of love and when he instantaneously passes from being a hounded debtor to feeling like a grandee for a day. Transformation in reverse also presents no difficulties for him. The notions of evolution and the logic of inner development are not applicable to Chlestakov, though he is in constant movement. Having taken on a certain modus of behavior Chlestakov momentarily achieves a perfection in it which, for a man capable of inner development, would have taken a life-time's effort to achieve (undoubtedly Chlestakov possesses a talent for imitation). But what has been acquired in an instant is lost as quickly, without leaving a trace. Having fallen asleep as a Most Important Personage, on waking he finds that he is again an insignificant government clerk and "an empty-headed fellow."

Here it would be appropriate to ask, what is actually the object of our scrutiny? We are not considering here Gogol's comedy as an artistic whole, in whose inner world Chlestakov exists only as a textual reality, as one of the elements in the architectonics of the play Gogol created. The subject of our scrutiny should probably be regarded as a study in that difficult subject, text pragmatics. It is not accidental that this area of inquiry very rarely attracts the attention of scholars. First of all, the notion of pragmatic links, as it was formulated by Peirce and Morris, when applied to complex semiotic systems, proves to be not precise enough. The relations between a sign and the people who receive and transmit information are not easy to determine because here even the word "relation" evidently has a different meaning from the one used in semantics and syntactics, a meaning far removed from terminological definition; and the notion "people" immediately prompts the questions: is the study of man in this instance the subject of a semiotic, sociological, psychological or some other description?[32]

The question is further complicated when historical material is the object of study; in this case difficulties are due not only to the vagueness of the concepts but also spring from the lack of recorded data which might allow us to pass a sufficiently complete judgement on the attitudes of various collectives towards texts that circulated in their midst. While the opinions of critics have been well documented, information about readers' attitudes is, as a rule, incomplete and fragmentary. The Middle Ages basically do not provide information about the addressee's attitude towards the texts, but tell us what his attitude ought to have been. Of course, even such scant data can be valuable material for reconstructions. However, the methods to be used for the latter have not, as yet, been fully worked out.

And yet the necessity for studies of what is called the pragmatic aspect is so vital and urgent that the difficulties, mentioned above, have to be considered not as reasons to reject research into this area, but as stimulating factors for it.

Evidently it would be appropriate to exchange the concept of "people" for the notion of a collective, organized according to the structural laws of a particular culture. In relation to a given culture this collective can be regarded as a certain kind of text. Then, the pragmatic links could be treated as the correlation of two texts, each with its distinctive organization and each occupying a hierarchically different place, but functioning within the limits of one cultural whole. Limiting our task even further, we assume it is advisable to isolate from the notion of a cultural collective something of a more particular nature: the structure of behavior of a historically definite and culturally specific group. Behavior is to be regarded both as a certain language and as the sum of historically recorded texts.

Our task, defined in this manner, on the one hand falls within the possible limits of a semiotic study and, on the other, comes close to the traditional aesthetic problem of the interrelationship between art and reality. If we observe the structures of behavior inherent in that or this culture as a complex hierarchical organization which creates, for its own particular social roles, the norms of "correct" behavior, as well as the acceptable aberrations from these norms, we have the possibility of isolating significant and insignificant elements in the real actions of historical figures and groups, and thus to reconstruct invariant types of historical behavior. Moreover we are taking into account the fact that each period in culture aims at organizing the behavior of the members of its collective and it does this by creating type-norms of "correct" behavior. These metatexts are a valuable source for the reconstructions we are proposing. But we must not forget that any description of behavior in any text of the period, whether it is the most precise legal injunction or the most realistic work of art, is not itself the object of our study as such, but rather merely a source for the reconstruction of the object, a source which has been encoded in a particular way so as to make that specific text. In this lies the difference between our approach and the essay-type discussions of literary heroes as types in Russian life, which were popular at the turn of the last century. A work of art can be studied from many points of view. In particular, the scholarly approach which regards a work of art as the result of a creative act on the part of the author differs completely from the one which considers it as material for the reconstruction of types of cultural behavior in a particular period. Naive mixing of the two is the more inadmissible in that it happens all the time.

Let us imagine a spectator, completely ignorant of European culture of the nineteenth to early twentieth century, who is standing in front of one of Rodin's statues. He will be much mistaken if, on the basis of this text, he attempts to imagine the clothes, gestures and behavior of the people who were the sculptor's contemporaries. He would have to interpret what he sees as an integral artistic act, a translation of the notions of a certain period into the language of a certain artistic structure. But let us imagine that this has been done as thoroughly as possible. Then, probably it would be possible to decode the period on the basis of the statue, including even its everyday aspect, but no longer in the initial, naive, sense.

The aim of this work is not the study of Chlestakov's image as a part of the artistic whole which is Gogol's comedy; but it is to use this profound creation of Gogol's synthesizing thought, in order to reconstruct those types of behavior which make up the larger cultural historical context, and in so doing to open a door, even if slightly, onto the problems of the pragmatics of Gogol's text.

In Chlestakov, the hero of *The Government Inspector*, it is easy to isolate features inherent to a more general type which was present in Gogol's mind as an essence of a higher order, and which manifests itself in various of Gogol's characters as hypostases. This creative archetype is a fact of Gogol's creative consciousness. However, it is possible to discover therein features with sufficiently clear resemblance to the behavior of certain historical figures; and these features are quite stable on the whole and exhibit a tendency to recurrence in different variations. This allows us to see both in Gogol's creative consciousness and in historical documents the manifestations of a more general historical form, of a certain cultural mask, a type of behavior which emerged historically within the framework of this particular culture. From among the numerous examples we shall select the most significant.

In 1812, a seventeen year old cornet, Roman Medoks, squandered 2,000 roubles of Government money and ran away from his regiment. He decided to avoid punishment with the help of a project in which adventurousness and "unusual lightness of thought," dreams about heroic enterprises and the most common kind of swindling were intertwined. Having faked documents in the name of Sokovnin, aide-de-camp to the Emperor and a lieutenant in the Horse Guards, who was serving as aide-de-camp to the Minister of Police, Balašov, he also provided himself with a faked instruction from the Minister for War, which accorded him the most far-reaching yet vague powers, to act in the Caucasus in the Emperor's name. Armed with this instruction he intended, like some new Minin,* to organize a volunteer corps, drawn from the mountain peoples of the Caucasus, and, at its head, to attack Napoleon, in this manner earning his pardon.[33]

---

*Kuz'ma Minin, a merchant who with Prince Dmitrij Požarskij organized an army to drive the Poles out of Moscow in 1612.

On his arrival in Georgievsk, Medoks received 10,000 roubles, presenting the counterfeit order of the Minister. Here he was received by the Governor, Baron Vrangel', and the commander of the Caucasus line, General Portnjagin, both experienced administrators, with complete trust. It is significant that when one of the officials of the Treasury Department expressed his doubt that such an important mission could have been entrusted to so junior (both in age and in rank) an officer, and the Treasury Department voiced its hesitation at being made to pay such a large sum, Vrangel' decisively stopped them and insisted that the required sum should be paid. Medoks was received as a person entrusted with the highest authority; he himself took parades and balls were given in his honor. In an attempt to delay his exposure, he informed the local postal department of his authority to check the Governor's correspondence, which allegedly had been given to him, and he told General Portnjagin that he had been commanded to conduct secret surveillance of Baron Vrangel', who, he alleged, was not trusted in Petersburg.

Having lost completely his grasp on reality, Medoks sent a report to Balašov about his actions, using the name of the non-existent aide-de-camp Sokovnin; however, the report was accompanied by a give-away letter, in which he emphasized the patriotic motives for his swindle and asked Balašov for protection and intercession, so as to enable him to bring to conclusion the matter of the "volunteer corps." At the same time he addressed himself to the Minister of Finance, Count Gur'ev, recommending himself as a person under Balašov's protection, and petitioned him for more money.

The insolence and the scope of this affair plunged the authorities in the capital into confusion, thus delaying the arrest of Medoks, whose tactics consisted in entangling as large a circle as possible of people in the highest positions.

When he was arrested, he called himself Vsevoložskij, and then Prince Golicyn, probably listing, one after another, all the aristocratic names that he knew.

On the Emperor's orders, Medoks was jailed for life in the fortress of St. Peter and St. Paul. In 1826 his fate suddenly changed. While still a prisoner in Schlüsselburg, he met there some of the men convicted in connection with the events of December 14. It is likely that it was at this point that he turned to the appropriate authorities, offering his services as an informer. At least in March of 1827 he was suddenly released and deported to Vjatka, through which the convicted Decembrists used to pass on their way to Siberia. Travelling by way of Vjatka, I.I. Puščin wrote to his family:

Here I learnt that one Medoks, who had been jailed in the Schlüsselburg fortress at the age of 18, and spent fourteen years there, was now

194

in Vjatka and at liberty. I made his acquaintance in prison.[34]

Medoks fled from Vjatka, after acquiring a passport in another name, and set off for the Caucasus, but was again stopped in Ekaterinodar. The Tsar gave an order to send him as a private soldier to Siberia; he ran away again, and from Odessa, where he lived on false documents, he wrote a letter in English to Nicholas, asking to be pardoned. All these peregrinations ended as follows: Medoks, a private in the Omsk regiment, suddenly turned up in Irkutsk, without the knowledge of his immediate superiors in the army, but enjoying the open patronage of the gendarmerie. In Irkutsk he showed a suspicious interest in the exiled Decembrists and their families, who had joined them in Siberia. He wormed his way into the household of A.N. Murav'ev, who had been exiled to Siberia but not stripped of his gentry status, and who had received, as a sign of the highest Imperial favor, permission to serve in the capacity of Mayor of Irkutsk.

S.Ja. Štrajch thinks that when he first appeared in Murav'ev's house, Medoks was already acting as *agent-provocateur*. There are, however, no grounds for such an assumption; as far as can be judged from the files for that period (and these constitute a well-preserved body of documents), they contain neither reports nor documentary evidence of Medoks' links with the secret police. Generally, Štrajch tends to rationalize Medoks' behavior, presenting him as a man purposefully following his path. But Medoks' character, as it emerges from the documents, seems to have been different.

While still in Schlüsselburg, Medoks, then a prisoner, who had spent years in jail and who had no hopes for a release, made the acquaintance of Jušnevskij, Puščin, M. and N. Bestužev, Pestov and Divov.* When he was later transferred to the fortress of St. Peter and St. Paul he found means to make the acquaintance of Fonvizin and Naryškin,* and while in Vjatka he became quite close with Jušnevskij, Štejngel', Švejkovskij and Barjatinskij.* The mystery surrounding his arrival in Vjatka and later in Irkutsk suggests the possibility of some sort of contacts with the gendarmerie. However, one has to keep in mind that, on the one hand, we are not in possession of any documents able to confirm such contacts, and on the other, that the Decembrists themselves, who were very careful in this respect, saw nothing strange in his appearance in their midst. Probably there is some quite normal explanation for his stay in Irkutsk.

Medoks' desire to penetrate the Decembrist milieu in Siberia was probably dictated by numerous considerations: he derived pleasure from

*A.P. Jušnevskij, I.I. Puščin, M.A. and N.A. Bestužev, P.G. Divov, M.A. Fonvizin, M.M. Naryškin, V.I. Štejngel', A.P. Barjatinskij, and the others were all arrested in connection with the Decembrist affair.

his meetings and conversations with highly educated people who sympathized with him. Medoks himself, as was noted already during his first arrest, had a good command of French, German and English,

> he was well versed in literature and history, art and drawing, he had a social adroitness and other advantages natural in a person of good breeding, and in particular he possessed a sound knowledge of his native tongue and a considerable skill in expressing himself in Russian, correctly and with ease.[35]

Besides, Medoks was absolutely without any means of support and enjoyed the financial help of A.N. Murav'ev and the Decembrist "ladies" (the most active was probably Jušnevskaja). The sums he used to receive were on the whole very small but for a man in his situation they were considerable. But most important of all was something else: here, it seemed to Medoks, he found himself in the world of that aristocracy, "the Sokovnins, the Vsevoložskijs, the Golicyns," which had always been the summit of his dreams. When he had learnt what sums the Volkonskij, Trubeckoj and Šeremet'ev families used to send to their relatives, it took his breath away. It seemed to him (especially when his attempt, through P.L. Šilling, to obtain Benckendorff's* favor had failed and he began to work out a plan of escape[36]), that through the mediation of the exiled Decembrists he could establish aristocratic connections that would be useful to him. He had a trait that make him and Nicholas I two of a kind, namely an exaggerated notion of the might, solidarity and wealth of those powers whose representatives he deemed the Decembrists to be.

In A.N. Murav'ev's house Medoks met the sister of the wife of the founder of the Union of Salvation, the Countess Varvara Michajlovna Šachovskaja, who for many years loved A.N. Muchanov and was loved in return. At first parental opposition and later the arrest and the exile of her lover interfered with their marriage. V.M. Šachovskaja came to her sister in Irkutsk, so as to be near her beloved and hoping that Nicholas I would permit them to marry (another obstacle was the fact that they were close relatives: Muchanov's sister was married to Šachovskaja's brother). Permission was not granted and Šachovskaja soon returned to Moscow, where after some time she died.

When he had seen Šachovskaja, Medoks became enamoured of her. There are no grounds to think, as does Štrajch, that there was no sentiment at all on his part and that the *agent provocateur* of the police simply played the part of a man in love. Medoks' diary bears witness to the contrary: he was truly in love, although his feeling is expressed in words that might have been borrowed from Popriščin's diary, with his famous

---

*General A.K. Benckendorff (1783 – 1844), head of the Third Department (the secret police) under Nicholas I.

exclamation: "the daughter. . .ah knavery," or from Benediktov's poetry:

> Thinking that she would be without her cap, I was admiring in advance the sight of her wonderful black hair, arranged in the Raphaelian manner; I was all aflame at the thought of seeing my adored one in her finery [. . .] She was in her cap, her bosom which but a minute ago I saw in my ideal dream all uncovered could not be seen under the tippet she was wearing. [37]

It is true that at the same time he attempts to start an affair with Jušnevskaja, explaining it in his diary by his passion for "soft females." However, Medoks' hopes were not fulfilled. Benckendorff refused Šilling's petition; in the Murav'ev household he was received merely as an acquaintance, he enjoyed a certain amount of trust on the part of the Decembrist wives, who used him to pass on correspondence, bypassing official channels, the exiles talked with him willingly, probably telling him certain events from their past life and their activity, but it goes that far and no further.

And then Medoks, who had become convinced that between Petrovskij Zavod and European Russia a fairly lively correspondence was being conducted through unofficial channels, with women serving as intermediaries, thought up a grandiose provocation. He turned to Benckendorff, and using the latter as an intermediary to address himself to the Tsar, informed Nicholas of a new colossal plot, organized by the Decembrists. The center of this plot was, according to Medoks' information, in Moscow, its participants were closely linked with the exiles and together they were preparing a new move. Supplying real information about the secret correspondence with Russia, he added invented documents, ciphers and codes, which, allegedly, served to further the dealings between the state criminals and their accomplices in both capitals. These false documents, like any counterfeit documents, are extremely interesting. We might add that in general when explaining the essence of a document as a cultural fact, counterfeits are as interesting as parodies are in explaining the essence of a work of art.

On the one hand, the counterfeits produced by Medoks reflect current and trivial notions about the essence of Decembrism just as Chlestakov's stories of Puškin mirror uneducated opinions about the nature of poetic creativity. The mysterious conspiratorial nature of the invented "Union" is sharply exaggerated; Medoks besides made use of some information about Masonic ritual: doctrines about the seven degrees, references to Knights Templar and false ciphers. On the other hand, however, one has to admit that Medoks skilfully put to use the conversations which had been conducted in his presence, though what had been said about the past he transferred into the future. Thus, he was obviously repeating somebody's words (and this is interesting for the content reconstruction of the conversations held among the exiled Decembrists), when he wrote about Michail Orlov: "No one can attract people better than he does. Once he was a unique (i.e., 'irreplaceable'—Ju. L.) man."[38] But by adding that Orlov "hasn't quite lost heart and that he could probably be useful," he tried to create the impression that the latter had been drawn into a new conspiracy.

It cannot be an accident that in the cipher compiled by Medoks Orlov was designated by the graphic sign for lightning. It is equally interesting that Jakuškin's cipher sign was the dagger. Passing on what were alleged to be Jušnevskij's words on the assignment of parts in the future action, Medoks characterized Jakuškin as follows: "Jakuškin and Jakubovič are daggers that have long since been sharpened." This opinion was in keeping with Jakuškin's behavior during "the Moscow conspiracy" of 1818 ("it seemed that he silently bared the dagger, ready to murder the Tsar"), but it bore no relation to Jakuškin's mood in 1832. Jušnevskij could describe in this manner only the Jakuškin of yore; Medoks changed the time and transformed a story about the past into a denunciation about the present.

And yet Medoks' denunciation does contain echoes of certain opinions. His testimony that some kind of writings by the exiles were making their way into the foreign press deserves attention, as this information preserved traces of the living intonation of real conversations.

> Jušnevskij laughed heartily when, from the issues of this journal [*Revue Britannique* —Ju. L.] he used to receive, they cut out his own article, afraid lest he become enlightened reading it.

Most probably Medoks behaved like a mediocre writer of historical romances, who, having invented a romantic context, makes the historical figures say things that were recorded in one of the sources. He invented the situation, but the words he had no doubt heard somewhere in the Decembrists' circle.

Also of interest is the project to publish a journal *Mithridate* (the name was probably suggested by the legend that Mithridates trained himself to take poison and therefore had no fear of poisonings), a French-language publication which was to refute the official lies of the Russian government. Some sort of conversation about the desirability of such a journal Medoks undoubtedly had heard, but he transformed a non-committal conversation into a well thought out political project.

The circle of persons slandered by Medoks is significant in yet another respect. The *agent provocateur* was convinced that the Siberian exiles enjoyed support among the highest echelons of the aristocracy, precisely those circles into which he had always dreamed of penetrating, moved by an acute feeling of social envy.[39] He listed, one after another, all the titled families which came into his head (just like Chlestakov, when he lists his Petersburg connections): Count Šeremet'ev, Prince Kasatkin-Rostovskij, Countess Voroncova and Countess Orlova. In addition, he dragged in those people he had heard about from the "state-criminals" as having been active in secret societies, but who escaped punishment: M. Orlov, adjutant-general S.P. Šipov, L. Vitgenštejn (to the latter Medoks "entrusted" the publication of *Mithridate*). It is significant that of the prisoners at Petrovskij Zavod Medoks "implicated" in the plot not the most resolute and politically active, but those who were rich and aristocratic: Trubeckoj, N. Murav'ev, Fonvizin, Jušnevskij, Švejkovskij, adding Jakuškin and Jakubovič as "regicides," and Muchanov, probably out of jealousy.

In accordance with a well-known psychological law, he dragged into his denunciation the object of his love, Countess Šachovskaja, as well as A.N. Murav'ev, who had given him financial support and welcomed him in his house.

The authorities in Petersburg reacted nervously to the denunciation. The point was that Medoks' notions of the essence of Decembrism, in principle, were shared by Nicholas I, who was equally convinced that behind the activists of December 14 stood conspirators from the aristocracy, and who was compelled to listen to Michail Orlov's lecture on contemporary politics, where he explained to the Tsar "the truly democratic essence" of the movement.[40] We shall deal later with the nature of this seemingly strange trustfulness, which ensured the Chlestakovs a grateful audience. A cavalry captain Vochin was sent to Siberia: his task was to collect on the spot with Medoks' help, proof of the plot's existence. Medoks was asked for proof and he prepared a false document, "a coupon," written in the invented ciphers, on presentation of which the secrets of the conspirators in Moscow allegedly would have to be revealed to him. This action achieved his aim: a recall from Siberia to European Russia. What would happen next he was probably not inclined to guess, perhaps indeed counting on his having revealed a plot, in whose existence he himself was beginning to believe, and perhaps he just wasn't thinking about a thing and pinning his hopes on the off chance.

In Moscow he immediately rushed to spend money, which he now had in abundance: he went to stay in the best hotel, ordered clothes for 600 roubles from a French tailor, demanded and received more money from Benckendorff and from Moscow's governor-general, married a rich bride, receiving a substantial dowry. Medoks' behavior aroused the suspicions of the commander of Moscow's district gendarmerie, General Lesovskij, who confided his doubts to Benckendorff; however, in Petersburg they persistently believed in the idea of a plot, though the falseness of Medoks' slander became more and more apparent. When finally, after six months of delays, Lesovskij demanded positive results from Medoks, the latter fled, telling his wife that he was going to visit his sister, but not forgetting to take with him the remainder of the dowry.

Having set out on a tour of Russia, on one occasion he pretended to be an official sent on an important assignment, on another, when he came to visit the relatives of the exiled Decembrists (for example the brothers of V.F. Raevskij in Staryj Oskol) he posed as a person who suffered for sharing the same ideas. On the way he wrote letters to Lesovskij, assuring the general of his devotion, but withholding information on his whereabouts. When his money ran out, he secretly returned to Moscow hoping to receive more from his wife. However, his wife's relations handed him over to the police and he was brought to Petersburg, under arrest. He tried to extricate himself by means of a new series of denunciations, now informing the government that the plot had built its nest in the gendarmes' corps: the official in charge of the Third Department, A.N. Mordvinov, being A.N. Murav'ev's cousin, prevented the matter from coming into the open, while Lesovskij's opposition was the chief cause of Medoks' failure. He even tried to convince the authorities that in order to discover the plot he had to live like a lord, to have his own coachman — without all this, the conspirators would not trust him and would not reveal their secrets to him. He also asked for a personal interview with the Tsar. However, all this was of no use. Medoks again found himself in the Schlüsselburg fortress, where he remained until 1856. He died in 1859.[41]

Somewhat different aspects of this historical-psychological type manifest themselves in the life story of Ippolit Zavališin. On June 22, 1826, when Nicholas was walking on Elagin island a cadet from the artillery school, Ippolit Zavališin, approached him and handed in a denunciation in which he accused his own brother Dmitrij, who had signed his final deposition on May 24 and was awaiting the decision about his fate in the fortress. Ippolit Zavališin accused his brother of high treason and the receipt of enormous sums of money from foreign powers in order to conduct subversive activity in Russia. A new case was opened. Ippolit Zavališin lived above his means and had accumulated large debts. Besides, the hope of instantaneous, and what seemed to him "sure", fortune, began to loom before him. Here is what D.I. Zavališin tells about the substance of the whole affair:

> Of course, he could see no secret papers whatsoever in my house, he could see only papers concerning the management of the quarter-mastership affairs during the round-the-world expedition; I had a lot of official papers, which weren't secret at all and for that reason they were lying quite openly on the table. [. . .] Among those papers, as was established later, he used to rummage. There were a lot of papers in foreign languages here: bills from consulates for various articles supplied to the expedition and bills of exchange. Ignorant of any foreign language, with the exception of French, Ippolit could not find out about the content of these papers. Seeing the government's subsequent irritation, directed against us, and even flagrant injustice

in relation to us, he thoughtlessly imagined that, as the government was thus disposed towards us, any testimony against us would be accepted without an inquiry, and for that reason (knowing that being a bad student he could not count on lawful promotion) he made up his mind to earn his promotion by falsely denouncing his brother.[42]

The falseness of the denunciation came to light, though Ippolit hastily reinforced it with a second denunciation, where he slandered a great number of completely innocent people. Kept under arrest during the investigation of his denunciation, Ippolit Zavališin informed General Kozen that he "expected to become aide-de-camp to the Emperor."[43] One had to be endowed with a truly Chlestakovian imagination to be able to conceive the possibility of such a jump from a cadet in an artillery school. However, fate had in store for him something different: the Emperor ordered that he be reduced to the rank of private and sent to the Orenburg garrison.

After his arrival in Orenburg Zavališin soon discovered the existence of a circle of freedom-loving youth [44] and suggested they should organize a society, for which he himself had composed the statutes, and then denounced them all to the authorities.

This second attempt to advance his career by means of a denunciation also proved a failure: Ippolit Zavališin received a harsher sentence than his victims — penal servitude for life. He served his sentence together with the Decembrists.

Ippolit Zavališin's fate bears less resemblance to a picaresque novel than the adventures of Roman Medoks do, but it fills out this historical-psychological invariant with some essential traits.

According to the testimonies in our possession, Ippolit Zavališin was an immature youngster (at the time of the submission of his first denunciation he was seventeen), who early learnt to make debts and who used to boast that "even before entering the school, he was well acquainted with all the taverns and pubs in Petersburg."[45] However, in the character testimonial compiled by General Kozen on the basis of Zavališin's own words, we read that "he has read more than one would have expected from a youth of his age; thanks to a good memory he can recite many poems by heart."[46] But something else is even more amazing: to the very same General Kozen Zavališin finds it imperative to state that he is a passionate admirer of Ryleev. This statement was made sometime at the end of June 1826, i.e., when Ryleev's fate had already been sealed and he may, indeed, have already been executed. It is true that we cannot say to what degree Zavališin's words could be treated as a "statement." Perhaps they were just the excited chatter of a narcissistic boy. But, in any case, it is significant that he chatted in *this* way.

A certain Kolesnikov, in his memoirs, provides several psychologically interesting details. He describes the proceedings which led to the sending of the victims of Zavališin's provocation in Orenburg, and the provocateur himself, to Siberia. In particular, the proceedings included writing down any distinguishing marks. A clerk in the military court, one Bulanov, who came from the same regiment as those sentenced, and who was their friend as well, "was so tactful and lenient that he did not wish either to undress or to measure us, but wrote down the distinguishing marks and the height of each of us from our own words," writes Kolesnikov. However, Zavališin suddenly demanded that Bulanov should write down that among the distinguishing marks "on his chest there is one birthmark in the shape of a crown, and on his shoulder, one shaped as a sceptre. This provoked general laughter."[47] With all the resentment that Zavališin's personality naturally evokes, the personality of a man whose moral defects reached the proportions of complete moral deformity,[48] the historian has no right to dismiss his words with a laugh. Here we suddenly encounter a belief which is well-known from the history of popular royal pretenders, one which reflects the firmly rooted popular faith that a true Tsar has to have "the Tsar's birthmarks" on his body. Behind this faith lies a profound mythological notion that the existing power is not the "real" power (but a "false Tsar," the "anti-Christ," a "werewolf"), and that the true Tsar is in hiding and perhaps, until his time is ripe, has no inkling of his Tsar-like nature. Thus in 1732 a beggar appeared in a village, who announced:

> "I am not a peasant, nor am I a peasant's son: I am an eagle, an eagle's son and I am destined to be the eagle [compare the tale of the eagle and the crow in *The Captain's Daughter*—Ju. L.]. I am the Tsarevich Aleksej Petrovič [...] I have a cross on my back and on my thigh a sword." The peasants took him to the wise man, who was famous for his ability to recognize people [it is an interesting notion that there is such a special ability "to know people," i.e., according to certain marks, to recognize their true nature—Ju. L.]. The wise man acknowledged that he was the true Tsarevich.[49]

Pugačev's followers demanded that he show them "the Tsar's marks" on his body: "You call yourself sovereign, and sovereigns have Tsar's marks on their bodies."[50] And Pugačev showed them the "eagles" on his body (probably marks of furuncles).*

If the popular formula of belief in one's special election sounds totally unexpected in the mouth of a nobleman from the capital and an officer (even if degraded to the ranks) in the 1820's (incidentally, this confirms yet again the schematic nature of our ideas about the chasm allegedly separating the consciousness of an educated nobleman from the world of folklore), one has to bear in mind that the idea of a great destiny was probably cultivated in the Zavališin family. Thus, not the semi-educated youngster Ippolit, but Dmitrij Zavališin, a man of encyclopaedic erudition, towards the end of his life begins his memoirs, and very seriously at that, by informing his reader that:

* See below, "Tsar and Pretender," pp. 262-3.

My christening was accompanied, as the saying goes, by especial solemnity. I was christened in the banner-hall, under the banners [here we have a word-play characteristic of texts with veiled predictions: *znamja* (banner), *znamenie* (sign). Ju. L.], in the presence of a bishop, the important personages from the town and delegations from various nations: Persians, Hindoos, Kirghiz, Kalmyks [it is difficult to imagine that Zavališin, who for many years carefully studied the Scriptures, and while serving his sentence translated anew, "for his own usage," the whole of the Bible from the original, in his narrative of the christening was not thinking of the adoration of the Magi. Ju. L.] ... In my family they used to tell me about the portents supposed to predict a brilliant future. One of the predictions was made by a certain phrenologist.

At this point in his memoirs Zavališin makes a note: "As early as 1803 my sister wrote to me saying that it is clear that Providence is guiding me towards some special goal, along an inscrutable road."[51] And though the aged Zavališin, giving this particular form to his story, as it were dissociates himself from those predictions, it is not to be doubted that all his past life was marked by the expectation of their fulfillment. It is very probable that Ippolit Zavališin too considered the moment when he described his special marks to be his "starry hour," when he would at last be recognized and his fate would change dramatically.

It is very interesting that these naive notions, derived from folklore, combined in Zavališin's mind with the Romantic worship of Napoleon, the cult of the chosen individual who is above moral taboos, obviously in a primitive version consistent with the intellectual level of a seventeen year old cadet, in whose mind folklore and Western culture were strangely intermingled.

Kolesnikov goes on to depict a tragi-comic scene: Ippolit Zavališin, already sentenced to penal servitude for life, his head shaven, bound in chains, on a "cable" (a kind of iron rod or a thick rope to which the prisoners were chained in twos; the Orenburg group was treated with much less ceremony than were the Decembrists, who travelled to Siberia in separate sledges), "with a certain comic haughtiness" announced to his fellow travellers, whose undoing he had brought about:

"You do not understand me; you are unable to comprehend my destiny." Taptikov and Družinin answered him laughing: "Perhaps you think you are going to become Napoleon?" "Why not?" he answered with malice, "know that if I succeed, then from Nerčinsk to the Tsar's palace I will pave my way with corpses, and my brother will be the first step to the throne."[52]

An amazing peculiarity of Zavališin is his ability to change in an instant: one minute he is the gloomy demon and Napoleon, next he is a free-thinker, throwing out of his cell the priest who came to offer him consolation: "Bare-headed priest how can you possibly understand this sacred and exalted idea [the idea that his road in life was like carrying the cross, Ju. L.]. Get out of here."[53] And half an hour later he begins to dance in his chains, between the bunks, repeating over and over to his fellow-sufferers: "You want to sleep and I want to dance the gallop,"[54] or he whistles, like a man with no cares in the world, as he walks along the road leading to his place of imprisonment. Or, on the one hand, in a letter to the Emperor, he describes his denunciation of his brother in this way: "Seeing my exalted sentiments of loyalty and love for the fatherland rejected, and my unprecedented sacrifice counted for nothing, I, burning with indignation and moved by various sentiments that agitated me strongly..."; but on the other hand he says the following, and to whom? to the general entrusted with guarding him: "If the Emperor, while reading my papers, was able to read what's in my heart, he would have sent me to the devil."[55]

I would wish to stress one more trait, which the group of characters that concerns us here seems to share: they are all Romantics in their subjective self-consciousness. We have already had occasion to mention that the Romantic model of behavior is endowed with special activeness. Easily reduced to simplified stereotypes, it is actively accepted by the reader as a program for his own behavior. If in Realism art imitates life, then in a Romantic situation life actively begins to resemble art.[56] It is not by chance that the Werthers* and Demons** triggered off an epidemic of imitation, something that cannot be said either about Nataša Rostova [in War and Peace] or about Konstantin Levin [Anna Karenina], or about Raskol'nikov [in Crime and Punishment] and Ivan Karamazov [The Brothers Karamazov]. However, a person who has chosen the Romantic norms as the program for his behavior and plays the role of a demon or a vampire has no power to change at will the stage where the drama of his life is being shown. Deeds, transposed from the ideal space of the Romantic text into far from ideal Russian reality, give birth to strange hybrids. G.A. Gukovskij noticed the Romantic in Gogol's government clerks: the hero of The Diary of a Madman, he wrote,

> is also, if I may say so, a Romantic, and the Romantic pose of Pop-riščin reads like a parody of Romanticism, a more vicious example of which it would be difficult to invent.[57]

Of course it is not only a parody. What appears as a parody in the text created by the poet's will, in the real text of human behavior appears as a deformation of the character's orientation, produced by the conditions that were thrust upon him by circumstances. With this is also connected the sharp divergence between self-evaluation and the evaluation

*Hero of Goethe's The Sorrows of Young Werther (1774).
**The outcast demon is the theme of Lermontov's narrative poem, The Demon (1839).

made by the outside observer in heroes of this type. A text, which from the subjective point of view reads as "the Demon," to the eyes of the outside observer can turn out to be Chlestakov or Ippolit Zavališin.

For this brand of Romanticism in Grušnickij's* variant, it is quite typical that behavior is not the outcome of the personality's organic needs and does not constitute one indivisible whole with it, but is "selected," like a role or a suit of clothes, and, as it were "put" on the personality. This makes possible the quick changes in behavior, as well as the absence in each new state of a memory of the one preceding it. Thus our skin, with any change, preserves the memory of that which has been, but a new suit has no memory of the old one. Not only some personalities, at certain periods but even whole cultures at certain stages, can exchange organic evolution for "a change of clothes." The price for this is the loss of historical and cultural memory.

The detailed treatment we have given our examples makes it unnecessary to add any more; it seems that already at this point one could say that the literary Chlestakov is linked with a definite historical-psychological type. What are the historical conditions in which such a type could emerge?

First of all, his emergence calls for the ready availability of a highly developed and organic culture, whence a man of the Chlestakovian type would be able to assimilate ready made texts and models of behavior. Earlier we connected Chlestakovism with Romanticism. It is essential to stress that Chlestakovism is not the generator of Romanticism (in a cultural sense it is not a generator at all), but its consumer. Chlestakovism, existing as a parasite on a highly developed culture, which it simplifies, needs a special environment—a situation of confrontation between an already formed highly developed culture, and a young culture in a superdynamic state.

Secondly, it is essential that against the background of this dynamism, fluidity and the absence of dominant conservative elements in the culture, the organic development of society is slowed down or, at a certain point in time, stopped completely. For example, having received a dynamic push in the times of Peter the Great, Russian social development became frozen during the reign of Nicholas I. The absence of a deeply rooted traditionalism in the state culture of that period created in certain bureaucratic spheres "an unusual lightness of thought," the notion that "all is permitted" and the belief that opportunities were unlimited. And the illusory nature of state-bureaucratic activity easily allowed lies to substitute for real activity. When transplanted into the psychology of separate individuals, its result was Chlestakovism.

Thirdly,.Chlestakovism is connected with a high degree of semioticity

---

*Minor, imitative, character in Lermontov's novel, *A Hero of Our Time.*

in society. Only where various types of social alienation, of "illusoriness," play a dominant role is that alienation of activity from results possible; an alienation without which the Chlestakov-type of fooling of oneself and of those around one, as a form of existence, is impossible.

Fourthly, Chlestakovism implies the existence of a despotic authority. Chlestakov and the Mayor, Medoks and Nicholas I (or Benckendorff) are neither antagonists, nor deceivers and deceived, but inseparable couples. On the one hand, only in conditions of an autocratic arbitrary rule, which breaks down even the norms of its own state "regularity," does there emerge that atmosphere of instability, and at the same time the illusion of unlimited possibilities, which nourishes the infinite ambitions of the Chlestakovs and the Ippolit Zavališins. On the other hand, autocracy, wasting enormous efforts in order to deprive itself of the real sources of information about what actually is happening in the society which it governs, is nevertheless in need of such information.[58] Strangling the press, falsifying statistics, transforming all kinds of official accountability into ritualized lies, the autocracy of Nicholas left itself one single source of information—the secret police. However, this put the autocracy in a situation not devoid of a special farce-like tragedy. It would be erroneous to think that Nicholas I's government, including the Third Department of His Imperial Majesty's chancellery, was staffed by blockheads, uneducated or completely incompetent people. In the Third Department there were businesslike and fairly reasonable officials; there were also people not lacking in education. Irrespective of how we evaluate their intellectual abilities, it is clear that they were far more broadminded than those insignificant individuals, the various Medokses, who served as their informants. However, the exploitation of ambitious minors, obscure visionaries and simply idle gossip-mongers and informers inevitably results in the actual level of administration descending to the level of the views held by such people.

One of the enigmas of *The Government-Inspector* is: why does the stupid and simpleminded Chlestakov succeed in making a fool of the Mayor, who is shrewd and, in his way, a man with experience in such matters; why does the simpleminded, frivolous and outwardly insignificant[59] Medoks make a fool of all those with whom fate brings him in contact, from generals and governors in the Caucasus to Benckendorff and Nicholas I? If one uses one single source of information, there is no possibility of rising above it.

In his fable *Razors*, published in 1829 (Gogol saw in it a connection with those people from the Decembrist circle who had been removed from office), Krylov wrote:

... The razors are very blunt!
How is it possible not to be aware of it? We are not as
Stupid as all that;

206

But I am afraid to cut myself with a sharp one. . .
They are afraid of clever people
And more willingly suffer fools at their side.[60]

The blockhead and the adventurer became the two figures of Nicholas's state. However, attracting the adventurer into the state service, the bureaucracy itself became servant of its own servants. It was dragged into the same circle of hare-brained schemes. Just as Chlestakovism represents a concentration of the traits of the period in one individual, so, in its turn, Chlestakovism, moving in the contrary direction and rising from below to the heights of the state-machine, shaped the image of the times.

Gogol had grounds when he insisted that Chlestakov, the incarnation of the idea of falsehood not as a moralizing abstraction but in concrete, historical and socio-cultural form ("this phantasmagoric character who, like deceit personified, flew away with the troika, God knows where" ["Instruction to those intending to act *The Government Inspector* properly"], IV, p. 118), was the main character of *The Government Inspector*. Is it necessary to remind the reader what associations the image of the troika had in Gogol's mind?* However the question how this real and historical type became transformed in Gogol's consciousness is beyond the scope of this article: it demands an analysis of Gogol's comedy as an independent text.

Earlier we discussed the activeness of the Romantic text. This does not mean of course that the literature of realism is passive in relation to the behavior of its readers. However, the nature of its activeness is different. Romantic texts are perceived by the reader as direct programs for behavior. Realist images, in this respect, are less tendentious. However, they *give a name* to types of behavior which exist spontaneously and unconsciously in the depths of a given culture, thus transplanting them into the sphere of the socially conscious. Chlestakov "is a type containing much of what is scattered in various Russian characters" ["Extract from a letter after the first performance of *The Government Inspector*"] (IV, p. 101). Having been constructed, named and having received definition in Gogol's work, Chlestakovism becomes transplanted in the world beyond the confines of Gogol's comedy onto a completely different level: it enters the category of behavior types of which a cultural awareness exists.

In certain respects it can be said that realism tends towards a greater degree of conventionality[61] than Romanticism. Presenting typified images, the realist work turns to material which, while still outside the artistic text, has undergone cultural treatment; the man behind the text

---

*In the play Chlestakov leaves town at the end of Act IV to the sound of the troika bells off-stage. In Gogol's novel *Dead Souls* there is a famous passage where Russia is compared to a galloping troika.

has already chosen his cultural role, has included his individual behavior in the category of some kind of social role. Introduced into the world of an artistic text, he acquires a double coding. Encoding oneself to be "the Demon " "Cain,"* "Onegin," "imagining herself to be the heroine of her beloved authors"** (*Eugene Onegin*, Ch. 3), the character also happens to be a government official, a petty officer or a provincial miss. The realist text in principle is oriented towards a situation of "an image within an image." It is not accidental that precisely in realist literature the quotation, the reminiscence, "new patterns on an old canvas" (the fact that Russian realist prose begins with [Puškin's] *The Tales of Belkin* is symbolic) occupy such a place, and in realist painting there are the themes of the mirror and the picture within a picture, and in realist theater—the situation of 'a stage on stage.' In Romantic art (if we discount the border area of Romantic irony) these situations are much less active. Of course, systems of citations are characteristic only of that stage of realist art at which it is engaged in working out its own language ; yet the orientation towards a double semiotic coding constitutes its basic trait. One side result of this situation is the fact that realist texts are a valuable source for judging the pragmatics of various types of social signs.

Thus if a Romantic text reorganizes the real behavior of the individual, the realist text reorganizes society's attitudes towards individual behavior, hierarchically organizing various types of behavior in relation to the scale of values current in a given culture; its activeness is manifest in the organization of the complete system of behavior for that culture. Of course, such a system of interactions is extremely complex. And while we were saying that the study of the pragmatics of artistic texts is one of the most complex problems that contemporary literary research is faced with, we must also add that the pragmatics of the realist text (as opposed to the pragmatics of folkloristic and medieval texts, where special rules exist for this purpose, and of Romanticism, in which a relatively strict pragmatic usage is present), is in terms of research task, the most complex of all.

Translated by Ruth Sobel

NOTES

1   Aksakov 1955 – 1956, III, p. 160 ("The history of my friendship with Gogol").
2   Ibid., p. 165.
3   Ibid.
4   Belinskij, PSS, III, p. 454.

Cain: A Mystery, by Byron (1821).
**Tat'jana in *Eugene Onegin*.

5   Ibid., p. 465.
6   Ibid., XII, p. 108.
7   Gogol', PSS, IV, p. 118.
8   Deržavin 1957, pp. 98 –99.
9   Karamzin 1966, p. 195.
10   Bestuževye 1951, p. 787.
11   Ibid.
12   Bestužev 1933, p. 271.
13   *Vosstanie*, III, p. 264.
14   Ibid., p. 224.
15   Zavališin 1908, p. 21.
16   Ibid., p. 22.
17   Ibid., p. 31.
18   Ibid., p. 41.
19   Ibid., p. 54.
20   Ibid., p. 87.
21   Ibid., p. 97.
22   *Vosstanie*, III, p. 237.
23   Romanovič-Slavatinskij 1870, p. 11.
24   *Zakony*, VI, No. 3890.
25   Tolstoj 1942, pp. 265 – 266.
26   *Pamjatniki* 1961, p. 193. It is significant that Puškin in *My Genealogy* begins
the history of favoritism in Russia with Menšikov ('My grandfather didn't peddle
pancakes. . .').
27   Barskov 1918, pp. 240 – 241. See also Jakubovskij 1968. Here for example
we are informed about Platon Zubov: 'After his death he left in silver coins alone
about 20 million roubles, though he admitted that "he himself knows not for what
purpose he puts away and saves money",' p. 300.
28   Pestel': "In his deviousness, his body movements, his height, even in his face he
was very like Napoleon" (*Ščukinskij sbornik*, 4. M., 1905, p. 39). S. Murav'ev-Apostol:
"He had an extraordinary resemblance to Napoleon I" (*Dekabristy* 1938, p. 485).
29   Gogol' PSS, IV, p. 48. Hereafter all the references to this edition are given in the
text (Roman numeral – volume, Arabic numeral – page).   An unusually interesting
testimony to the connection between a socially humble situation and the psychological reaction of hate towards oneself and the desire for regeneration (not rebirth
– the Tolstojan thirst for rebirth is connected with a completely different ideological-
psychological complex), for ceasing to be oneself, right up to the mythological
thirst to "change one's name," we find in Vjazemskij's letter to Žukovskij, dated
December 13, 1832.   Vjazemskij was not "a little man" and self-deprecation was
deeply alien to him.   In 1826 he had written:

> They claim that people are egoists.
> Where is egoism? Who is a complete 'I'?
> Who is not in debt to this word?
> In a new edition it looks
> Like the dictionary's anachronism.
>
> (*Koljaska*)

The more acutely he must have felt like a faceless cog when, under pressure from the
state, he was compelled to join government service. Vjazemskij wrote to Žukovskij:
'Here's a plot for you for a fantastic novel *dans les moeurs administratives*: an official
who goes mad at the sound of his name, who is persecuted by his name, whose name
flashes in his eyes, sounds in his ears, seethes in his spit; he spits with disgust,

209

rejecting his name, secretly and in silence takes on another name, for example that of his superior, signs with this new name an important paper, which then is sent on and results in important consequences; for this inadvertent falsehood he is put on trial etc. Here's a plot for you, to fill your leisure hours. But I, being superstitious, will not take it up, for fear that it might happen to me.' (*Russkij archiv*, 1900, Bk. I, p. 367). One is struck by the coincidence of many features between this "fantastic Russian tale" and Gogol's *The Diary of a Madman*. As Vjazemskij's letter coincides chronologically with the time when Gogol' began to work on this tale, we may assume that the latter, through the mediation of Žukovskij, had become acquainted with the subject. *The Diary of a Madman* is in many respects the tragic parallel to *The Government Inspector*. That escape from oneself and flight towards the heights of life, which Chlestakov provides for himself thanks to his "unusual lightness of thought" and to a fat-bellied bottle of Madeira, Popriščin achieves by paying the price of madness. However, the basic parallel is obvious. Popriščin, depressed by his humbleness, does not strive to change the world. Moreover, the world, in his consciousness, is unshakeable to such a degree that it is precisely the news of social changes, the amending of the law of succession and the vacant Spanish throne, which cause his madness. He wants to become an "anti-self" and, taking this to the very limit, promotes himself king. (Chlestakov acting in Russian conditions, due to the censorship, stops at the rank of Field-Marshal and the governorship of the State Council; compare the plot of *The Golden Fish**). The scene of name-changing and paper-signing ("in the most important place, where the departmental director signs" [*The Diary of a Madman*, "Ferdinand VIII"], III, 209), coinciding with Vjazemskij's idea, marks the moment of Popriščin's transformation. The conviction that true life is on the far side of the door ("I would like to see at close quarters how these gentlemen live, all these quibbles and court jokes, how they are, what they are doing in their own circle," "I would like to catch a glimpse of the drawing room, whose open door you sometimes see," III, 199) at first gives birth to the passion of a peeping Tom – the psychological reservoir for denunciations, and then brings forth the desire to become the oppressor oneself and to see the humiliation of others ("in order to see how they would run to and fro," III, 205.) The desire to become an "anti-self" in order to humiliate one's present self is characteristic of other heroes of Gogol. Compare the Mayor's words: "Well, why would one like to be a general? Because if it happens that you have to go somewhere, military couriers and aide-de-camps ride before you everywhere: horses! [they cry] and there at the post-stations everyone is waiting: all these titular councillors, captains, mayors, and you don't give a damn: you dine somewhere with a governor, and there: stand mayor! ha, ha, ha (bursts into laughter, dies of laughter) that's what's appealing, you rascals." [*The Government Inspector*, Act V, Sc. 1.] (IV, 82.) The instantaneous awakening of the man in Popriščin, which Gukovskij has described, makes him a tragically torn hero.

30 Compare Chlestakov's ideas about the essence of the creative process: "How strangely Puškin writes. Just imagine: in front of him there's a glass of rum, the best, costing about 100 roubles a bottle: such rum as is kept only for the Austrian Emperor [it is assumed that the rum for the Austrian Emperor is also kept in a cellar, only its price is particularly high. Ju. L.] and then, when he starts writing his pen only goes: tr. . . tr. . . tr. . . Recently he has written a play, *The Cholera Medicine*, one's hair simply stands on end. One of our clerks [in the variants 'one

---

*In Puškin's version of the fairy tale the old woman rises to the rank of queen but reverts to her previous miserable status when she asks the magic fish to make her mistress of the ocean.

departmental director'] went mad when he read it" [*The Government Inspector*, Act III, sc. 6 (second redaction)] (IV, 294).

31 Compare Barthes 1972, pp. 58 – 61 ("Wine and milk").

32 The "pragmatic poetics" of E. Čaplevič bears witness to the kind of muddle that can arise under the banner of "pragmatic research." See Čaplevič 1974.

33 See Štrajch 1925, 1929, 1930.

34 Puščin 1956, p. 100

35 Štrajch 1925, p. 31.

36 An entry in Medoks' diary for April 28, 1831: "If Šilling's aid brings no success, then I will have to go away, not waiting for favors and without asking permission." (Ibid., p. 42)

37 Ibid., pp. 36 – 37. R. Medoks' diary, published by Štrajch (see Štrajch 1930) does not confirm the publisher's idea that Medoks' feelings towards Šachovskaja were a pretence and that denunciation was his sole objective. In order to make his version look more convincing Štrajch claims, completely arbitrarily, that the diary was written for show in the Murav'ev household and that, allegedly, parts of this diary were left lying about in their drawing room. All these conjectures are wholly arbitrary. Equally unfounded is the claim that the well-known scholar Šilling was an *agent provocateur* of the Third Department. (On Šilling see Alekseev 1972.) Roman Medoks was not an agent of the Ochrana in the times of Zubatov, as Strajch presents him. He was a "Gogolian man," who found himself in the cultural world of the people of the Puškin period. He was blinded by the civilized refinement of this world, by its spirituality and moral loftiness. The poverty-ridden Siberian life of the Murav'evs amazed him by the degree of material unconcern. He felt both attraction and an acute envy towards this world. The "natural" result was falling in love with Šachovskaja and the denunciation of A.N. Murav'ev. Both these impulses were equally sincere and in equal measure were the logical consequences of Medoks' psychological complex.

38 Ibid., p. 63.

39 In general, envy plays a prominent part among Medoks' motives. It can be gleaned from his denunciation of Jušnevskij, from his words that instead of a well-deserved death he "enjoys both life and his wife, who is still a lady; the dungeon he lives in is a dungeon in name only, in reality he is in an academy." (Štrajch 1930, pp. 62 – 63.) The last words are characteristic, in that they convey the atmosphere of conversations conducted during the Petrovskij Zavod period. The Decembrists, as yet, had not grasped with what malice and envy Medoks watched for their weaknesses, he who never had a penny from anyone and who spent 14 years in a cell, not receiving any help whatsoever even in Irkutsk, a man devoured by boundless ambitions, yet still wearing a private's uniform and penniless.

40 *Krasnyj archiv* 1926, p. 160.

41 In connection with the psychology of social defectiveness, Medoks invites comparison with the central character in Bulat Okudžava's novel *Merci, or the Adventures of Šipov* (see Okuažava 1971).

42 Zavališin 1908, p. 252.

43 Cited from the introductory article by P.E. Ščegolev in Kolesnikov 1914, p. XII.

44 See Kolesnikov 1914, published with some cuts by the censor; complete text RO IRLI, f. 604 /Bestuževye/ed. chr. 18[5587]; Rabinovič 1958; Lotman 1959.

45 Kolesnikov 1914 p. XI.

46 Ibid.

47 Ibid., p. 22.

48 For the historian of culture it is, however, interesting that I. Zavališin's action was unanimously evaluated as something ugly. Neither Nicholas I nor the president of the court presiding at the trial of the Orenburg society, General Essen, nor the

inhabitants of the town, soldiers and peasants, could hide their disgust towards him. Even in a milieu of petty provincial officials, where morals were far from high, he aroused aversion. Kolesnikov has preserved the following scene: when the convicts, who had come in chains from Orenburg to Ufa, were brought into the building of the provincial government, a semi-ruined building, where, around jars of pomade which served as ink-pots, sat the copyists and the clerks with tattered elbows, "all the copyists at once stopping their squeaking pens turned to us with noticeable curiosity. One put his pen behind his ear, another stuck it between his teeth, yet another held it in his hand, but all rose immediately from their places and surrounded us. Their first question, uttered by several voices, was 'which of you is Zavališin?' [. . .] Stepping forward and smiling caustically with a kind of theatrical importance, he answered 'What do you want? I am at your service.' The clerks surveyed him from head to foot and immediately stepped back; one of them said 'Nothing at all, we just wanted to find out what kind of an animal you are.'" (Ibid., p. 64) We must remember that the very existence of Kolesnikov's notes is due to the initiative of the Decembrist V. Štejngel', who did everything so that this unparalleled witness would reach the conscience of posterity. It is not an accident that Kolesnikov's notes are one of the very early monuments of Decembrist memoir-writing; they were written in 1835.

49 Čistov 1967, p. 126.
50 Ibid., p. 149.
51 Zavališin 1908, p. 10.
52 Kolesnikov 1914, p. 76.
53 Ibid., p. 75.
54 Ibid., p. 76.
55 Ibid., p. XI.
56 Lotman 1973.
57 Gukovskij 1959, p. 310.
58 Compare M. Lunin's words, "The people think despite their profound silence. The proof that they do are the millions which are spent in order to overhear the opinions which they are barred from expressing." Both the desire not to let the people express their thoughts and the intention "to overhear" these thoughts are equally typical of an autocracy.
59 "His face was white and clear, his thinning hair, both on his head and his eyebrows was very light brown, his eyes were grey, he had a smallish sharp nose; when he spoke, he stammered." (Štrajch 1930, p. 32.)
60 I.A. Krylov 1944-46, III, p. 181.
61 For the way we understand the problem of conventionality in art see *Filosofskaja ènciklopedija [Philosophical encyclopaedia]*, Vol. 5, M., 1970, article "Convention in Art," together with B.A. Uspenskij, pp. 287–288.

GOGOL'S "TALE OF CAPTAIN KOPEJKIN": RECONSTRUCTION OF THE PLAN AND IDEO-COMPOSITIONAL FUNCTION

Ju.M. Lotman

"The Tale of Captain Kopejkin"* is still a somewhat enigmatic interlude in *Dead Souls*. The usual explanation treats of it as an inserted novella, "which has a relatively superficial relationship to the theme," but which

> Gogol needed for ideological reasons. He shows that even in the "highest" society there is no justice. The minister, through whom Captain Kopejkin, who has lost an arm and a leg in the Napoleonic Wars and who no longer has the means to support himself, asked for "the royal favor," offered only promises,[1]

and later had recourse to repression. Those authors who touch upon this problem see in Kopejkin a "little man," the victim of autocratic-bureaucratic licence: "In 'The Tale of Captain Kopejkin' Gogol severely criticized and exposed the higher bureaucracy."[2] How this exposure is connected to the basic theme of the *poèma*** is still obscure. Clearly it is not fortuitous that in a whole series of critical works concerned with the conception of *Dead Souls*, "The Tale" is not considered at all.[3]

That the satire of "The Tale" is directed against the Petersburg bureaucracy is beyond question. It was precisely "The Tale" that caused the difficulties with the censorship which complicated the publication of *Dead Souls*. The depiction of Kopejkin as a "little man," however, is open to doubt. It is a source of some bewilderment why Gogol, if this was his purpose, should have portrayed not an invalid soldier (compare, for example, the figure of the discharged soldier in Pogodin's tale *The Beggar* [1826], or in Nikolaj Polevoj's *Tales of a Russian Soldier* [1829],[4] but a captain and an officer. An army captain was a rank of the ninth class which gave the right to hereditary nobility and consequently to the ownership of serfs.[5] The choice of such a hero for the role of positive

---

*"The Tale of Captain Kopejkin" is told by the postmaster in Chapter 10 of Part One of *Dead Souls* (Gogol, *Dead Souls*, translated by David Magarshak, Penguin Classics, 1967, pp. 209–215; quotations from *Dead Souls* are from this edition). The postmaster suggests that Čičikov, the hero of the novel, might in fact be Captain Kopejkin. The first part of *Dead Souls* was published in 1842.

**Gogol described *Dead Souls* not as a novel, but as a *poèma*, i.e. a long narrative poem.

213

character is strange for the Natural School* and especially for a writer with such an acute "sense of rank" as Gogol. N.L. Stepanov's idea that the figure of Captain Kopejkin is "the expression of the deep dissatisfaction of the *broad mass of the people*"[6] (my italics, Ju. L.) also seems exaggerated.

The conception of the "Tale" as an inserted novella, mechanically introduced into the text of the novel without any thematic connection to its main development, goes against the author's own statements: the banning of the "Tale" by the censorship reduced Gogol to despair. Moreover, the author insisted more than once that "The Tale of Captain Kopejkin" was an organic part of the work. Neither made sense without the other. In a letter to Nikolaj Jakovlevič Prokopovič of April 9, 1842, Gogol wrote: "They have removed the whole episode with Kopejkin, which I need very badly, more even than they think."[7] The next day he wrote to Pletnev:

> The destruction of the Kopejkin episode has disturbed me greatly! It is one of the best parts of the *poèma*, and without it there is a rent which I am incapable of patching or sewing up. [8]

The same day he wrote to the censor Nikitenko: "It is one of the best passages. And I find it quite impossible to patch up the gap which has opened in my *poèma*."[9] So, on the one hand, commentators suggest that "it has a relatively superficial relationship to the theme," but, on the other, the author insists that it is one of the best passages, removal of which creates a gap that cannot be sewn up.

It is indicative that, in order to retain the "Tale," Gogol was prepared to weaken the element of denunciation, which he would hardly have done if, in the absence of any thematic link to the main action, he needed it solely for this denunciatory tone. In the letter to Pletnev, quoted above, Gogol wrote:

> I resolved that I should rather re-write it than lose it completely. I threw out all the generals and made the character of Kopejkin clearer, so that it is now obvious that it was all his own fault, and that people behaved correctly towards him.

What, then, is the connection of the inserted novella to the artistic world of Gogol's *poèma* as a whole?

The theme of *Dead Souls* was given to Gogol by Puškin. We do not, however, know the details of the idea which Puškin handed over. Moreover, it is difficult to imagine that the poet just said two or three sentences

---

*The name given to those writers including Gogol, the young Turgenev and Dostoevskij and others who under the aegis of Belinskij in the mid to late 1840's turned to prose and the "physiological" description of life among the lower classes.

to Gogol, characterizing the knavery of a crafty entrepreneur. It was probably a question of a verbal improvisation, during which Puškin developed in Gogol's presence the thematic possibilities inherent in a confrontation of this kind. It is difficult to imagine that a writer, suggesting the theme of a major work to another writer, would not have thrown in a few words on how he himself would have developed the intrigue, arranged the clash of characters, constructed certain episodes. It is just as difficult to credit psychologically that Gogol would have been aroused by two or three coldly spoken sentences: what probably took place was an absorbing conversation. We can attempt to reconstruct certain outlines of it. It is difficult to imagine that Puškin spoke on themes that had never previously concerned him and which he had never touched upon, in one form or another, in his own work: there is a logic to the development of artistic ideas, and, as a rule, a new thought is a transformation of some initial invariant. In this sense, the various themes of an author can very often be depicted as a single theme, manifest through a certain sum of variants. The difficulty lies in formulating the rules of this transformation, rules which permit the establishment of identity between themes which are superficially quite different. Consequently, in Puškin's plans, thematic features may be distinguished which are also present in the tale about the dead souls. Besides, from what we know of Puškin's creative manner we can be sure that he was extremely restrained in conversations about plots which he had "in his frame." As a rule he discussed only plans which he had definitively abandoned or "was giving away." We are interested, then, in those plots which Puškin had thought about, but which, at the time when he gave Gogol the idea of *Dead Souls* had already been abandoned. Let us examine some of them.

The theme of the robber had long engaged Puškin's interest.

The question of the literary roots of this theme, on the one hand, and of its links with the social problems of Russian life and the biographical observations of Puškin himself, on the other,[10] has been examined relatively fully in the critical literature.

It is sufficient for us at this point to note that the image of the robber went hand in hand in Puškin's consciousness with the figure, not without autobiographical traits, of a high-ranking personage, who was represented now as a Byronic hero, now as a Petersburg dandy, now transformed into an eighteenth century nobleman. Sometimes these two characters went side by side in a single plot development, sometimes they merged into a single figure, or resulted from the splitting of a single figure. Behind these figures lay the Romantic typology of characters and the division of heroes into the disappointed individualists who had lost their thirst for life and who combined boundless pride with a premature spiritual death, and the passionate children of nature, at one with their wild and passionate people, naive, indomitable, cruel and ingenuous. The first

215

easily took on the features of the rebel belonging to the highest society and civilization; the second was associated with the popular insurgent. Let us leave out of account *The Captive of the Caucasus*,* where the opposition between, on the one hand, the Captive, belonging to the world of civilization, destroyed "by premature aging of the soul,"[11] and, on the other, the wild and free mountain dwellers still only hints at the contrast which interests us; the contrasting pair of characters we have described first appears when the hero of the unrealized plan of the *Poem of the Volga robbers* is divided into Girej in *The Fountain of Bachčisaraj* [1824] and the Robber in *The Robber Brothers* [1825]. While he was working on the central chapters of *Eugene Onegin* [i.e. 1824–1826], this contrast took on the character "Petersburg Dandy vs. Robber." The clear parallelism between the robber from the ballad *The Bridegroom* [1825] and the Onegin of Tat'jana's dream is convincing evidence of the connection between these images in Puškin's consciousness. If, however, we recall that a series of associations links these two texts with a third, *The Songs of Sten'ka Razin* [1826], it becomes obvious that Puškin is interested in those aspects of the robber which link him to the popular potential for rebellion.

While working on the final chapters of *Eugene Onegin* [1828–1829] Puškin was deeply taken with Bulwer Lytton's novel *Pelham, or the Adventures of a Gentleman* [1828], particularly the figure of the dandy. There is no doubt, however, that what also appealed to him was the fact that in the course of the novel's development the cream of English dandyism encounters heroes from the criminal world, as a result of which the problem of "the gentleman and the robber" is foregrounded.

The ending of *Eugene Onegin* is somewhat unexpected, even for the author himself: it is known that Puškin considered the sixth chapter to be the end of the first part of the novel. This leads us to suppose that he thought of the second part as being of roughly the same length as the first.** We do not intend to speculate about how the novel might have continued (particularly since quite enough hypotheses on this topic have already been advanced). Let us merely consider certain general indications of the abandoned plan. Presumably the novel was shortened not by discarding episodes after the final meeting of Onegin and Tat'jana, but by reducing the part between the duel and this meeting. The evidence of Juzefovič, so often cited by commentators, according to which Onegin was to have been among those in Senate Square*** and to have perished in Siberia or in the Caucasus, is too short and imprecise to use for any

---

*Puškin's first Romantic narrative poem (1822).
***Eugene Onegin* consists of eight completed chapters. In addition there is an unnumbered fragment entitled "Onegin's Journey," written 1829–1830, and the fragment entitled "chapter ten" (written in autumn 1830).
***On December 14, 1825, i.e. a Decembrist.

216

concrete reconstructions of the text. All this ideologically extremely weighty part of the narration Puškin could have fitted into a single paragraph, as for example he did with the ending of *The Shot*. If we learnt of the events referred to there from someone else's telling, we could well imagine the dramatic conflicts in the camp of the rebellious Greeks, and the scene of the execution of Vladimirescu, and the flight of Ypsilanti, who abandoned his fellows–the whole chain of events which led to the tragic battle of Skulyani. These events were well known to Puškin and, at the time, caused him much concern. It would be easy to imagine plot developments which might have followed the introduction into the thick of these historical events of the sombre romantic figure of Sil'vio. And yet Puškin, as we know, reduced all this to the laconic phrase: "He [Sil'vio] was in charge of a detachment of Hetairists and killed in the battle of Skulyani" (*The Shot*, VIII, 1, 74)*. As for chapter ten [of *Eugene Onegin*] it is impossible to judge from the extant manuscripts how it is linked thematically and genetically to "Onegin's Journey" (the compositional placing of the chapter precisely as the "tenth," i.e. the last, has no bearing on determining its function in the plot, since the final chapter was, one may assume, envisaged as a sort of appendix, set outside the plot, as it were Onegin's diary, from which it evidently derives). This assumption might indeed explain the mention of Puškin in the third person–the only one in the novel!–("Puškin was reading his fairy tales"), and the note of irony, which stung the Decembrists but has been ignored by commentators, in the passage about the men of December 14, a note which is highlighted by the contrast with the emotionally charged lines about Napoleon.

In the final text of "Onegin's Journey," the shortened and re-worked one that is familiar to us, events are demonstratively absent; during Onegin's journey *nothing happens* to him. This justifies the refrain: "Ennui, ennui!" And yet Puškin's original plan could hardly have been like this. Evidence of this is provided, for example, by the chronological inconsistency – Onegin's unjustifiably long and unexplained trip south: he left Petersburg "on July 3" (1821) (*Eugene Onegin*, Variants, VI, 476), and arrived in the Crimea "three years aft(er) m(e)" (idem, VI, 489). Puškin was in the Crimea from August 15 until mid-September 1820. Therefore Onegin turned up in the Crimea in summer or autumn 1823. What was he doing for two years on the Volga and in the Caucasus?

At the same period, in the late 1820s and the 1830s, Puškin was obviously interested in ideas for a large-scale adventure story. Traces of this can be found in several details of the extant text of "Onegin's Journey": Puškin leads his hero from Moscow, via the Makar'ev fair** along the Volga to the Caucasus. If we bear in mind that there is no plot

---

*References here and below are to Puškin PSS.
**i.e. the great Nižnij Novgorod fair.

217

motivation for such an itinerary, it creates a strange impression: in Puškin's time, no one travelled to the Caucasus that way, and Puškin himself was quite unfamiliar with this route which was not associated for him with any *personal* memories. However, the Volga did have firm folkloric and literary associations: with the robber theme, with the images of Stepan Razin* and Pugačev.** Both these images are reflected in the extant text – in the songs of the barge haulers:

> . . . they sing (. . .)
> Of that robber refuge
> Of those daring raids
> How St(en'ka) Raz(in) in olden days
> Bloodied the Volga's waves.
>
> They sing of those uninvited guests
> Who burned and hacked. . . (*Eugene Onegin*, Variants, VI, 499).

The Caucasus was also steeped in associations of romantic brigandage. If we add that, in one version at the beginning of his journey (Novgorod), and in another at the end (Odessa, the suggestion of A. Gerbstman) Onegin was to visit the military settlements, that Petersburg and Odessa were the places where hero and author met, and possibly (this supposition emerges from chapter ten), where the hero met the "wise" members of the Union of Welfare, there emerges a succession of colorful scenes which provide a basis against which to unfold a complex plot which would have placed Onegin between the world of nobility culture in all its fullness and complexity, and the world of popular "robber" freemen. Simultaneously there arose the psychological antithesis of the "gentleman" and the "robber." All this reconstruction is extremely hypothetical, but it fits in with Puškin's interest in combining an adventure plot on many planes with a wide picture of Russian society, an interest which is clearly evident in the majority of Puškin's unfinished plans of this period.

The period around 1830 is remarkable in Puškin's work for the wealth and variety of his unrealized plans Some of them have reached us in the form of plans and drafts, others are known only by their title. In many of these cases even the most general reconstruction of what Puškin had in mind seems impossible. If, however, we imagine that on a certain abstract level these plans could be regarded as variants of a single archeplot, and if we learn to recognize the archetypal images behind the transformations of Puškin's creative thought, then we may hope to obtain sufficient additional data to make relatively probable reconstructions.

---

*Sten'ka Razin, popular figure in Russian folklore, led a peasant revolt in the Volga region in 1670. Executed in 1671.

**Emel'jan Ivanovič Pugačev (1726 – 1775) led a widespread popular revolt in the Volga region and the Urals in the reign of Catherine the Great. In 1773 he declared himself to be Peter III, Catherine's deceased husband. Executed in 1775.

The antithetical pair "gentleman--robber" is evident in a whole series of Puškin's plans. Among them are the drafts for a narrative poem based on Jan Potocki's *The Manuscript found in Saragossa* [1803–1815] (the fragment beginning "Al'fons mounts his horse" [1836]; possibly also the plan about the Wandering Jew: "A lamp in a Jewish hovel..."); reflections of the Pelham plot (see below); and, probably, the plot about the outsider [*kromešnik*]. Moreover, the antithetical images may merge into a single contradictory whole, the gentleman-robber. For its part, the image of the gentleman has the tendency to split into "Mephistopheles" and "Faust," images of the spirit of evil and of the bored intellectual. When they synthesize, demonic devilish features emerge in the "gentleman"; when they subdivide, the antithesis is between evil activity and passively egoistic inactivity. In the merged form, this image often has traits of Bonapartism, and this, of course, leads to the possibility of separating out the antithesis: "evil, egoistic activity and good, altruistic activity." The motivating force for characters of the first kind is egoism (= self-interest), and for the second, altruism (= love). In various combinations the features of this archetype (the dandy) are apparent in Onegin, in Sil'vio (in merged form), and in the form of antithetical contrast: Mephistopheles and Faust (in *A Scene from Faust* [1825]), Pavel and Varfolomej (in "A Secluded House on Vasil'evskij Island" [1829]), the demon in love and the young man (the plan of "A Demon in Love"), Švabrin and Grinev [in *The Captain's Daughter*, 1835]. On another level of the archeplot, the possibility of the synthesis of the gentleman and the robber could produce variants of the "Dubrovskij" type [*Dubrovskij*, 1832] (with the accent on the altruistic variant) or the "Herman" type [*The Queen of Spades*, 1833] (with the accent on the egoistic variant of the "gentleman"). Against this background the reconstruction of several of the plans is possible. Particularly significant here are the outline plans for "A Novel at the Caucasian Waters" [1831] and "A Russian Pelham" [1834–1835]. These last two are close to that circle of ideas which, evidently, had been budded from the Onegin stem. They are characteristic too inasmuch as here the theme "hero of the Onegin type vs. robber" is organically interwoven with the Decembrist theme.

In the plan for "A Novel at the Caucasian Waters" there is the first mention of "Pelham": "Jakub.(ovič) pays court through his brother Pelham—refusal—duel" (VIII, 2, 966).[12] The name Pelham was inserted by Puškin later, and its sense is not absolutely clear. However, in general, the shift of the plot from one stratum to another is characteristic: the society milieu, the robber milieu, the Decembrist milieu (the main hero is the Decembrist Jakubovič; evidently Puškin intended to change his name later, retaining Jakubovič just as a prototype). The plot knots are those of a typical adventure story: courtship, abduction, duel, attacks by the Circassians, the help of loyal natives. Evidently the old plot of *The*

Captive of the Caucasus was to be re-worked again: in one of the variants of the plan there is the note: "...betrays him to the Circassians. He is released (by a Cossack girl or a Circassian girl)" (Plan for "A Novel at the Caucasian Waters," VIII, 2, 967). In this plan, Jakubovič is close to the image of Dubrovskij – the combination of gentleman and robber in a single person. This evokes a connected doubling – Dubrovskij as Desforges lives in the house of Troekurov, but as the robber chieftain he lives in the forest, by day he is a Frenchman, by night he robs landowners, by night he is Dubrovskij, robber and popular avenger. Jakubovič by day is a Russian officer at the Caucasian waters, in love with Alina; by night he is a Circassian, taking part in the raids on Russian settlements. Note that the combination of the image of the robber with the motif of being in love and of abducting the beloved will be exceptionally persistent.

It is, however, the plan for "A Russian Pelham" that is of the greatest interest to us. This plot has been studied by several commentators.[13] For the most part, however, two particular aspects of it have evoked interest: the intriguing characterization of the "Society of the *wise* (I(l'ja) Dolg(orukov), S.(ergej) Trub(eckoj), Nik(ita) Mur(av'ev) etc.)" (Variants to "A Russian Pelham," VIII, 2, 974); and the search for prototypes and historical realia. The questions why the hero is called a Russian Pelham, and how, in the light of this one might reconstruct the plot, have not been discussed.

The hero of Bulwer Lytton's novel is an aristocrat and a dandy, a leader of fashion, and part of the novel takes place in the highest society circles of Paris and London. The other part of the hero's life takes place, however, in the haunts of the most dubious society. In Puškin's plan, the fate of the "Russian Pelham" (later called Pelymov), which takes him through all strata of contemporary society, links him to the robber-nobleman Fedor Orlov. This figure, who plays a key role in Puškin's plan, has not, strange as it may seem, attracted the attention of commentators. Fedor Fedorovič Orlov, the brother of Aleksej Fedorovič and Michail Fedorovič Orlov,[14] was a historical figure and a personal acquaintance of Puškin. They had met in Kišinev and were on very friendly terms.[15] We know little of the life of Fedor Orlov, and the fact of his becoming a brigand, caught and pardoned only through the intercession of his brother Aleksej, the favorite and personal friend of Nicholas I, is attested to only in Puškin's notes. It is usually supposed that naming the hero Fedor Orlov is only a conventional indication of the prototype who provided the author with the basis for the literary conflict he planned. This is, however, probably not the case. First of all, let us establish precisely the time when Puškin began work on the plot of the novel. Usually this is established from the evidence of the watermark on the paper ("1834") and is given as "probably 1834."[16]

This date can be corroborated by more precise evidence. The idea came to Puškin, as far as we can judge, soon after the death of Fedor Orlov (in one of the plans the hero of the novel, Pelymov, is called "the executor of Fedor Orlov's will," cf. Variants to "A Russian Pelham," VIII, 2, 975). Orlov died in the autumn of 1834. The announcement published by his brother Michail Fedorovič Orlov in No. 84 of *Moscow News* [*Moskovskie Vedomosti*] for 1834 is evidence of this:

> Announcing with great sorrow the passing of my brother, Colonel Fedor Fedorovič Orlov, I, the undersigned, declare that I completely renounce that part of his estate which passes to me after his death, and, not intending to take possession of it, I offer it for the paying off of his creditors, if they appear with legal documents. Retired Major-General Michail, the son of Fedor, Orlov.[17]

The newspaper announcement adhered to a set formula: it signified a refusal to pay the debts of a dead relative, for it was quite clear that after the death of Fedor Orlov, there remained no property, only debts.

It is unlikely that the story of Fedor Orlov's brigandage and of his rescue through the intervention of his brother Aleksej Fedorovič, the personal friend of Tsar Nicholas, whose intercession saved another brother, the Decembrist Orlov, from Siberia, is invented, though we have not managed to discover documentary evidence. In 1831, however, Fedor Orlov aroused the interest of the Third Department, which collected information about his debts and his behavior (cf., for example, "On the financial claim of the tailor German against Lieutenant-Colonel Orlov"[18]; case records of 1831, unfortunately these records have not survived). Fedor Orlov was a passionate gambler, a fiery, reckless man. In one of the variants of Puškin's plan the motif of his suicide is introduced: "he even becomes a brigand, he slits the throat of Ščepočkin; he shoots himself (or disappears)" (Variants to "A Russian Pelham," VIII, 2, 975). The actual circumstances of the death of Fedor Orlov are unknown to us. Even if he died a natural death, Puškin did not sin against the psychological truth of his character or against biographical accuracy, but merely displaced certain circumstances. He knew, of course, the episode of Fedor Orlov's notorious attempted suicide in 1812. A.Ja. Bulgakov noted in his diary on January 24, 1812:

> Yesterday the youngest son of Count Fedor Grigor'evič Orlov, Fedor, lost 190,000 at cards and shot himself; but since the pistol was very tightly packed and loaded with three bullets, the barrel blew up and the shot backfired. The attempted suicide was miraculously saved; but his whole face was disfigured. Yet he survived. It will be strange to say in twenty years' time: here is a man who shot himself in 1812. [19]

Puškin became interested in his old acquaintance not only because he was a reckless fellow, one of the most renowned "scapegraces" in the guards. This was a new variant of the type of the "nobleman-robber" which had aroused Puškin's attention. After Dubrovskij-Švabrin, Fedor Orlov was a new link in the chain of Puškinian heroes of this type.

The real Fedor Orlov, however, had one characteristic which sharply distinguished him in this company: he was a hero of the Napoleonic war of 1812, and an invalid, who had lost a leg in battle.

Of the circumstances of Fedor Orlov's military life we know the following. N.N. Murav'ev wrote in his notes:

At Borodino there were four Orlov brothers, all of them brave and strong. Aleksej served as captain in the Horse Guards. His horse was killed under him, and he was left on foot among the enemy cavalry. Four Polish uhlans who surrounded him, gave him a few wounds with their lances, but he bravely stood his ground and parried their shots with his broadsword; exhausted by his wounds, he would soon have fallen, if he had not been saved by his comrades, the Princes Golicyn, from the same regiment. His brother, Fedor Orlov, who served in one of the hussar regiments, galloped up to the French cavalry and with his pistol killed an enemy officer right in front of the column Soon after that he lost a leg to enemy cannon. This, at least, is how people related deeds of bravery which I myself did not witness. The third Orlov brother, Grigorij, who was in the Cavalier Guards, and was adjutant to a general, also lost a leg to a cannon. I saw them carrying him away. He sat on his horse, supported under the arms by Cossacks, his severed leg was dangling from below the knee, but the expression on his face had not changed at all, and did not even display suffering. The fourth Orlov brother, Michail, who was then Toll's adjutant, also displayed remarkable fearlessness, but was not wounded.[20]

N.N. Murav'ev is an exceptionally precise memoirist, who distinguishes between what he has seen himself and the reports of others. Therefore certain inaccuracies, which have crept into his evidence (Fedor Orlov did not lose a leg at Borodino) do not lessen the value of his testimony: they bear witness to the fact that around the names of the Orlov brothers, including Fedor, there existed a Guards folklore (all four brothers served in the Guards), surrounding them with an aura of bravery and heroism.

Fedor Orlov lost his leg later. The historian of the Sumy Hussar (later the third Dragoon) regiment, describing the unsuccessful battle of Bautzen [May 20–21, 1813], which was indeed almost catastrophic for the Allies, reports:

It is impossible not to mention, however, the particularly brave attack by junior captain Orlov with one squadron of the Sumy regiment. Catching sight of an attack by the French cavalry, he and his squadron cut their way into the centre of it (. . .) During this glorious exploit Orlov lost a leg, but his bravery was recognized and he was awarded the Order of St. George, fourth class.[21]

Later, on April 20 1820, Fedor Orlov, who was already serving in a Life-guard regiment of uhlans, was promoted by Imperial order from captain to colonel,[22] but in point of fact was not in his regiment, but with his brother, Michail Orlov. Going on sprees and playing cards, he was not, however, immune to the currents of the time, and joined the Masonic lodge of the "United Friends" in Petersburg, which became famous in the history of Decembrism.[23] He treated the politico-economic conversations of his brother Michail with irony, however, preferring a game of billiards. On March 1, 1823 he was discharged from the service "fully" "for his wounds, with the right to wear uniform,"[24] which, obviously, resulted from Michail Orlov's disgrace and the break up of the Kišinev* circle.

Thus, when Puškin was musing over the plan for "A Russian Pelham," preparing to include Fedor Orlov in the novel, his imagination was struck by the image of a lame robber with a wooden leg, a hero of the 1812 war.

Puškin's work on "A Russian Pelham" coincided with the period of his most intensive personal contact with Gogol. In "An Author's Confession," Gogol tells how Puškin persuaded him to take on a large-scale narrative,

> and to persuade me he gave me his own plot, which he had wanted to use himself for something like a *poèma*, and which, he said, he would not have given to anyone else. This was the plot of *Dead Souls*.[25]

This conversation took place most probably in the autumn of 1835. On October 7 of the same year, Gogol, obviously continuing their conversation, wrote to Puškin that he had "already begun to write *Dead Souls*."[26] Autumn 1835 is the time when Puškin stopped working on "A Russian Pelham." One may suppose that this was the "plot" of the "something like a *poèma*" which Puškin gave Gogol, saying that it "give(s) you complete freedom to travel with your hero all over Russia, and to introduce a large number of different characters."[27] Evidently, Puškin did not just relate to Gogol (nor, we can be more certain, did he read them from his papers) the extant plans of "A Russian Pelham" – he improvised on this theme. At some stage he may have recalled the case, which he knew from P.I. Bartenev, of swindling with dead souls (this case was also known to Gogol himself).[28] In any event, the authoritative evidence of Gogol himself unambiguously indicates that the plot given him by Puškin was not an idea which only fleetingly concerned the poet, a plan which had just come into his head. Yet there are no traces of plans of anything more like *Dead Souls* among Puškin's extant manuscripts. Moreover, Puškin always "thought on paper," and his most ephemeral plans were

---

*Orlov's circle in Kišinev began to be investigated in February 1822: its members were arrested or demoted.

expounded in the form of manuscripts. And the manuscripts of his final years are well preserved, the mysterious disappearance from them of any traces of the "given away" plot would itself need explanation.

Gogol, of course, had no intention of simply re-telling Puškin's plot in his own words: it is not only the coincidences which are of great interest, but also the non-coincidences, which make it possible to assess the profound differences between the creative worlds of Puškin and Gogol. The closest point of contact between Puškin's plan and Gogol's realization of it is in the figure of Fedor Orlov–Captain Kopejkin. The image of Kopejkin was gradually adapted to the conditions of the censorship, first by self-censorship, then by the pressure exerted on the author by the censor Nikitenko. In this respect, it is the early versions that are of the greatest interest. In them, Kopejkin retains features which link him to Dubrovskij: Kopejkin turns out to be not simply a robber chieftain, but the head of an enormous detachment ("in a word, my good sir, he has simply a (sort of) army").[29] The special place of Kopejkin among a series of popular avenger-robbers in the literature of those years comes from the fact that his vengeance is purposefully aimed at the bureaucratic state:

> There is no way through on the roads, and all this is, in fact, so to say, aimed only at the government. If someone is driving by on some, that is his own, business,—well, he'll just ask why, and let him be on his way. But as soon as there is some government fodder, provisions or money, in a word (you can imagine) everything which bears, as it were the name "government," there's no quarter given. Well, you can imagine, this is a terrible loss for the exchequer.[30]

It is remarkable that in this entire episode the absurd accusations which are directed at Čičikov though bizarre with regard to him, closely recall episodes of the "brigandly" biography of Fedor Orlov in Puškin's plans: both of them (the former in the imagination of the provincial ladies, the latter in Puškin's plan, which probably bore some reflection of reality) abduct a young woman. This detail is fundamental in Puškin, appearing in various forms in all the known plans for "A Russian Pelham"; and it is fundamental among the accusations the provincial ladies make against Čičikov.

What, then, is the precise relationship of Čičikov to Captain Kopejkin? Is it merely the strange association of ideas in the head of the postmaster of the town of N., who ignores the fact that both Čičikov's arms and legs are in place, which justifies the appearance of this character in *Dead Souls*? Čičikov is an entrepreneur, an entirely new figure in Russian literature of those years. This does not mean that he has no literary relatives. Let us look which literary names are recalled in connection with Čičikov, or which associations he evokes in the novel, without distinguishing, for the time being, the serious from the parodic (a parodic association is a serious one turned inside out).

224

1. Čičikov, as the Romantic society hero. Čičikov "was on the point of making a reply probably no worse than those uttered in our modern novels by the Zvonskys, the Linskys, the Lidins and the Gremins." [*Dead Souls*, p. 176.][31] After a little drink he began to "read to Sobakevich Werther's letter to Charlotte."[32] Also part of this level of the novel is the letter to Čičikov from an unknown lady.

2. Čičikov, as the Romantic robber. He bursts in on Korobočka, in the words of the lady agreeable in all respects, "like Rinaldo Rinaldini." He is Captain Kopejkin, he is the robber on the run from lawful prosecution in the neighboring province, he is also a maker of false banknotes.

3. Čičikov, as the demonic personality. He is Napoleon who has been

let out from the island of St. Helena and he was now wandering all over Russia in the guise of Chichikov, though he was not really Chichikov at all. Of course, the officials did not really believe it, but it did make them wonder and, thinking it over each for himself, they found that Chichikov's face, when he turned round and stood sideways, was very much like a portrait of Napoleon. The chief of police, who had served in the campaign of 1812 and had seen Napoleon personally, could not but admit that he was not an inch taller than Chichikov and that Napoleon could certainly not be said to be too fat, though he was not too thin, either.[33] [*Dead Souls*, p. 216]

4. Čičikov, the Antichrist. After the comparison of Čičikov with Napoleon, there follows the tale about the prediction

of a prophet who had been for three years in prison; the prophet had come from no one knew where in bast-shoes and an uncovered sheep-skin smelling terribly of stinking fish, and announced that Napoleon was Antichrist and was kept on a stone chain behind six walls and seven seas, but that later on he would break his chain and gain possession of the whole world. The prophet was very properly put in prison for his prediction.[34] [*Dead Souls*, pp. 216–217]

Leaving this last point to one side for the time being, we can note the following: the image of Čičikov is a synthesis of the characters bequeathed by the Puškin tradition: the Romantic society hero (variant – the dandy) and the robber. Moreover, Puškin had already noted the possibility of merging these images in the figure of the knight of profit, money-grubber and demonic egoist, Hermann. The depiction of the resemblance of Čičikov and Napoleon is a parodic quotation of the corresponding passage in *The Queen of Spades*: Hermann has "Napoleon's profile"; "he sat on the window-ledge with arms folded, frowning menacingly. In this position he was amazingly reminiscent of the portrait of Napoleon" (VIII, 1, 244, 245).

Čičikov is surrounded by literary projections, each of which is both parodic and serious: a new man in Russian reality, he is both spirit of evil and man of the world, the embodiment of egoism, Hermann, a knight of profit, and a noble robber (he robs, like Kopejkin, only the exchequer). Synthesizing all these literary traditions in a single figure, he simultaneously debases them parodically. But it is not just a question of literary parody: Gogol more than once stressed that the ordinary and the insignificant are more terrible than majestic literary evil. Čičikov, the anti-villain, anti-hero, anti-robber, man without features ("neither fat nor thin"), turns out to be Antichrist himself who will in time conquer the entire world. He signifies the time when vice ceased to be heroic and evil majestic. Absorbing all Romantic images, he renders them all colorless and worthless. Yet he has the closest connection of all to Hermann in *The Queen of Spades.* Just as the essence of Dubrovskij (and the Utopianism of that image) is revealed by projection on to Grinev-Švabrin, on the one hand, and onto Pugačev, on the other, so Hermann was expanded into Pelham and Fedor Orlov, the principle of culture and the principle of money, deceit, knavery and brigandage. Čičikov retained only the hopeless prose of adventurism for the sake of money. And yet his link to the robber is close and organic. It is no accident that the name Kopejkin is involuntarily associated with the chief slogan of his life: "Look after the kopecks" [*kopi kopejku*]. The hymn to the kopeck is the only patrimonial inheritance of Čičikov:

A classmate or friend may cheat you and be the first to leave you in the lurch when you're in trouble, but money will never let you down, whatever trouble you may be in. With money in your pocket you can do anything and money will see you through everything.[35] [*Dead Souls*, p. 236.]

It was precisely the association evoked by the sound of his name (and Gogol's sense of this was extremely acute),[36] which must have attracted Gogol's attention to the songs about the robber Kopejkin. The songs about "The Thief Kopejkin" in the notes of Petr Vasil'evič Kireevskij* were familiar to Gogol. [37] It is most likely that, although neither the collectors[38] nor Gogol had any reliable information about the chieftain Kopejkin, Gogol may have known the oral legend about the soldier Kopeknikov (which is, of course, a version of the name Kopejkin, distorted when noted down in French), who became a robber "against his will," when Arakčeev refused to help him, and his father directed that he should provide for himself.[39]

The hero of popular songs, the robber Kopejkin, the soldier "Kopeknikov" sent away by Arakčeev, Fedor Orlov, the invalid hero of 1812 who became a robber, merged into the complex figure of Captain Kopejkin. Yet another detail of the relationship of Kopejkin to Čičikov is significant: Kopejkin, a hero of the anti-Napoleonic wars, and Napoleon are two

*(1808 – 1856), prominent Slavophile and folklorist.

antithetical figures who together characterize the Romantically heroic epoch of 1812. The synthesis and parodic diminution of these images give birth to the "hero of the kopeck," Čičikov. One might recall that Puškin too linked the Napoleonic epoch and the era of money as two links in one chain:

> The world has changed in the thunder of new glory.
>
> . . . . . .
> Witnesses of yesterday's fall,
> The young generations have hardly come to their senses.
> Gathering the late fruit of harsh experience,
> They rush to balance income and expenditure.
> They have no time to joke, to dine with Temira. . .
> ("To a Grandee," 1830, III, 1, 219)

The synthetic relationship of Čičikov to the earlier literary tradition does not, however, detract from the fundamental novelty of this character. Čičikov was conceived of by Gogol as a hero who was to undergo future rebirth. How this possibility itself is motivated leads us to aspects of Gogol's artistic thinking that are new for the nineteenth century. The villain in eighteenth century Enlightenment literature retained the right to our sympathies and our belief in his possible regeneration since Nature, which lay at the base of his character, was good, though perverted by society. The Romantic villain expiated his guilt by the grandiose scale of his crimes; the grandeur of his soul secured him the sympathies of the reader. In the final analysis, he might turn out to be an angel who had strayed from his path, or even a sword in the hands of heavenly justice. The Gogolian hero carries the hope of rebirth, because he has reached the limit of evil in its extreme, base, petty and *funny* manifestations. The comparison of Čičikov with the robber, Čičikov with Napoleon, Čičikov with Antichrist makes the former a comic figure, removes from him the aura of literary nobility (the parodic theme of Čičikov's attachment to "noble" service, "noble" behavior and so on, follows a parallel path through the tale). Evil is given not only in its pure form, but also in its insignificant forms. This is already the most extreme, and the blackest, kind of evil, in Gogol's view. And precisely in its blackness is hidden the possibility of just as full and absolute a rebirth. Such a conception is organically linked to Christianity, and forms one of the bases of the artistic world of *Dead Souls*. This relates Čičikov to the heroes of Dostoevskij.

The analogy between Herman (Napoleon + the murderer, a variant of the robber) and Raskol'nikov [in *Crime and Punishment*] (the same combination of features which makes up the image of a man who has joined battle with the world of wealth and who strives to subjugate it)[40] has already been discussed. The connection between these images and

227

Čičikov is less immediately apparent. Dostoevskij, however, in creating Raskol'nikov, certainly, perhaps subconsciously, had the hero of *Dead Souls* in mind.[41]

The antithesis "dandy – robber" is extremely important for Dostoevskij. Sometimes it appears quite openly (for example in the pair: Stavrogin – Fed'ka [*The Devils*]; in general, precisely because Stavrogin is drawn as a "Russian gentleman," his image is subsumed in the tradition of characters with a dual existence, appearing now in society circles, now in the slums, amidst the dregs of society). Sometimes it appears in a complex transformation.

Such a distribution of images is part of a wider tradition: the relationship "gentleman – robber" is fundamental for Balzac (Rastignac – Vautrin), Hugo, Dickens. In the final analysis it goes back to the mythological figure of the werewolf, leading two contrary ways of life by day and by night. Because of its tendency at times to divide into two different and mutually hostile characters, at times to merge into a single contradictory image, this archetype has an enormous potential semantic capacity, thereby allowing different cultural contexts to fill it with different content, while at the same time retaining a certain semantic constant.

Translated by Julian Graffy

NOTES

1 Sokolov 1970, p. 641.
2 Stepanov 1955, p. 218.
3 Cf., for example, Kuprejanova 1971, where the place of the "Tale" in the novel is defined as follows: "One should also bear in mind that the middle rank backwoods landowners portrayed in *Dead Souls* were not at all, in Gogol's estimation, the 'generals' of Russian life, he saw in them rather the 'privates,' i.e. the most commonplace and ordinary of men. By 'generals,' Gogol meant the ruling state apparatus, its highest bureaucratic spheres. Actually as generals they appear in the first volume of *Dead Souls* only in the 'Tale of Captain Kopejkin'" (ibid, p. 69). This is all she has to say of the role of the "Tale" in the novel. The inadequacy of this interpretation of the "Tale" is clearly apparent to the critic herself. At least, when she transferred pages from the article quoted above word for word into a monograph published later, Kuprejanova excised the sentence which contained the allusion to the "Tale of Captain Kopejkin" (cf.: Kuprejanova and Makogonenko 1976, p. 303).
4 Polevoj's tale is particularly significant, since it contains a definite correspondence with chapter X of *Dead Souls*, which is evidence that while working on the "Tale" Gogol had in his mind Polevoj's story, which he probably read in 1834. Here the retired soldier-invalid says of Napoleon: "Is it true, your honour, that they have now sent him beyond the sea, beyond the ocean, across the seething ocean deep? Somehow I don't believe it! For, by all that's holy, they say He's the Antichrist, and that the end of the world is nigh, and he'll escape again" (quoted from *Russkie povesti* volume 2, p. 47). Compare, in Gogol, the words of the "prophet," who announced that Napoleon was Antichrist and was kept on a stone chain, behind

228

six walls and seven seas, but later he would break his chain and gain possession of the whole world" (*Dead Souls*, Ch. 10, pp. 216–217). For all the similarity of the basic plot situation – a hero-invalid, left helpless – a textual coincidence of this kind emphasizes the *conscious artistic* reasons for Gogol's making Kopejkin an officer.

5   Titular Counsellor Bašmačkin [the hero of Gogol's story *The Overcoat*] also belongs to the ninth class. Yet precisely here there is a significant difference, evidence of the importance of the "poetics of rank" to Gogol. In the civil service, nobility, and consequently the right to own serfs, began (before the edict of June 11, 1845, which complicated this procedure) from the eighth class, but for the military from the first commissioned officer rank, i.e. from the fourteenth class. Bašmačkin is called an "eternal titular counsellor" – he can never step across the barrier which divides him from the nobility. This places a deep social divide between him and Kopejkin. It is not by chance that Collegiate Assessor Kovalev [the hero of Gogol's story *The Nose*], who is only one rank higher than Bašmačkin, i.e. he belongs to the eighth class, is a man of a completely different world and a different social psychology. Moreover, there was no juridical sense of a social difference between "*Major*" Kovalev and *Captain* Kopejkin, and in fact military uniform afforded Kopejkin a far more respected position in the society of the time than the undress uniform of Kovalev, who, though he called himself a major "so as to give himself more nobility and weight," was in fact a collegiate assessor.

6   Stepanov 1955, p. 217.

7   Gogol, PSS, XII, p. 53.

8   Ibid., p. 54.

9   Ibid. Cf.: "I cannot contemplate publishing my manuscript without Kopejkin" (ibid., p. 55).

10   For a survey of critical literature, see Sandomirskaja 1966, pp. 370–379.

11   Letter to Gorćakov, October/November, 1822, Puškin, PSS, XIII, 52. [Subsequent references to this edition will be given in the text together with the English title of the work referred to].

12   For analysis of the plot of "A Novel at the Caucasian Waters," see: Izmajlov 1975; Sidjakov 1973, pp. 104–107. The possibility of a synthesis of various tendencies in the image of Jakubovič is demonstrated by the fact that in oral tales about him Puškin could merge the autobiographical element with the brigandly, that is to say he could improvise about himself as a robber. Cf. Puškin's words in a letter to A.A. Bestužev of November 30, 1825: "Jakubovič (. . .) is a hero of my imagination." "When I lie to women, I assure them that I joined his band of brigands in the Caucasus" (Puškin, PSS, XIII, 244).

13   Cf.: Sidjakov 1973, pp. 150–155; Kazancev 1967.

14   Puškin was acquainted with four of the five (by two mothers) illegitimate, later legitimized sons of Catherine the Great's grandee Fedor Grigor'evič Orlov: Aleksej, Michail, Fedor and Grigorij. [On M.F. Orlov, see above Part Two, Ch. 1.]

15   Cjavlovskij 1931, p. 66 seq.

16   Sidjakov 1973, p. 148.

17   Quoted from a cutting of the Poltorackij archive, Lenin Library, manuscript department, fond 233 (Poltorackij), collection 39, storage unit 9, sheet 1.

18   Central State Archive of the October Revolution, fond 109, 1831–1832, inventory, fond III, section 2, dispatch office.

19   *Russkij archiv* 1867, pp. 1362–1363. Bulgakov wrote the same thing to his brother in a letter, see *Russkij archiv* 1900, book II, No. 5, p. 7. The note was made in January and consequently the last sentence has nothing to do with the war, and signifies: "Here is a man who shot himself twenty years ago."

20   *Russkij archiv* 1885, part III, No. 10, p. 259.

21   Golodolinskij 1902, part II, p. 132; cf. also, part III, No. 346 in the *List of officers for 1814*.
22   Bobrovskij 1903, p. 310.
23   *Russkaja starina* 1907, No. 7, p. 208.
24   Bobrovskij 1903, p. 310.
25   Gogol, PSS, VIII, p. 440 ("Author's Confession"). For a detailed analysis of Gogol's "Puškinian plans," see Vacuro 1977.
26   Gogol, PSS, X, p. 375.
27   "Author's Confession," ibid., VIII, p. 440.
28   For a digest of data see the commentaries by V.A. Ždanov and È.È. Zajdenšnur, Gogol, PSS, VI, pp. 900–901.
29   Gogol, PSS, VI, p. 528, *Dead Souls* (second redaction).
30   Ibid., pp. 528–529.
31   Ibid., p. 166. (*Dead Souls*, Ch. 8)
32   Ibid., p. 152. (*Dead Souls*, Ch. 7) "Werther's letter to Charlotte": two Russian poems on this theme are known, by V. Tumanskij and A. Merzljakov (?).
33   Gogol, PSS, VI, p. 206. (*Dead Souls*, Ch. 10)
34   Ibid.
35   Ibid., VI, p. 225. (*Dead Souls*, Ch. 11)
36   Compare the etymologization of the names Zavališin [Squire Lie-a-Bed], Poležaev [Squire Take-a-Nap], Sopikov [Mr. Snooze] and Chrapovickij [Mr. Snore] (*Dead Souls*, Ch. 9, VI, p. 190) in connection with the semantics of dream.
37   Cf.: Kireevskij 1977, pp. 225–226 and 302.
38   "Who and when was the thief Kopejkin?" Kireevskij asked Jazykov. (Kireevskij 1935, p. 63; in publishing Kireevskij's letters, M.K. Azadovskij did not comment upon this name.)
39   The text of this "anecdote" was published in *Revue des Études Franco-russes*, 1905, No. 2. Mention of this publication is made by Leone Pacini Savoi in the article "La 'Povest' o kapitane Kopejkine'," Rome, 1958. Cf.: Stepanov 1959, 1, p. 18.
40   The fact that heroes of this kind enter into a struggle with Gold, striving to subjugate it, gives them yet another feature, that of knighthood. This quality has a tendency to divide into the Don Quixote knight (Kostanžoglo [in *Dead Souls*], Štol'c [in Gončarov's *Oblomov*]) and the Baron in [Puškin's] *The Covetous Knight*. Through Pljuškin this last is also comparable with Čičikov.
41   See Belyj 1934, pp. 99–100; Ju.M. Lotman, "The Theme of Cards and the Card Game in Russian Literature of the Nineteenth Century," *PTL. A Journal for Descriptive Poetics and Theory of Literature*, Vol. 3, No. 3, 1978.

THE POETICS OF EVERYDAY BEHAVIOR
IN RUSSIAN EIGHTEENTH CENTURY CULTURE

Ju.M. Lotman

The title of the present work calls for some explanation. To treat everyday behavior as a special kind of semiotic system may in itself give rise to objections. Indeed to speak of the poetics of everyday behavior amounts to claiming (for the historical and national cross-section of culture indicated in the title), that certain forms of ordinary daily activity were consciously oriented towards the laws and norms of literary texts and were lived through as direct aesthetic experiences. If this thesis could be proved, it could become one of the most important typological features for the culture of the period under investigation.

It cannot be said that everyday behavior as such has been neglected by scholars. In ethnographical studies it is seen as a natural object for description and investigation. The theme is a traditional one also for researchers concerned with relatively remote periods such as the ancient world, the Renaissance or the Baroque period. The history of Russian culture can also lay claim to several works which are still significant, from Kostomarov's *Description of the Domestic Life and Customs of the Great Russian Nation in the Sixteenth and Seventeenth Centuries* [Kostomarov 1860] to Romanov's *The People and Customs of Early Russia* [Romanov 1947].

The following observation follows from what we have said: the further a culture lies from us historically, geographically or culturally the more clearly can we see that its particular everyday life-style is a specific object of scientific study. This may be linked with the fact that the documents which record the norms of everyday, ordinary behavior for a particular social group as a rule originate with foreigners or are written for them. Such documents take for granted an observer who is located outside the given social group.

There is an analogy here with descriptions of everyday speech: when this is first recorded and investigated the descriptions are nearly always oriented towards an outside observer. As we shall see, this parallel is no accident. Both everyday behavior and one's own language are semiotic systems which are perceived by their immediate bearers as "natural," as belonging to Nature rather than to Culture. Their semiotic and conventional character is apparent only to an outside observer.

What we have said so far would seem to run counter to the title of this work since an aesthetic experience of everyday behavior would seem to be possible only for an observer who perceives such behavior as one of several semiotic phenomena in culture. The foreigner who experiences the alien pattern of everyday life as something exotic may perceive it aesthetically; whereas the immediate bearer of the culture as a rule simply does not notice its special features. However, in eighteenth century Russia, the culture of the nobility had undergone such a transformation in the very essence of everyday behavior that it had acquired features which were usually alien to it.

In any community with a relatively developed culture people's behavior is organized around a basic opposition:

1. On the one hand, usual, everyday, ordinary conduct, which is felt by the members of the group themselves to be "natural," the only possible, normal kind of behavior;

2. On the other hand, all types of ceremonial, ritualistic, and non-practical modes of behavior. This may be connected with the state, with worship or some other ritual; these types of behavior are perceived by the bearers of the culture as having an independent significance.

The bearers of the culture learn the former as they do their native language, being as it were immersed in its usage directly without noticing when, where or from whom they acquired familiarity with this system. It seems to them that mastery of this system is so natural that it cannot be called into question. Even less likely is it that anyone might take it into his head to compile for them grammars of the language of everyday life, metatexts describing the "correct" norms. The second type of behavior, however, is learned as one does a foreign language, by using rules and grammars: first its norms are assimilated and then on this basis "texts of behavior" can be constructed. The first type of behavior is acquired spontaneously, unawares, the second is assimilated consciously from teachers and mastery over it is, as a rule, marked by a special act of initiation.

After Peter the Great, the nobility in Russia experienced a change that was far more profound than a mere development in their way of life. The area which is normally left to unconscious, "natural" behavior became something to be learnt. Manuals appeared dealing with the norms of everyday conduct since the whole of the existing structure of everyday behavior was renounced as incorrect and replaced by a "correct," European, pattern.

The result was that a member of the Russian nobility of Peter's time and after was like a foreigner in his own country: even when fully grown up he had to learn artificially what people usually absorb in early childhood by direct experience. The alien and the foreign became the norm.

To conduct oneself correctly was to behave like a foreigner, that is to act in an artificial way according to the norms of an alien life-style. It was as necessary to bear these norms in mind as it was to know the rules of a foreign language in order to be able to use it properly. *The True Mirror of Youth* [*Junosti čestnoe zercalo*, 1767], desiring to portray the ideal of courteous behavior, suggested that one should imagine oneself to be in the society of foreigners: "One should explain what one needs elegantly in pleasant and polite words as if one were speaking with some foreigner, so that one becomes accustomed to this sort of thing." [1]

This sort of cultural inversion did not by any means amount to the "Europeanization" of the way of life in any straightforward sense of this expression, since the forms of everyday behavior and the foreign languages which were imported from the West and became the normal means of communication among members of the *Russian* nobility, altered their function in this process. In the West they were native and natural and, consequently, subjectively imperceptible. Obviously the ability to speak Dutch did not particularly increase a person's prestige in Holland. But transferred to Russia, European everyday norms acquired high prestige, they increased a person's social status as did knowledge of foreign languages. In *The True Mirror of Youth*, quoted above, we read:

> Young people who have returned from abroad and have learned languages at great expense, should keep practising them and should make every effort not to forget them, and further improve their knowledge of them by reading useful books and associating with others for this purpose. They should also do some writing and composition in order not to forget the languages.
> Those who have not been abroad and who come from school or elsewhere to the court should behave meekly and humbly before everyone and be willing to learn from whoever they can. They should not be haughty keeping their hat on as if welded to their heads. They ought not to rush about or be boastful as if they respected no one.[2]

Such a picture makes it obvious that, contrary to the widely held view, Europeanization emphasized the non-European features of the way of life rather than eliminating them, for in order to be constantly aware of one's own behavior as foreign, it was necessary *not to be* a foreigner (a foreigner does not feel his behavior to be foreign), one had to assimilate the forms of the European life-style while retaining the outsider's, "alien," Russian attitude to them. One did not have to become a foreigner, but to behave *like* one. It comes as no surprise, then, that the acquisition of foreign customs, far from eliminating antagonism to foreigners, occasionally intensified it.

A direct result of these changes in the attitude to daily life was the ritualization and semioticization of those spheres which in the non-inverted culture were perceived as "natural" and not significant. The

233

result was the very opposite of the "privacy" which so forcibly struck Russian observers of European life (cf. Count Peter Tolstoj's* remarks about Venice: "They do not accuse one another of anything and have no fear of one another. Everybody does what he chooses"[3]). The image of European life was duplicated in the ritualized game of playing at European life. Everyday behavior was turned into a set of signs for everyday behavior. The degree of this semioticization, of the conscious, subjective perception of the way of life as a sign increased sharply. Daily life took on features of the theater.

It is entirely typical of the Russian eighteenth century that the members of the nobility passed their lives as if they were plays, conceiving themselves to be forever on the stage, the people on the other hand tended to look on the gentry as if they were mummers, whom they watched from the pit. An interesting indication of this was the use of European (gentry) clothing for masquerades during Yuletide. Thus, at the beginning of the nineteenth century at Yuletide V.V. Selivanov recalled crowds of peasant mummers, village and household serfs, coming into their master's house which was open to them at that time. Their gear consisted of peasants' sheepskin coats *turned inside out*, or they wore clowns' clothing which was not used in normal times (bast caps and suchlike). However, along with this they also used their masters' regular clothing obtained on the quiet from the housekeeper: "Some of the master's old uniforms and other garments for men and women that were kept stored away."[4]

It is indicative that in cheap popular prints of the eighteenth century, with their tendency to depict their subjects as it were in a theater framed with side-curtains, "borders" and footlights, the folk characters, *inasmuch as they were actors*, are portrayed in the clothing of the gentry. In a well-known print entitled "Please leave me," the pancake-seller is drawn with beauty spots on her face while her suitor has a tie-wig and beauty spots and wears the dress uniform and cocked hat of a member of the nobility.[5]

The reason for regarding the way of life of the gentry as more highly semioticized comes not only from the fact that, having made it "his own," the Russian nobleman of the post-Petrine period also felt it as "alien." This dual attitude to one's own behavior turned it into a game.

This feeling was intensified because many features of popular life-style were preserved all through society. It was not only the lesser land-owners in the provinces who switched back easily to the norms of the traditional popular life-style and behavior, but also the great magnates, even Peter the Great and Elizabeth.** And so there were two possible

---

*Count P.A. Tolstoj (1645 – 1729) kept a diary of his journey to Italy in 1697 – 1699.
**Daughter of Peter the Great, she reigned from 1741 – 1762.

types of behavior, the one being neutral or "natural" and the other specifically gentlemanly and at the same time consciously theatricalized. It was typical of Peter that for himself he preferred the former, and even when he did take part in the ritualized performances, he would reserve for himself the role of producer, the person who organized the game. He would demand that his courtiers take part, but personally he kept out of it. However, this love for "simplicity" did not make his behavior any closer to that of the people, rather it indicated something that was the direct opposite. For the peasant, holidays and festivals were associated with a transition into a sphere of more ritualized behavior. A church service, the unfailing mark of any festival, a wedding and even a simple entertainment in a tavern signified entry into a set ritual which even laid down what, to whom and when one should say or do anything. For Peter, however, leisure meant a transition to non-ritualized, unofficial behavior. (A peasant festival in particular, involved some form of public spectacle: a crowd of uninvited people would gather "to watch" outside the house where a wedding was taking place. Peter's leisure activities, however, took place behind closed doors, in the narrow circle of "his own" people). This opposition is neutralized in the case of the parodic ritual: being an anti-ritual it tends to intimacy and the enclosed group, but being a ritual, though one turned inside out, it tends towards publicity and openness. During the Petrine period there was a confusion of the most varied forms of behavioral semiotics: official church ritual, parodies of church ritual in the blasphemous rites of Peter and his friends, the prac-tice of foreign modes of conduct in everyday life, intimate unofficial behavior which was consciously opposed to ritual;[6] all this set against the background of the popular life-style made it possible to perceive the category *style of behavior*. We may compare this with the fact that the colorful and disordered state of the lexis of the language at the beginning of the eighteenth century sharpened the sense of the stylistic significance not only of speech levels, but of every individual word (not only of beha-vior, but also of each action), so preparing the way for the strict classi-fying and ordering of the mid-eighteenth century.

And so after the first step, the semioticization of daily life, there followed a second, the creation of styles within the framework of the norm of ordinary life. This was expressed in particular in the fact that stylistic constants of behavior were laid down for definite geographical zones. When he travelled from St. Petersburg to Moscow, from his estate near Moscow to another more remote one, or from Russia to Europe, a nobleman often unconsciously, but always unerringly changed his style of behavior. The process of style-formation in this sphere proceeded also in another direction, that of social differentiation. Differences in styles of behavior emerged between a government servant and one who was retired, between military and civil personnel, between the court nobility and the

The Behavior Patterns of the Gentry

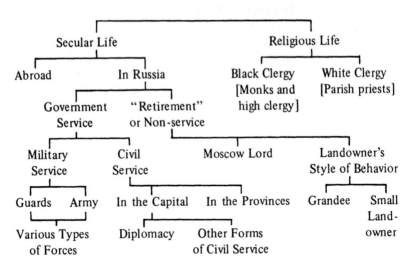

(Only those basic varieties of behavior, as practiced by members of the Russian nobility in the eighteenth century, that were realized as a consequence of choice between alternative possibilities, are taken into account.) No attempt has been made to adjust the typology for age differences.

nobleman from outside the capital. His way of speech, deportment and clothes unfailingly indicated what place any person occupied in the stylistic polyphony of everyday life. Gogol quoting in letters (and later in his play *The Gamblers*) the expression: *"Rute, rešitel'no rute! prosto karta foska!"* ["A run of luck, definitely a run of luck! it's just a low card!"] declared that this sentence was "real army usage and in its own way not without merit"; i.e. he made it clear that neither a civil servant on the one hand nor a guards officer on the other would speak this way.

This stylistic coloration was brought out by the fact that any particular form of behavior was the result of choosing one of the possible alternatives. The existence of this choice, the possibility of replacing one pattern by another, was the basis of the gentry's life-style. The life system of the Russian gentry was constructed like a tree-structure. And, the gentry, having achieved, by the second half of the eighteenth century, the freedom to enter government service or to live in retirement, to live in Russia or abroad, went on trying to increase the number of "branches" of the tree. The government, however, especially under Paul I and Nicholas I, took active steps to reduce to zero the opportunities for individual patterns of behavior, for choosing one's own style and personal path. It aimed at turning life into service, clothes into uniform.

The main opportunities for types of behavior among the nobility are represented by the scheme above (see diagram).[7] The existence of *choice* is what decisively separates the behavior of the gentry from that of the peasantry, which was regulated by the agricultural calendar and was the same within the bounds of each of its phases. It is curious to note that from this point of view the behavior of a noble woman was in principle nearer to that of the peasant than to that of her male counterpart, since it did not include any points of individual choice but was determined by her age.

The emergence of styles of behavior naturally made behavior resemble the aesthetically experienced phenomena, and this in turn caused people to seek models for the daily conduct of their lives in the sphere of art. For someone who had not yet assimilated European forms of art, his models could only be such forms of visual performance as were familiar to him — the church liturgy and the fairground puppet theater. However, the former enjoyed such authority that its use in everyday life would be a parodic and blasphemous performance. We find a striking example of the use of forms from the popular theater for the organization of the daily routine of the life of a member of the gentry in the rare little book *The Genealogy of the Golovins, the Owners of the Village of Novospaskoe, assembled by Peter Kazanskij, Bachelor of the Moscow Theological Academy* (see Kazanskij 1847). In this curious publication compiled from the domestic archive of the Golovin family which included materials greatly reminiscent of those that were available to Ivan Petrovič Belkin when he set about writing *A History of the Village of Gorjuchino*,* there is, in particular, a description of the life of Vasilij Vasil'evič Golovin (1696–1781), compiled on the basis of his own notes and family legends. Golovin's tempestuous life (he studied in Holland, knew four European languages and Latin and was one of Catherine I's** gentlemen-of-the-bedchamber; he got into trouble in connection with the Mons affair,*** underwent torture under Biron****[8] and, having got out of there by means of an enormous bribe, settled down in the country) is of interest because of the theater he made of his daily life. It was a mixture of fairground puppetry, folk incantations and spells, and Christian ritual.

---

*In *The History of the Village of Gorjuchino* which Puškin wrote in the autumn of 1830, Belkin, who had figured as narrator in *Tales of Belkin* written just before, discovers papers in the attic of his house which enable him to set about his "history."

**Widow of Peter the Great. She reigned from 1724–1747.

***In the last year of Peter the Great's reign, William Mons won influence over Catherine, Peter's wife, and used his position for corrupt ends. Peter ordered his execution in 1724.

****Ernst-Johann Biron, favorite of Empress Anne (1730–1740), known for his cruelties.

The following is an extensive quotation:

> He would get up in the morning before sunrise and then he would read through the midnight and morning services with his favorite church-reader Jakov Dmitriev. After the morning observances his butler, steward, the elected delegate of his serfs and his headman would come before him with various reports and communications. They usually entered and departed at the command of his house-maid Pelageja Petrovna, a woman of proven honesty. She would begin by pronouncing the words: "In the name of the Father, the Son and the Holy Ghost" and those present would answer: "Amen!" Only then would she say: "Enter and be sure to come in quietly, humbly, with care and reverence, with purity and with prayer, when you come to our lord and master with your reports and to receive your instructions. Bow low to his grace and remember, watch very carefully!" "I greet you," replied their master, "my friends, you who are free from torment and torture, untested and unpunished!" This was what he always said. "Well, what's been happening? Is everything all right, my children, are all our affairs prospering?" The first to answer this question, with a low bow, was the butler. "In the holy church and the most precious vestry, in your lordship's house, in the stables and cattleyard, in the peacock-house and the stork-house, everywhere in the gardens, the bird ponds and in all the other places, by Our Saviour's grace, my master, all has been preserved by God, and is in good order." After the butler, the steward began his report. "In your lordship's cellars, barns, granaries and store-houses, in your sheds and crop-drying barns, apiaries and poultry-yards, ham-stores and drying-rooms, by Our Lord's grace everything, my master, is safe and sound. Fresh spring water from the holy well at Grigorovo has been fetched as your lordship commanded on the skewbald horse and put into a glass bottle, placed in a wooden vat, surrounded on the inside with ice and closed up with stones piled up on top of it." The delegate reported as follows: "Throughout the night, my master, your noble house has been patrolled, both kinds of rattle have been sounded, the signal has been rung and the sounding-board has been struck loudly; the horn, sir, has been blown at intervals and all four men have talked to each other in loud voices, the night birds have not been flying about nor making eerie noises, they have not frightened the young masters, nor have they pecked at the master's window-putty; they have not landed on the roofs or been messing about in the loft." The headman ended up with his report: "In all four villages by God's grace all is well and in good order. Your lordship's peasants are thriving, their cattle are in good health, the four-footed beasts are at their pasture, the domestic fowl are astir, no earthquakes have been reported, nor have there been any heavenly manifestations. The cat Van'ka[9] and the woman Zažigalka[10] are living at Rtiščev and by your honour's command receive some unwinnowed grain each month, they sigh daily over their misdemeanour and, my master, with tears beg that your august anger should be replaced by mercy and that you should forgive your guilty slaves.

We omit the description of the painstakingly elaborate daily ceremonial consisting of household prayers, the church liturgy and the rites of breakfast, dinner and the dessert, each of which provided a regularly repeated spectacle.

Preparations for going to bed would begin [between 3 and 4 in the afternoon — Ju. L.] with the command to close the shutters, from inside the Jesus prayer was read: "Lord Jesus Christ, son of God, have mercy upon us!" — "Amen!" came the reply from several voices from outside and at this word the shutters would be closed with a terrific bang and the iron bolts shot home. At this point the butler, steward, the delegate and the headman would arrive. The only person allowed into the master's study was the butler who passed the orders on to the others. The delegate's instructions were as follows: "Listen to our lord's command: see that you stay awake all night, patrol around our master's house, sound the rattles as loudly as possible, blow the horn, make the sounding-board hum, keep the piercing rattle going, hit the signal bell, do not wander about yawning, and remember carefully: you must see that the birds do not fly about making eerie sounds that might frighten the little children, or peck at the master's window-putty, perch on the roofs or mess about in the lofts. Be watchful, lads, be sure not to forget anything!" "We hear," was the response. These were the headman's instructions: "Tell both ranks of policemen that they should guard and keep a strict eye on all the populations, young and old alike, unceasingly protect the inhabitants from fire, and be ever vigilant, and watch for disturbance in any of the villages of Celevo, Medvedki and Goljavino, or any disorder on the rivers Ikša, Jachroma and Volguša. They should watch out for any strange manifestations in skies above or any fearsome earthquakes below their feet. If any such thing should come to pass or some other wonder befall them, then they should take no thought or action themselves, but at once go to their lord and report it all to his noble grace and commit it all firmly to memory." Vorob'eva, a maid, passed the steward's instructions on to him: "Our lord and master has commanded you to look after the provisions and to send a horse to Grigorovo for holy water. Place it in a vat, enclose it in ice, cover it all round and pile stones on it, with purity and prayer. Take good care of the people, look after the cattle, do not be careless or chatter idly. Remember this well!" this concluded the issue of orders. It was Vorob'eva who usually locked and unlocked the doors of the rooms. She would take the keys to the master himself and placing them at the head of his bed would say: "Rest, master, with Jesus Christ, sleep, master, under the protection of the Most Holy Mother of God, may your guardian angel stand over you, my master." Then she gave instructions to the maids on duty: "Mind the cats,[11] do not clatter about, do not speak loudly, do not fall asleep during the night, watch out for eavesdroppers, put out the light and be sure not to forget anything!"

After he had read the regulation evening prayers Vasilij Vasil'-evič would go to bed and crossing himself would say: "The servant of God lays himself to rest, he bears upon him Christ's seal and confirmation, he is guarded by the Mother of God's indestructible wall and defence, the Baptist's blessed right arm, the all-powerful and omnipotent cross of my guardian angel, the faces of the incorporeal powers and the prayers of all the saints. The cross is my stronghold, I drive out the Demon and root out all his enemy host, now and forever and unto the ages of ages. Amen!" At night in

Novospaskoe there was a tremendous din to be heard, banging, ringing, whistles and shouting, and the crashing and running of the four men on duty and the same number of watchmen on their rounds. If something prevented the master from going to sleep quickly, he did not go to bed and was out of sorts the whole night. In that case he would either begin reading aloud his favorite book, '*The Life of Alexander of Macedon*' by Quintus Curtius, or would sit down in a large armchair. . .and utter the following words, gradually raising and lowering his voice: "Satan, my enemy, depart from me into the empty places, into the thick forests and the earth's abysses where the light of God's countenance never goes! O Satan, my enemy! Depart from me and remove yourself to the dark places, to the bottomless seas, to the wondrous mountains, empty of dwellings and men, where the light of the Lord's countenance never goes! Damned ugly mug, begone and take yourself off to hell, depart from me you damned ugly mug and go to the outer darkness of hell and into the thrice-bottom-most fires of hell and never come here again. Amen! Amen! Amen! I say unto you, vanish utterly, thrice-damned one, thrice-pagan and thrice-accursed one! I blow upon you and I spit!" On completing the incantation, he would get up from his chair and begin pacing about through all seven of his rooms, banging his rattle. . . These peculiarities naturally aroused curiosity and many people watched him through chinks in the walls. But this situation too could be dealt with. The maids would start to shout out humorous and facetious remarks and they would throw cold water over the eavesdroppers from the upper windows. The master would approve of their actions saying: "The thief is getting his deserts, it is nothing to do with them, thrice-accursed ones! thrice-pagan! thrice-damned! untried! untortured! and unpunished!", stamping both his feet and repeating the same thing over and over again.[12]

What we have here is indeed a theater with its fixed and regularly repeated performances and texts. However, this was still *folk* theater with the rhymed monologues of the puppet-show and with a typical ending when the audience has water thrown over it from the stage. The "master" is on the stage, a character very well-known from the folk theater and popular prints. He is moreover in part also the "black magician" who makes incantations and reads aloud Latin interspersed with puppet-show verses in Russian. This fusion of the comic with the menacing and frightening in the performance is highly typical.

But the master was not just an actor, he was a spectator too, and for his part watched the carnivalized ritual into which he had turned the daily routine of his life. He enjoyed playing at the same time both menacing and comic roles and made sure that the others also did not depart from the style of the game. It is unlikely that he, being an enlightened astronomer and geographer, who had travelled all over Europe, talked with Peter the Great, was the grandson of Sophia's* favorite, V.V. Golicyn, believed outside the game that his favorite cat Van'ka had continued to "live out" dozens of years in exile and "to sigh over his crime

*Peter the Great's half-sister, who was Regent during Peter's minority.

240

daily." But he preferred living in this conventionally based pretend world, rather than in the one where, as he wrote in his calendar, "I, poor sinner that I am, have had my nails tidied up, which had been mutilated."[13]

Subsequently we can observe how the system of genres which took shape in the aesthetic consciousness of the high culture of the eighteenth century began to affect the behavior of the Russian gentry actively, creating the tree-structure system of *genres of behavior*.

Striking evidence of this process is the tendency to divide up the space of everyday living into scenic areas, the transition between these being accompanied by a change in the behavioral genre. Before Peter's time the binary opposition of ritual and non-ritual space in the world and in the area of human habitation was a familiar notion. This opposition was realized at various levels as "dwelling house – church," "area outside the altar – altar,"* "black corner – red corner in the peasant's hut"** and so on. This was carried over into the construction of the landowner's house as the division into living rooms and reception rooms. However, later on there emerged a tendency on the one hand to convert the reception rooms into living space and on the other to differentiate the living space. The move from the winter quarters to the summer residence – the switch within a matter of hours from the Classical or Baroque halls in the palace to a village "log cabin" or a "medieval" ruin, a Chinese village or Turkish kiosk, and in Kuskovo*** the move from the "Dutch cottage" to the "Italian cottage," – signalled a change in the type of behavior, speech and place. It was not only the palaces of the Tsars and great lords, but also the much more modest estates of the ordinary gentry that were filled with summer-houses, grottoes, temples for solitary contemplation, hideaways for lovers and suchlike. As the residence became a stage set (another parallel with the theater was that the change in space was accompanied by a change in the music that went with it), it might, if necessary, be made simpler and cheaper: instead of a construction of special space (as was the case in the outstanding architectural ensembles) there could be signs of such a construction which were within the means of the ordinary landowner as well.

A later development in the poetics of behavior was the evolution of the category of the role. Just as a theatrical role is the invariant of its typical performances, so an eighteenth century man would choose a certain type of behavior for himself that simplified his real, everyday life-style and elevated it to a certain idealized form. This role as a rule involved the selection of a historical figure, a statesman, man of letters or character from a poem or tragedy. This figure came to be the idealized double of the actual man, in some sense displacing his patron saint. His

---

*In an Orthodox church the altar area is screened off from the main body of the church by the "royal doors."

**The "red corner" in a peasant's hut was where the icons and icon lamp hung.

***The estate of the Šeremet'evs, near Moscow.

programme of behavior was oriented on the chosen personality and labels such as the "Russian Pindar," the "Northern Voltaire," "our La Fontaine," the "New Sterne" or "Minerva," "Astraea," the "Russian Caesar" or the "Fabius of our day" became something like additional personal names. ("Minerva," for example, became Catherine the Great's literary name.)

This tendency, while, on the one hand, it built up a person's subjective self-assessment and organized his behavior and, on the other, determined how his contemporaries perceived his personality, also entailed an integrated programme for personal conduct which in some respect predicted the nature of his future actions and how they would be received. This gave rise to anecdotal epics which were built up on the principle of accumulation. The role or mask was the thematic pivot onto which more and more new episodes from the anecdotal biography could be strung. This kind of behavior text was in principle open-ended: it could be infinitely expanded, being enriched by ever more new "incidents."

The number of these possible roles was by no means unlimited and in fact was not even very large. In many ways it recalls the set of characters in various kinds of literary texts and theatrical productions.

First of all there are roles derived from ordinary neutral behavior by the quantitative exaggeration of all its characteristics or by turning them inside out.

Among the characteristic masks from this set, the variant of the "warrior" [bogatyr'] was typical of the eighteenth century. This role was created by the quantitative increase of certain of a person's normal, neutral characteristics. The eighteenth century teems with giants. Puškin's description of Peter the Great as a "miracle-worker giant"* clearly derives from the eighteenth century and in anecdotes about Lomonosov his physical strength, which was out of the ordinary, the heroic scale of his amusements, etc. are unfailingly emphasized. The portrayal of Suvorov as a "miracle-warrior" [čudo-bogatyr'] belongs here (cf. "you have *doubled* the warrior's stride" [my italics – Ju. L.]; "warrior's" means twice as much as is usual[14]). The most complete embodiment of this tendency was the epic of anecdotes about Potemkin. This evolved into a complete picture of a man whose natural endowments were *all* abnormally large. It included stories of his monstrous appetite and digestion. (These were very much in the spirit of Rabelais and the Russian popular print "He ate gloriously and drank to his heart's content." The Russian versions completely lost the overtones of political caricature characteristic of the French originals, reverting to their roots in the fair-ground popular humor.) Cf. stories such as:

During the last century, in the Tavrida Palace, Prince Potemkin

*In his poem "The Feast of Peter the Great" (1835).

was passing through the washroom with Lavašev and Prince Dol-gorukov. They saw a magnificent bath made of silver.

Lavašev: "What a fine bath!"

Prince Potemkin: "If you can *fill* it (this is what appears in the written version, but a different word appears in the oral version), I'll give it to you as a present."[15]

The audience was meant not only to admire the generous sweep of Potemkin's imagination, but also to assume that he, as the legal owner of such a magnificent bath, might himself easily perform such a feat. Potemkin's legendary character had another aspect: it was no accident that Puškin, hearing that Denis Davydov's article had been submitted to the censor Michajlovskij-Danilevskij to be approved, said: "One might just as well have sent Prince Potemkin to learn from eunuchs how to deal with women."[16] This background serves to emphasize how immense were his political schemes, his banquets and feasts, his extravagance, thieving and bribe-taking, his magnanimity, generosity and patriotism. In fact any anecdote, whether about his criminal or heroic features, could join into the biographical epic of anecdotes about Potemkin, but only if these features are magnified to the fullest possible extent.

Another typical role that organized several biographical legends and actual biographies is that of the wit, humorist and buffoon. It too is associated with the world of the puppet theater and the popular print. Such, for example, is the biography of A.D. Kop'ev,* episodes from which as retailed by his contemporaries, generally, are no more than random anecdotes about a wit who manages to extricate himself from awkward situations by his bold replies. Vjazemskij even while narrating episodes from Kop'ev's "biography" pointed out that these actions and responses were attributed to other people as well (to A.N. Golicyn) or might even be well known French anecdotes. The mask or role has a force or attraction and the legendary biography becomes a text that tends to expand by absorbing a variety of anecdotes about wits.

S.N. Marin's** case is especially interesting in this connection. He was a military man who had been hit by four grapeshot bullets at Austerlitz (in the head, hand and two in the chest) and was awarded the golden sword for bravery and promoted to the rank of staff-captain. At Friedland he was wounded by a shell fragment in the head and received the Cross of St. Vladimir and was rewarded with an aide-de-camp's aiguillettes. In 1812 he was duty general under Bagration and died at the end of the campaign from wounds, ill-health and exhaustion. He had been an active politician and a participant in the events of March 12, 1801***; he had met and talked with Napoleon to whom he conveyed the Russian Emperor's letter; and lastly he was a satirical poet. But all

*A.D. Kop'ev, minor writer of the late eighteenth century.
**S.N. Marin, 1775–1813.
***The palace coup when Paul was assassinated.

this was pushed into the background in the eyes of his contemporaries by his reputation as a joker and a wit. This is the image of Marin which entered the consciousness of historians of Russian culture at the beginning of the nineteenth century.

The "Russian Diogenes," the "new cynic" was another widespread type that incorporated a combination of philosophical contempt for wealth with poverty, breaking the norms of propriety and, as a necessary concomitant, desperate drinking. The stereotype for this was created by Barkov* and subsequently provided the overall pattern for the image and behavior of Kostrov,** Milonov and dozens of other literary figures.

A person who oriented his conduct on a definite role made his life resemble a sort of improvised performance in which solely the type of behavior of each character was predictable, not the plots and situations arising from their conflict. The action was open-ended and could be prolonged by an endless accretion of episodes. This way of structuring one's life gravitated towards the folk theater and was ill-adapted for understanding tragic conflicts. A striking example was the biography of Suvorov which had a mythology built around it. In constructing this idealized myth about himself Suvorov was clearly orienting himself on Plutarch's characters, principally Caesar. This exalted image might, however, at times, in letters to his daughter or when he was dealing with soldiers, be replaced by the figure of a Russian warrior. (In letters to his daughter, the well-known "Suvoročka," the stylized descriptions of the military operations bear such a striking resemblance to the fantastic trans-formations of the scene of battle in Captain Tušin's mind in *War and Peace* that Tolstoj must have been familiar with this source.)

However, Suvorov's behavior was guided by two norms rather than one. The second was clearly oriented on the role of the buffoon. Endless anecdotes relate to this role, recounting his eccentricities, his cockcrows and his comic escapades. The combination of two mutually incompatible roles in the behavior of one and the same person may be associated with the importance of contrast in the poetics of the pre-Romantic period. (See the fragment from Batjuškov's notebook [17]: "Recently I happened to become acquainted with a strange man, *one of many*!" See also, "My Uncle's Character" by Griboedov[18]; or the extract from Puškin's high school diaries for December 17, 1815: "Do you want to see a strange man, an eccentric?"[19])

The unpredictability of such a person's behavior came about because his interlocutors could never guess which of two possible roles would be actualized. While the aesthetic effect of behavior oriented on one constant

*I.S. Barkov (1732–1768), translator and author of ribald poetry.
**E.I. Kostrov (d. 1796), poet, translator among other things of Apuleius' *The Golden Ass*.

role lay in the fact that in different situations a *single* mask would be sharply expressed, here the effect lay in the fact that the audience was constantly surprised. For instance, Prince Esterhazy who had been sent by the Vienna Court to hold talks with Suvorov complained to Komarovskij: "How can you talk with a man from whom you cannot get any sense?" He was even more amazed at the next meeting: *"C'est un diable d'homme. Il a autant d'esprit, que de connaissance."*[20] ["A devil of a man. He has as much wit as he has knowledge."]

The next step in the evolution of the poetics of behavior may be described as the transition from role to plot. A plot is not just a chance component of everyday life. Indeed, the emergence of plot as a definite category that organizes narrative texts in art may in the final analysis be explained by the need to choose a behavior strategy in extra-literary activity.

For everyday behavior can acquire ultimate meaning only if the particular string of individual acts at the level of reality can be correlated with a sequence of actions which, having an overall meaning and finality, functions at the code level as a generalized sign for the situation, or succession of individual acts and their results, i.e. as a plot. The presence in the consciousness of a particular community of a totality of plots makes it possible to encode real behavior, to classify it as significant or not, and to attribute meaning to it. The lowest units of semiotic behavior (gesture and individual act), as a rule, acquire their semantic and stylistic value, not in isolation, but in relation to categories of a higher level: plot, style and genre of behavior. The sum total of all the plots that encode the behavior of an individual in a particular epoch can be defined as the mythology of everyday and social behavior.

In the last third of the eighteenth century, a time when in post-Petrine Russian culture a mythology of this kind was evolving, the chief source for behavior plots was high literature which did not treat of everyday matters: the ancient historians, Classical tragedies, and in some cases, the lives of the saints.

To regard one's life as a text which is organized according to the rules of a particular plot implies laying heavy emphasis on the "unity of the action" and focussing one's life on one immutable goal. The theatrical category of the "ending," the fifth act, took on special significance. Structuring one's life as a sort of improvised performance in which the actor was required to keep within the bounds of his role created a text without an ending. In it more and more new scenes added to and varied the course of events. The introduction of a plot immediately introduced the idea of an ending and at the same time endowed the ending with a determining meaning. Death and destruction, as the subject of constant reflections, came to be seen as the crowning event to a life. This naturally activated heroic and tragic models of behavior. By identifying yourself with the hero of a tragedy you not only acquired a type of behavior but also a type of dying. Concern with the "fifth" act became a distinctive feature of the "heroic" life at the end of the eighteenth and the beginning of the nineteenth centuries.

> I was born so that the whole world should be the spectator
> Of my triumph or my ruin...[21]

These verses by Lermontov demonstrate with exceptional clarity the idea of the individual as an actor playing out the drama of his life before a mass of spectators (Romantic exaggeration manifests itself here in the fact that the "whole world" is the audience), and the idea that the culmination of one's life is to be identified with the theatrical notion of the fifth act (triumph or ruin). Hence Lermontov's constant preoccupation with the finale of his life: "The end, how sonorous this word is."

> Nor shall I be forgotten when I die. My death
> Will be terrible: alien lands
> Will be amazed at it, but in my own country
> All will curse even my memory.[22]

In the early morning of December 14, 1825, when the Decembrists went out onto Senate Square, A.I. Odoevskij* cried out: "We shall die, brothers, oh how gloriously we shall die!" The rising had not yet begun, and there was no reason at all to expect failure. However, a heroic end did indeed give the character of high tragedy to the event, exalting the participants in their own eyes and in those of future generations to the level of characters from a dramatic plot.

In this connection Radiščev's career is of exceptional interest. The circumstances of his death are still unexplained.**

The reports of threats supposedly addressed to Radiščev by Zavadovskij, or even by A.R. Voroncov,*** which have appeared many times in the scholarly literature, are not trustworthy. Of course, Radiščev could easily have aroused hostility by some careless action or word. However, to anyone who is in the least familiar with the political climate—"the glorious beginning of the days of Alexander"—it is obvious that this was not a time when a courageous project, written at government command (and no other "dangerous" activities were attributed to Radiščev during these months!), might provoke any really serious repression.**** Puškin's

*Prince A.I. Odoevskij (1802–1839), poet, follower of Ryleev, condemned to hard labor.
**On A.N. Radiščev, see above, Part I, Ch. 1, p. 26. He committed suicide in 1802.
***Count P.V. Zavadovskij (1739–1812) was chairman of the Commission on the Revision of the Laws to which Radiščev was appointed member in 1801. Count A.R. Voroncov (1741–1805), Radiščev's lifelong friend and protector.
****Radiščev's "Project for a civil code," which has not survived, made radical proposals for reforms.

246

version is clearly tendentious.* There is a hint of irrepressible irony in it which was evoked by the lack of proportion between Zavadovskij's utterance ("said to him in friendly reproof") and Radiščev's reaction ("Radiščev *saw* a threat. He went home distressed and terrified. . .") [my italics, Ju. L.]. Puškin's article has not yet received a generally accepted interpretation, and until this is done and its purpose properly explained, it is highly risky to use excerpts from it. One thing is clear: Radiščev was a brave man and it would have been impossible to scare him with the shadow of a danger, an ambiguous threat. His suicide was not brought about by fear. It is hardly worth seriously refuting. Štorm's anecdotal argument to the effect that with regard to Radiščev's suicide "everything was of significance, even the gradual deterioration in the weather recorded in the meteorological bulletin of *The St. Petersburg Gazette* for the 11th and 12th of September."[23] It was not only the weather that played a fateful role in Radiščev's life at this point, in Štorm's view, not only his disappointment at his failure to improve the condition of the peasants, but also circumstances "concerning him personally." According to him, one of these, "without doubt," was that one of Radiščev's distant relatives had been convicted of fraud.[24]

All attempts to find actual grounds in his biography for this tragic act in the autumn of 1802 have led nowhere.

Yet this act, though there were no grounds for it in the biographical circumstances of the last months of the writer's life, fits neatly into a long chain of his numerous meditations on this theme. In his *Life of Fedor Vasil'evič Ušakov* [1789], in *A Journey from St. Petersburg to Moscow* [1790], and his treatise, *On Man, his Mortality and Immortality* [1792] and other works, Radiščev keeps coming back to the problem of suicide. These thoughts are, on the one hand, linked with the ethics of the eighteenth century materialists and, directly contrary to the Church's teaching, affirm a person's right to dispose of his own life. On the other hand, the problem has not only a philosophical, but also a political aspect: the right to commit suicide and the liberation of the individual from the fear of death, puts a limit to his obedience and restricts the power of tyrants. Free of the obligation to live under any conditions however bad, the individual becomes free in an absolute sense and thereby nullifies the power of despotism. This notion occupied an extremely large place in Radiščev's political system and he returned to it again and again. "Oh my dear friends! rejoice at my ending: it will be the end of sorrow and torment. You who have been wrenched away[25] from the yoke of prejudice, remember this, that misery is no longer the lot of one who has died."[26]

This thought was not unique to Radiščev. In *Vadim of Novgorod* by Knjažnin** Vadim's last remark to Rjurik runs as follows:

---

*Puškin tells that Radiščev was driven to suicide by Zavadovskij's threats of punishment for his Project. ("Aleksandr Radiščev," 1836.)

**Ja.B. Knjažnin (1742–1791) wrote his tragedy *Vadim of Novgorod* in 1789.

Surrounded by your victorious army,
You in your crown who have the power to behold everything at
   your feet,
What are you compared with one who dares to die?[27]

Cf. also the ending of *Marfa Posadnica* by F. Ivanov:*

Marfa: .... "In the Tsar you see a monster, in me an exemplar:
          Having lived without baseness, die without baseness"
          (stabs herself). [28]

The readiness to face death is what distinguishes a man from a slave in Radiščev's view. In the chapter "Mednoe" [in his *Journey from St. Petersburg to Moscow*] addressing the serf footman who is both his debauched master's accomplice and his victim, the author writes: "Noble thoughts are foreign to your mind. *You do not know how to die* [my italics, Ju. L.]. You will bow down and be a slave in spirit as in estate." [29] The image of Fedor Ušakov's courageous death** reminded Radiščev, "of people who bravely take their own lives." The last exhortation the author put into Ušakov's mouth was, "that you should be steadfast in your thoughts in order to face death unflinchingly." [30]

Radiščev regarded heroic behavior on the part of the individual as of enormous significance as it provided an educative spectacle for his fellow citizens, for he constantly reiterated that man is an imitative animal. This visual, demonstrative aspect of personal conduct made the theatrical element in the life of an individual especially relevant if he laid claim to be a "teacher...of moral fibre" and an "example of courage." [31]

A man born with tender feelings, endowed with a powerful imagination, impelled by ambition, comes forth from amidst the people. He mounts the rostrum. All eyes are fixed on him, everyone impatiently awaits his utterance. Applause or ridicule worse than death awaits him.[32]

The blend of the visual and theatrical with the set of ideas of heroic death discussed above gave Addison's tragedy *Cato*** a special meaning for Radiščev. It was the hero of this work that became a sort of code for Radiščev's own conduct.

In the chapter "Krestcy" in *A Journey from St. Petersburg to Moscow* Radiščev put the following words into the mouth of the virtuous father:

This is my last will and testament. If outrageous fortune hurl upon you all its slings and arrows, if there is no refuge left on earth for your virtue, if, driven to extremes, you find no sanctuary from

*F. F. Ivanov (1777–1816), his tragedy on the subject of Martha, Mayor of Novgorod (1809) was extremely popular.
**F. V. Ušakov (1747–1770), follower of Helvetius, took poison when his death agonies became unbearable.
***Joseph Addison (1672–1719), his tragedy on the theme of Cato of Utica was produced in 1713 and had enormous success.

248

oppression; then remember that you are a man, call to mind your true greatness, seize the crown of bliss which they are trying to take from you. Die. As a legacy I leave to you the words of the dying Cato. [33]

Which words "of the dying Cato" did Radiščev have in mind? Ja. L. Barskov in the commentary of the Academy edition assumed that "he had Plutarch's account of Cato's dying speech in mind."[34] * The most recent commentators share this view. [35] However, it is clear that the reference is to the final monologue from Addison's tragedy, the monologue about which Radiščev wrote later in Siberia:

> I have always derived the utmost satisfaction in reading the meditations of people standing at the edge of the grave, on the threshold of eternity, and, having thought over the cause of their ending and the motives acting upon them, I have derived much that I have been able to find nowhere else. . .You know the monologue of Shakespeare's Hamlet and that of Cato in Addison's play. [36]

Radiščev quoted this monologue in his own translation at the end of the chapter "Bronnicy" in *A Journey from St. Petersburg to Moscow*:

> But a certain mysterious voice says to me, that 'something will forever live.'
> "The stars shall fade away, the sun himself
> Grow dim with age, and nature sink in years;
> But thou shalt flourish in immortal youth,
> Unhurt amidst the wars of elements,
> The wrecks of matter, and the crush of worlds."

Radiščev provided this extract with the remark: *"The Death of Cato*, Addison's tragedy, Act V, scene 1." [37]

The connection between the nobleman's speech at Krestcy and this extract is obvious and a constant one for Radiščev. The idea of readiness to commit suicide is only a variant of the theme of the heroic feat. And this in its turn is associated with faith in the immortality of the soul:

> It does happen, and many cases have been reported, that men, who are told that they must die, face the meeting with advancing death with calm assurance and fortitude. We have seen and do see people who take their own lives courageously. In very truth you need courage and spiritual strength to meet your own annihilation with an unflinching eye. . .It is sometimes the case that such a person sees beyond the bounds of the grave and expects to rise again. [38]

Thus Radiščev's suicide was not an act of desperation, an admission of defeat. It was a long premeditated act of defiance, a lesson in patriotic

*Cato is supposed to have said: "Now I am my own master."

fortitude and unwavering love of freedom. It is difficult now to reconstruct in detail his attitude to the political situation at the beginning of Alexander's reign. By the autumn of 1802 he had evidently come to the conclusion that he had to perform some feat calculated to arouse and mobilize Russian patriots. Though we read in his childrens' reminiscences that during his last days he was in a state of agitation and once even said: "Well, my dear children, what if I am again exiled to Siberia?", if one bears in mind all that he did at the beginning of Alexander I's reign, such an assumption seems to be so ill-founded that one might naturally conclude as did his son Pavel: "Mental breakdown was becoming more and more marked."[39] Pavel Radiščev was young when his father died, and when he wrote his memoirs, in spite of his unfeigned and touching admiration for his father's memory, he quite failed to understand the essence of Radiščev's views. The words recorded in the memoirs were obviously not occasioned by mental sickness. Most probably Radiščev was in an excited state of mind having decided that the time had come for the final achievement, "the fifth act of his life." However, at a given moment he had not decided what form this act of protest would take or whether it would be bound up with his death. But the inertia of the long contemplated action evidently triumphed. Puškin had grounds for saying that from the time of Ušakov's deathbed conversations with Radiščev, "suicide had become one of his favorite themes for meditation."[40]

We may assume that Radiščev's view of himself "as a Russian Cato" determined not only his own behavior, but also the view his contemporaries took of his action. Addison's tragedy was well-known to the Russian reader. So, for instance, book VIII of the journal *Hippocrene* [*Ippokrena*] for 1801 contained a characteristic selection of materials as well as a full prose translation (by Gart [Hart? – Trans.]) of Addison's tragedy entitled "The Death of Cato or the Birth of the Roman Autocracy. A Tragedy by the famous Addison"; we find also extracts entitled "Brutus" and "Hamlet's Thoughts on Death." It is interesting to find Cato's and Hamlet's monologues juxtaposed, an association which we are already familiar with from Radiščev. This is what is said about Brutus:

> Certain of your strict rules imply that you have sinned in shedding Caesar's blood; but these honest people are mistaken. *What mercy does the life of one who seizes excessive power deserve from one who would rather kill himself than accept enslavement* [my italics, Ju. L.].[41]

The hero of Suškov's tale, *A Russian Werther** killed himself leaving behind him on his small table Addison's *Cato* open at the passage quoted in the chapter "Bronnicy." S. Glinka,** who admired Radiščev (one of his friends, the writer's son, described Glinka as one of Radiščev's

*M. V. Suškov (d. 1799), his *A Russian Werther* was published in 1801.
**S. N. Glinka (1775 – 1847), writer and publisher.

"greatest devotees"), at the time when he was a young cadet, had only three possessions, the books *A Journey from St. Petersburg to Moscow, Vadim of Novgorod* and *A Sentimental Journey* [by Sterne]. Once he was put in the guardhouse:

> Cato's noble deed in turning his dagger against himself when Julius Caesar had him put in chains, whirled round in my head, and I was ready to dash my head against the wall.[42]

Both the image of Cato, and Cato as portrayed by Addison, constantly attracted Karamzin. In his review of *Emilia Galotti* published in the *Moscow Journal** he described Emilia as a "heroine who speaks in Cato's language about human freedom." "Thereupon Emilia called for a dagger in her fanaticism believing that suicide was a sacred deed."[43] Later Karamzin was to call Martha Posadnica "the Cato of her republic."

In his *Letters of a Russian Traveller*, Karamzin quoted the same lines from Voltaire which Radiščev's son later recalled when trying to explain the motives for his father's action:

Quand on n'est rien et qu'on est sans espoir,
La vie est un opprobre et la mort un devoir. . .

[When one is nothing and without hope, Life is a burden and death a duty.]

Elsewhere Karamzin wrote: "Addison's fine tragedy is particularly good where Cato speaks and acts."[44] Karamzin included "Cato the suicide" among the ancient heroes in his *Historical Eulogy Addressed to Catherine II,*[45]* and in 1811 he wrote in the Grand duchess Catherine Pavlovna's album a quotation from Rousseau where Cato is called "a god among mortals."[46] Of special interest here is that in an article by Karamzin published in *The European Gazette*, and which was a coded reaction to Radiščev's death,[47] we find an elaborate polemic not with Radiščev, but directed against a false reading of the ideas and images in Addison's *Cato*:

> Budgell,** a perceptive English writer, was a relation of the great Addison. They shared the publication of *The Spectator* and other journals. All the pieces in *The Spectator* signed X were by him. Addison tried to help Budgell make money, but he was a spendthrift; he was completely ruined after Addison's death and finally threw himself into the Thames leaving in his room the following note:
> What Cato did and Addison approv'd cannot be wrong!
> We know that Addison wrote the tragedy "Cato's Death." So moral an author would not have approved of suicide in a Christian, but allowed himself to praise it in Cato, and the fine monologue: "It

---

*Karamzin wrote his review of Lessing's tragedy in 1791.
**Eustace Budgell (1686 – 1737), Addison's cousin and collaborator.

must be so. . .Plato, thou reasonst well," released the unfortunate Budgell from the pangs of conscience which might have saved him from suicide. Good authors! think of the consequences of what you write! [48]

Karamzin condemned the very principle of constructing one's life according to a dramatic plot and at the same time showed clearly that he had had no trouble in deciphering Radiščev's action.

To approach one's own life as if it were a plot marked a change in the poetics of behavior from elemental creativity into consciously regulated activity. The next step was the attempt, typical of the period of Romanticism, to fuse the biographical and artistic texts into one. Poems began to be joined together into lyrical cyles to form "poetic diaries" and "novels of one's own Life," and the biographical legend became an essential condition for the perception of any text as artistic. The trend towards fragmentation in Romantic texts has long been noted. However, it is vital to emphasize that this fragmentation was compensated for by plunging the text, once it had been fixed graphically (in print or manuscript), into the context of oral legend about the author's personality. This legend proved to be the most powerful factor regulating both the poet's actual behavior and the way in which the audience perceived this behavior itself and the writer's works as well.

The development of the poetics of behavior to the absolute limit during the Romantic era was necessarily followed by a demonstrative exclusion of this category by the realist writer. The poet's life recedes from the realm of the artistically significant facts (the best evidence for this is the appearance of parodic pseudo-biographies like that of Koz'ma Prutkov*). In losing to some extent the element of play, art stops leaping over the footlights, it no longer steps off the pages of the novel into the realm of the author's and readers' real lives.

However, the disappearance of the poetics of behavior was not destined to be long. Having disappeared with the last of the Romantics in the 1840's, it was resurrected in the years between 1890 and 1900 in the biographies of the Symbolists, "žiznestroitel'stvo" ["life-construction"], "the theater for one actor," "the theater of life" and other manifestations of twentieth century culture.

Translated by N.F.C. Owen

NOTES

1   *Junosti čestnoe zercalo*, 1767, p. 29.
2   Ibid, pp. 41–42.
3   *Russkij archiv*, 1888, vol. I, book 4, p. 547.

*Koz'ma Prutkov was the collective pseudonym of a group of writers including A.K. Tolstoj. Koz'ma Prutkov "died" in 1863.

4   Selivanov 1881, p. 115.

5   The idea that the clothing of the gentry was theatrical costume rather than everyday gear is illustrated by the fact that even in the twentieth century actors in the Russian folk theater performed in ordinary jackets which were decorated with orders, ribbons and shoulder-straps to indicate they were theatrical costumes. In P.G. Bogatyrev's description of folk theater costumes it is not only Tsar Maximilian or King Mamaj, but also Anika the Warrior, Zmejulan and others who have ribbons across their shoulders and shoulder-straps on them, in order that the actor on the stage "should not look like the surrounding audience," as P.G. Bogatyrev remarks (see: Bogatyrev 1923, pp. 83–84). It is interesting to set this against the same author's statement that in the Czech puppet-theater "the puppeteer quite deliberately makes the speech of upper class people incorrect" (ibid., p. 71). Obviously the theatrical clothes are incorrect too as compared with normal dress. They are made from materials *that seem* to be real, but are not in actual fact. In this respect they are like the clothes used to dress the bodies of the dead (for example, *bosovki* –shoes without soles), which were made up specially before funerals and which like the theatrical costumes *represented* high quality clothing. For the consciousness still closely linked with the pre-Petrine tradition, the theater continued to be a "spectacle" [*igrišče*], a sort of masquerade and carnival, in particular, it is marked by the obligatory feature of dressing up or change of costume. If we recall that from a popular (i.e. traditional pre-Petrine) point of view the fact of changing clothes was invariably perceived as of the Devil and only permitted at definite points in the calendar (Yuletide), and then only as a form of magical play with the powers of darkness, then it is natural that the theatricalization of the way of life of the gentry and its perception as a constant carnival (an endless festival and a permanent masquerade) was accompanied by a definite religious and ethical attitude towards that kind of life. On the other hand it is no surprise there was a tendency for the aestheticized life-style of the gentry to absorb peasant life into its orbit, and this came to be seen through the prism of the idyll. Again we find a great many attempts to create theatricalized images of the Russian peasantry in real life (against the back-ground of and in contrast with actual peasant life). Such were the round dances by peasant girls wearing silk sarafans, which were performed along the banks of the Volga during Catherine the Great's voyage; such were Šeremet'ev's theatrical villages, or the Klejnmichel family who dressed up in Georgian peasant costume at a ball and touchingly thanked Arakčeev for his kind help.

Elizabeth Petrovna's coronation provided a conspicuous example of the erosion of the boundaries between stage performance and life; it was accompanied by dressing up and a switch of sex and age roles. The coronation was marked by splendid masquerades and spectacles. On May 29, 1742 in the palace on the Jauza the opera *La Clemenza di Tito** was put on. Since the role of Tito was meant to be taken as an allusion to Elizabeth, the part was taken by a woman dressed up as a man, Signora Giorgi. The audience in the hall, moreover, because of the masquerade that was to follow the performance was in masquerade dress. If we bear in mind that on the day of the coup Elizabeth was wearing a male guardsman's dress uniform and that the usual arrangement for mask balls at her court was for men to dress up as women (especially the young cadets), and the women as men, then it is easy to imagine how all this must have looked to the peasants who were spectators, and the servants and the crowd on the streets. (See Arapov 1861, p. 44).

6   If the average, neutral behavior of the European "burgher" when trans-planted to Russia was transformed by becoming of much greater semiotic significance, then the transformations in the behavior of Russians visiting Europe at

*by Johann Adolph Hasse (1699 – 1783)

that time are no less interesting. In some cases this was a continuation of the pre-Petrine tradition and the semiotic significance was sharply increased. Close attention to the sense of a gesture or ritual, the perception of any and every detail of behavior as a sign in these cases are understandable: the individual saw himself as a representative, an accredited person, and incorporated the laws of diplomatic protocol into his daily conduct. The European observers, however, assumed that this was in fact the normal behavior of Russians.

But the reverse transformation was also possible: behavior could be markedly deritualized and, against the background of the European life-style, appeared more natural. Thus, Peter the Great while being quite at home with the restrictive norms of diplomatic ritual, during his travels abroad preferred to astonish the Europeans by the unexpected simplicity of his behavior, more direct not only than the usual norms of "royal" behavior but also than the "burghers." For instance, during his visit to Paris in 1716 he demonstrated his understanding of the usual ritual: although burning with impatience to see the city he did not go out of the house until the king had visited him. During the Regent's visit, he invited him into his room, but went in first and was the first to sit down in an armchair (the Regent also sat in an archchair while they conversed, but Prince Kurakin remained standing while he interpreted); when, however, he paid a return call on the seven-year old Louis XV, seeing the latter coming down the steps towards the coach, "Peter jumped out, ran to the king, picked him up and carried him up the steps into the hall." (S.M. Solov'ev, book IV, p. 365).

7   The diagram indicates the possibility of a career in holy orders. This was not very typical, but was not totally excluded. Members of the nobility are to be found both among the white and the black clergy in the eighteenth and the beginning of the nineteenth centuries. One essential feature of the eighteenth century is not reflected in the diagram: the attitude to suicide changed decisively in post-Petrine Russia. Towards the end of the century aristocratic youth was swept by a veritable wave of suicides. Radiščev saw in man's freedom of choice between life and death a promise of liberation from political tyranny. This topic was actively discussed in literature (by Karamzin and "Russian Werthers") and the press. And so by adding yet another alternative the very fact of existence became the result of personal choice.

8   "He was held in detention for about two years until 1758, the third day of March, and while there he suffered terrible torture and was subjected to indescribable torments. While he was being lifted onto the rack he had his shoulder-blades dislocated, hot irons passed along his back, red-hot needles stuck under his fingernails, was beaten with a knout and, finally, returned to his family in a mutilated state." "Unfortunately for posterity it is not known what was his actual crime," was the melancholy comment of Petr Kazanskij (see Kazanskij 1847, pp. 57–58).

9   This was the master's favorite cat. Once it had climbed into a basket of fish and eaten a fish of an exceptionally delicious kind that had been prepared for the master of the house. It had got stuck there and choked. The servants reported the cat's crime but not the fact that it was dead, and the master sent it into exile (note added by Kazanskij).

10   This was the name of the woman whose carelessness caused Novospaskoe to burn down in 1775. Vasilij Vasil'evič was so frightened by this fire that he ordered all his household serfs to do their cooking in a special room, but as he had more than three hundred, it is no surprise that the command was not able to be carried out (ibid.).

11   There were seven cats in Vasilij Vasil'evič's rooms. They were able to wander about freely during the day, but at night they would be fastened to a table with seven legs. One maid was detailed to be in charge of each cat. If it happened that one of the cats broke away from the table and came to the master, then cats and

254

girls would be subjected to punishment (ibid.).

12 Kazanskij 1847, pp. 60 –70.

13 Ibid., p. 58. Cf.: "Count P.M. Skavronskij, a famous man of great wealth,. . . surrounded himself with singers and musicians: he spoke with his servants to music, in recitative; the butler would announce in a velvety baritone that his meal was served. The coachman talked with him in sonorous octaves, the postilions used descants and altos, the footmen were tenors etc. During formal dinners and balls his servants formed trios, duets and choirs while they attended the guests. The master himself responded likewise in musical form." (Pyljaev 1897, p. 88).

14 Suvorov's instructions to Miloradovič; see Miljutin 1852, vol. I, p. 588. For the tendency in medieval texts to construct outstanding characters as possessing the same set of qualities as other people, but in superlative degree see Birge Vitz 1975; this kind of construction is based on a belief in the immutability of the role allotted to a man from above. However, the tradition it created of "heroic" ["bogatyrskij"] images (= models) influenced the behavior of people even when the role became the result of an active choice made by a man himself.

15 Vjazemskij 1929, p. 194.

16 *Russkij arhiv* 1880, III, book 2, p. 228, note.

17 See Batjuškov 1934, pp. 378 – 380.

18 See Griboedov 1956, pp. 414 –415.

19 See Puškin PSS, XII, pp. 301 – 302.

20 Komarovskij 1914, p. 90.

21 Lermontov 1954, vol. II, p. 38. ("To *," 1832)

22 Ibid., vol. I, p. 185. ("June 11, 1831," 1831)

23 Štorm 1968, p. 439. See my review of the first edition (Lotman 1966). "The second, corrected edition" did not take account of criticism of the first, and only added considerably to the number of errors. We will note only that the author considered it fitting to conclude the book "with some unpublished lines in the spirit of the Radiščev tradition" from a poem by an unknown author, hinting that it was probably Puškin. Unfortunately, the lines quoted are standard knowledge, being an extract from Vjazemskij's poem "Negodovanie" [*Indignation*]. These verses are just as "unpublished" as their author is "unknown." What we have here before us is no chance error, but an unmistakable case of dilettantism, which forms a fitting conclusion to Štorm's book.

24 Ibid., p. 383.

25 The word *istorgnutyj* appears in the printed text by mistake for *istorgnutye* [i.e. singular instead of plural].

26 Radiščev PSS Vol II, p. 101 (*On Man, his Mortality and Immortality*); cf. Montesquieu 1748, book I, chapter VIII.

27 Knjažnin 1914, p. 63.

28 F.F. Ivanov 1824, part II, p. 89.

29 Radiščev PSS, Vol. I, p. 351. [English translation of *A Journey from St. Petersburg to Moscow*, see Radiščev 1958, p. 190. References in square brackets given below are to this edition.]

30 Radiščev PSS, Vol. I, p. 184 (*The Life of F. V. Ušakov*).

31 Ibid., p. 155.

32 Ibid., p. 387 [p. 231] ("Eulogy on Lomonosov").

33 Ibid., p. 295 [p. 123].

34 Ibid., p. 485.

35 Kulakova & Zapadov 1974, p. 157.

36 Radiščev PSS, Vol. II, pp. 97–98   (*On Man, his Mortality and Immortality*).

37 Ibid., Vol. I, p. 269 [p. 91].

38 Ibid., pp. 183 – 184 (*Life of F. V. Ušakov*).

39   See Radiščev 1959, p. 95. Radiščev was in fact ill in August 1802 (see his letter to his parents of August 18, PSS, Vol. III, p. 535). However there is absolutely no reason to think that reference is being made to *mental* illness. This is just as much a euphemism as is the reference to his death from consumption in the official papers.

40   Puškin PSS, Vol. XII, p. 31 ("Aleksandr Radiščev," 1836).

41   *Ippokrena*, VIII, 1801, pp. 52–53.

42   Glinka 1895, p. 103.

43   *Moskovskij Žurnal*, part I, 1791, p. 67.

44   Karamzin, 1964, Vol. I, p. 573.

45   Karamzin 1848, Vol. I, p. 312.

46   *Letopis'* 1859, book 2, p. 167.

47   For evidence in support of this assumption and the text of the note see Lotman 1962, pp. 53–60.

48   *Vestnik Evropy*, 1802, no. 19, p. 209.

PART THREE

257

TSAR AND PRETENDER: *SAMOZVANČESTVO*
OR ROYAL IMPOSTURE IN RUSSIA AS A
CULTURAL-HISTORICAL PHENOMENON

B. A. Uspenskij

1. Although *samozvančestvo*, or royal imposture, is not an exclusively Russian phenomenon, in no other country has it been so frequent, or played such a significant role in the history of people and state. [1] To write the history of Russia and avoid the question of royal imposture is impossible: in the words of Ključevskij, "royal imposture in Russia, ever since the first False Dmitri * made his appearance, became a chronic malady of the state from that moment on; almost until the end of the eighteenth century, hardly a single reign passed without a pretender." [2] From the beginning of the seventeenth century and even up to the middle of the nineteenth, it would be hard to point to more than two or three decades in which a pretender did not put himself forward, and indeed, in some periods, pretenders can be counted by the dozen. [3]

The root-causes of this phenomenon have not yet been fully explained. For the most part scholars have attempted to solve the question of royal imposture by reference to either a social or a political perspective: on the social level it is seen as a specific and persistent form of anti-feudalism, and on the political level as a struggle for power. Neither of these approaches, however, elucidates the *specific* nature of royal imposture as a cultural phenomenon: as we shall see below, royal imposture in the broader sense of the term is by no means invariably linked to social movements, nor does it necessarily involve a struggle for political power. If we are to grasp the essence of royal imposture, we clearly have to uncover those cultural mechanisms which pre-condition the phenomenon, i.e., to examine in a historical light the ideological conceptions of Russian society. An important step in this direction was taken by K. V. Čistov, who has convincingly demonstrated the connection between royal imposture and the utopian legend of the Tsar-Deliverer: indeed, Čistov sees royal imposture as a realization of this legend. [4] While wholly accepting Čistov's conclusions, we should point out, however, that his explanation is not exhaustive. This

---

*Claiming to be Dmitri, the youngest son of Ivan the Terrible, who had in fact been murdered in 1591, the False Dmitri marched on Moscow in 1605 and held the throne for less than a year.

approach, in fact, explains not so much the appearance of pretenders, as the social reaction to it, i.e. the response and support which they enjoyed among the populace; in addition, it highlights an important aspect of the phenomenon, namely *belief* in the pretender. Moreover, the question of royal imposture cannot be explained without delving further into the psychology of the pretenders themselves, i.e. into the whole complex of notions which directly motivated their actions. In this paper we shall attempt to show that it was *religious* notions which lay at the root of this psychology; in other words, we shall examine the religious aspect of royal imposture as a phenomenon of Russian culture.

2. It is quite clear that the psychology of royal imposture is directly connected with the question of attitude to the Tsar, i.e. the special way in which royal power was understood. Pretenders made their appearance in Russia only after there were Tsars, i.e. after the establishment and stabilization of royal power (no instances of pretenders claiming a *princely* throne are known). Moreover, the special nature of the attitude to the Tsar is determined by the understanding of royal power as being sacred, having a divine nature. It might even be suggested that royal imposture, as a typically Russian phenomenon, is connected precisely with the process of sacralization of the monarchy (which in turn is connected with the Byzantinization of monarchic power). Furthermore, the appearance of pretenders may actually be evidence of the start of the process of the sacralization of the monarch [5]; it is perhaps no accident that the first pretender appeared in Russia soon after the rite of anointing (along with that of crowning) was added to the accession ceremony. Anointing confers, as it were, a special charismatic status on the Tsar: as the anointed one, the Tsar is likened to Christ (Greek: *christos*, "the anointed one") and consequently, from the beginning of the eighteenth century, could even be called "Christ." [6]

We should remember that the word "tsar" in early Russia was regarded as a sacred word and has the same feature of non-conventionality in relation to the linguistic sign that all sacred lexis has in general; by the same token, the act of calling oneself Tsar can in no way be viewed as a purely arbitrary act of will.[7] Captain Margeret writes in his notes in 1607:

> Now, concerning the title which they take, they think that there is none more solemn than the one they have, "Tzar." They call the Roman Emperor "*Tsisar*," deriving it from Caesar; other sovereigns they call "*kroll*," following the example of the Poles; the Persian suzerain they call "*Kisel Bacha*" and the Turkish, "*Veliqui Ospodartursk*," i.e. the Great Lord of Turkey...According to them, the word Tzar is to be found in the Holy Scriptures. For wherever mention is made of David, or Solomon, or other kings, they are called "Zar David" and "Zar Solomon"...For this reason they maintain that the name of Tzar which it once pleased God to confer on David, Solomon and other rulers of Judah and Israel is the most authentic, and that

the words "Tsisar" or "Kroll" are merely a human invention and acquired by feats of arms. [8]

In this way the name Tsar is acknowledged to be a creation not of man, but of God; consequently the title of Tsar is seen as distinct from all other titles in as much as it is of divine nature. Even more important is the fact that this word is applied to God Himself: in liturgical texts God is often called "Tsar," and hence the characteristic parallelism, bequeathed to Christian religious consciousness, as it were from the earliest times, between Tsar and God [9], a parallelism which finds expression in such paired phrases as *Nebesnyj* Tsar (King of Heaven—referring to God) and *zemnoj* Tsar (Earthly Tsar—referring to the Tsar); *Netlennyj* Tsar (Incorruptible Tsar, i.e. God) and *tlennyj* Tsar (Corruptible Tsar, i.e. the Tsar).[10] Cf. also the naming of the Tsar as *zemnoj bog* (Earthly God), which is attested to in Russian from the sixteenth century onwards. [11]

In such conditions as these the very fact of calling oneself Tsar—irrespective of the fact of wielding actual power or not—has an undeniably religious aspect to it, and either way betokens a claim to possess sacred qualities. It is typical that the False Dmitri was called, like Christ, *"pravednoe solnce"* (sun of righteousness)[12] ; the Barkulab chronicle speaks of him thus: "for he is assuredly the true Tsar of the East, Dmitri Ivanovič, the sun of righteousness." [13] This is, as far as we know, the first case of such a title being applied to a Tsar. [14] In this sense, arbitrarily to proclaim oneself Tsar may be compared with proclaiming oneself saint, a custom found, for example, among the Russian sects of the *chlysty* (the flagellants) and the *skopcy* (the castrates). Indeed, in certain cases these two tendencies coincide: the well-known Kondratij Selivanov, whom the *skopcy* saw as the incarnation of Christ, was at the same time believed to be the Emperor Peter III.[15] * According to the teaching of the *skopcy*, "in the beginning was the Lord Sabaoth, then Jesus Christ, and now the Lord and Father, Peter Feodorovič, God of Gods and Tsar of Tsars." [16] Similarly Akulina Ivanovna, "mother of God" to the *skopcy*, was acknowledged to be both Mother of God and the Empress Elizabeth Petrovna, ** and accordingly the mother of Kondratij Selivanov, since he was Tsar and God[17] ; another "mother of God" to the *skopcy*, Anna Sofonovna, considered herself to be the Grand duchess Anna Feodorovna, the wife of the heir to the throne, the Tsarevich Constantine Pavlovič.*** [18]

In general, along with the pretenders who took the name of a Tsar, there were in Russia also pretenders who took the name of a saint, or who claimed to have special powers from on high; in a sense these are pheno-

---

*Peter III (Peter Fedorovič) reigned from 1761-1762. He was succeeded by his wife Catherine the Great.

**The Empress Elizabeth, who reigned from 1741-1761, was the daughter of Peter the Great and aunt of Peter III.

***Brother of Alexander I. He renounced his claim to the throne.

mena of the same order. Thus, for example, in the first half of the eighteenth century there appeared in Siberia a self-styled Prophet Elijah[19] (we should, incidentally, note in this connection that Kondratij Selivanov, whom we discussed above, was also at times called the Prophet Elijah).[20] At the end of the seventeenth century, Kuz'ma Kosoj (El'čenin), who led one of the Old Believer movements in the Don country, proclaimed himself "pope"[21] and maintained that he had to place Tsar Michail on the throne[22]; what is more, he acknowledged Michail to be God Himself.[23] According to other sources, he considered himself to be Tsar Michail, i.e. both Tsar and God together.[24] Self-styled Tsar Michails, as well as people who thought it their mission to put Tsar Michail on the throne, have turned up in Russia at later dates too, right up to our own times.

3. The notion that royal power is established by God accounts for the distinction made in those days, and in particular in the seventeenth century, between "righteous" (*pravednyj*) and "unrighteous" (*nepravednyj*) Tsars: *pravednyj* signifies not "just" (*spravedlivyj*), but "the right one" (*pravil'nyj*). Thus Ivan Timofeev distinguishes in his *Chronicle* between Tsars who are genuine ("most true," "most original," Tsars "by nature") and those who are Tsars in outward appearance only ("unreal," who "make an assault" on tsardom "by means of pretence").[25] Neither usurpation of the throne, nor even legitimate accession to the throne through the rite of coronation is sufficient to make a man Tsar. It is not conduct, but *predestination* which marks the true Tsar; so a Tsar may be a tyrant (as, for example, Ivan the Terrible) yet this in no way means that he is not in his rightful place. A distinction is therefore drawn between Tsars by the grace of God and Tsars by act of will, only the former being acknowledged as true Tsars; in other words, a distinction is made between the non-conventional and the conventional senses of the word *tsar*. The False Dmitri, then, in contrast to Ivan the Terrible, is not, from Ivan Timofeev's point of view, a Tsar at all: although he was legitimately enthroned, he is in fact only a *samocar'*, a "*self-styled Tsar*."[26] Similarly Boris Godunov,[*] according to the same author, "imposed himself on us. . .by his own volition,"[27] and so Ivan Timofeev does not recognize him as Tsar; and he has the same attitude towards Vasilij Šujskij.[**][28]

On the other hand, Tsar Michail Fedorovič,[***] as Avraamij Palicyn emphasizes in his *Tale* [****] "was chosen not by men, but in truth by God";[29] and moreover he does not understand this in the sense that God's will guided Michail Fedorovič's election in the Assembly of the Land, but rather that he was destined by God even before his birth and

---

[*]Reigned 1598-1605.
[**]Vasilij IV, a bojar who held the throne from 1606-1610.
[***]Tsar Michail, the first of the Romanov dynasty, was elected Tsar in 1613. The Assembly of the Land was abolished by Peter the Great.
[****]Avraamij Palicyn (1555-1627) completed his *skazanie* in 1620.

anointed from his mother's womb."³⁰ The Assembly of the Land simply divined, as it were, his predestination ³¹ (it should be noted, by the way, that the early Russian scribes provide no practical indications whatsoever on how to distinguish a true Tsar from a false one).

Similarly in the *Epistle to the Ugra* by the Archbishop of Rostov, Vassian (Rylo), dated 1480 and addressed to Ivan III, the author sees the Tatar Khan (Achmat) as a false Tsar. He calls him a pretender and usurper who "captured our land like a robber, and ruled over it *although he was neither a Tsar nor descended from Tsars*," and contrasts him with Ivan, who is the true Tsar, "the sovereign-ruler confirmed by God":

> And yet what prophet prophesied and what apostle or prelate taught this man, so unpleasing to God, this wicked man who *calls himself Tsar* to submit to you, the great Christian Tsar of all Russian lands?³²

It must be borne in mind that during the period of Tatar rule the Khan was called "Tsar" in Russia, yet now this Tsar is called a *pretender* (we shall return to this question later). Cf. also a similar formulation in the denunciatory epistle from the clergy, headed by Iona (the future Metropolitan), to Prince Dmitrij Šemjaka in 1447, appealing to him to submit to Prince Vasilij the Blind:

> Lord, we must dare to say this: will you be overcome by spiritual blindness through your infatuation with what is temporal and ephemeral, and the totally illusory honour and glory of being prince and ruler: that is, to hear yourself addressed by the title of Prince and yet not to have it bestowed by God? ³³

In this case too, self-styled power (power by outward appearance only) is contrasted with God-given power (power by inner nature), and power conferred on oneself with power conferred by God; it is worth noting in this connection that it was precisely Vasilij the Blind who was the first of the early Russian princes more or less consistently to call himself "Tsar" and "autocrat" (*samoderžec*). ³⁴ Indeed, it is Metropolitan Iona ³⁵ himself who calls him Tsar, and who is probably the author of the epistle of 1447 quoted above; thus, in this instance too, the point at issue is royal power by divine election.

If true Tsars receive power from God, then false Tsars receive it from the Devil. ³⁶ Even the church rite of sacred coronation and anointing do not confer grace on a false Tsar, for these actions are no more than outward appearances; in reality the false Tsar is crowned and anointed by demons acting on the orders of the Devil himself.³⁷ It follows therefore that if the real Tsar may be likened to Christ (see above) and perceived as an image of God, a living icon, ³⁸ then a pretender may be regarded as a false icon, i.e. an *idol*. Ivan Timofeev in his *Chronicle* writes of the False Dmitri:

All obey this man who dwells beyond the borders of the Russian land; all willingly submit to him *though he is an idol, and pay homage to him as to a Tsar.* [39]

Thus the Tsar as icon is seen in opposition to the pretender as idol.

4. The idea of a true Tsar's being divinely preordained, of his being marked by divine election, is clearly apparent in the exceptionally persistent notion of special "royal signs," usually the cross, the eagle (i.e. the Tsar's coat of arms) or the sun-signs, which are supposed to be found on the Tsar's body, and which attest to his elective status. This belief has played an important part in the mythology of royal imposture: according to numerous historical and folklore sources it was precisely by virtue of these "royal signs" that the most diverse pretenders—for example, the False Dmitri, Timofej Akundinov,* Emel'jan Pugačev** and others—demonstrated their royal descent and their right to the throne; and it was especially the marks on their bodies that made others believe in them and support them. [40] Thus, for example, a beggar who turned up in 1732 in the Tambov province proclaimed:

> I am no peasant and no son of a peasant; I am an eagle, the son of eagles, and my destiny is to be an eagle. I am the Tsarevič Aleksej Petrovič...I have a cross on my back and a birthmark in the form of a sword on my thigh... [41]

Compare the evidence of the Pugačev investigation:

> He had been at Eremina Kurica's [the name of a Cossack] for two days, when the latter called Emel'ka*** to the bathhouse and Emel'-ka said to him: "I have no shirt." Eremina Kurica replied: "I'll give you mine." Then the two of them went alone to the baths. When they arrived and Emel'ka undressed, Eremina Kurica saw the scars of a disease on Emel'ka's chest, just under the nipples, and asked him: "What's that you have there, Pugačev, on your chest?" And Emel'ka replied to Eremina Kurica: "Those are the marks of a sovereign." Hearing this, Eremina said: "That is good, if it is so."

Further on in the same deposition we read:

> When we had sat down, Karavaev said to Emel'ka: "You call your-self a sovereign, yet sovereigns have the royal signs on their bodies," whereupon Emel'ka stood up and, ripping open the collar of his shirt, said: "There! If you do not believe that I am the sovereign, just look—here is the royal sign." First of all he showed the scars under his nipples left by an illness, and then the same kind of mark on his

---

*Claiming to be the son of Vasilij Šujskij (Vasilij IV), he was executed in 1653.

**Emel'jan Pugačev (1726–1775) was the leader of the most widespread and serious popular revolt under Catherine the Great.

***i.e. Pugačev.

left temple. The Cossacks—Šigaev, Karavaev, Zarubin, Mjasnikov—looked at the signs and said: "Well, now we believe you and recognize you as sovereign."[42]

In 1822 a certain townsman by the name of Starcev wrote to Alexander I about a man who maintained that he was Paul I.

> I know that he bears upon his body, on his back between the shoulder-blades, a cross the like of which none of your subjects can have except those of supreme power; for this reason it must be supposed that he has a similar sign also on his chest. Now since he is vouchsafed such a cross on his body he cannot be a man of simple birth, neither can he be a nobleman: he must almost certainly be the father of Your Imperial Majesty... [43]

In 1844 a peasant by the name of Kljukin stated that he had been in the baths with a man who called himself the Tsarevič Constantine Pavlovič, and "I saw the hairs on his chest formed in the shape of a cross, which no man has, save one of royal blood."[44] Such examples are very common and it would be easy to adduce many more. There is no reason in such cases to suspect a conscious attempt at mystification: for there is no doubt that the pretenders themselves were convinced that the presence of such a mark on their bodies specifically attested to their having been singled out.

The notion of divine election, of the belief that the Tsar is mystically preordained, most likely explains not only the specific conception of royal power in early Russia, which we discussed above, but also the psychology of the pretender. In the absence of any clear-cut criteria on how to distinguish between a true and a false Tsar, the pretender could evidently to some degree believe in his predestination, in his election. It is significant that the most striking pretenders—the False Dmitri and Pugačev—crop up precisely at those moments when the natural (i.e. hereditary) order of succession has been broken and when the actual occupier of the throne could in fact be regarded as a pretender. Boris Godunov who, in Ivan Timofeev's words, acceded to the throne "by an act of his own will" (see above) could be regarded in this way, as, of course, could Catherine the Great, who had no right to the Russian throne at all. The presence of one pretender (a pretender on the throne) provokes the appearance of others; and there is a kind of competition between pretenders, each of whom claims to be marked (elect). At the basis of this psychology, however paradoxical it may seem, there lurks the conviction that it is not man, but God who must judge who is the real Tsar.[45] It follows, therefore, that royal imposture is a quite predictable and logically justified consequence of the conception of royal power which we have been discussing.

However, the specific psychology of royal imposture is based to a considerable degree on a *mythological act of identification*.[46] It is indicative in this connection that Pugačev, who called himself Petr Fedorovič,* should have called his closest associate, I.N. Zarubin-Čika, "Count Černyšev."**[47] In addition, the other self-styled Peter III—the *skopec* Kondratij Selivanov, discussed above—had his own "Count Černyšev" (this was another leader of the *skopcy*, A.I. Silov[48]). The case of the "mother of God" to the *skopcy*, Akulina Ivanovna, who, as mentioned above, called herself "Empress Elizabeth" (at the end of the eighteenth century, i.e. after Elizabeth Petrovna's death) is exactly analogous. She had a close associate who called herself E.R. Daškova;[49] the fact that the real, not self-styled E.R. Daškova*** was an associate not of Elizabeth, but of Catherine, only serves to underline the purely functional role of such an appellation. In these cases the *name* has become, as it were, a function of the *position*. No less remarkable in this context is the portrait of Pugačev in the Moscow Historical Museum, where Pugačev is painted over the portrait of Catherine:[50] if a portrait is a pictorial parallel to a person's name, then the repainting of a portrait is equivalent to an act of renaming.[51]

5. Thus the very concept of royal power in early Russia presupposed an opposition between true, genuine Tsars and Tsars in outward appearance only, i.e. pretenders. In this sense the behavior of a pretender is viewed as carnival behavior: in other words, pretenders are seen as mummers (*rjaženye*).

Furthermore, royal imposture is obviously connected with the "game of Tsar" which was played in Muscovy in the seventeenth century; people would play at being the Tsar, i.e. would *dress up* as Tsars and act out the attendant ceremonies. Thus in the record book of the Muscovite court for February 2, 1634 we read:

> The same day, Prince Matvej, Prince Ofonasej and the Princes Ivan and Ondrej Šechovskie were brought before the Tsar, where the following was said to them: In the year 7128 [i.e. 1620, B.A.U.] Ondrej Golubovskoj laid a charge against you to the Sovereign Tsar and Grand Prince Michajlo Fedorovič of all Russia**** that one evening you went to Ilejka Bočkin's house and that you, Prince Ofonasej, Prince Ondrej, Prince Ivan and Ilejka Bočkin did in a rascally and cunning [i.e. playful] way call you, Prince Matvej, Tsar, and that you, Prince Matvej, did call the prince and his comrades your bojars; indeed, you yourselves confessed to such rascality. The bojars' verdict was that you should be condemned to death for that misdeed. And then his Majesty the Tsar and Grand Prince Michajlo Fedorovič

---

*i.e. Peter III, husband of Catherine the Great.
**Count Z.G. Černyšev, d. 1784, and his brother Ivan, held high positions under Catherine.
***Princess E.R. Daškova was one of the outstanding women of her time.
****i.e. Michail Romanov.

of all Russia, at the entreaty of His Majesty's father, the Great Sovereign and Most Holy Patriarch of Moscow and all Russia, Filaret Nikitič, was merciful to you and spared your lives. His Majesty commanded that you be sent for your great crimes to separate prisons in the towns downriver [from Moscow].

But now His Majesty the Tsar and Grand Prince Michajlo Fedorovič of all Russia, in blessed memory of his father, the Great Sovereign and Most Holy Patriarch of Moscow and all Russia, Filaret Nikitič, has taken pity on you and ordered you to be reprieved from disfavor and brought back from Moscow to appear before the Sovereign. Henceforth you, Prince Matvej, and your comrades are to redeem your great crimes through service. [52]

Another such case has been preserved in the archive of the Ministry of Justice. On the Wednesday of the first week of Lent in 1666, a landowner from Tver' by the name of Nikita Borisovič Puškin made a petition in Moscow, in which he called down on his peasants 'the Sovereign's word and deed':

> It seems the peasants from my villages around Tver', to wit from the villages of Vasil'evskoe and Michajlovskoe, have got up to some kind of unholy mischief: they chose one of their number—I do not know whom—as their leader, and *having given him a high-ranking title*, went with him this Shrovetide Saturday and made an uproar with flags and drums and rifles.

The evidence for the case revealed that the peasants "called one of their number a man of high rank—the Tsar;" moreover, they paraded their elected Tsar, Mit'ka Demidov, "through the village on a litter with a funnel placed on his head,"

> and carried before him *varenec* [boiled soured milk, the ritual repast of Shrovetide, B.A.U.]; they also tied a sheaf of straw to a pole [cf. the carrying and burning of sheaves of straw or a scarecrow stuffed with straw in ritual processions at Shrovetide, B.A.U.], and the customary basket [sic, B.A.U.], and tied a garment instead of a standard to another pole and carried with them instead of a rifle, roofing-timbers.

Next the peasants chose as their Tsar, instead of Mit'ka Demidov, Perška Jakovlev, who unleashed a royal punishment upon his subjects:

> In the village of Michajlovskoe, at Perška's command, his brother peasants beat a certain peasant—I forget his name—with sticks, and the peasant pleaded with them, saying: "Sire, have mercy;" and Perška was wearing a green caftan at the time with a shoulder-belt and a maiden's fox-fur hat upon his head. And for a flag they tied a woman's veil to a pole. [53]

267

Both of these peasant "Tsars" had two fingers of their right hands cut off. Both they and their accomplices were whipped "mercilessly" and exiled together with their families to Siberia.[54] It is highly significant that all these events should have taken place at Shrovetide and be characterized by the typical attributes of Shrovetide festivities (the sheaf of straw, the *varenec*, etc.). Dressing up as Tsar similarly emerges as one of the aspects of Shrovetide mummery.[55] Unfortunately we do not know at what season of the year the Šachovskie princes 'played at tsar,' but we have every reason to suspect that it happened at Yuletide or at Shrovetide.

'Playing at Tsar' is reflected not only in historical but also in folklore and ethnographical documents. We find a characteristic description of the game in a fairy-tale recorded in the Perm' province:

> The boy grew not year by year, but hour by hour. He started playing with his friends. They began to *play at Tsar*. The blacksmith's son said to his friends: "Shout to the river to flow backwards! The one who succeeds will be Tsar!" They all shouted and shouted, but nothing happened; then he gave a shout, and the river began to flow backwards. They played the same game again: "Shout to the forest to bow down to the damp earth!" The others shouted and shouted, but nothing happened; he gave a shout, and the forest bowed down. "So, I am Tsar a second time!" They played a third time: "Shout to the animals in the forest to be silent!" [Omission in the text.] "So, lads, I'm Tsar for the third time! I can kill whoever I like since no court can try me," he said. So they agreed to this.[56]

Here we have a very clear reflection of the sacred properties of the Tsar: 'playing at Tsar' in this context is seen as playing at being a sacred, omnipotent being.

The 'game of Tsar' is essentially a variant of royal imposture, though one completely divested of any kind of political pretensions whatsoever: it is royal imposture in its purest form, so to say. It was no accident that the 'game of Tsar' was ruthlessly punished in the seventeenth century, and the fact that despite persecution the game was still played and even left its mark in folklore is extremely significant.[57]

6. The extent to which the 'game of Tsar' was found in early Russia is demonstrated by the fact that it could be played not only by pretenders, but also by real Tsars, who forced *another* man to be the false, inauthentic Tsar—a Tsar in outward appearance only. Thus Ivan the Terrible in 1567 forced his equerry, the bojar Ivan Petrovič Fedorov (Čeljadin), who was suspected of conspiracy, to be dressed up in the Tsar's clothes, given the sceptre and other insignia of royalty and be seated on the throne; after which, having bowed down to the ground before him and paid him all the honors befitting a Tsar, Ivan killed the travesty Tsar with his own hand. This is how Šlichting describes the incident:

When he [I.P. Fedorov] arrived at the palace, the tyrant caught sight of him and immediately commanded that he be given the raiment which he [Ivan] was wearing himself and that he should be arrayed therein, that he be given the sceptre which sovereigns are wont to hold, and then ordered him to mount the royal throne and take his seat in the place where the Grand Prince himself always sat. As soon as Ioann [I.P. Fedorov] had done this, albeit with vain protestation (there is after all no sense in trying to justify oneself before a tyrant), and had seated himself on the royal throne in the princely raiment, the tyrant himself rose, stood before him and, baring his head and bowing, knelt before him, saying: "Now you have what you sought, what you aspired to – to be Grand Prince of Muscovy and to occupy my place. So now you are the Grand Prince; rejoice now and enjoy the power after which you thirsted." Then after a short pause he began again, thus: "However, as it lies in my power to seat you upon this throne, so does it also lie in my power to unseat you." Thereupon, seizing a knife he thrust it into his chest several times and made all the soldiers there at the time stab him with their daggers. 58

This scene is full of the most profound symbolism: Ivan accuses Fedorov of unlawfully claiming the Tsar's throne and yet makes him Tsar, but Tsar in outward appearance only – a *pretender*-Tsar. Such behavior is fairly typical of Ivan in general and – as we shall see below – is not by any means necessarily linked with the desire to rid himself of an unworthy man or quench his thirst for revenge; rather it is connected with the masquerading and dressing up so typical of Ivan and his entourage: [59] in fact, with the game which outwardly might remind one of playing the holy fool, but which is in reality radically different from it. [60]

Even more indicative is the incident when in 1575 Ivan crowned Simeon Bekbulatovič Tsar, handed over to him all his royal ceremonial and all the royal insignia, himself assuming the name of Ivan of Moscow and playing the role of a simple bojar; in the words of the chronicler:

Ivan Vasil'evič was pleased to make Simeon Bekbulatovič Tsar of Moscow. . .and crowned him Tsar, and himself assumed the name of Ivan of Moscow, left town and went to live in Petrovka; he handed over all his royal ceremonial to Simeon, while he himself travelled simply, like a bojar, in a cart and when he came into Simeon's presence he would seat himself far away from the royal throne, together with the bojars. [61]

According to some sources, Simeon Bekbulatovič even underwent the sacred rite of coronation, [62] but even this could not make of him a genuine, authentic Tsar. [63] The enthronement of Simeon Bekbulatovič was directly bound up with the institution (or to be more precise, with the reinstatement) of the *opričnina*, which also had many features of the masquerade to a marked degree: while Ivan entrusted the *zemščina* to Simeon Bekbulatovič, he himself controlled the *opričnina*:[64] the term *zemščina* (from *zemlja* = land, earth) is correlated with the original land, while the word *opričnina* signifies that which is separate, unconnected, on the outside.[65] We should point out that I.P. Fedorov too was the head of the *zemščina* government,[66] so that in both cases the person at the head of the *zemščina* plays the part of the travesty Tsar; and this, of course, is no mere coincidence.

It is highly significant, moreover, that Simeon Bekbulatovič should have been a direct descendant of the Khans of the Golden Horde, i.e. of those who in their time wielded the real power over the territory of Russia and who *called themselves Tsar* (we have already mentioned that the Tatar Khans were called precisely this);[67] the Tsarevich Bekbulat, father of Simeon Bekbulatovič, was the grandson of Achmat, the last Khan of the Golden Horde—the very man of whom Vassian Rylo wrote in his *Epistle to the Ugra* in 1480 that he was a false Tsar, a pretender (see above)—and was, in addition, one of the strongest claimants to the Khanate of the fragmented Tatar Horde.[68] So it was that Ivan placed the Tatar Khan on the throne of Russia. *The role of travesty, pretender-Tsar is played by one who would formerly have possessed the right to call himself Tsar and to rule over the Russian state*; such a Tsar is now revealed to be a false Tsar, a Tsar in outward appearance only—and by the same token, the previous Tatar Khans are also seen as false Tsars, not true ones.[69] What we have before us is as it were the last stage in the struggle with Tatar rule, a semiotic stage. In his time, having overcome the Khan (Tsar), the Russian Grand Prince became Tsar, i.e. began to take the name used by the Khans; and now it was the Khan who became the *pretender*-Tsar.[70] It was quite in character that Ivan the Terrible should have behaved like this; for he was the first Russian Tsar officially crowned Tsar, i.e. the first monarch to enjoy the *formal* right to assume the title of Tsar of Russia.

It could be said that in each case, both in that of I.P. Fedorov and in that of Simeon Bekbulatovič, the 'game of Tsar' had a symbolic character for Ivan the Terrible and served the function of a *political 'unmasking'*: in the first case an actual person (I.P. Fedorov, accused of laying claim to royal power) was unmasked, and in the second, a state principle (the rule of the Tatar Khans). In both cases it was the *head of the zemščina* who was subjected to being unmasked.

We know of another Tsar who indulged in this game: Peter the Great. In much the same way as Ivan designated Simeon Bekbulatovič Tsar while he himself became a subject, so Peter designated F.Ju. Romodanovskij "Prince-Caesar" [*knjaz'-kesar'*], calling him *korol'* (*konich* [sic], king) and "His Majesty," while he called himself the latter's "serf and lowliest slave," and was awarded various ranks and promotions by him.[71] Setting out in

1697 on his journey abroad, Peter entrusted the government of Moscow to Prince-Caesar Romodanovskij, and in his letters from abroad addressed him as monarch, emphasizing his own subject status.[72] All the highest ranks—those of Colonel (1706), Lieutenant-General and *šoutbejnacht*, i.e. Rear-Admiral (1709)—were awarded to Peter by the Prince-Caesar.[73] Nobody dared drive into Romodanovkij's courtyard—the sovereign himself used to leave his gig at the gates [74]—and in their mock ceremonies Peter would kiss Romodanovskij's hand.[75]

This "game" also had its point of symbolic unmasking. It is character-istic, for example, that at the wedding of the Tsar's jester, Šanskij, in 1702, Romodanovskij should have been dressed in the robes of a seven-teenth century Tsar of Russia, while Nikita Zotov was dressed as the Patriarch:[76] this parody of the Russian Tsar as it were anticipates Peter's assumption of the title of Emperor.[77] After F.Ju. Romodanovskij's death (in September 1717), the title of 'Prince-Caesar' was inherited by his son, I.F. Romodanovskij (from April 1718); at the wedding of the 'Prince-Pope,' P.I. Buturlin, in 1721—that is, just before Peter was proclaimed Emperor!—I.F. Romodanovskij again appeared in the costume of Tsar of Russia, his wife was dressed as Tsarina and the crowd of servants wore traditional Russian costume.[78] In this connection we should remember that both Romodanovskijs were known as adherents of traditional Russian customs and in their private lives kept up the traditional bojar ways.[79] Broadly speaking, the Prince-Caesar may be considered an equivalent of the Prince-Pope: the Prince-Caesar being a parody of the Tsar, and the Prince-Pope a parody of the Patriarch; just as the parody of the image of the Tsar preceded the assumption of the title of Emperor, so the parody of the image of the Patriarch preceded the abolition of the Patriarchate [1721]. At the same time we have here a parody of the very principle (ultimately derived from Byzantium) of the coexistence of the priesthood and monarchy, i.e. the division of power into eccle-siastical and secular, a division which was in opposition to the one-man power of Peter.[80] Finally, we should not forget that the Romodanovskij family, unlike the Romanovs, traced their descent from Rjurik. Thus, in this case too—as in that of Simeon Bekbulatovič—the role of the monarch is played by one who could previously have laid claim to the title.

Moreover, for both Ivan the Terrible and Peter the Great, this masquerade is intimately bound up with the notion of royal imposture, and can be seen as simply another aspect of the same phenomenon. Its basis is the opposition between genuine and apparent Tsars (pretenders) mentioned above: in all these cases the true, real Tsar, by shedding the *external* signs of his status as Tsar and forcing another to play what is to all intents and purposes the role of pretender, is in fact emphasizing as it were his own *authentic* right to the royal throne, independent of any formal attributes of kingship. Ivan and Peter clearly shared the conception

271

of royal power which we discussed above, and indeed their behavior derives from that conception. It is indicative that Ivan should have renounced the throne several times in the course of his reign (in 1564 in connection with the institution of the *opričnina*, and in 1575 in connection with its reinstatement and the installation of Simeon Bekbulatovič as Tsar), as if in the full certainty that, come what might, he still remained the true and genuine Tsar: a Tsar by nature, "by the will of God, and not by the unruly whim of mankind," as he puts it himself in his letter to Stephen Batory.[81] In just the same way Ivan could, in a critical situation, ostentatiously abandon Moscow, leaving his throne behind him (in 1564 he left Moscow for Aleksandrovskaja Sloboda) and nonetheless still remain Tsar.[82]

It is also significant that both Ivan and Peter should have named another man not only *Tsar*, but *saint*; their contemporaries – not without justification – saw overt blasphemy in this.[83] Bearing in mind the sacred nature of the title of Tsar, we can say that we have essentially the same type of behavior in both cases.

7. It should be borne in mind that any kind of masquerade or dressing up was inevitably thought of in early Russia as *anti-behavior*; i.e. a sinister, black-magic significance was attributed to it in principle. This is quite plain from the example of the mummers of Yuletide, Shrovetide, St. John's Night and other festivals, who, it was assumed (by participants in the masquerade as well as spectators!), depicted devils, or unclean spirits; correspondingly, the dressing up was accompanied by extremes of disorderly behavior, often of an overtly blasphemous character.[84]

This is how imposture too, and, evidently, "the game of Tsar," was perceived in early Russia. Dressing up in the Tsar's clothes should be seen in this context as a typical case of anti-behavior, to which, on the level of content, there corresponds the blasphemous attempt to procure sacred attributes through outer simulation. It is no accident that Ivan and Peter took part in this masquerade, for they were both Tsars of whom anti-behavior was on the whole typical, whether expressed by dressing up or by the blasphemous imitation of church rituals – cf. in this connection Ivan's "*opričnyj* monastery"[85] and Peter's "Council of All the Fools."[86] In this sense the link between the installation of Simeon Bekbulatovič as Tsar and the institution of the *opričnina*, [or *opričina*], mentioned above is highly typical: the word *opričnina* means both "separate, unconnected," and at the same time "on the outside" [*kromešnoe*]; it is, therefore, by the same token connected with the *other world*, the travesty element of demons. Thus the *opričniki* were seen as *kromešniki* [people on the outside] (cf. *t'ma kromešnaja* [outer darkness] as a term for purgatory), i.e. as special kinds of mummers, who assumed diabolical appearance and diabolical behavior.[87] And indeed the manner in which the *opričniki* acted recalls the behavior of mummers at Yuletide or other festivals:

thus, Ivan's *opričnyj* monastery in Aleksandrovskaja Sloboda – in which the *opričniki* dressed up in monks' habits and the Tsar called himself the Abbot of this carnival monastery – would seem in all probability to have arisen under the influence of those Yuletide games of which the icon-painter of Vjaz'ma, the *starec* Grigorij, wrote in 1651, in his petition to Tsar Aleksej Michailovič. In Vjaz'ma, he wrote,

> there are various vile games from Christmas Day to the vigils of epiphany, during which the participants designate some of their number saints, invent their own monasteries and name for them an archimandrite, a cellarer and *starcy*.[88]

In exactly the same way the blasphemous entertainments indulged in by Peter, exemplified above all by the ceremonies of the Assembly of All the Fools, were originally intended primarily for Yuletide and Shrovetide (they soon, however, extended for the whole period from Christmas to Lent), and correspondingly contained elements of Yuletide and Shrovetide ritualism.[89] It should be noted in addition that by forcing his people to wear "German," i.e. European, clothes, Peter had in the eyes of his con-temporaries transformed his entourage into mummers (just as Ivan's *opričniki* had appeared in their time as mummers too): it was said that Peter had "dressed people up as devils."[90] Indeed, European dress in pre-Petrine times was perceived as a "mockery," a masquerade, and on icons devils could be depicted in German or Polish dress.[91]

By the same token, royal imposture as a specific type of behavior falls wholly into the traditional Russian situation which presupposes, along with correct, normative behavior, some form or other of anti-behavior (see above, Part I, Chapters 1 and 2); in other words royal imposture is part of the tradition of anti-behavior in Russia.

8. Royal imposture, then, is perceived in early Russia as anti-behavior. The fact that the False Dmitri was regarded as a sorcerer ("a heretic"), i.e. that features characteristic of the behavior of sorcerers were ascribed to him in the popular consciousness, is indicative of this. Indeed, it is precisely this kind of view of him which is reflected in the historical songs about the False Dmitri, for example:

> The unfrocked Griška, son of Otrep'ev, stands
> Before his crystal mirror
> And in his hands he holds a book of magic
> And casts spells, this unfrocked Griška, son of Otrep'ev,[92]

and:

> He distributes Lenten food to the people,
> While he himself eats non-Lenten food [on a Friday!];
> He makes his bed on the icons there are around him
> And tramples underfoot the miracle-working crosses.[93]

Similar views were seemingly held even during the False Dmitri's lifetime: an anonymous account of 1605 states that after the False Dmitri's appearance in the political arena Boris Godunov sent emissaries to the Polish Sejm and "they spread the rumor that Dmitri is the son of a priest and is a widely-known sorcerer." Later on, the same rumor was put about by Boris in Moscow, too; from the same account we learn that on his way to Moscow the False Dmitri captured Griška Otrep'ev, "the great and widely known magician, of whom the tyrant Boris spread the rumour that he was the real Dmitri." [94] In any case the evidence provided by folklore sources is thoroughly corroborated by the tales about the Time of Troubles,* in which, for example, we find the "heretical book" (i.e. book of magic or sorcery) which the False Dmitri was said to be constantly reading; [95] it is stated that he began "to eat veal and other unclean foods on Wednesdays and Fridays."[96] No less characteristic are the rumours that a *skomoroch*'s** mask hung instead of icons on the False Dmitri's wall, and that icons lay about under his bed;[97] *skomorochi* and sorcerers were identified with each other in early Russia, and besides, during the act of sorcery icons were placed on the ground, and icons or the cross were trodden on, and so on. [98]

Historical songs about the False Dmitri tell of how he sets off to the bathhouse at the time when people are going to church; this is also a characteristic of the behavior of sorcerers, inasmuch as in early Russia the bathhouse was thought of as an "unclean place," a kind of antipode to the church—and so of course sorcerers could be recognized by the fact that they went to the bathhouse instead of going to church.[99] See, for example:

> The time had come for the Great Day,
> For the Great Day, for Christ's Day,
> And in Ivan-the-Great's bell-tower
> The biggest bell of all was rung.
> All the bojar-princes went to the liturgy,
> To Christ's midnight Easter service,
> But that thief Griška the Unfrocked went to the bathhouse
> With his sweetheart Marinuška Jur'evna;
> All the bojar-princes are praying to God;
> That thief Griška the Unfrocked is washing in the bathhouse
> And fornicating with his sweetheart Marinuška.
> The bojar-princes come back from the service;
> That thief Griška the Unfrocked comes from the bathhouse
> With his sweetheart Marinuška Jur'evna.100

---

*The period between the death of Fedor (eldest son of Ivan the Terrible) in 1598 and the accession of Michail Romanov in 1613.
**See above. p. 46.

Cf.: All the people went to Christian mass,
But Griška the Unfrocked and his Tsarina Mariška,
Marina Ivanovna, daughter of the Prince of Lithuania—
They didn't go to Christian mass;
They went to the steam-baths,
To the clean wash-tub,
And steamed themselves in the steam-bath.
They washed themselves in the wash-tub
During Christ's midnight Easter service.
The people come away from Christian mass,
But Griška the Unfrocked comes from the steam-bath
With his Tsarina Marina Ivanovna.[101]

The description of the model intended to represent hell, which the False Dmitri is supposed to have erected for his amusement is particularly interesting in this connection. In the *Tale of the Reign of Tsar Fedor Ioannovič* we read:

And so that accursed heretic, ever thirsty for power in this brief life and in the one to come, built for himself the image of his eternal dwelling, the like of which has never been in the realm of Russia since the beginning of the world; what he desired, that did he inherit. He made a great pit right opposite his palace on the other side of the Moskva river and placed a great cauldron of pitch there, prefiguring his own future place, and placed above it three great and awesome bronze heads; their teeth were made of iron and inside there was noise and clanging, and by some cunning contrivance the jaws were made to yawn open like the jaws of hell, and the teeth were pointed and the claws were like sharp sickles ready to clutch at you. When they began to yawn it was as if a flame spurted out of the gullet; sparks were continually shooting out of the nostrils and smoke was ceaselessly issuing from the ears. From inside each head could be heard a great noise and clanging, and people looking at it were terrified. And out of the mouth hung down a great tongue, at the end of which was an asp's head, which looked as if it wanted to swallow you up. The accursed one, foretelling his eternal dwelling-place with his father the Devil and Satan, was very fond of that hellish place and was always looking at it out of his palace windows, so as to achieve his heart's desire, the outer darkness of hell; and what he coveted, that did he inherit. And that accursed heretic ordered those Orthodox Christians who denounced his accursed heresy to be thrown into it to their death.[102]

This description corresponds fairly closely to the iconographic representation of hell as a fire-breathing serpent (see such depictions on Russian icons of the Last Judgement, for example).

The False Dmitri was accordingly given a sorcerer's burial: whereas his accomplice, Basmanov, who was killed together with him, was buried near a church, the False Dmitri was buried in a "God's house" [ubogij] dom] or skudel'nica* (i.e. where suicides were buried). Subsequently,

---

*Collins 1671, p. 22, describes these burial places as follows: "[the corpses]

275

however, the corpse was exhumed and burnt.[103] The reason for the exhumation was doubtless the idea that the earth would not accept the body of a sorcerer, i.e. the earth's anger was feared.[104] Compare also the statement that when the False Dmitri's body was exhibited "for shame," before being interred,

> the earth itself did abhor it, and the beasts and the birds abhorred such a foul body and would not come to eat of it. . . the earth disdained to carry upon it the accursed and vile corpse, and the air was poisoned and would not send rain from the heavens; where the accursed corpse lay, the earth brought forth no fruit and the sun would not shine because of the foul stench, and the stench covered all the fruits and they dried up; and the Lord took away from the earth both wheat and grapes until the corpse had disappeared.[105]

Foreigners' accounts of the vilification of the False Dmitri's body are also significant:

> for further ridicule they threw a hideous and shameless *mask* on the belly of the dead sovereign. . . , and stuffed a reed-pipe into his mouth. . .with which to bribe the door-keeper of Hell.[106]

The mask and the pipe were seen as the attributes of the inverted world of the sorcerer and were intended to demonstrate the False Dmitri's adherence to that world; at the same time we see here an exchange between top and bottom, which is characteristic of mummers who aim to resemble unclean spirits.[107] Compare also the characteristic rumours of devils playing like *skomorochi* over the False Dmitri's body;

> And as his body lay in the field many people in the middle of the night, even until cockcrow, heard much dancing and playing of bells and pipes, and other devilish games being enacted over his accursed body; for Satan himself was rejoicing at his coming. . .[108]

It is characteristic that even the False Dmitri, recognizing Boris Godunov as a false Tsar, i.e. a pretender (he ordered his body to be transferred from the Archangel'skij Cathedral and interred outside the Kremlin, in the Church of St. Ambrose), should see a sorcerer in him and "fearing spells and magic, gave orders to demolish. . .to its foundations" Boris's palace.[109]

Pretenders, then, are perceived as sorcerers, and elements of antibehavior are attributed to them. And conversely Peter the Great, whose conduct seemed to his contemporaries nothing more nor less than antibehavior,[110] is perceived essentially as a pretender: popular rumour, even during Peter's lifetime, proclaimed him to be not a genuine

are sent to the *Bosky* or *Boghzi Dome* (i.e. God's House) which is a great pit in the fields arched over, wherein they put an hundred or two hundred and let them rest till Midsummer, and then the popes go and bury them, and cover them with earth."

("natural") Tsar, but rather *a substitute Tsar* who had no right to the throne. Here, for example, is one of the many testimonies which express just such a view: in 1722

> the *starica* Platonida said of his Imperial Majesty: *he is a Swede put in the place of the Tsar*, for just fancy—he does what is displeasing to God; christenings and weddings are celebrated 'against the sun,'[111] and images are painted of Swedish people,[112] and he does not abstain during Lent,[113] and he has taken a liking to Swedish dress,[114] and he eats and drinks with Swedes and will not leave their kingdom...[115] and the Grand Prince Peter Alekseevič was born already with teeth of a Swedish woman, he is the Antichrist.[116]

Rumors to the effect that a substitute had been exchanged for the real Tsar (either while he was abroad or else in infancy) and that another man sat upon the throne in his stead—i.e. a pretender, a Tsar in outward appearance only—were widespread in Peter's reign and were extraordinarily persistent.[117] These rumors stimulated the appearance of a whole succession of pretenders who played the role of the legitimate heir of the authentic, real Peter; for the most part they were False Aleksejs, giving themselves the name of the Tsarevich Aleksej Petrovič.[118] It is remarkable that the first False Aleksej appeared even during the lifetime of Aleksej Petrovič (in 1712, i.e. six years before his execution).[119] This seemingly testifies to the fact that viewing Peter as a "substituted" Tsar could be transferred to his son: in as much as Peter is seen as a false Tsar, his son may be seen as the false heir; it was presumed that the real Peter had a real heir who was called Aleksej Petrovič.[120] The absence of pretenders playing the role of Peter himself is entirely understandable if we bear in mind the widespread opinion that Peter had been *killed* when he was "substituted"; this opinion is one component of the legend of the "substitute" Tsar.[121]

Thus, along with the myth of the return of the Tsar-Deliverer (which has been analysed in connection with the question of royal imposture by K.V. Čistov), there existed the fairly persistent myth of the *pretender on the throne*, which was based on a specifically Russian concept of royal power, i.e. on the distinction between true and false Tsars. The coexistence of these myths considerably assisted the spread of royal imposture in early Russia.

Translated by David Budgen

NOTES

1   Cf. Čistov 1967, p. 29.
2   Ključevskij 1956-9, vol. III, p. 27.
3   Čistov 1967, pp. 32, 179-80.
4   Čistov 1967.

277

5   On the history of the process of sacralization of monarchic power in Russia, see Živov & Uspenskij 1981.

6   Feofan Prokopovič specifically justifies the legitimacy of such a title in his *Discourse on the Tsar's Power and Honour* and subsequently in his *Inquiry upon the Pontifex* and *Discourse on the Coronation Day of Catherine the First* (see Feofan 1760-74, I, p. 252 & II, pp. 178-9; Feofan 1721, p. 37). For the history of the naming of the Russian monarch as "Christ," see specially Živov & Uspenskij 1981, II -4.

7   The religious connotation of the word "tsar" can be traced back also in sporadic instances of its use in the titles of the Russian princes before the title of Tsar was officially assumed (see Vodov 1978).

8   Margeret 1607, pp. 25-6, quoted in Ustrjalov 1859, I, p. 254. [Translation from the French. Margeret's spelling of titles has been preserved.]

9   The Archpriest Avvakum wrote in his exegesis of Psalm XLIV: "Christ. . .by command of the Father on high is anointed by the Holy Ghost and is filled with grace and truth. It is for this reason that he is called Christ, or the Anointed One, or Tsar" (RIB, XXXIX, col. 459).

10   The opposition between the "corruptible Tsar" and the "incorruptible" one (God) dates from a work by the sixth century Byzantine writer Agapitos, which was widely quoted in early Russian writing. The twenty-first chapter of this work in which it is said that the Tsar is like men in his corruptible nature, but like God in his power, found its way into the early Russian *The Bee* [*Pčela*] (Semenov 1893, pp. 111-2). We find reflections of this opposition in the chronicle story of the murder of Andrej Bogoljubskij (PSRL, I, 1, col. 370 & II, col. 592); in an extract from Iosif Volockij's *Letter to the Grand Prince* (Iosif Volockij 1959, p. 184); and in the sixteenth discourse of the same author's *Enlightener* [*Prosvetitel'*] (Iosif Volockij 1855, p. 602). In the latter the monarch is directly named "corruptible [mortal] tsar" (ibid., p. 420). Aleksej Michailovič often called himself this, for example in his epistle to the Troice-Sergievo Monastery, 1661 (AAE, IV, No. 127, p. 172).

11   The practice of calling the Tsar "earthly God" is also Byzantine in origin (cf. the same appelation in the works of the eleventh century Byzantine writer Kekavmenos: Kekavmen 1972, p. 275). Foreigners were the first to report that the Russians considered their Tsar to be the "earthly God," e.g. Pastor Oderborn in his pamphlet on Ivan the Terrible, 1588 ("*irrdliche Gott*": see Oderborn 1588, fo. d 3; in the Latin edition the word used for this quality is *divinitas*: see Oderborn 1585, fo. x 4); Isaac Massa in his description of Siberia of 1612 (Alekseev 1932, p. 252); Jurij Križanič in his *Politika* of 1663-6 (Križanič 1965, p. 206). In Russian sources the title of "earthly God" or "earthly divinity" as applied to the monarch is recorded later, from the mid-eighteenth century onwards (see Živov & Uspenskij 1981, II-5).

12   "Righteous sun" is a name often given to Christ in liturgical texts (see, for example, the Christmas troparion, the troparion for the feast of the Purification of the Mother of God, the fourth and fifth verses of the Easter canon, etc.). In the new edition of the liturgical texts established after Patriarch Nikon's reforms, the corresponding expression is 'sun of righteousness.' [Cf. Malachi, 4. 2.]

13   Vajtovič 1977, p. 198.

14   Cf. Simeon Polockij's address to Tsar Aleksej Michailovič of 1656: "We greet you, Orthodox Tsar, righteous sun" (Tatarskij 1886, p. 49).

15   Kel'siev 1860-2, III, pp. 62-98.

16   Ibid., p. 75; cf. also p. 81.

17   Ibid., pp. 63, 81, 106 − 7. "The *skopcy* believe that their Redeemer [Kondratij Selivanov] was incarnate of the Empress Elizabeth Petrovna, of blessed memory, who, according to their mythology, was like the real Mother of God, a pure

virgin at the birth, before the birth and after the birth, since she conceived and bore the Redeemer, according to the Gospel, not from the will of the flesh, but from the Holy Ghost. The most widely held opinion among them is that the Empress Elizabeth was delivered of her burden in Holstein, and then, on her return to Russia, being predestined for a saintly and ascetic life, in fact ruled for only two years (although others maintain she did not rule at all) and gave up her throne to one of her favorites who bore a perfect likeness to her in both her facial features and her spiritual virtues; while she herself retired to the province of Orlov, where she settled in the house of a peasant *skopec* and lived out the remainder of her days under the name of a simple peasant woman, Akulina Ivanovna, in fasting, prayer and good works, and on her death was buried in the garden there, where her relics remain to this day. Other *skopcy* relate that Elizabeth Petrovna's delivery took place in Russia, and that her son, Peter III, the Redeemer, was despatched the moment he was born to Holstein, where on reaching adolescence, he underwent castration." (Ibid., p. 63)

18   Ibid., p. 108.

19   See Pokrovskij 1972.

20   When in the 1790's Kondratij Selivanov was in hiding from the authorities among the Fedoseev Old Believers of the Moscow province, he was treated with great respect, since he led an ascetic life and kept silent. Subsequently, at the investigation, the Old Believer Ivan Gavrilov testified as follows: "We called him, in our local speech, Elijah the Prophet, or Enoch, or John the Divine" (Mel'nikov 1872, p. 47). This could not possibly be simply a rhetorical trope, since such appellations would normally be totally inadmissible among the Old Believers (they consider it sinful, for example, to call people by the sobriquets of their patron saints: to address Nikita, say, as "Nikita Sokrovennyj [the Concealed]," if his nameday is the day of the Holy Nikita Sokrovennyj, see Mel'nikov PSS, IV, p. 251). It is characteristic in this context that Kondratij Selivanov should have proclaimed himself not only God and Tsar, but prophet too, stating that: "I am God of Gods, Tsar of Tsars and prophet of prophets" (Kel'siev 1860-2, III, p. 81; appendices, p. 12).

21   S.M. Solov'ev 1960-66, VII, p. 429.

22   Družinin 1889, pp. 97, 148, 267, 277.

23   That is, prince Michael, mentioned in the Old Testament; according to the prophecy of Daniel, he was called upon to destroy the unfaithful (Daniel 12, 1). Concerning the legend of Tsar Michail, see A.N. Veselovskij 1875; Istrin 1897, pp. 180 ff.; cf. the evidence of Kuz'ma Kosoj at the investigation (1687): "He claims to be Grand duke Michail and, on the evidence of the Holy Scripture and the testimony of various holy books, the Lord God Our Saviour Himself" (Družinin 1889, p. 277). In defence of his plenary powers Kuz'ma Kosoj stated that he had a book which was written in God's own hand before the making of the world and the creation of the universe, and showed a transcript from this book (ibid., p. 97; cf. Supplement to AI 1841-2, XII, p. 133, no. 17).

24   Čistov 1967, p. 90; cf. Supplement to AI 1841-2, XII, p. 139, no. 17. In addition, the biblical prince Michael, mentioned in the Book of the Prophet Daniel, could be associated with the Archangel Michael and at the same time with the Tsar Michail Fedorovič, the founder of the Romanov dynasty. Thus a founder of the Old Believers, Father Lazar', compared Michail Fedorovič with the legendary Tsar (Prince) Michael (Subbotin 1875-90, V, p. 225), while a certain Old Believer, Martyn son of Kuz'ma, stated under torture in 1682: "when Tsar Michail Fedorovič reigned, it was not he, but the Archangel Michael" (S.M. Solov'ev 1960-66, VII, p. 428). As N.N. Pokrovskij points out, the legend of the Tsar Michail "unleashed on the reigning tsar (and sometimes the entire dynasty after Aleksej Michajlovič) an enormous accumulation of eschatological views which had grown up over the centuries in popular consciousness" (Pokrovskij 1974, p. 167).

25 RIB, XIII, cols. 300, 393.
26 Ibid., col. 351.
27 Ibid., cols. 326, 336, 356.
28 See Val'denberg 1916, pp. 362, 364, 365, 369, 372.
29 RIB, XIII, col. 1237.
30 Ibid., col. 1247.
31 See Val'denberg 1916, p. 366.
32 PSRL, VI, p. 228; cf. VIII, p. 211.
33 AI, I, p. 79, No. 40; cf. also p. 82. The "spiritual blindness" of Dmitri; Šemjaka is evidently contrasted here with the physical blindness of Vasilij the Blind (whom Šemjaka blinded in 1446).
34 See especially the *Discourse Selected from the Holy Scriptures which is in Latin* [*Slovo izbranno ot svjatych pisanij eže na latyne*], 1460-1, in the edition of Popov 1875, pp. 384, 394 (Prince Vasilij is called 'Tsar' in this work twelve times in all). The title of 'Tsar' applied to Vasilij the Blind is used also by Metropolitan Iona in his epistle to Pskov (RIB, VI, no 90, col. 673; though in the other copy of this epistle the words 'of the Russian Tsar' as applied to Vasilij the Blind do not occur: see AI, I, no. 60, p. 107), and he is also called this in the chronicle for 1472 (PSRL, XXV, p. 260; Popov 1875, p. 379). The history of Russian princes' being honored with the title of 'Tsar' has been researched by Vodoff (1978); for the term *samoderžec* [autocrat] see Sokol'skij 1902, p. 68, note 3; Ostrogorskij 1935, p. 168.
35 See Iona's epistle to the Pskovians (RIB, VI, no. 90, col. 673), supposedly dated 1461, but possibly earlier (on the question of the date see Golubinskij 1900-17, II, 1, p. 498, note 2).
36 See Val'denberg 1922, pp. 223-4.
37 See Ivan Timofeev's *Chronicle* [*Vremennik*], RIB, XIII, col. 373.
38 Maxim the Greek wrote in his epistle (about 1545) to the young Ivan the Terrible that "the earthly Tsar was none other than the living and visible form (that is, the spirit embodied) of the Tsar of Heaven Himself" (Maksim Grek 1859 – 62, II, p. 350; Ivanov 1969, no. 217); and Metropolitan Filipp Kolyčev said to Ivan: "If, O Tsar, you are revered as the image of God, you were nevertheless created with the clay of the earth" (Sokol'skij 1902, p. 198). No less significant is the fact that Patriarch Nikon protested specifically at the Tsar's being called "God's likeness" (Zyzykin 1931-9, II, p. 14). The Patriarch of Jerusalem, Dosifej (Dositheus), also links the righteousness of the Tsar with his status as the image of God, in his document [*gramota*] to Tsar Fedor Alekseevič dated 27 June 1679 (Kapterev 1895, p. 239). This idea, generally, has its roots in Byzantium (see Živov & Uspenskij 1981, III-2).
39 RIB XIII, col. 367.
40 See Čistov 1967, pp. 44, 66, 67, 71, 86, 118, 126, 127, 148-9, 185, 210.
41 Esipov 1880, p. 434; Čistov 1967, p. 126.
42 Pugačev 1935, pp. 123, 125-6; Čistov 1967, pp. 148-9.
43 Kubalov 1924, p. 167; Čistov 1967, p. 185.
44 Čistov 1967, p. 210. This motif of the "royal marks" turns up unexpectedly after the French Revolution, when a runaway French convict appeared in Russia exhibiting a royal lily (the mark with which capital offenders were branded in pre-Revolutionary France) and went around assuring Russian landowners that this was how the princes of the blood were distinguished; this fabrication was remarkably successful (Pingaud 1886, p. 89; Lotman 1980, p. 45). Ippolit Zavališin (the brother of the Decembrist) – an adventurer who clearly believed in his own divine election – demanded upon his arrest that note be taken of special marks on his body: "that he had a birthmark in the form of a crown on his chest, and on his shoulders another in the form of a sceptre" (Kolesnikov 1914, p. 22; see also above, Part II, Chap. 5, pp. 202-4). Clearly belief in the royal marks was not only widespread among the

common folk but was shared by very different classes of Russian society.

45 Ancient Rome provides us with a typologically similar picture: with the violation of the natural order of succession, the usurper or adopted son who gets the throne pretends to refuse power, i.e. does not consider himself Emperor, as it were, and in fact presents himself as a false monarch. He accepts power only when a sign from God (a victory over his rival, for example), or social opinion, endorses his authority and his mystical power. It is precisely from the moment of this first manifestation of supreme power that the days of his rule are calculated; and by the same token, the day of his predecessor's death does not always coincide with the successor's *dies imperii*: see Béranger 1953 (this book was kindly brought to my notice by M.L. Gasparov).

46 On mythological identification in general, see Lotman & Uspenskij 1973, pp. 285, 296, 299, 300 et passim.

47 Pugačev 1975, pp. 55, 57, 127-39, 152, passim, nos. 50, 54, 156-76, 198 passim. Moreover, Zarubin-Čika was called Ivan Nikiforovič Černyšev, in contrast with the real Count Zachar Grigor'evič Černyšev.

48 See Livanov 1868-73, I, pp. 207-8; Čistov 1967, p. 182.

49 Livanov 1868-73, I, p. 426; Čistov 1967, p. 182.

50 Babenčikov 1933.

51 The phenomenon of mythological identification is seen most graphically among the *skopcy* and the *chlysty* who see in actual people the direct incarnation of the Lord of Sabaoth, of Christ or of the Mother of God, and give these people the corresponding names. In the same way the *Pavlikiane* ["Paulicians"] (who are in many ways similar to the *chlysty* and may well have a common origin) called themselves after the Apostle Paul and his disciples and fellow workers; they saw themselves as their incarnations (see Javorskij 1928, p. 506).

52 RIB IX, pp. 550-1; cf. also p. 529.

53 See Polosin 1926, pp. 59-61.

54 Ibid., p. 62.

55 Compare, for example, the description of the Shrovetide processions in the reminiscences of A.K. Lelong: "At about two o'clock they would harness two or three sledges and on one of them would put a vat or barrel instead of a mattress, and on this would sit Vissarion Rodionovič (a peasant) dressed up in a cloak made of matting and a hat, similarly adorned with bast feathers. He would ride on ahead, while other sleighs rode behind, full to bursting with our house servants, who would be singing and playing the accordion. This convoy would go round the whole village and be joined by other mummers from the village on their own sleighs; they would go round other villages, singing, and be joined by still more people on sleighs and in disguise. Under the leadership of our Vissarion, an enormous convoy would be formed" (Lelong 1913, no. 7, p. 65). Just as characteristic was the custom of dressing up as a priest at the end of Shrovetide and imitating the church ritual of the burial service (see, for example, Šejn 1898-1900, p. 333; M.I. Smirnov 1927, pp. 22-3). The same kind of travesty can be observed in the Yuletide rituals as well (see Gusev 1974; cf. the petition of the *starec* Grigorij, quoted below, which tells us that at Yuletide "they designate some of their number saints, invent their own monasteries and name for them an archimandrite, a cellarer and *starcy*").

It is very significant that in the case of 1666 quoted above, there was a *maiden's* cap on the head of the peasant "Tsar" Perška Jakovlev: dressing up in the clothes of the opposite sex — and especially men dressing up as women — is characteristic of mummers at Shrovetide, Yuletide and other times.

56 Zelenin 1914, no. 40, p. 271.

57 In connection with the "game of Tsar" Makarov's reminiscences of a certain landowner from Čuchloma are interesting: "Of his many cynical and sorcerous

pranks I shall relate only one which was known at that time in the district of Čuchloma as "The Entry into Jerusalem." He once gathered together his serfs and his house-servants of both sexes, even the children, and positioned them in two rows along the road leading from his estate to the nearest village over a distance of several hundred yards. Ordering each to take up a palm branch, he mounted an old nag and rode at walking pace from the village to the manor-house past the two rows of his subjects, who waved their branches over him" (Makarov 1881-2, I, p. 28). Unfortunately, the memoirist makes no mention as to the season in which the performance took place. In as much as the Tsar is seen as a living image of God (see above), the "game of Tsar" is indirectly linked with the likeness to the Divinity; whereas what we have here is a *direct* imitation of God. It is not impossible that the behavior of this landowner reflects memories of the ritual "ride on a donkey" performed by the Patriarch on Palm Sunday (a ritual which had lapsed since 1696), or of the triumphal reception of Peter in Moscow after the victory of Poltava (December 21, 1709), when he was met by children dressed in servers' robes, waving palm branches and singing "Blessed is he that cometh in the name of the Lord"; in one instance Christ was represented by the Patriarch and in the other by the Tsar.

58   Šlichting 1934, p. 22.   A similar account of I.P. Fedorov's execution is given by Oderbom (Oderbom 1588, f.v. M3, fo. R2-f.v. R2; Guagnini 1578, f.v. 28-f.v. 30). See also Karamzin 1830-1, IX, p. 113; for typological analogies see Frejdenberg 1973, p. 492.

59   In addition this disguise very often bears the character of a symbolic *unmasking*. Thus, for example, when in 1570 Ivan the Terrible flew into a rage with the Archbishop of Novgorod, Pimen the Black, he ordered him to be arrayed as a *skomoroch*. Cf. Šlichting's account: ". . . he ordered that his tiara be snatched from his head; he also divested him of his episcopal vestments as well as stripping him of his rank as a bishop, saying: 'It is not fitting that you be a bishop, but rather a *skomoroch*. Therefore I will give you a wife in marriage.' The tyrant ordered that a mare be brought forth, and turning to the bishop said: 'Receive from me this wife, mount her now, saddle her, set out for Muscovy and enter your name on the reigster of the *skomorochi*.' Then, when the bishop had climbed on the mare Ivan ordered that his feet be tied to the animal's back; and having sent him out of town in this fashion, he commanded him to follow the Moscow road. When he had already gone some way, Ivan sent for him to appear before him again and gave him a musical instrument to hold, bagpipes and a stringed lyre. 'Practice in this art,' said the tyrant, 'for there is nothing more for you to do, especially now that you have taken a wife.' And so this bishop, who had no idea before this of how to play the lyre, rode off on the command of the tyrant in the direction of Moscow on the back of the mare, strumming on the lyre and blowing the pipes" (Šlichting 1934, pp. 29-30; cf. Karamzin 1830-1, IX, p. 172). According to other sources the Tsar threatened the Archbishop that he would make him lead a bear about, as the *skomorochi* do (Guagnini 1578, fols. 34-5; Olearius 1906, pp. 127-9). The priest-figure and the *skomoroch* are perceived as antipodes, and by dressing the archbishop up as a *skomoroch*, Ivan is, as it were, attaching him to the inverted world of anti-behavior: if the mummers during the Yuletide and Shrovetide rituals can dress up as priests (see above), then here we have a case of the opposite – of the priest becoming a mummer.

60   For a discussion of the similarities and differences between Ivan's behavior and that of the Holy fool [*jurodivyj*], see above, Part I, Chap. 2.

61   S.M. Solov'ev 1960-66, III, p. 565; Lileev 1891, pp. 25-6; Nikolaev 1904, pp. 466-7.   Cf. the petition handed to Simeon Bekbulatovič by Ivan the Terrible and his sons on October 30, 1575, which observes all the rules of epistolary etiquette laid down for addressing the monarch: "Unworthy Ivan Vasil'ev and his children, little Ivan and little Fedor, do petition thee, great Lord and Prince Semion [sic]

Bekbulatovič of all Russia, that thou, O Lord, shouldst show them mercy..." The petition concludes in the manner proper in such cases with the words: "How, O Lord, dost thou decree? We petition thee, O Lord, for everything. O Lord, have mercy, take pity!" (*Poslanija* 1951, pp. 195-6).

62 Lileev 1891, pp. 26, 36; cf. however Nikolaev 1904, pp. 467-8.

63 The fact that Simeon Bekbulatovič was legitimately installed as Tsar is confirmed by the latest text of the oath of allegiance to Boris Godunov (in 1598) and to his son Fedor Borisovič (in 1605): those swearing allegiance undertook not to wish "the Tsar Simeon Bekbulatovič" to be ruler of Moscow (S.M. Solov'ev 1960-66, IV, pp. 353, 421). It is also significant that the False Dmitri ordered Simeon Bekbulatovič to take the tonsure, seeing in him a claimant to the throne (Nikolaev 1904, p. 470).

64 Cf. the evidence of the Chronicles: "And so Tsar Ivan Vasil'evič became an ally of those who do multiply the sins of Orthodox Christianity and was filled with anger and violence: he began maliciously and mercilessly to persecute the serfs in his power and to shed their blood; and the kingdom which was entrusted to him by God he divided into two parts: one part he made over to himself, and the other he entrusted to Tsar Simeon of Kazan'. Then he went away from several small towns and went to one called Starico, where he took up residence. He called his half the *opričniki* and Tsar Simeon's part the *zemščina*; and he ordered his half to assault, slaughter and plunder the other half..." (S.M. Solov'ev 1960-66, III, p. 733, note 85; cf. Popov 1869, p. 284; Lileev 1891, pp. 22-3). See also the commentary by Ja.S. Lur'e in *Poslanija* 1951, p. 634, note 2. Simeon Bekbulatovič ruled from October 1575 to July 1576.

65 The term *opričnina* was not invented by Ivan the Terrible: it is met earlier in business documents, signifying a separate territory (see Sreznevskij 1893-1912, II, col. 694; Djuvernua 1894, p. 122, S.M. Solov'ev 1960-66, II, p. 484). However, in Ivan's time – and possibly even earlier – the word had a second meaning associated with the "outer [darkness]" [*kromešnyj*], i.e. the inverted, demonic principle; this will be discussed in more detail below.

66 See S.B. Veselovskij 1969, pp. 93-4.

67 The naming of the Tatar Khan as "Tsar" was reflected in the title of the Russian monarch. Thus, Ivan the Terrible, and the Russian monarchs following him, were called "Tsar of Kazan'" and "Tsar of Astrachan'" (after the capture of Kazan' in 1552 and of Astrachan' in 1557): the Khanate (or kingdom) of Kazan' split away from the Golden Horde in 1445 and that of Astrachan' came into being after the collapse of the Golden Horde in 1480, i.e. both Khanates were in one way or another connected with the Golden Horde.

68 Lileev 1891, p. 3; Nikolaev 1904, p. 466.

69 In his capacity as Khan of Kasimov, Simeon Bekbulatovič was related by direct line of succession to the Khans of the Golden Horde and was called Tsar even before he was installed on the Russian throne (see Vel'jaminov–Zernov 1863-6, II, pp. 1, 13-14, 15-16, 20-21, 25). Ivan the Terrible made him Tsar or Khan of Kasimov in 1567; prior to this he was called, like his father, Tsarevich: evidently in his capacity as descendant of the Khans (or Tsars) of the Golden Horde. The rulers of the kingdom of Kasimov in general held the title of Tsarevich, except for those who were already Khans before their installation as ruler of Kasimov; these retained the title of Tsar (Khan). Simeon Bekbulatovič (even before he was converted to Orthodoxy and while he still bore the name Sain-bulat) was the first ruler of Kasimov personally to receive the title of Tsar (Khan). See ibid., pp. 25-6.

The kingdom of Kasimov was created by Vasilij the Blind in 1452 as a reaction to the recently formed kingdom (or Khanate) of Kazan', and the rulers of Kasimov were appointed by the choice of the ruler of Moscow: power was not hereditary and was conferred on the person who was considered most useful to Moscow. Kasimov (the former town of Gorodec) was so named in the same year, 1452, after the prince of the Golden Horde, Kasim, the son of the Khan Udu-Muhammed, who went over to Vasilij the Blind in 1446, for protection against his brother Muchmutek, the Khan of Kazan' (immediately after the latter had formed the kingdom of Kazan' in the autumn of 1445: see Vel'jamino-Zernov 1863-6, I, pp. 3-4). In 1449 Kasim defeated the troops of the Khan of the Golden Horde, Seid-Achmat, and in 1467 led an unsuccessful campaign against Kazan'. Thus the kingdom of Kasimov may be seen as a kind of Muscovite model of the Golden Horde.

70   The assumption by the Russian Grand Prince of the title of Tsar is connected with the fall of the Byzantine Empire, an event which led to the idea of Moscow as the new Constantinople, or the Third Rome (see above, Part I, Chap. 1).

Moreover, in its time, the title of Tsar united the Emperor (*basileus*) of Byzantium, to whom Russia was culturally subject (the Russian church lay under the jurisdiction of Constantinople), and the Khan of the Golden Horde, to whom the Russian lands were politically subject; both of these rulers were called "Tsar" in early Russia. During Tatar rule the Russian church prayed for the Tatar "Tsar," i.e. he was named in the liturgy (see Prochorov 1978, pp. 53, 84); we may assume that before the Tatar-Mongol conquest the prayer for the Tatar "Tsar" had been preceded by prayer for the Greek "Tsar," i.e. the Emperor of Byzantium. After the collapse of the Byzantine Empire and of the Golden Horde (with the subsequent conquest of the Tatar lands), the Grand Prince of Moscow emerges as the successor not only of the Tsar (Emperor) of Byzantium, but also of the Tsar (Khan) of the Golden Horde. On the one hand, with the fall of Byzantium the Grand Prince was the only Orthodox ruler left (with the exception of the ruler of Georgia, which was distant and peripheral), i.e. the only independent ruler of the Orthodox *oikoumene* [inhabited, i.e. civilized, world]; it was generally assumed that there was only one Tsar in the Orthodox world (see RIB VI, supplement, no. 40, col. 274 ff.; cf. D'jakonov 1889, pp. 25-6; Savva 1901, p. 200 ff.), and this position, formerly occupied by the Emperor of Byzantium, was now occupied by the Prince of Russia. On the other hand, the territory which had formerly belonged to the Golden Horde now belonged to the Grand Prince. Thus the Russian Tsar now united in his own person both the Tsar (Khan) of the Golden Horde and the Tsar (Emperor) of Byzantium: if in a territorial sense he was successor to the Tatar Khan, then in a semiotic sense he was successor to the Greek Emperor.

71   Semevskij 1885, p. 283; Petrov 1918, p. 132. Peter's first letter to Romodanovskij addressing him as "king" is dated May 19, 1695. It begins with the words *"Min Her Kenich* [My Lord King]. The letter written by Your Illustrious Majesty, my most merciful sovereign, in the capital town of Presšpurch [Presburg] on the 14th day of May, was handed to me on the 18th day, for which sovereign mercy of yours we are bounden to shed our blood, even to the last drop..." The letter is signed "The eternal slave of your most Illustrious Majesty bombadier *Piter*" (Peter 1887-1977, I, no. 37, pp. 29-30). Later on, similar letters frequently occur.

In his *History of Tsar Peter Alekseevič and of Those Persons Close to Him*, Kurakin recounts that already in 1689, at the time of the military exercises, Peter had proclaimed F.Ju. Romodanovskij to be Tsar of Presburg, with his residence in Preobraženskoe, in the small town Presburg (Plezpurch) on the river Jauza, and I.I. Buturlin to be Tsar of Semenovskoe with his residence in Sokolinyj court on Semenovskoe meadow (Kurakin 1890-1902, I, p. 65). Subsequently, in the mock battles of Kužuchovo in 1694 Buturlin was referred to as "the Polish King" (Željabužskij 1840, pp. 32-3; Bogoslovskij 1940-8, I, p. 195); he suffered a defeat by Romodanovskij, who by this act emerged, as it were, as the Russian potentate (they were both, however, referred to as 'generalissimus' as well). It is highly significant that in these mock battles (at Semenovskoe in 1691 and Kožuchovo in 1694) Peter took part on Romodanovskij's side, acting as his subordinate, and so consequently Romodanovskij's victory over Buturlin was in fact predetermined (see Bogoslovskij 1940-8, I, pp. 125-8, 196-206). In addition, in these contexts Buturlin had under his command a concentration of the old Muscovite troops (*strelcy*), whereas Romodanovskij had the new-style soldiers (*soldaty*); the former played a passive, and the latter an active, role, i.e. Buturlin's forces were doomed to defeat beforehand (see ibid., pp. 195, 197, 199, 206). According to Željabužskij, it was precisely after his victory in the Kozuchovo mock battle of October 1694 that Romodanovskij received his "new appellation" and began to be called '*gosudarič*'* (Željabužskij 1840, p. 39). In his speech to the troops after this victory, Romodanovskij is mentioned as "Our Most Elevated Generalissimus, Prince Fedor Jur'evič of Presburg and Paris and conqueror of All the Jauza" (Bogoslovskij 1940-8, I, p. 201). Wittram supposes that Romodanovskij had the title of "*gosudar*'" in May 1692 (Wittram 1964, I, p. 110), basing his supposition on the letter from the shipwrights of Pere-jaslavl' which states that Peter was building a ship on the orders of "his Lord [*gosudar*'], Generalissimus Prince Fedor Jur'evič" (see Bogoslovskij 1940-8, p. 143); this context is not, however, very significant, in as much as the word "*gosudar*'" could in this case refer to the title of "generalissimus."

72 M.M. Ščerbatov writes of Romodanovskij: "Some time before his departure for foreign parts, he [Peter] gave the title of "Prince-Caesar" to this man [Romo-danovskij], while he himself pretended to be his subject, and in so doing set an example of obedience. Having accepted from him various ranks and, supposedly, instructions, he left him ruler of Russia when he himself went to foreign parts in 1697; and when he returned he continued both the title and his ostensible respect to him: he would call him "Lord" [*gosudar*'] both verbally and in writing, and he used his [Romodanovskij's] sternness and severity to repress the arrogance of the bojars and to track down and punish crimes even unto his death" (Ščerbatov 1774, p. 15). Golikov tells us that, on going abroad in 1697, Peter "founded a new govern-ment": "The Great Lord entrusted the government of the state to his most faithful bojars, Prince Romodanovskij and Tichon Nikitič Strešnev, and gave them as assistants the most loyal of his bojars, namely Lev Kirilovič Naryškin and the Princes Golicyn and Prozorovskij. And so that the Chief Ruler, Prince Romodanovskij, should be the more respected, he gave him the title of Prince-Caesar and Majesty, and himself pretended to be subject to him" (Golikov 1788-9, I, p. 290).

After the victory of Poltava Peter considered it his duty to congratulate Romo-danovskij, in as much as it meant that thenceforth Petersburg would become the residence of "His Majesty": "We congratulate Your Majesty on this victory which is unprecedented in the entire world. And now beyond any doubt the desire of Your Majesty to take up residence in Petersburg has been attained through this final downfall of the enemy" (Peter 1887-1977, IX, I, p. 246, no. 3281).

73 Petrov 1918, p. 135; Verchovskoj 1916, I, p. 92.

74 Petrov 1918, p. 138.

75 Jul' 1900, p. 297.

76 Golikov 1788-9, II, p. 76; Semevskij 1885, pp. 286-7.

77 It is essential to bear in mind that Peter could have been called Emperor long before he officially assumed the imperial title in 1721. Feofan Prokopovič specifi-cally remarks on this in his encomium on Peter, dated 1725, when he recalls how "with our entreaties we persuaded him to assume the title of 'Great' and 'Emperor'";

*'son of the sovereign' or 'little lord': *gosudar*' could mean either 'sovereign' or 'lord'.

Feofan adds: "which is what he was already, and was called by everyone" (Feofan 1760-74, II, p. 163). Indeed, Peter is addressed as "Emperor" and "Father of the Fatherland" as early as 1708 in a speech delivered to him on behalf of all the clergy (Charlampovič 1914, p. 462, note 4, with a reference to the Archive of the Typographical Library, no. 100, fol. 20). From that time on this title is frequently used to refer to Peter. Some examples follow. In 1709, on the occasion of the victory of Poltava, a publication appeared under the title of *The Wonderful Public Apotheosis of the most Praiseworthy Valour of the Hercules of All the Russias...of Our Great Sovereign, Tsar and Grand Prince Peter Alekseevič, Emperor and Autocrat of All the Russias, Great, Small and White* (Pekarskij 1862, II, no. 160; Bykova & Gurevič 1955, no 26). In 1713 in the title of the *Book of Mars... [Kniga Marsovaja]* it is stated that it was printed "by order of the Emperor, Peter the First, Autocrat of All the Russias," and on the frontispiece of this volume there appears a portrait of Peter done by Aleksej Zubov in 1712 with this inscription: "Peter the First, Most August [*prisnopribavitel'*] Emperor, Tsar and Autocrat of All the Russias" (Pekarskij 1862, II, no 233, p. 291; Bykova & Gurevič 1955, no. 68; Peter 1973, p. 206. The word *prisnopribavitel'* [literally: 'Eternally increasing'] means 'most august,' cf. *augustus* from Latin *augeo*, 'I increase, add'). Peter is referred to as 'Emperor' (but not as 'Tsar') in Serban Kantemir's *Panegyrical Burnt Offering [Panegiričeskoe vsesožženie]* of 1714 (Pekarskij 1862, II, no. 249; Bykova & Gurevič 1955, no. 85); it is noteworthy that in the manuscript of this work, preserved in the Library of the Academy of Sciences, the word '*Autocrat*' [*samoderžec*] is used instead of 'Emperor' (Bykova, Gurevič & Kozinceva 1972, no. 20): apparently the word 'Emperor' was inserted during the process of publication. The title of the book *The Laurea or Crown of Immortal Glory [Ljavrea ili Venec bezsmertnyja slavy]* (1714) uses the words "His Imperial Majesty" (Pekarskij 1862, II, no. 266; Bykova & Gurevič 1955, no. 112); in just the same way Peter is called 'Emperor' in both editions of the *Book of Command or of Maritime Rights in the Navy [Kniga ordera ili vo flote morskich prav]*, which came out in the same year, 1714 (Pekarskij 1862, II, nos. 247, 249; Bykova & Gurevič 1955, nos. 75, 79). See also Bykova & Gurevič 1955, nos. 243, 310, 320 (= Pekarskij 1862, II, no. 394), 366, 606 (= Pekarskij 1862, II, no. 478); Bykova & Gurevič 1958, nos. 126, 128, 130, 131, 136, 138 (= Pekarskij 1862, II, no. 453), 149 (= Pekarskij 1862, II, no. 478); Pekarskij 1862, II, nos. 380, 450, 483. 1718 saw the publication of the *True Document of His Caesarine Roman Majesty...on whom the aforementioned Caesar in this his Document conferred the title of Caesar [Cesar'] of all the Russias*; this Document was referred to on the occasion of Peter's being presented with the imperial title (Pekarskij 1862, II, no. 388; Bykova & Gurevič 1955, no. 298). We should also mention the portrait of Peter in the collection of the State Russian Museum, presumably to be dated 1697, which bears the inscription: *Petrus Alexandrowitz Moscowitarum Imperator cum magna legatione huc regio montem venit medio May. Anno M: DCXCVII;* i.e. "Peter Aleksandrovič, Emperor of Muscovy, came here to the region of mountains together with the Great Embassy in the middle of May 1697" (Peter 1973, p. 119). Even earlier, in 1696, on the occasion of the victory of Azov, a medal was struck with a portrait of Peter and bearing the inscription: *Petrus Alexii fil, Russor. Mag. Caes.* (Bajer 1738, p. 267), where the word *Caes[ar]* signifies 'Emperor'. In 1709 the Viennese court expressed its disapproval of the Tsar's assumption of the title of 'Emperor'; in 1710 the Austrian ambassador to Russia, General Velček (Weltschek) notified Vienna to acknowledge the title of '*Majestät Kayser'*, i.e. the imperial title (Florovskij 1972, p. 390).
78 Berchgol'c 1902-3, I, pp. 115-7; Petrov 1918a, p. 121. The wedding of the Prince-Pope took place on September 10, 1721, and Peter became Emperor on October 20 of the same year.

79 Petrov 1918, p. 138; idem 1918a, pp. 123-4.

80 It should be emphasized that *'kesar''* stands in the same relation to 'tsar' as 'pope' [*papa*] to 'patriarch'. Indeed, if *pope* signifies the supreme pontiff of Rome, then *kesar'* in Church Slavonic signifies the Roman Emperor: see above, Part I, Chap. 3, note 5. Thus Prince-*kesar'*, like Prince-Pope, would on the face of it appear to be Rome-orientated; however, just as the Prince-Pope in fact represents the Russian patriarch, so the Prince-*kesar'* represents the Russian Tsar.

81 *Poslanija* 1951, p. 213.

82 It is indicative that in 1682, at the time of the Revolt of the *Strel'cy* and the disputes with the Old Believers, the Tsarevna Sophia Alekseevna broke off the discussions and threatened to leave Moscow with the two young Tsars (Ivan and Peter)* (S.M. Solov'ev 1960-66, VII, p. 288); this threat had the desired effect. Cf. in this connection Peter's own departure in 1689 for the Troice-Sergievo Monastery.

When, however, Patriarch Nikon did the same thing (in 1658 Nikon, having quarrelled with Aleksej Michailovič, ostentatiously left the patriarchal throne and retreated to the Monastery of the Resurrection), he ceased to be considered Patriarch. The difference in attitude to secular and ecclesiastical power is thrown into particular relief here: in a certain sense the Tsar emerges as a more sacred figure than the Patriarch, in as much as he is Tsar by nature and not by virtue of his having been installed upon the throne.

83 Similarly, Ivan the Terrible mockingly called Nikita Kazarinov Golochvastov an "angel" (see the testimony of Kurbskij in his *History of the Grand Prince of Muscovy*, RIB, XXXI, col. 308; cf. Karamzin 1830-1, IX, p. 186). In an exactly comparable way Peter the Great later named one of the participants in his fools' performances (Vasilij Sokovnin) "a prophet," and this directly corresponds to the blasphemous tendency of Peter's merrymaking (cf. Kurakin's testimony in his *History of Tsar Peter Alekseevič and of Those Persons Close to Him*: Kurakin 1890-1902, I, p. 73). In conditions where the non-conventionality of the sign is prevalent this kind of linguistic behavior is highly significant.

84 Cf., for example, the eloquent description of Yuletide mummers in the Petition of 1636 from the priests of Nižnij-Novgorod, apparently drawn up by Ioann Neronov: "On their faces they place shaggy and beast-like masks and the like in clothing too, and on their behinds they fix tails, like demons made visible, and they wear shameful members on their faces, and goat-like bleat all manner of devilish things and display their shameful members, and others beat tabors and clap and dance and perform other improper deeds" (Roždestvenskij 1902, pp. 24-6); the features described here correspond exactly to the iconographic image of the demon, which is also characterized by the tail, the shagginess and the interchange between top and bottom (the face and the sexual organs). In just the same way the behavior of the mummers in the picture represented here corresponds to the idea of devilish behavior. The description of Yuletide games which appears in the Life of Ioann Neronov is no less characteristic: "In those days the ignorant used to assemble for games of devilry...putting on their faces various frightening masks in the guise of demons' faces" (Subbotin 1875-90, I, p. 247). Numerous ethnographic descriptions testify that the mummers themselves called their masks "the mask of the Devil," "the devil's mug," "the devil's grimace" and so on, and by the same token considered that donning them constituted a terrible sin which would require future atonement. Very often, therefore, any kind of Yuletide mask at all, whatever it represented, was seen as a devil's mask (see, for example, Efimenko 1877-8, I, p. 138; Maksimov, 1908-1913, XVII, pp. 39-40). In early Russia a particular form of penance was

---

*i.e. Ivan V and his half-brother Peter I (the Great); Sophia, their elder sister, was Regent until 1689.

laid on those who donned a mask.

It is no accident, therefore, that the *opričniki* of Ivan the Terrible, whose form of behavior was to a significant degree based on the principles of anti-behavior (see below), should have danced in masks: it is well-known that Prince Michajlo Repnin preferred death to the donning of the sinful *"maškara"* (RIB, XXXI, col. 279; S.M. Solov'ev 1960-66, III, p. 541). Kurbskij testifies that the Tsar ordered that Repnin be killed in church, near the altar, during the reading of the Gospel; this is, of course, highly significant: the wearing of a mask was shown in this case to be the antipode to the church ritual.

85   See Šlichting 1934, p. 27; Polosin 1963, p. 154; Karamzin 1830-1, IX, pp. 98-9; Skrynnikov 1975, p. 123. Metropolitan Filipp (Kolyčev) viewed the wearing of monastic cowls by the *opričniki* as sacrilege. See Karamzin 1830-1, IX, pp. 98, 118-9.

86   See Semevskij 1885, pp. 282-336; Wittram 1964, I, pp. 106-10.

87   Kurbskij, for example, often calls the *opričniki* "kromešniki" (see especially RIB, XXXI, cols. 155, 273, 306, 307, 323) and puts into the mouth of Metropolitan Filipp Kolyčev the following words addressed to the Tsar: "If thou wilt promise to repent of thy sins and dismiss from thy presence that Satanic regiment which thou hast assembled to the great detriment of Christianity, that is to say, those *kromešniki*, though they are called *aprišnicy [opričniki]*, I will bless thee and forgive thee, and will return...to my throne" (RIB, XXXI, col. 316). On this subject S.B. Veselovskij wrote: "The words *oprič'* and *krome* are synonymous. In those days the idea of the after-life, of "the kingdom of God," was a realm of eternal light beyond the confines of which (outside *[oprič']* which, without *[krome]* which) was the kingdom of eternal gloom, "the kingdom of Satan"... The expressions *kromešnyj* and *kromešnik*, formed by analogy with the words *oprič'*, *opričnyj* and *opričnik*, were not merely a play on words, but at the same time branded the *opričniki* as the progeny of hell, as servants of Satan. Kurbskij, too, on many occasions in his writings, calls the adherents and servants of Tsar Ivan, and in particular his *opričniki*, "the Satanic regiment," from which it followed, or was implied, that Tsar Ivan was like Satan" (S.B. Veselovskij 1963, p. 14; cf. also Karamzin 1830-1, IX, p. 95 and note 140). In exactly the same way Ivan Timofeev also recounts in his *Chronicle [Vremennik]* that the Tsar laid "dark," i.e. infernal, signs on his *opričniki*: "He separated his favorites, who were as wolves, from those he hated, who were as sheep, and laid on the chosen warriors dark signs: he clothed them all in black from head to foot, and ordered that they also have their own horses, identical in color to their clothing; he made all his men in every way like demonic servants" (RIB, XIII, col. 272). That it is possible to put such an interpretation on the word *opričnik* seems to be inherent in the word itself: *opričnik* seems to be etymologically connected with the Ukrainian *oprišok* ('robber'), and this corresponds to the connection between robbers and the world of outer darkness *[kromešnyj]* and of sorcery (cf. the widespread association of robbers with sorcerers). In this context the name introduced by Ivan is highly significant: it is surely this that also explains the prohibition in 1575 of the name *opričnina* (see S.M. Solov'ev 1960-66, III, p. 565; Polosin 1963, p. 183; Štaden 1925, p. 110; Skrynnikov 1975, p. 190).

88   Kapterev 1913, p. 181. The custom of dressing up as a monk at Yuletide was partially kept up even into the twentieth century (see Zavojko 1914, p. 138; Čičerov 1957, p. 210, and also the description of the 'monk game' in, for example, M.I. Smirnov 1922, p. 58). The information given by the chronicler of Piskarev (in the beginning of the seventeenth century) about the entertainments indulged in by the young Ivan the Terrible in 1545-6 is very interesting in this connection: "And he also amused himself in this way: he would do the spring ploughing and sow buckwheat with his bojars, and his other amusements were walking on stilts and *dressing*

up in a shroud" (see Materialy 1955-9, II, pp. 73-4). This should be compared with those ethnographical accounts which testify that Yuletide mummers sometimes dressed up in "the clothes of the deceased" and pretended to be corpses (see, e.g. Zobnin & Patkanov 1899, p. 517); cf. also the Yuletide game of 'dead-man', in which one of the participants also imitated a dead person (see Gusev 1974, p. 50 ff; Maksimov 1908-1913, XVII, p. 14ff.; Zavojko 1917, p. 24). Both corpses and representatives of the Devil belong to the 'other world' and can be directly associated with each other; thus in a broad sense mummers depict all dwellers of the 'other world.'

Thus the *opričniki* should evidently be associated with mummers and in this sense identify with the 'other world' of outer darkness [*kromešnyj*]. It is, moreover, characteristic that the *opričniki* should, in their turn, perceive the representatives of the *zemščina* as belonging to another, alien world: for which very reason, it was as if in their eyes they did not even exist. Cf. Štaden's testimony: "The *opričniki* did indescribably terrible things to the *zemskie* [members of the *zemščina*] so as to extort from them money and goods. Even the field of battle [i.e. God's judgement*] had no force in this case: all those who fought on the side of the *zemskie* acknowledged themselves to be defeated; though they were alive they were thought of as if they were dead..." (Štaden 1925, p. 86). Thus the *opričniki* consider the *zemskie* to be no better than *corpses*: the *opričnina* and the *zemščina* belong to different worlds, which are opposed to each other in the same way as the 'other world' and this world are.

The *opričniki* were supposed to avoid associating with the *zemskie* (see Štaden 1925, p. 93), and this forcibly reminds one of those restrictions on association which were common in the case of denominational disagreements (cf. the Old Believers' later refusal to have contact with the Nikonites for eating, drinking and praying); it was most likely this that Ivan Timofeev had in mind when he wrote in his Chronicle that Ivan the Terrible, in founding the *opričnina*, "in his anger, by division and splitting into two, divided a united people and as it were created two faiths" (RIB, XIII, col. 271). The *opričniki* moreover cut themselves off from their parents and in so doing automatically became outcasts, standing in opposition to the rest of the world. The punishment for contact between an *opričnik* and a member of the *zemščina* was death for both, so association with a representative of the opposite party was just as dangerous as contact with a representative of the 'other world.'

89   Kurakin, in his *History of Tsar Peter Alekseevič...*, describes Peter's jesting entertainments as "Yuletide pranks," remarking, however, that the Patriarch of All the Fools "prolonged his celebration from Christmas throughout the entire winter until Shrovetide, visiting all the noble households of Moscow and the suburb and the houses of the best-known merchants, and chanting the way they usually do in church" (Kurakin 1890-1902, I, p. 72 ff.); the behavior of the travesty "Patriarch" is, moreover, extremely reminiscent of the behavior of Yuletide carol-singers. Information on this jesting celebration at Yuletide can also be found in Željabužskij 1840, p. 59, cf. pp. 225, 279; Bassevič 1866, pp. 119-20; Jul' 1900, pp. 128-9; Korb 1906, p. 109 ff.; and Berchgol'c II, pp. 10-11; III, p. 186. Golikov, following Strahlenberg, enumerates all that Peter was accused of and mentions in particular "His Majesty's celebration at Yuletide" (Golikov 1788-9, I, p. 3; cf. Strahlenberg 1730, pp. 231-2); it is quite clear that the "Assembly of All the Fools" could indeed be seen as a Yuletide performance. According to Berchgol'c, Yuletide celebrations in 1724 were signalized by all the senators and members of the Imperial Colleges being dressed up in disguise and being obliged to wear masks and the appropriate costumes even in their audience chambers (Berchgol'c 1902-3, IV, pp. 16-17).

Even later in the eighteenth century jesting performances were often associated

*Whichever side won in a battle to settle a dispute was taken to have been granted success by God's judgement.

289

with either Yuletide or Shrovetide and included features of the corresponding rituals. So, for example, the public masquerade 'Minerva Triumphant' which took place in Moscow in 1763 after Catherine the Great's accession was arranged to coincide with Shrovetide. Porošin describes the Yuletide games which Catherine organized in Petersburg, in which men dressed up in women's clothing (Porošin 1881, col. 560), in a similar way to that of Yuletide mummers. Dressing up in the clothes of the opposite sex was in general characteristic of court masquerades in the eighteenth century (see for example Catherine 1906, pp. 100-1; Porošin 1881, col. 555, Chrapovickij 1901, p. 205).

90 Lileev 1895, p. 208; Roždestvenskij 1910, p. xxxiv.

91 See Uspenskij 1976, p. 290. In exactly the same way the prominent Old Believer Ivan Smirnov testified in the 1720's that Peter was making "the male sex female, to the extent that he orders the male sex to let their hair grow long and to shave their beards" (P.S. Smirnov 1909, p. 160); as already pointed out, assuming the attributes of the opposite sex is typical in general of mummers: men disguising themselves in women's clothing, imitating women and so on. Such an opinion as the one quoted above must have been reinforced by the behavior of Peter himself, who was prone to all kinds of disguises and to the assumption of other names or titles which corresponded to them ('Sergeant Peter Michajlov', 'bombardier' or 'captain Piter', and so on).

92 Miller 1915, p. 590.

93 Ibid., p. 621.

94 Dimitrij Ioannovič 1908, pp. 13, 17.

95 RIB, XIII, col. 827.

96 RIB, XIII, col. 56. Apart from the prescriptions laid down for fasting on Wednesdays and Fridays, the Russians and the other Eastern Slavs placed a special prohibition on veal (see Zelenin 1927, p. 116). According to Šlichting, who records that Muscovites ate no veal at all, Ivan the Terrible ordered that people who sampled veal out of hunger should be burnt at the stake (Šlichting 1934, p. 39): thus it is quite clear that a doctrinal significance was seen in this prohibition.

97 See Ustrjalov 1859, II, pp. 196, 238.

98 See, e.g., Maksimov 1908-1913 XVIII, pp. 128, 146; idem X, p. 184; Nikitina 1928, pp. 309-10; Zelenin 1927, p. 45; Efimenko 1877-8, II, p. 221.

99 Nikitina 1928, pp. 311-2.

100 Miller 1915, p. 585.

101 Ibid., p. 591; cf. also pp. 587, 588, 589, 593, 595, 597, 601, 602, 620, 624.

102 RIB, XIII, cols. 818-20. Cf. also in *Another Story [Inoe skazanie]*: "And he created for himself in this transient life an entertainment which was also a token of his eternal dwelling-place in future ages, the like of which no-one in the state of Russia or in any other state, save in the infernal kingdom, has ever before seen on earth: an exceedingly vast hell, having three heads. And he made both its jaws of bronze which jangled greatly; and when it opened wide its jaws, the onlookers saw what seemed like a flame spurt from inside them and a great jangling noise issued from its gullet; its teeth were jagged and its claws seemed ready to grab, and out of its ears flames seemed to be bursting forth; and the accursed one placed it right on his Moskva river as a reminder of his sins, so that from the highest vantage points in his residence he could gaze upon it always and be ready to settle in it for endless ages with other like-minded associates" (RIB, XIII, cols. 55-6).

103 S.M. Solov'ev 1960-66, IV, p. 455; Olearius 1906, p. 238.

104 For customs associated with the burial of "unclean" bodies in general, see Zelenin 1916.

105 RIB, XIII, col. 831; cf. col 59.

106 Ustrjalov 1859, I, p. 347; cf. S.M. Solov'ev 1960-66, IV, p. 455.

107 Cf. the description of the Yuletide mummers in the Petition of 1636 from the priests of Nižnij-Novgorod quoted above, note 84. The reed-pipe stuck into the False Dmitri's mouth "for payment to the gate-keeper at the entrance to hell" seems to be a travesty substitute for the money which was ordinarily placed with the deceased so that he would be received into the next world (on this custom see Uspenskij 1978, p. 108, note 32); moreover, the money was sometimes placed in the deceased's *mouth* (see Collins 1671, p. 21; PSRL, I, col. 178; cf. also Fischer 1921, p. 173 ff., Niederle 1912-21, I, pp. 266-8). In addition, the whistle could also have corresponded functionally to the so-called "permit," which, it was supposed, was destined for the gate-keeper of Paradise, who was usually thought to be either St. Nicholas or St. Peter (Uspenskij 1978, pp. 94-5).

108 RIB, XIII, col. 831; cf. col. 59.

109 Dimitrij Ioannovič 1908, pp. 25, 31. For our purposes here it is sufficient to note that pretenders were *perceived* as sorcerers, in as much as they were seen as self-appointed, travesty Tsars. The question arises as to how far anti-behavior was inherent in these pretenders and how far it was attributed to them by public opinion. It must be supposed that this was a question of the degree of self-awareness of the pretender, which varied in each actual case. As we have already said, many pretenders undoubtedly believed that they were genuine Tsars, yet among them there were also some adventurers who were perfectly well aware of the unlawfulness of their claims. *A priori* it must be assumed that anti-behavior was in the main characteristic of the pretenders in the second category, i.e. those who perceived themselves as mummers.

110 See especially on this Uspenskij 1976.

111 What is meant here is walking around the lectern against the sun (in other words, anti-clockwise) in the course of the celebration of a christening or a wedding; this practice was introduced by Patriarch Nikon, whereas previously the accepted form of this ritual movement was in the opposite direction, 'sun-wise.' The opponents of Nikon's reforms considered this change a blasphemous violation of the ritual, imparting to it the nature of a demonic action.

112 This refers more particularly to the spread of the art of secular portraiture. Formerly only icon-painting was allowed in Muscovite Russia, i.e. it was permitted to depict only the saints, not ordinary people.

113 What is presumably meant here is the violation of fasts, a common feature of life in Petrine Russia, and the exemption of soldiers from fasting, which was introduced into Russia on Peter's insistence.

114 That is, the enforced introduction of foreign dress under Peter.

115 Formerly it was forbidden to eat, drink or pray with persons of another faith (foreigners); this prohibition survived among the Old Believers.

116 Esipov 1861-3, II, p. 41.

117 See Čistov 1967, pp. 91-112; Golikova 1957, pp. 122-61, 168-76, 172-219, 266-75.

118 See Čistov 1967, pp. 114-30.

119 Ibid., pp. 118-9.

120 Such a duality, as we have seen, is quite characteristic for the ideology of imposture: just as the pretender Peter III (Pugačev) had his own 'Count Černyšev' (see above), so the "pretender" Peter the Great was assumed to have a pretender heir, Aleksej Petrovič.

121 Čistov (1967, pp. 113-4), who thinks that the historical image of Peter did not correspond to the Utopian image of the Tsar-Deliverer, explains this phenomenon differently – and in our opinion unconvincingly. Inasmuch as Peter was perceived as a Tsar by "indirect" line of succession, and as a "substitute" Tsar, his historical image bears no relation at all to the problem: the real Peter who existed in the

consciousness of his contemporaries has nothing whatsoever to do with the person who *should have been* occupying his place.

THE SYRIAC QUESTION IN SLAVONIC LITERATURE:
WHY SHOULD THE DEVIL SPEAK SYRIAC?

B. A. Uspenskij

There are indications in Slavonic literature that the Devil speaks Syriac. This motif occurs more than once, for example in the Life of St. Hilary, included in the Macarian Menology at 21st October. While exorcising a possessed camel, the saint asks the evil spirit "in Syriac": "Fearest thou not me, guileful devil, being entered into such a vessel?" In another episode Hilary is visited by a demoniac; the onlookers are amazed "that the man, who knew no tongue but his native German, and the Latin, began to answer the saint's questions in the tongue of Palestine ... The devil answered him in Syriac, confessing that from the first he had entered into him." [1]

Likewise the Fool in Christ Andrew of Constantinople, when a young man came to him for instruction, "turned the young man's speech to Syriac, and sat and conversed with him as much as he desired." [2]

Notwithstanding the opinions of certain scholars, linguistic behavior of this kind is not peculiar to devils (as A.I. Jacimirskij considered [3]) or to Fools in Christ (the opinion of A.M. Pančenko [4]); nor are there grounds for regarding the case in point as linguistic anti-behavior, i.e. the assumption of a foreign tongue as glossolalia. We cannot avoid the conclusion that in the examples quoted the devil speaks. Syriac not so much on account of its incomprehensibility or some other negative characteristic of the language as on account of its antiquity: the use of Latin by demons in mediaeval Catholic literature forms a perfect analogy (cf. the Catholic legend where a demoniac is brought to a monk who demands that the demon should speak to him in Latin [5]). Thus, in the apocryphal *Questions of how many parts Adam was created in*, [6] we find the assertion that God "will judge the earth in Syriac." In the treatise "Of letters" by the monk Chrabr it is maintained that Syriac was the language that God originally created, and that it was spoken by Adam and by all people until the Tower of Babel: "for God made not the Hebrew tongue first, nor the Latin, nor the Greek, but the Syriac, which Adam spoke, and from Adam to the Flood, and from the Flood until God divided their tongues at Babel ..."[7]). Chrabr is clearly using Greek sources: the opinion that Syriac is the oldest of all languages was expressed, for example, by Theodoret of Cyrrhus in his commentary on Genesis, where he refers to the Syriac origin of the first biblical names (Adam, Cain, Abel and Noah) and of the word "Hebrew";[8] this opinion was attacked by George Hamartolos, who considered Hebrew, and not Syriac, to be the oldest language.[9] It is characteristic also that the Life of St. Cyril (Constantine) the Philosopher, according to its most likely interpretation, ascribes to Cyril a knowledge of Syriac and an acquaintance with the Syriac version of the Scriptures. [10]

Translated by Ralph Cleminson

NOTES

1 *Velikie Minei Četii*, October, col. 1721-1722.
2 Ibid. col. 121.
3 Jacimirskij 1913, book 3, p. 97.
4 Lichačev & Pančenko 1976, p. 125.
5 "The reader said to the evil spirit: 'I shall recognise you as the evil spirit that dwells in this peasant if you speak to me in Latin.' And he began to speak and made a mistake in his Latin, and the brother derided him for his bad grammar. But the evil spirit answered: 'I can speak Latin as well as you, but this peasant's tongue is so coarse and unfitted for speech that I can scarcely speak with it for its coarseness.'" (Karsavin 1915, p. 66)
6 "Voprosy ot skol'kich častej sozdan byl Adam," in Tichonravov 1863, II, p. 452.
7 Kuev 1967, pp. 189-190; cf. also pp. 193, 196,199, 203, 206, 209, 212, 216, 219, etc.
8 Jagić 1896, p. 25; Kuev 1967, p. 68.
9 Istrin 1920-30, I, pp. 57-58.
10 Vaillant 1935; Jakobson 1944; Jakobson 1954, pp. 68-70; Horálek 1956; Ivanova 1969.

ON THE ORIGIN OF RUSSIAN OBSCENITIES

B.A. Uspenskij

The study of Russian obscene language is beset with special highly characteristic difficulties. Most characteristic of all is the taboo attached to the subject, which, strange as it may seem, extends also to scholars working in the fields of lexicography, phraseology and etymology. And yet expressions of this kind are of particular interest to the etymologist and philologist in view of their archaic nature which gives the opportunity to reconstruct elements of proto-Slavonic phraseology. The taboo extends also to a number of words semantically related to the obscene vocabulary;[1] this is particularly true of Russian, in contrast to the Western European languages in which words of this type are free from taboo. There is no contradiction between the taboo attaching to obscene and related words and their active use in the context of anti-behavior which tends to break cultural prohibitions.

This attitude towards obscene language is determined by a specific sense of the non-arbitrary nature of the linguistic sign in the case in question. It is significant that prohibitions against this sort of expression are absolute, not relative, in character, a fact which reveals their essential independence of the context: the uttering (or writing) of obscenities is regarded as inadmissible on principle—even when it is attributed to a third person, as in the case of the repetition of someone else's words for which the speaker (or writer) cannot be held responsible. In other words, the text cannot be translated to the level of metatext, and cannot be just quotation: in any context the words in question retain as it were a *direct* connection with their content, and consequently whoever utters them is in every case directly responsible for them.[2] But this sort of attitude towards the linguistic sign is characteristic first and foremost of sacred lexis: indeed, this specific sense of the non-arbitrariness of the linguistic sign is characteristic precisely of the sacred, and is responsible for the taboo attaching to expressions within it; hence, paradoxically, the vocabulary of degradation approaches that of religion.

This attitude to obscene language may be explained by supposing that obscenities had a strongly expressed ritual function in Slavonic paganism; the attitude towards this phraseology survives in the language, though the function itself is lost.

Indeed, the use of obscene language is represented in a wide variety of agricultural, nuptial, etc. rituals of evident pagan origin—that is in ceremonies connected in one way or another with *fertility*: obscene language is an essential component of such rites and is unquestionably ritualistic in character. At the same time the use of obscenities is markedly anti-Christian; and this is also connected with their pagan origins. In consequence, obscene language was regarded in early Russian literature as a feature of diabolical behavior, cf. for example the description of heathen games in the *Petition of the priests of Nižnij Novgorod* of 1636:

> Moreover, sire, they abuse one another shamefully, their father and their mother whorishly, in the mouth* [?] and in the throat, defiling their tongues and their souls with the most shameful filthiness.

In the middle of the sixteenth century Metropolitan Daniel, denouncing those who spent their time "engaged in foul speech and in the shameful devices of Satan," wrote:

> but you, who are a Christian, do that which is hateful to God; you dance and leap, speak whorish words, and are guilty of many other mockeries and foul speech, play the zither, and bowed instruments, and pipes, and whistles, and do great service to Satan;

in his words, "where there is foul talk and blasphemy, there is a gathering of demons, where there are games, there is the devil, and where there is dancing, there is Satan." Obscene language is presented here along with other characteristic features of heathen behavior denounced in didactic writings against the "double faith."** Cf. also the Hypatian Monastery of the Trinity's instruction to its agents (seventeenth century), which prescribes that the monastery peasants "should not curse with obscene or any foul words, and should not play devilish games, or pipes or zithers or wind instruments or domras or any games"; examples could be multiplied. The *Tale of Bygone Years*, describing the pagan rituals of the Radimiči, Vjatiči and Severjane,*** mentions "shameful speech" as a specific feature of heathen conduct. It is also worth noting the opinion expressed in early Russian literature that an obscene expression "is a Jewish word": in the Christian perspective "Jewish," like "Hellenic," could be identified with paganism, and consequently the heathen Slavonic gods could be treated as "Jewish"—we find references to the "Jewish heretic Perun"**** and to "Chors***** the Jew," for example. At the same time the house-spirit, a personage of evident pagan origin, was

*Russian, *v rod* is here translated as if it were *v rot*.
**Russian, *dvoeverie* – the coexistence of Christianity and paganism.
***Slavonic tribes.
****God of thunder.
*****God of the sun.

credited with a propensity for obscene swearing.

It is important to realize that there are occasions when obscene language was the functional equivalent of prayer. Thus to escape from a wood- or house-spirit or from a devil, one was advised either to say a prayer or to use obscene language (in the same way as one turned either to a priest or to a sorcerer in order to counteract witchcraft); moreover obscene language was at times regarded as relatively the stronger means, i.e. there could be occasions when prayer was of no avail and only cursing was effective. Likewise, both prayers and obscenities were means of finding buried treasure: in some localities it was considered necessary to pray in order to take possession of treasure guarded by evil spirits, and in others to curse. In just the same way the magical ritual of *opachivanie** used to free a locality of an epidemic (identified with evil spiritual forces) was accompanied sometimes by noise, shouting and cursing, and at other times by prayer. Insofar as the evil spirits represent the old heathen gods, one may suppose that obscene swearing goes back to heathen prayers or incantations.[3] There is a particularly clear correspondence between obscene language and pagan religion among the Serbs, who avert hail by throwing a *hammer* at the clouds, *swearing as they do so*. It is well known that in Slavonic (and Indo-European) mythology the hammer is an attribute of the thunder god; it must be assumed that the obscenities bear some relation or other to him as well.

In order to understand the role of obscene language in pagan religion it is of particular interest that writings directed against obscenity declare that an obscene word is an offence firstly to the Mother of God, secondly to the mother of the person to whom it is addressed, and thirdly to

> the third mother, the earth, by whom we are fed, and nourished, and clad, and given thousands of good things, and to whom by the commandment of God we shall return, that is in our burial.[4]

One copy of the apocryphal *Conversation of the Three Hierarchs* includes the question "Why is it not meet for Orthodox Christians to swear?" and the answer:

> Because of the most holy Mother of God, Christ's mother; secondly our own mother, of whom we were born and saw the light, thirdly Mother Earth, from whom we were taken and to whom we shall return.

This is considered to be a Russian interpolation in a text of Greek provenance. Cf. also the apocryphal *Jerusalem Scroll*, where Our Lord says:

---

*A nocturnal ceremony in which a plough was drawn round the village by naked women.

I command you not to swear and not to pronounce My name in vain and not to let fall from your lips foul, abusive and obscene words. So great is this sin, that I cannot forgive it, for it is not only your own mother that you put to shame—you shame your own mother, and the Mother of God, and damp Mother Earth.

Likewise the spiritual song "Of the drunkard" ("Basil the Great") says that an obscene word offends Mother Earth and the Mother of God. In the same way the specialist on Belorussian culture, A.E. Bogdanovič, noting the Belorussians' "concept of the earth as universal mother" remarks: "it is therefore considered reprehensible, among other things, to use obscene language, as this dishonours Mother Earth."

Particularly characteristic in this connection is the magical practice of copulation with the earth which undoubtedly has a pagan origin. (This practice may explain the ritual rolling on the ground which forms part of some agricultural rites). Significantly, an offence of this nature against Mother Earth is considered on a par with an insult offered to one's *parents*. In an early Russian penitential we read: "If anyone abuses or beats his father or mother, or lies upon the earth playing as upon his wife, 15 days [of penance]." Cf. also the unmarried girls' appeal for husbands addressed to the feast of the Intercession of the Mother of God, which plays upon the inner form of the name of the feast (*Pokrov*, lit. "covering") and moreover likens the girl to the earth, understood as a female organism: "Father Pokrov, cover (*pokroj*) the earth with snow, and me with a bridegroom." The concept of the earth as a female organism is also to be found in one of A.N. Afanas'ev's "forbidden stories," where the world is compared to a woman's body: the breasts are "the Mountains of Sion," the navel "the navel of the world," and the vulva "the outer darkness." The motif of copulation with the earth has evident mythological roots and betrays a link with the basic myth of the god of thunder, as may be seen, for example, in the wedding lament:

Break open, thunder-arrow,
[Break open] also the mother, the damp Mother Earth.
Fall apart, damp Mother Earth,
On all four sides.

Similarly in the pagan religion of antiquity, the earth was thought of as a female organism, and the harvest as giving birth; hence the phallic processions and ritual obscenities (Greek: *aiskhrologia*) of classical antiquity. Exactly the same explanation can be given for the ritual nakedness as part of agricultural magic which occurs both in Slavonic rituals and those of classical times.

The following account, from the province of Jaroslavl', is interesting with regard to the association of Mother Earth with the Mother of God:

During the drought (of 1920–1921), when some of the peasants began to break up the lumps and clods of earth in the ploughed fields with mallets, they met fierce opposition from their womenfolk, who asserted that by so doing they were "beating the most holy Mother of God herself."

In other cases analogous prohibitions were motivated by the fear that Mother Earth would bear no corn or by reference to the earth's *pregnancy*.

The association of the earth with the Mother of God was sometimes reflected in icon-painting: in the fourteenth-century icon of the Synaxis of the Mother of God from Pskov (Tret'jakov Gallery), the Mother of God on the grass is an allegory of the earth. (This icon is sometimes associated with the heresy of the Shearers.*) Finally let us note that at the yearly service of the *chlysty* sect,** during the singing of songs in honor of "damp Mother Earth," the "Mother of God" emerges from underground and communicates the participants with berries. Maria Timofeevna Lebyatkin in Dostoevskij's *The Devils* says:

> "'If you don't mind my saying so,' I says, 'God and nature are one and the same thing'. . .Meanwhile one of our lay sisters, who lived in our convent as a penance for uttering prophecies, whispered to me as we were coming out of church: 'What is the Mother of God, do you think?' 'She's the great Mother,' I said, 'the hope of the human race.' 'Yes,' she said, 'the Mother of God is great mother earth, and therein lies a great joy for men.'"***

As we have seen, ethnographical data provide direct confirmation for this account.

Finally, it should be noted that in Slavonic pagan religion worship of Mother Earth is connected with the worship of the adversary of the thunder god, above all with the worship of Mokoš' as a feminine hypostasis opposed to the god of thunder, cf. the wedding lament quoted above, which includes the motif of the thunder-arrow breaking open damp Mother Earth. With the coming of Christianity the cult of Mokoš' was transferred both to St. Paraskeva Pjatnica (who may consequently be thought of as "mother of earth and water") and to the Mother of God, in consequence of which the Mother of God is associated with damp Mother Earth. It is significant in this connection that Russian spiritual songs may attribute the commandment not to use obscene language both to Pjatnica and to the Mother of God.

Translated by Ralph Cleminson

---

*See above, p. 12.
**See above, p. [32]n.
***Fyodor Dostoevsky, *The Devils* [*The Possessed*], translated by David Magarshak, Penguin Books, London 1982, p. 154.

NOTES

1   It is characteristic that in the West Slavonic languages Sl. *jebati* has the meaning "to curse, swear," i.e. the semantics of the word may refer to the general meaning of expressing oneself in obscenities.

2   This sort of attitude is reflected in the spiritual song "Of the drunkard" ("Basil the Great"):

> What man, though it be but once,
> Shall speak an obscene oath,
> *In jest or not in jest,*
> To the Lord it is the same.

3   Very curious in this connection are the indecent inscriptions on the resonator of the cathedral of St. Sophia in Novgorod, which were made before the firing, i.e. in the middle of the eleventh century.*   In all probability this is not a case of deliberate sacrilege, but a syncretistic combination of Christian and pagan worship: the resonators gave to the Christian prayers, sung in the church, a supplementary pagan meaning – without the worshippers' knowing!

4   There may be a reflection of this text in the folk-legend about the origin of obscene language, where this is connected with incest: "Every man has three mothers: his own mother and two great mothers, damp Mother Earth and the Mother of God. The devil led one man astray, he killed his father and married his mother; from that time on he began to swear, naming his mother in his cursing, and that sin has been on the earth ever since."

*A resonator (*golosnik*) is a clay jar inserted into the thickness of the wall in order to improve the acoustics of a church.

300

SOURCES

The papers in this volume were published in Russian in the following publications:

Part One

1. *Trudy po russkoj i slavjanskoj filologii*, XXVIII, Tartu, 1977.

2. *Voprosy literatury*, 3, 1977.

3. *Chudožestvennyj jazyk srednevekov'ja*, ed. V. A. Karpusin, Moscow, 1982.

Part Two

1. *Literaturnoe nasledstvo dekabristov*, eds. V. G. Bazanov, V. E. Vacuro, Leningrad, 1975.

2. Jurij M. Lotman, *Testo e Contesto*, Bari, 1980.

3. Ju. M. Lotman, *Stat'i po tipologii kul'tury*, Tartu, 1973.

4. Ibid.

5. *Trudy po russkoj i slav'janskoj filologii*, XXVI, Tartu, 1975.

6. *Trudy po znakovym sistemam*, 11, Tartu, 1979.

7. Ibid., 8, Tartu, 1977.

Part Three

1. Chudožestvennyj jazyk, op. cit.

2. *Vtoričnye modelirujuščie sistemy*, Tartu, 1979.

3. *Struktura teksta–81*, Moscow, 1981.

301

REFERENCES

The abbreviations used in the following bibliographic references are: AN SSR = Academy of Sciences of the USSR; *ČOIDR* = *Čtenija v obščestve istorii i drevnostej rossijskich pri Moskovskom universitete*; L. = Leningrad; LGU = Leningrad State University; M. = Moscow; Pgd. = Petrograd; TGU = Tartu State University; *TODRL* = *Trudy otdela drevnerusskoj literatury*; St. P. = St. Petersburg; *UZ* = *Učenye zapiski;* GBL = Lenin State Library.

AAÈ (1836)
  Akty, sobrannye v bibliotekach i archivach Rossijskoj imperii archeografičeskoju ekspedicieju Imperatorskoj Akademii nauk. 4 vols. St.P.
ADRIANOVA-PERETC, V.P. (1928)
  "Do istoriji parodiji na Ukrajini v XVIII vici ('Služba pyvorezam' 1740 roku)," *Zapiski istorično-filologičnogo viddilu Vseukrajs'koj Akademij nauk*, XVIII. Kiev.
ADRIANOVA-PERETC, V.P. (1936)
  "Obrazcy obščestvenno-političeskoj parodii XVII-načalu XIX v.," *TODRL*, III.
ADRIANOVA-PERETC, V.P. (1936a)
  Prazdnik kabackich jaryzek. Parodija-satira vtoroj polovinoj X VIveka. L.
ADRIANOVA-PERETC, V.P. (1937)
  Očerki po istorii russkoj satiričeskoj literatury X VII veka, M/L.
ADRIANOVA-PERETC, V.P. (1954)
  Russkaja demokratičeskaja satira X VII veka. M/L.
AFANES'EV, A.N. (1865-1869)
  Poetičeskie vozzrenija slavjan na prirodu. 3 vols. M.
AFANES'EV, A.N. (1897)
  Narodnye russkie skazki A.N. Afanas'eva Ed. A.E. Gruzinskij. 2 vols. M. Revised ed. 5 vols. M. 1913-1914.
AFANAS'EV, A.N. (1936-1939)
  Narodnye russkie skazki A.N. Afanas'eva. Ed. M.K. Azadovskij, N.P. Andreev, Ju.M. Sokolov. 3 vols. M.
AI (1841-1842)
  Akty istoričeskie; sobrannye i izdannye archeografičeskoju komissieju. 5 vols. St. P.
AKSAKOV, S.T. (1955-1956)
  Sobranie sočinenij v 4-ch tomach. M.
ALEKSEEV (1863)
  "Rasskaz Petra Velikogo o patriarche Nikone. Vsepoddanejšee pis'mo protoiereja Alekseeva k imp. Pavlu Petroviču," *Russkij archiv*, 8-9.
ALEKSEEV, M.P. (1932)
  Sibir' v izvestijach zapadnoevropejskich putešestvennikov i pisatelej. Vvedenie, teksty i kommentarij. Vol. I. *XIII-XVII vv.* Irkutsk.
ALEKSEEV, M.P. (1972)
  "Puškin i nauka ego vremeni," in *Puškin. Sravnitel'no-istoričeskie issledovanija.* L.
ALEKSEEV, Petr (1818)
  Cerkovnyj slovar', ili istolkovanie rečenij slavenskich drevnich, takož inojazyčnych bez perevoda položennych v svjaščennom pisanii i drugich cerkovnych knigach. 5 parts. Pt. III. St. P.
ALMAZOV, A.I. (1894)
  Tajnaja ispoved' v pravoslavnoj vostočnoj cerkvi. Vol. III. Odessa.

ANNENKOV, P. (1874)
A.S. Puškin v Aleksandrovskuju epochu. St. P.

ANIČKOV, E.V. (1914)
Jazyčestvo i drevnjaja Rus'. St. P.

ARAPOV, Pimen (1861)
Letopis' russkogo teatra. St. P.

ARTAMONOVA, Z. (1933)
"Neizdannye stichi N.A. L'vova," *Literaturnoe nasledstvo*, 9-10.

ARZAMAS (1933)
Arzama i arzamasskie protokoly. L.

AZADOVSKIJ, M. (1924)
Besedy sobiratelja. Irkutsk.

BABENČIKOV, M. (1933)
"Portret Pugačeva v Istoričeskom muzee," *Literaturnoe nasledstvo*, 9-10.

BACHTIN, M.M (1965)
Tvorčestvo Fransua Rable i narodnaja kul'tura srednevekov'ja i Renessansa.
M. (English: M. Bakhtin, *Rabelais and His World*, Cambridge, Mass. 1968,
1971.[2])

BACHTIN, M.M. (1975)
Voprosy literatury i èstetiki. M. (English: M.M. Bakhtin, *The Dialogic Imagination: Four Essays*, Austin 1981).

BAJER [BAYER], G.S. (1738)
*Kratkoe opisanie vsech slučaev, kasajuščichsja do Azova ot sozdanija sego
goroda do vozvraščenija onago pod Rossijskuju deržavu.* Translated from the
German by I.K. Taubert. St.P.

BAKLANOVA, N.A. (1951)
" 'Tetradi' starca Avraamija," *Istoričeskij archiv*, VI.

BARSKOV, Ja.L. (1918)
"Pis'ma imp. Ekaterinu II k grafu P.V. Zavadovskomu," *Russkij istoričeskij
žurnal*, 5.

BARSOV, E.V. (1883)
*Drevnerusskie pamjatniki svjaščennogo venčanija carej na carstvo v svjazi s
grečeskimi ich originalami. S istoričeskim očerkom činov carskogo venčanija
v svjazi s razvitiem idei carja na Rusi.* M.

BARTHES,Roland (1972)
Mythologies. London.

BASARGIN, N.V. (1917)
Zapiski. Prague.

BASSEVIČ (1866)
Zapiski o Rossii pri Petre Velikom, izvlečenye iz bumag grafa Basseviča. Translated from the French by I.F. Ammon. M.

BATJUŠKOV, K.N. (1934)
Sočinenija. [M/L].

BATJUŠKOV, K. (1936)
Stichotvorenija. L.

BAZANOV, V.G. (1949)
Vol'noe obščestvo ljubitelej rossijskoj slovesnosti. Petrozavodsk.

BAZANOV, V. (1964)
Učenaja respublika. M/L.

BEKAREVIČ, N.M. (1901)
"Dnevniki raskopov kurganov . . ." In, *Kostromskaja starina. Sbornik iz-
davaemaja Kostromskoj gubernskoj učenoj archivnoj komissiej*, V. Kostroma.

BELINSKIJ, V.G. (1953-1959)
Polnoe sobranie sočinenij. 13 vols. M/L.
BELKIN, A.A. (1975)
Russkie skomorochi. M.
BELOGOLOVYJ, N.A. (1898)
Vospominanija i drugie stat'i. M.
BELYJ, A. (1934)
Masterstvo Gogolja. M/L.
BÉRANGER, J. (1953)
Recherches sur l'aspect idéologique du principat. Basel.
BERCHGOL'C, F.V. (1902-1903)
Dnevnik kamer-junkera F. V. Berchgol'ca, 1721-1725. Translated from the German by I.F. Ammon. 4 parts. M.
BESSONOV, Petr (1871)
Belorusskie pesni s podrobnymi ob"jasnenijami ich tvorčestva, i jazyka, s očerkami narodnogo obrjada, obyčaja i vsego byta, I. M.
BESTUŽEV, N.A. (1933)
Stat'i i pis'ma. M/L.
BESTUŽEVYE (1951)
Vospominanija Bestjuževych. M/L.
BIRGE VITZ, E. (1975)
"Type et individu dans l' 'autobiographia' médiévale," *Poétique,* 24.
BOBROVSKIJ, P.O. (1903)
Istorija lejb-gvardii ulanskogo eja veličestva godudaryni imp. Aleksandry Feo-dorovny polka. Supplement to Vol. II. St. P.
BODJANSKIJ, O. (1863)
"Kirill i Mefodij. Sobranie pamjatnikov, do dejatel'nosti svjatych pervoučitelej i prosvetitelej slavjanskich plemen otnosjaščich," ČOIDR, 2.
BOGATYREV, P.G. (1923)
Narodnyj teatr. Češskij kukol'nyj i russkij narodnyj teatr. (Sborniki po teorii poetičeskogo jazyka, VI). Berlin/St. P.
BOGATYREV, P.G. (1940)
Lidové divadlo české a slovenské. Prague.
BOGATYREV, P.G. (1971)
Voprosy teorii narodnogo iskusstva. M.
BOGOSLOVSKIJ, M.M. (1940-1948)
Petr I. Materialy dlja biografii. 5 vols. [L.]
BOGUSLAWSKI, Wojciech (1965)
Mimika. Warsaw.
BYKOVA, T.A. and GUREVIČ, M.M (1955)
Opisanie izdanij graždanskoj pečati, 1708-janvar' 1725 g. M/L.
BYKOVA, T.A. and GUREVIČ, M.M (1958)
Opisanie izdanij, napečatannych kirillicej, 1689-janvar' 1725 g. M/L.
BYKOVA, T.A., GUREVIČ, M.M. and KOZINCEVA, R.I. (1972)
Opisanie izdanij, napečatannych pri Petre I. Svodnyj katalog. L.
ČAADAEV, P Ja. (1871)
[M. Žichanev], "K biografii P. Ja. Čaadaeva," *Vestnik Evropy,* 7.
ČAADAEV, P Ja. (1913-1914)
Sočinenija i pis'ma P. Ja. Čaadaeva. 2 vols. M.
ČAPLEVIČ, Eugenius (1974)
"Celosten li strukturnyj analiz?", *Voprosy literatury,* 7.
CATHERINE (1906)

Zapiski imperatricy Ekateriny II. St. P.

CATHERINE (1901-1907)
Sočinenija imperatricy Ekateriny II. 12 vols. St. P.

ČECHOV, A.P. (1960-1963)
Sobranie sočinenij i pisem v 12-ti tomach. M.

ČERNOV, S.N. (1960)
U istokov osvobodiťnogo dviženija. Saratov.

CHARLAMPOVIČ, K.V. (1914)
Malorossijskoe vlijanie na velikorusskuju cerkovnuju žizn'. Vol. I. Kazan'.

CHRAPOVICKIJ, A.V' (1901)
Dnevnik s 18-go janvarja 1782 po 17-oe sentjabrja 1793 goda. 2nd ed. M.

ČIČEROV, V.I. (1957)
Zimnij period russkogo zemledeľčeskogo kalendarja X VI-XIX vekov. (Očerki po istorii narodnych verovanij). M. (*Trudy instituta ètnografii AN SSSR,* NS, XL).

ČISTOV, K.V' (1967)
Russkie narodnye sociaľno-utopičeskie legendy X VII-XIX vv. M.

CJAVLOVSKIJ, M.A. (1931)
Kniga vospominanij o Puškine. M.

CJAVLOVSKIJ, M.A. (1962)
Staťi o Puškine. M.

COLLINS, Samuel (1671)
The Present State of Russia. London. (Russian translation by P. Kireevskij: Samuil Kollins, *Nynešnee sostojanie Rossii,* M. 1846).

CORNEILLE, Pierre (1963)
Oeuvres complètes. Paris.

DAL', V.I. (1869)
Tolkovyj slovar' živogo velikorusskogo jazyka. [St.P.]. [1869]; 2nd ed. 4 vols. 1880 – 1882.

DANIIL ZATOČNIK (1932)
Slovo Daniila Zatočnika po redakcijam XII i XIII vv. i ich peredelkam. Podgotovil k pečati N.N. Zarubin. L.

DAVYDOV, Denis (1822)
Opyt teorii partizanskogo dejstvija. 2nd ed. M.

DAVYDOV, Denis (1962)
Sočinenija. M.

DEKABRISTY (1938)
Dekabristy. Letopisi. Gosudarstvennyj literaturnyj muzej, Bk. 3. M.

DEKABRISTY (1951)
Dekabristy. Poèzija, dramaturgija, proza, publicistika, literaturnaja kritika. Ed. Vl. Orlov. M – L.

DEMKOV, N.S. (1965)
"Neizdannoe satiričeskoe proizvedenie o duchovenstve," *TODRL,* XXI.

DERŽAVIN, G.R. (1957)
Stichotvorenija. L.

DIMITRIJ IOANNOVIČ (1908)
Istoričeskoe i pravdivoe povestvovanie o tom, kak moskovskij knjaz' Dimitrij Ioannovič dostig otcovskogo prestola [1605 g]. Czech text of 1606 with foreword and translation by V.A. Francev. Prague. (*Starina i novizna,* Bk. XV, St.P. 1911).

D'JAKONOV, M. (1889)
Vlasť moskovskich gosudarej. Očerki po istorii političeskich idej drevnej

Rusi do konca XV veka. St.P.

DJUVERNUA, A. (1894)
Materialy dlja slovarja drevnerusskogo jazyka. M.

DMITRIEVA, R.P. (1955)
Skazanie o knjaz'jach Vladimirskich. M—L.

DMITRIEVA, R.P. (1976)
"O tekstologičeskoj zavisimosti meždu različnymi vidami rasskaza o potomkach Avgusta i darach Monomacha," *TODRL* Vol. XXX.

DOPOLNENIJA (1846—1875)
Dopolnenija k Aktam istoričeskim, sobrannye i izdannye archeografičeskoj komissiej, 12 Vols. St.P.

DOSTOEVSKIJ, F.M. (PSS)
Polnoe sobranie sočinenij v 30-ti tomach. L. 1972.

DRACULA (1964)
Povest'o Drakule. Ed. Ja.S. Lur'e. M—L.

DREUX DU RADIER (1779)
Ljubovnyj leksikon. Translated from the French by A.V. Chrapovickij. 2nd ed. [M.]. (French original: *Dictionnaire d'Amour,* The Hague, 1741).

DRUŽININ, V.G. (1889)
Raskol na Donu v konce XVII v. St.P.

DURNOVO, N.D. (1939)
"Dnevnik." In, *Dekabristy. Zapiski otdela rukopisej Vsesojuznoj biblioteki imeni V.I. Lenina,* 3.

DURNOVO, N.D. (1914)
"Dnevnik." In, *Vestnik obščestva revnitelej istorii,* No. 1.

EFIMENKO, P.S. (1877)
"Materialy po ètnografii russkogo naselenija Archangel'skoj gubernii," *Izvestija Obščestva ljubitelej estestvoznanija, antropologii i ètnografii pri imperatorskom Moskovskom universitete,* Vol. 30 (*Trudy ètnografičeskogo otdela,* V. 1).

EFIMENKO, P.S. (1878)
"Materialy po ètnografii russkogo naselenija Archangel'skoj gubernii," ibid. (*Trudy ètnografičeskogo otdela,* V. 2).

EFIMOV, N.I. (1912)
Rus'—novyj Izrail. Teokratičeskaja ideologija sovremennogo pravoslavija v dopetrovskoj pis'mennosti. Kazan'. (*Iz ètjudov po istorii russkogo cerkovno-političeskogo soznanija,* 1).

ENGEL, J.J. (1804)
Ideen zu einer Mimick. Vol. I. Berlin.

ESIPOV, G. (1861—1863)
Raskol'nič'i dela XVIII stoletija. Izvlečennye iz del Preobraženskogo prikaza i Tajnych rozysknych del kanceljarii G. Esipovym. 2 vols. St.P.

ESIPOV, G. (1880)
Ljudi starogo veka. Rasskazy iz del Preobraženskogo prikaza i Tajnoj kanceljarii. St.P.

ETKIND, E. (1970)
Razgovor o stichach. M.

FAMINCYN, A. (1889)
Skomorochi na Rusi. St.P.

FEOFAN (1721)
Feofan Prokopovič. *Rosysk istoričeskij, koich radi vin, i v jakovom razume byli i naricalis' imperatory rimstii, kak jazyčestii, tak i christianstii, pontifeksami ili archierejami.* St.P.

FEOFAN (1760 – 1744)

Feofana Prokopoviča, archiepiskopa Velikogo Novgoroda i Velikich Luk, svjatejšego pravitel'stvujuščego sinoda vice-prezidenta, a potom pervenstvu-juščego člena, Slova i Reči poučitel'nye, pochval'nye i pozdravitel'nye. 4 vols. St.P.

FEOFAN (1961)

Feofan Prokopovič, *Sočinenija,* M. – L.

FET, A. (1890)

Moi vospominanija, Part I. M.

FISCHER, A. (1921)

Zwyczaje pogrzebowe ludu polskiego. Lwów.

FLOROVSKIJ, A.V. (1972)

"Stranicy iz istorii russko-avstrijskich diplomatičeskich otnošenij XVIII v." In, *Feodal'naja Rossija vo vsemirno-istoričeskom processe,* M.

FILARET (1885 – 1888)

Filaret [Drozdov], *Sobranie mnenij i otzyvov po učebnym i cerkovno-gosudar-stvennym voprosam.* 5 vols. M.

FONVIZIN, D.I. (1959)

Sobranie sočinenij v dvuch tomach. M. – L.

FREJDENBERG, O.M. (1973)

"Proischoždenie parodii," *UZ TGU,* 308 *(Trudy po znakovym sistemam,* VI).

GAL ARD, Jean (1974)

"Pour une poétique de la conduite," *Semiotica,* X, 4.

GAL'KOVSKIJ, N.M. (1913 – 1916)

Bor'ba christianstva s ostatkami jazyčestva v drevnej Rusi. 2 vols. Moscow – Char'kov.

GENLIS (1818)

Dictionnaire critique et raisonné des étiquettes de la cour, ou l'esprit des éti-quettes et des usages anciens, comparés aux modernes, par Madame la Com-tesse de Genlis. Paris.

GERASIMOV, M.K. (1910)

"Slovar' uezdnogo Čerepoveckogo govora," *Sbornik otdelenija russkogo jazyka i slovesnosti imp. Akademii nauk,* LXXXVII, 3.

GERŠENZON, M.O. (1923)

Istorija molodoj Rossii. Moscow – Prague.

GIBBENET, N. (1882 – 1884)

Istoričeskie issledovanija dela patriarcha Nikona. 2 parts. St.P.

GILMAN, S.L. (1974)

The Parodic Sermon in European Perspective. Aspects of Liturgical Parody from the Middle Ages to the Twentieth Century. Wiesbaden.

GINZBURG, L. (1964)

O lirike. M – L.

GIZEL', Innokentij (1778)

Sinopsis. St.P.

GLINKA, S.N. (1895)

Zapiski Sergeja Nikolaeviča Glinki. St.P.

GOETHE, J.W. (1803)

"Regeln für Schauspieler." In, J.W. Goethe, *Kunsttheoretische Schriften und Übersetzungen,* Vol. 17. *Schriften zur Literatur,* Pt. 1. Berlin, 1970.

GOETHE, J.W. (1955)

"Pravila dlja akterov." In, *Chrestomatija po istorii zapadno evropejskogo teatra,* ed. S. Mokul'skij. M.

GOGOL', N.V. (PSS)
Polnoe sobranie sočinenij. 14 vols. M. 1937 – 1952.

GOL'DBERG, A.L. (1976)
"K istorii rasskaza o potomkach Avgusta i o darach Monomacha," *TODRL*, XXX.

GOLIKOV, I.I. (1788 – 1789)
Dejanija Petra Veligogo. 12 parts. M.

GOLIKOVA, N.B. (1957)
Političeskie processy pri Petre I po materialam Preobraženskogo prikaza. M.

GOLODOLINSKIJ, P. (1902)
Istorija 3-go dragunskogo Sumskogo ego korolevskogo vysočestva naslednogo princa datskogo polka. 3 vols. II. M.

GOLUBINSKIJ, E. (1900 – 1917)
Istorija russkoj cerkvi. Vol. I, 2nd ed. (Part 1, M. 1901; part 2, M. 1904); Vol. II (Part 1, M. 1900; part 2, M. 1917).

GRABAR', Igor' E. (ed.) (1953-1964)
Istorija russkogo iskusstva. M/L.

GRIBOEDOV, A.S. (PSS)
Polnoe sobranie sočinenij. 3 vols. St. P. 1911 – 1917.

GRIBOEDOV, A.S. (1956)
Sočinenija. M.

GROSSMAN, Leonid (1926)
Puškin v teatral'nych kreslach. Kartiny russkoj sceny 1817 –1820 godov. L.

GROSSMAN, Leonid (1958)
Puškin. M.

GRUMM-GRŽIMAJLO, A.G. and SOROKIN, V.V. (1963)
"'Obščestvo gromkogo smecha'. K istorii 'Vol'nych obščestv' Sojuza Blagodenstvija." In, *Dekabristy v Moskve*, M.

GUAGNINI (1578)
Alexander Gwagninus Veronensis, *Sarmatiae Europeae descriptio, quae Regnum Poloniae, Lituaniam, Samogitiam, Russiam, Masoviam, Prussiam, Pomeraniam, Livoniam et Moschoviae, Tartariaeque partem complectitur.* [Cracovia].

GUKOVSKIJ, G.A. (1959)
Realizm Gogolja. M – L.

GUKOVSKIJ, G. and ORLOV, V. (1933)
"Podpol'naja poèzija, 1770 – 1800-ch godov," *Literaturnoe nasledstvo*, 9 – 10.

GUSEV, V.E. (1974)
"Ot obrjada k narodnomu teatru (Evoljucija svjatočnych igr v pokojnika)." In, *Fol'klor i ètnografija. Obrjady i obrjadovyj fol'klor.* L.

HARDER, M.-B. (1968)
Schiller in Russland. (Materialen zu einer Wirkungsgeschichte, 1789 – 1814). Berlin – Zurich.

HERZEN, A.I. (1954-1964)
Sobranie sočinenij v 30-ti tomach. M.

HORÁLEK, Karel (1956)
"Sv. Kirill i semitskie jazyki." In, *For Roman Jakobson. Essays on the Occasion of his Sixtieth Birthday.* The Hague.

IOFFE, I.I. (1944 – 1945)
"Russkij renesans," *UZ LGU*, 72 (Serija filologičeskich nauk, 9).

IOSIF VOLOCKIJ (1855)
Prosvetitel'. Kazan'.

IOSIF VOLOCKIJ (1959)
Poslanija Iosifa Volockogo. Eds. A.A. Zimin and Ja.S. Lur'e. M-L.

ISTRIN, V. (1897)
Otkrovenie Mefodija Patarskogo i apokrifičeskie videnija Daniila v vizantijskoj i slavjano-russkoj literaturach. Issledovanija i teksty. M.

ISTRIN, V.M. (1920 – 1930)
Knigi vremennyja i obraznyja Georgija mnicha. Chronika Georgija Amartola v drevnem slavjanorusskom perevode. Tekst, isledovanie i slovar'. 3 vols. Pgd.-L.

IVANOV, A.F. (1969)
Slovar' govorov Podmoskov'ja. M.

IVANOV, A.I. (1969)
Literaturnoe nasledie Maksima Greka. Charakteristika, atribucija, bibliografija. L.

IVANOV, F.F. (1824)
Sočinenija i perevody. M.

IVANOV, V.V. and TOPOROV, V.N. (1965)
Slavjanskie jazykovye modelirujuščie semiotičeskie sistemy (Drevnij period). M.

IVANOVA, T.A. (1969)
"Ešče raz o 'russkich pis'menach'. (K 1100-letiju so dnja smerti Konstantina-Kirilla)," *Sovetskoe slavjanovedenie*, 4.

IZMAJLOV, N.V. (1975)
" 'Roman na kavkazskich vodach.' Neosuščestvlennyj zamysel Puškina." In, N.V. Izmajlov, *Očerki tvorčestva Puškina*. L.

JACIMIRSKIJ, A.I. (1913)
"K istorii ložnych molitv v južno-slavjanskoj pis'mennosti," *Izvestija otdelenija russkogo jazyka i slovesnosti*, XVIII, book 3, pp. 1 – 102; book 4, pp. 16 – 126.

JAGIĆ, V. (ed.) (1883)
Quattuor evangeliorum versionis paleoslovenicae. Codex Marianus glagoliticus. Borolini.

JAGIĆ, V. (1896)
Rassuždenija jugoslavjanskoj i russkoj stariny o cerkovno-slavjanskom jazyke. Codex slovenicus rerum grammaticarum. St. P.

JAKOBSON, R. (1944)
"Saint Constantin et la langue syriaque." In, *Annuaire de l'Institut de Philologie et d'Histoire orientales et slaves*, VII. Brussels.

JAKOBSON, Roman (1954)
"Minor Native Sources for the Early History of the Slavic Church," *Harvard Slavonic Studies*, II.

JAKOBSON, Roman (1975)
Puškin and his Sculptural Myth. Translated from the Czech and edited by John Burbank. The Hague-Paris.

JAKUBOVSKIJ (1968)
Karlik favorita, istorija žizni Ivana Andreeviča Jakubovskogo karlika svetlejšego knjazja Platona Aleksandroviča Zubova, pisannaja im samim. Munich.

JAVORSKIJ, Ju. (1928)
"Legenda o proischoždenii pavlikian." In, *Stat'i po slavjanskoj filologii i russkoj slovesnosti (Sbornik obščestva russkogo jazyka i slovesnosti, CI, 3)*. L.

JUL', Just (1900)
Zapiski Justa Julja, datskogo poslannika pri Petre Velikom. Translated from the Danish by Ju. N. Ščerbačev. M.

JUNOSTI ČESTNOE (1767)

Junosti čestnoe zercalo, ili pokazanie k žitejskomu obchoždeniju, sobrannoe ot raznych avtorov poveleniem ego imperatorskago veličestva gosudarja Petra Velikogo. St. P.

KANTEMIR, Antioch (1956)
Sobranie stichotvorenij. L.

KAPNIST, V.V. (1960)
Sobranie sočinenij v 2-ch tomach. M-L.

KAPTEREV, N.F. (1895)
"Snošenija Ierusalimskich patriarchov s russkim pravitel'stvom," *Pravoslavnyj Palestinskij Sbornik*, 43 (vol. 15). St. P.

KAPTEREV, N.F. (1909)
Patriarch Nikon i car' Aleksej Michajlovič. Vol. I. Sergiev Posad.

KAPTEREV, N.F. (1913)
Patriarch Nikon i ego protivniki v dele ispravlenija cerkovnych obrjadov. Vremja patriaršestva Iosifa. 2nd ed. Sergiev Posad.

KAPTEREV, N.F. (1914)
Charakter otnošenij Rossii k pravoslavnomu Vostoku v XVI i XVII stoletijach. 2nd ed. M.

KARAMZIN, N.M. (1830–1831)
Istorija Gosudarstva Rossijskogo. 12 vols. 3rd ed. St. P.

KARAMZIN, N.M. (1848)
Sočinenija Karamzina. St. P.

KARAMZIN, N.M. (1862)
Neizdannye sočinenija i perepiska N.M. Karamzina. St. P.

KARAMZIN, N.M. (1964)
Izbrannye sočinenija v druch tomach. M-L.

KARAMZIN, N.M. (1966)
Polnoe sobranie stichotvorenij. M-L.

KARSAVIN, L.P. (1915)
Osnovy srednevekovoj religioznosti v XII –XIII vekach, preimuščestvenno v Italii. Pgd. (*Zapiski istoriko-filologičeskogo fakulteta Imperatorskogo Petrogradskogo universiteta*, CXXV).

KARSKIJ, E.F. (1962)
Trudy po belorusskomu i drugim slavjanskim jazykam. M.

KATENIN, P.A. (1911)
Pis'ma P.A. Katenina k N.I. Bachtinu. (Materialy dlja istorii russkoj literatury 20-ch i 30-ch godov XIX veka). St. P.

KAZAKOVA, N.A. and LUR'E, Ja.S. (1955)
Antifeodal'nye eretičeskie dviženija na Rusi XI V–načala XVI veka. M.-L.

KAZANCEV, P.M. (1967)
"K izučeniju 'Russkogo Pelama' A.S. Puškina," *Vremennik Puškinskoj komissii, 1964.* L.

KAZANSKIJ, Petr (1847)
Rodoslovnaja Golovinych, vladel'cev sela Novospaskogo. M.

KAZOKNIEKS, Mara (1968)
Studien zur Rezeption der Antike bei russischen Dichtern zu Beginn des XIX Jahrhunderts. Munich.

KEKAVMEN (1972)
Sovety i rasskazy Kekavmena. Sočinenie vizantijskogo polkovodca XI v. Ed. G.G. Litavrin. M.

KEL'SIEV, V. (1860–1862)
Sbornik pravitel'stvennych svedenij o raskol'nikach, sostavlennyj V. Kel'-

sievym. I –IV. London.

KIREEVSKIJ, P.V. (1935)
Pis 'ma P. V. Kireevskogo k N.M. Jazykovu. M-L.

KIREEVSKIJ, P.V. (1977)
Sobranie narodnych pesen P.V. Kireevskogo. Zapisi jazykovych v Simbirskoj i Orenburgskoj gubernijach. I. L.

KIRŠA DANILOV (1958)
Drevnie rossijskie stichotvorenija, sobrannye Kiršeju Danilovym. M-L.

KIZEVETTER, A.A. (1912)
Istoričeskie očerki. M.

KLJUČEVSKIJ, V.O. (1956 – 1959)
Sočinenija v vos'mi tomach. M.

KNJAŽNIN, Ja. (1914)
Vadim Novgorodskij. Tragedija Ja. Knjažnina s predisloviem V. Sadovnika. M.

KOLESNIKOV, V.P. (1914)
Zapiski neščastnogo soderžaščije putešestvie v Sibir' po kanatu. St. P.

KOMAROVSKIJ, Graf E.F. (1914)
Zapiski. St. P.

KORB, Ioann Georg (1906)
Dnevnik putešestvija v Moskoviju (1698 i 1699 gg.). Translated by A.I. Malein. St. P.

KOROLENKO, V.G. (1914)
Sovremennaja samozvanščina (Polnoe sobranie sočinenij, vol. III). St. P.

KOSTADINOVA, L., FLOROVA, V. and DIMITROVA, B. (1968)
B'lgaro-ruski naučni vr''zki. XIX –XX vek. Dokumenti. Sofija.

KOSTOMAROV, N.I. (1860)
Očerk domašnej žizni i nravov velikorusskogo naroda v XVI i XVII stoletijach. St. P.

KOTLJAREVSKIJ, A. (1868)
O pogrebal'nych obyčajach jazyčeskich slavjan. M.

KOTOŠICHIN, Grigorij (1906)
O rossii v carstvovanie Alekseja Michajloviča. 4th ed. St. P.

KOTOŠICHIN (1980)
Grigorij Kotošixin, *O Rossii v carstvovanie Alekseja Michajloviča*. Text and commentary by A.E. Pennington. Oxford.

KOZMA OF PRAGUE (1962)
Koz'ma Pražskij, *Češskaja chronika*. M.

KRIŽANIČ, Jurij (1965)
Politika. Ed. V.V. Zelenin. M.

KRYLOV, I.A.
Sočinenija. Vol. I. M.

KUBALOV, B. (1924)
"Sibir' i samozvancy. Iz istorii narodnych volnenij v XIX v." *Sibirskie ogni*, 3.

KUEV, Kujo M. (1967)
Černorizec Chrab''r. Sofija.

KUKULEVIČ, A.M. (1939)
"Russkaja idillija N.I. Gnedič, 'Rybaki,' " *UZ LGU, serija filologičeskich nauk*, 46/3.

KULAKOVA, L.I. and ZAPADOV, V.A. (1974)
A.N. Radiščev. "Putešestvie iz Peterburga v Moskvu". L.

KUPREJANOVA, E.N. (1971)
" 'Mertvye duši' N.V. Gogolja. (Zamysel i ego vploščenie)," *Russkaja literatura*,

3.

KUPREJANOVA, E.N. and MAKOGONENKO, G.P. (1976)
Nacional'noe svoeobrazie russkoj literatury. L.
KURAKIN, F.A. (1890 – 1902)
Archiv knjazja F.A. Kurakina. 10 vols. St. P.-Saratov-M.-Astrachan'.
KURBSKIJ, A.M. (1914)
Sočinenija knjazja A.M. Kurbskogo. St. P.
KUZ'MINA, V.D. (1962)
Devgenievo dejanie. M.
LABZINA, A.E. (1914)
Vospominanija Anny Evdokimovny Labzinoj. St. P.
LEBEDEV, A. (1965)
Čaadaev. M.
LEBEDEV, L. (1981)
"Novyj Ierusalim v žizni svjatejšego patriarcha Nikona," *Žurnal Moskovskoj patriarchii*, 8.
LE BR[E]UN (1718)
Conférence de Monsieur le Br[e]un sur l'expression générale et particulière enrichie de figures. Amsterdam.
LEHMANN, P. (1922)
Die Parodie im Mittelalter. Munich.
LEHMANN, P. (1923)
Parodistische Texte. Beispiele zur lateinischen Parodie im Mittelalter. Munich.
LELONG, A.K. (1913 – 1914)
"Vospominanija," *Russkij archiv*, 1913, Nos. 6 – 7, 1914, Nos. 6 – 8.
LERMONTOV, M. Ju. (1954)
Sočinenija v 6-ti tomach. M-L.
LETOPIS' (1859)
Letopis' russkoj literatury i drevnosti [5 vols. 1859-1863].
LICHAČEV, D.S. (ed.) (1962)
Slovo o polku Igoreve. Pamjatnik XII veka. M-L.
LICHAČEV, D.S. (1967)
Poètika drevnerusskoj literatury. L. (1971,[2] 1979[3]).
LICHAČEV,D.S. (1972)
"Kanon i molitva Angelu Groznomu voevode Parfenija Urodivogo (Ivana Groznogo)." In, *Rukopisnoe nasledie Drevnej Rusi. Po materialam Puškinskogo doma*. L.
LICHAČEV, D.S. and PANČENKO, A.M. (1976)
"Smechovoj mir" Drevnej Rusi. L.
LILEEV, N.V. (1891)
Simeon Bekbulatovič, chan Kasimovskij, velikij knjaz' vseja Rusi, vposledstvii velikij knjaz' Tverskoj, 1567 –1616 g. (Istoričeskij očerk). Tver'.
LILEEV, M.I. (1895)
Iz istorii raskola na Vetke i v Starodub'e X VII –X VIII vv. I, Kiev. (*Izvestija istoričesko-filologičeskogo instituta knjazja Bezborodko v Nežine*, XIV).
LIVANOV, F.V. (1868 – 1873)
Raskol'niki i ostrožniki. Očerki i rasskazy. 4 vols. St. P.
LJUBOV' (1798)
Ljubov'. Knižka zolotaja. Gl[eb] Gr[omov]. St. P.
LOTMAN, Ju.M. (1958)
"Voennye vzgljady A.N. Radiščeva," *UZ TGU*, 127 (*Trudy po filosofii*, IV).
LOTMAN, Ju.M. (1958a)

"Andrej Sergeevič Kajsarov i literaturno-obščestvennaja bor'ba ego vremeni," *UZ TGU*, 63.

LOTMAN, Ju.M. (1958/1959)

"Neue Materialen über die Anfange der Beschaftigung mit Schiller in der russischen Literatur," *Wissenschaftliche Zeitschrift der Ernst Moritz Arndt-Universität Greifswald, Gesellschafts- und sprachwissenschaftliche Reihe*, 5/6.

LOTMAN, Ju.M. (1959)

"Matvej Aleksandrovič Dmitriev-Mamonov – poèt, publicist i obščestvennyj dejatel'," *UZ TGU*, 78.

LOTMAN, Ju.M. (1960)

"P.A. Vjazemskij i dviženie dekabristov," *UZ TGU*, 98.

LOTMAN, Ju.M. (1962)

"*Slovo o polku Igoreve* i literaturnaja tradicija XVIII – načala XIX v." In, Lichačev 1962.

LOTMAN, Ju.M. (1962a)

"Istočniki svedenij Puškina o Radiščeve (1819 – 1822)." In, *Puškin i ego vremja*, I. L.

LOTMAN, Ju.M. (1963)

"Tarutinskij period Otečestvennoj vojny 1812 goda i razvitie russkoj osvoboditel'noj mysli," *UZ TGU*, 139.

LOTMAN, Ju.M. (1965)

"O ponjatii geografičeskogo prostranstva v russkich srednevekovych tekstach," *UZ TGU*, 181 (*Trudy po znakovym sistemam* II)

LOTMAN, Ju.M. (1966)

"V tolpe rodstvennikov," *UZ TGU*, 78.

LOTMAN, Ju. M. (1973)

Stat'i po tipologii kul'tury. Tartu.

LOTMAN, Ju. M. (1975)

"Tema kart i kartočnoj igry v russkoj literature načala XIX veka," *UZ TGU*, 365 (*Trudy po znakovym sistemam* 7). English: "Theme and Plot: The Theme of Cards and the Card Game in Russian Literature of the XIXth Century," *PTL: A Journal for Descriptive Poetics and Theory of Literature* 3, 1978.

LOTMAN, Ju. M. (1977)

" 'Zvonjači v pradednjuju slavu'," *UZ TGU*, 414 (*Trudy po russkoj i slavjanskoj filologii* XXVIII).

LOTMAN, Ju. M. (1980)

Roman A.S. Puškina "Evgenij Onegin". Kommentarij. L.

LOTMAN, Ju. M. and USPENSKIJ, B.A. (1970)

"Uslovnost' v iskusstve." In, *Filosofskaja Ènciklopedija*, Vol. 5. M.

LOTMAN, Ju. M. and USPENSKIJ, B.A. (1971)

"O semiotičeskom mechanizme kul'tury," *UZ TGU* 284 (*Trudy po znakovym sistemam* V). English: 'On the Semiotic Mechanism of Culture," *New Literary History*, IX, 2, 1978.

LOTMAN, Ju. M. and USPENSKIJ, B.A. (1973)

"Mif - imja - kul'tura," *UZ TGU* 308 (*Trudy po znakovym sistemam* VI). English: "Myth - Name - Culture." In, *Semiotics and Structuralism. Readings from the Soviet Union*. Ed. Henryk Baran. White Plains, 1976.

LOTMAN, Ju. M. and USPENSKIJ, B.A. (1974)

"K semiotičeskoj tipologii russkoj kul'tury XVIII veka." In, *Chudožestvennaja kul'tura XVIII veka. Materialy naučnoj konferencii*. M.

LOTMAN, Ju. M. and USPENSKIJ, B.A. (1975)

"Spory o jazyke v načale XIX v. kak fakt russkoj kul'tury," *UZ TGU* 358

(Trudy po russkoj i slavjanskoj filologii XXIV).

LOVJAGIN, A. (1905)
"Potemkin." In, *Russkij biografičeskij slovar'*. St. P.

MAKAROV, N. (1881 – 1882)
Moi semidesjatiletnie vospominanija i s tem vmeste moja polnaja predsmertnaja ispoved'. 4 parts. St. P.

MAKSIM GREK (1859 – 1862)
Sočinenija. 3 vols. Kazan'.

MAKSIMOV, S.V. [1908 – 1913]
Sobranie sočinenij. 20 vols. St. P.

MANDEL'ŠTAM, O. (1928)
O poezii. L.

MANDEL'ŠTAM, O. (1964 – 1981)
Sobranie sočinenij. 4 vols. Washington - New York - Paris.

MANDEL'ŠTAM, O. (1979)
The Complete Critical Prose and Letters. Edited by Jane Gary Harris. Ann Arbor.

MAN'KOV, A.G. (1968)
Zapiski inostrancev o vosstanii Stepana Razina. L.

MARGERET, Jacques (1607)
Estat de l'Empire de Russie et Grand Duché de Moscovie, avec ce qui s'y est passé de plus mémorable et tragique pendant le règne de quatre empereurs: à sçavoir depuis l'an 1590 jusques en l'an 1606, en septembre par le Capitaine Jacques Margeret. Paris. (1668,[2] 1860,[3] 1946[4]).

MATERIALY (1955 – 1959)
Materialy po istorii SSSR. 7 vols. M.

MEL'NIKOV, P.I. (Andrej Pečerskij) PSS
Polnoe sobranie sočinenij. 7 vols. 2nd ed. St. P. 1909.

MEL'NIKOV, P.I. (1872)
Materialy dlja istorii chlystovskoj i skopčeskoj eresi. ČOIDR, 3.

MEL'NIKOV, P.I. (1879)
Delo po povodu stichotvorenija Tred'jakovskogo. ČOIDR, 1.

MEL'NIKOV, P.I. (1910)
"O sovremennom sostojanii raskola v Nižegorodskoj gubernii (1854 g.)." In, *Dejstvija Nižegorodskoj gubernskoj učenoj archivnoj komissii*, IX (*Sbornik v pamjati P.I. Mel'nikova (Andrej Pečerskij)*). Nižnij Novgorod.

MEŠČERSKIJ, N.A. (1958)
Istorija indejskoj vojny Iosifa Flavija v drevnerusskom perevode. M-L.

MILJUTIN, D.A. (1852)
Istorija vojny Rossii s Franciej v carstvovanie imperatora Pavla I v 1799 g. St.P.

MILLER, Vs.F. (1915)
Istoričeskie pesni russkogo naroda XVI –XVII vv. Pgd. (*Sbornik obščestva russkogo jazyka i slovesnosti*, XCIII).

MODZALEVSKIJ, B.L. (1928)
"K istorii 'Zelenoj lampy'." In, *Dekabristy i ich vremja*, Vol. I. M.

MOISEEVA, G.N. (1980)
Drevnerusskaja literatura v chudožestvennom soznanii i istoričeskoj mysli Rossii XVIII veka. L.

MOKUL'SKIJ, S. (ed.) (1955)
Chrestomatija po istorii zapadnoevropejskogo teatra. 2 vols. M.

MONTESQUIEU, Charles de (1748)
De l'esprit des lois. Paris.

MÜLLER, Ludolf (1962)
Des Metropoliten Ilarion Lobrede auf Vladimir den Heiligen und Glaubens-bekenntnis. Wiesbaden.

MURAV'EV, N.N. (1885)
"Zapiski N.N. Murav'eva," *Russkij archiv*, 9.

MURAV'EV APOSTOL, M.I. (1922)
Dekabrist M.I. Murav'ev-Apostol. Vospominanija i pis'ma. Prague.

MYSLOVSKIJ, P.N. (1905)
"Iz zapisnoj knizhki P.N. Myslovskogo." In, *Ščukinskij sbornik*, 4.

NARODNAJA GRAVJURA (1976)
Narodnaja gravjura i fol'klor v Rossii XVII –XIX vv. (K 150-letiju so dnja roždenija D.A. Rovinskogo). Materialy naučnoj konferencii (1975). M.

NEČKINA, M.V. (1947)
A.S. Griboedov i dekabristy. M.

NEČKINA, M.V. (1955)
Dviženie dekabristov. Vol. I. M.

NIEDERLE, L. (1912–1921)
Slovanské starožitnosti. Oddíl kulturní. Život starých Slovanů. Díl. I–III. Prague.

NIKITENKO, A.V. (1955)
Dnevnik v trech tomach. I. M.

NIKITINA, N.A. (1928)
"K voprosu o russkich koldunach," *Sbornik Muzeja antropologii i ètnografii AN SSSR*, VII.

NIKOLAEV, A. (1904)
"Simeon Bekbulatovič." In,*Russkij biografičeskij slovar'.* St. P.

NIKOL'SKIJ, K. (1885)
O službach russkoj cerkvi, byvšich v prežnich pečatnych bogoslužebnych knigach. St. P.

NIKOL'SKIJ, N.K. (1930)
Povest' vremennych let kak istočnik dlja istorii načal'nogo perioda russkoj pis'mennosti i kul'tury. K voprosu o drevnejšem russkom letopisanii. I. L.

O BOR'BE (1865)
"O bor'be christianstva s jazyčestvom v Rossii," *Pravoslavnyj sobesednik,* August.

ODERBORN, P. (1585)
P. Oderbornius, *Ioannis Basilidis Magni Moscoviae Ducis vita.* Wittenberg.

ODERBORN, P. (1588)
Wunderbare, erschreckliche unerhörte Geschichte und warhaffte Historien: nemlich, des nechst gewesenen Grossfürsten in der Moschkaw Joan Basilidis (auff ire Sprach Iwan Basilowitz genandt) Leben. In drey Bücher verfast und aus dem Latein verdeutscht durch Heinrich Räteln zu Sagan. Hörlitz.

OKUDŽAVA, Bulat (1971)
"Mersi, ili pochoždenija Šipova," *Družba narodov,* 12.

OLEARIUS, Adam (1656)
Opisanie putešestvija v Moskoviju i čerez Moskoviju v Persiju i obratno. Translated from the German by A.M. Lovjagin. St.P. 1906. English: *The Travels of Olearius in Seventeenth Century Russia.* Translated and edited by Samuel H. Baron. Stanford. 1967.

OLENINA, V. A. (1938)
"Vospominanija o dekabristach. Pis'ma V.A. Oleninoj k P.I. Barten'evu."

315

In, *Dekabristy*. *Letopis' gosudarstvennogo literaturnogo Muzeja*, III.

OSTROGORSKIJ, G. (1935)

"Avtokrator i Samodržac. Prilog za istoriju vladalačke titulature u Vizantiji i u južnich Slovena," *Glas Srpske Kral'evske Akademije*, CLXIV, 84.

PAMJATNIKI (1927)

Pamjatniki istorii staroobrjadčestva X VII v. Book I, No. 1. L. (*Russkaja istoričeskaja biblioteka*, XXXIX).

PAMJATNIKI (1961)

Pamjatniki russkogo prava, I. *Zakonodatel'nye akty Petra I*. M.

PANČENKO, A.M. (1973)

Russkaja stichotvornaja kul'tura XVII veka. L.

PEČERIN, V.S. (1932)

Zamogil'nye zapiski. M.

PEKARSKIJ, P. (1862)

Nauka i literatura v Rossii pri Petre Velikom. 2 vols. St.P.

P'ESY (1974)

P'esy škol'nych teatrov Moskvy. *Rannjaja russkaja dramaturgija*. (*X VII – pervaja polovina X VIII v.*). M.

PETER (1887 –1977)

Pis'ma i bumagi imperatora Petra Velikogo. 12 vols. St.P. – M.

PETER (1973)

Portret petrovskogo vremeni. *Katalog vystavki*. L.

PETROV, A. (1918)

"Romodanovskij, knjaz' Fedor Jur'evič." In, *Russkij biografičeskij slovar'*. Pgd.

PIERLING, P. (1896 – 1912)

La Russie et le Saint-Siège. *Etudes diplomatiques*. 5 vols. Paris.

PINGAUD, Léonce (1886)

Les Francais en Russie et les Russes en France. *L'ancien régime-L'émigration-Les invasions*. Paris.

POÈTY (1790 – 1810)

Poèty 1790 - 1810-ch godov. L. 1971. (Biblioteka poèta, bol'šaja serija).

POÈTY XVIII VEKA

Poèty X VIII veka. L. 1972.

POKROVSKIJ, N.N. (1972)

"Sibirskij Il'ja-prorok pered voennym sudom prosveščennogo absoljutizma," *Izvestija Sibirskogo otdelenija AN SSSR, serija obščestvennych nauk*, 6/2.

POKROVSKIJ, N.N. (1974)

"Predstavlenija krest'jan-staroobrjadcev Urala i Sibiri XVIII veka o svetskich vlastjach," *Ežegodnik po agrarnoj istorii vostočnoj Evropy 1971 g.* Vilnius.

POLEVOJ, N. (1934)

Materialy po istorii russkoj literatury i žurnalistiki tridcatych godov. L.

POLOSIN, I.I. (1926)

"'Igra v carja'. (Otgoloski Smuty v moskovskom bytu XVII v.)," *Izvestija Tverskogo pedagogičeskogo instituta*, I.

POLOSIN, I.I. (1963)

Social'no-političeskaja istorija Rossii X VI –načala X VII v. M.

POPOV, A. (1869)

Izbornik (chrestomatija) slavjanskich i russkich sočinenij i statej vnesennych v chronografy russkoj redakcii. M.

POPOV, A. (1875)

Istoriko-literaturnyj obzor drevnerusskich polemičeskich sočinenij protiv

316

latinjan (XI-X Vv.). M.

POROŠIN, Semen (1881)
Zapiski, služaščie k istorii ego imperatorskogo vysočestva Pavla Petroviča naslednika prestolu Rossijskago. 2nd ed. St.P.

POSLANIJA (1951)
Poslanija Ivana Groznogo. Eds. D.S. Lichačev & Ja.S. Lur'e. M–L. English: The Correspondence between Prince A.M. Kurbsky and Tsar Ivan I V of Russia, 1564 - 1579. J.L.I. Fennell, ed. Cambridge, 1963.

POTANIN, G.N. (1899)
"Ètnografičeskie zametki na puti ot g. Nikol'ska do g. Tot'my," Živaja starina, IX, 4.

PREDTEČENSKIJ, A.V. (1951)
"Zapiska T.E. Boka." In, Dekabristy i ich vremja. M–L.

PRISELKOV, M.D. (1918)
"N.F. Kapterev," Russkij istoričeskij žurnal, 5.

PROCHOROV, G.M. (1978)
Povest'o Mitjae. Rus'i Vzantija v epochu Kulikovskoj bitvy. L.

PROKOF'EV, E.A. (1953)
Bor'ba dekabristov za peredovoe russkoe voennoe iskusstvo. M.

PROKOPIJ OF USTJUG (1893)
Žitie prepodobnogo Prokopija Ustjužskogo. St.P.

PSRL
Polnoe sobranie russkich letopisej. 30 vols. St.P.–Pgd.–M. 1841–1965.

PUGAČEV (1935)
Vosstanie Emel'jana Pugačeva. L.

PUGAČEV (1975)
Dokumenty stavki E.I. Pugačeva, povstančeskich vlastej i učreždenij 1773 – 1774 gg. M.

PUŠČIN, I.I. (1956)
Zapiski o Puškine. Pis'ma. M.

PUŠKIN, (PSS)
A.S. Puškin. Polnoe sobranie sočinenij. 16 vols. M. 1937 – 1949.

PVL (1950)
Povest'vremennych let. Ed. V.P. Adrianova-Peretc. 2 parts. M–L.

PYLJAEV, M.I. (1897)
Staroe žit'e. Očerki i rasskazy. 2nd ed. St.P.

PYPIN, A.N. (1908)
Obščestvennoe dviženie v Rossii pri Aleksandre I. St.P.

RABINOVIČ, M.D. (1958)
"Novye dannye po istorii Orenburgskogo tajnogo obščestva," Vestnik AN SSSR, 7.

RADIŠČEV, A..N. (PSS)
A.N. Radiščev, Polnoe sobranie sočinenij. 3 vols. M–L. 1938–1952.

RADIŠČEV, A.N. (1958)
A Journey from St. Petersburg to Moscow. Translated by Leo Wiener. Ed. with introduction and notes by R.P. Thaler. Cambridge, Mass.

RADIŠČEV, A.N. (1959)
Biografija A.N. Radiščeva, napisannaja ego synov'jami. M–L.

RAEVSKIJ, V.F. (1956)
"Dnevnik." In, Literaturnoe Nasledstvo, 60/1.

REICHLER, Claude (1979)
La Diabolie, la séduction, la renardie, l'écriture. Paris.

RIB
Russkaja istoričeskaja biblioteka. 39 vols. St.P. 1872 – 1927.

RICCOBONI, A.F. & SCHRÖDER, F.L. (1821)
Vorschriften über die Schauspielkunst. Leipzig.

ROMANOV, B.A. (1947)
Ljudi i nravy drevnej Rusi. L. (1966²)

ROMANOVIČ-SLAVATINSKIJ, A. (1870)
Dvorjanstvo v Rossii ot načala XVIII veka do otmeny krepostnogo prava. St.P.

ROŽDESTVENSKIJ, N.V. (1902)
*K istorii bor'by s cerkovnymi besporjadkami, otgoloskami jazyčestva i porokami
v russkom bytu XVII v.* (*Čelobitnaja nižegorodskich svjaščennikov 1636 goda v
svjazi s pervonačal'noj dejatel'nostju Ivana Neronova*). *ČOIDR,* book 2.

ROŽDESTVENSKIJ, T.S. (1910)
"Pamjatniki staro-obrjadčeskoj poèzii," *Zapiski Moskovskogo archeologičeskogo instituta,* VI.

RUSOV, N.N. (1911)
Pomeščič'ja Rossija po zapiskam sovremennikov. M.

RUSSKIE POVESTI
Russkie povesti XIX veka, 20-ch – 30-ch godov. Vol. 2. M – L. 1950.

RYLEEV, K.F. (1934)
Polnoe sobranie stichotvorenij. L.

RYLEEV, K.F. (1954)
"Rasskazy o Ryleeve rassyl'nogo 'Poljarnoj zvezdy'." In, *Literaturnoe nasledstvo,* 59. M.

RYLEEV, K.F. (1971)
Polnoe sobranie stichotvorenij. L.

ŠACHMATOV, A.A. (1908)
"Predislovie k Načal'nomu kievskomu svodu i Nestorova letopis'," *Izvestija
otdelenija russkogo jazyka i slovesnosti imp. Akademii nauk,* XIII.

ST. FRANCIS (1903)
I Fioretti del glorioso messere Santo Francesco e de suoi Frati. Ed. G.L. Passe-
rini. Florence.

ŠAMBINAGO, S. (1906)
Povesti o Mamaevom poboišče. St.P. (*Sbornik otdelenija russkogo jazyka i
slovesnosti imp. Akademii Nauk,* LXXXI).

SANDOMIRSKAJA, B.V. (1966)
"Poèmy." In, *Puškin. Itogi i problemy izučenija.* M – L.

SAUSSURE, Ferdinand de (1962)
Cours de linguistique générale. Paris. Russian: F. de Sossjur. *Trudy po jazyko-
znaniju.* M. 1977.

SAVVA, V. (1901)
*Moskovskie cari i vizantijskie vasilevsy. K voprosu o vlijanii Vizantii na obrazo-
vanie idei carskoj vlasti moskovskich gosudarej.* Kharkov.

SAVVAITOV, P.I. (1872)
"Graf Aleksej Andreevič Arakčeev, rasskazy iz ego žizni svjašč[ennika] sela
Gruzina, [N.S.] Il'inskogo. Soobšč. P.I. Savvaitov." *Russkaja starina,* V.

Sb. RIO
Sborniki russkogo istoričeskogo obščestva. St.P.

ŠČEGOLEV, P.E. (1912)
Puškin. Očerki. St.P.

ŠČEGOLEV, P.E. (1931)
Iz žizni i tvorčestva Puškina. M – L.

ŠČERBATOV, M.M. (1774)
Tetrati zapisnyja vsjakim pis'mam i delam, komu čto prikazano i v kotorom čisle ot E.I. V. Petra Velikago 1704, 1705 i 1706 godov s priloženiem primečanij o službach tech ljudej, k kotorym sej gosudar' pisyval. [St.P.]
SCHILLER, Charlotte von (1862)
Charlotte von Schiller und ihre Freunde. Band 2, Stuttgart.
ŠEJN, P. (1895)
"Ešče o parodii v narodnych tekstach," *Ėtnografičeskoe obozrenie,* XXV, 2.
ŠEJN, P. (1898 – 1900)
Velikoruss v svoich pesnjach, obrjadach, obyčajach, verovanijach, skazkach, legendach i t.p. Vol. I, part 1 – 2. St.P.
SELIVANOV, V.V. (1881)
Predanija i vospominanija. St.P.
SEMENOV, V. (1893)
Drevnjaja russkaja Pčela po pergamennomu spisku. St.P. *(Sbornik Obščestva russkogo jazyka i slovestnosti,* 54).
SEMEVSKIJ, M.I. (1885)
Slovo i delo, 1700 – 1725. 3rd ed. St.P.
ŠEREMETEVA, M.E. (1928)
Svad'ba v Gamajunščine, kalužskogo uezda. Kaluga.
SEVER'JANOV, S. (1904)
Suprasl'skaja rukopis'. Vol. I. St.P. *(Pamjatniki staroslavjanskogo jazyka,* II, 1).
SIDJAKOV, L.S. (1973)
Chudožestvennaja proza A.S. Puškina. Riga.
ŠILDER, N.K. (1897 – 1898)
Imperator Aleksandr Pervyj, ego žizn i carstvovanie. 4 vols. St.P.
ŠILLER (Schiller), F. von (1955 – 1957)
Sobranie sočinenij v 7-ch tomach. Translated by V. Levik. M.
SIVKOV, K.V. (1950)
"Samozvančestvo v Rossii v poslednej treti XVIII v.," *Istoričeskie zapiski,* 31.
SKAZANIJA (1834)
Skazanija sovremennikov o Dimitrii Samozvance. III. St. P.
SKRYNNIKOV, R.G. (1975)
Ivan Groznyj. M.
ŠLICHTING, A. (1934)
Novoe izvestie o Rossii vremeni Ivana Groznogo. 'Skazanie'' Al'berta Šlichtinga. Ed. A.I. Malein. L.
SLOVCOV, P.A. (1971)
"Poslanie k M.M. Speranskomu." In, *Poèty 1790 – 1810-ch godov.* L.
SLOVO (1952)
Slovo o polku Igoreve. L.
SMIRNOV, M.I. (1919)
"Starye bogi," *Doklady Perejaslavl'-Zalesskogo naučno-prosvetitel'nogo obščestva,* 4.
SMIRNOV, M.I. (1922)
Ėtnografičesk[ie] materialy po Pereslavl'-Zalesskomu uezdu Vladimirskoj gubernii. Svadebnye obrjady i pesni, pesni krugovye i prochodnye, igry. Legendy i skazki. M. *(Otčety po obsledovaniju pridorožnych rajonov severnych železnych dorog,* 14.)
SMIRNOV, M.I. (1927)
"Kul't i krest'janskoe chozjajstvo v Pereslavl'-Zalesskom uezde. Po ètnografi-

319

českim nabljudenijam," *Trudy Pereslavl'-Zalesskogo istoriko-chudožestvennogo i kraevednogo muzeja*, I. *Staryj byt i chozjajstvo Pereslavskoj derevni*.

SMIRNOV, P.S. (1909)
Spory i razdelenija v russkom raskole v pervoj četverti XVIII veka. 1909.

SMIRNOV, S. (1914)
Drevnerusskij duchovnik. Issledovanie po istorii cerkovnogo byta. M.

SMIRNOV, Vas. (1920)
"Narodnye pochorony i pričitanija v Kostromskom krae." In, *Vtoroj ètnografičeskij sbornik (Trudy Kostromskogo naučnogo obščestva po izučeniju mestnogo kraja*, V). Kostroma.

SMIRNOV, Vas. (1927)
"Narodnye gadan'ja Kostromskogo kraja (očerk i teksty)," *Trudy Kostromskogo naučnogo obščestva po izučeniju mestnogo kraja*, XLI. *(Četvertyj ètnografičeskij sbornik)*. Kostroma.

SOKOLOV, A.N. (1970)
Istorija russkoj literatury XIX veka (pervaja polovina). M.

SOKOL'SKIJ, V. (1902)
Učastie russkogo duchovenstva i monašestva v razvitii edinoderžavija i samoderžavija v Moskovskom gosudarstve v konce XV i pervoj polovine XVI vv. Kiev.

SOLOV'EV, S.M. (1894 – 1896)
Istorija Rossii s drevnejšich vremen. 25 books. St. P.

SOLOV'EV, S.M. (1960 – 1966)
Istorija Rossii s drevnejšich vremen v XV knigach. M.

SREZNEVSKIJ, Vs. (1893)
"Musin-Puškinskij sbornik 1414 goda v kopii načala XIX v." *Zapiski imperatorskoj Akademii nauk*, LXXII, Appendix 5.

SREZNEVSKIJ, I.I. (1893 – 1912)
Materialy dlja slovarja drevnerusskogo jazyka po pis'mennym pamjatnikam. 3 vols. St. P.

ŠTADEN, G. (1925)
O Moskve Ivana Groznogo. Zapiski nemca-opričnika. Translated by I.I. Polosin. M.

STEPANOV, N.L. (1955)
"Gogol'." In, *Istorija russkoj literatury*. Vol. VII. M – L.

STEPANOV, N.L. (1959)
"'Povest' o kapitane Kopejkine' i ego istočniki," *Izvestija AN SSSR otdelenie literatury i jazyka*, 1.

ŠTORM, Georgij (1968)
Potaennyj Radiščev. Vtoraja žizn' "Putešestvija iz Peterburga v Moskvu." 2nd ed. M.

ŠTRAJCH, S.Ja. (1925)
Provokacija sredi dekabristov. Samozvanec Medoks na Petrovskom zavode. 2nd ed. M.

ŠTRAJCH, S. Ja. (1929)
Roman Medoks. Pochoždenija russkogo avantjurista XIX veka. 2nd ed. M. (1930 ^{3}).

STRAHLENBERG, Ph.J. von (1730)
Das Nord- und Ostliche Theil von Europa und Asia. Stockholm.

SUBBOTIN, N.I. ed. (1875 – 1890)
Materialy dlja istorii raskola za pervoe vremja ego suščestvovanija. 9 vols. M.

SUMAROKOV, A.P. (1935)
Stichotvorenija. L. (Biblioteka poèta)

TATARSKIJ, I. (1886)
Simeon Polockij (ego žizn' i dejatel'nost'). *Opyt issledovanija iz istorii pro-sveščenija i vnutrennej cerkovnoj žizni vo vtoruju polovinu XVII veka.* M.
TATIŠČEV, V.N. (1950)
Izbrannye trudy po geografii. M.
TICHONRAVOV, N. ed. (1863)
Pamjatniki otrečennoj russkoj literatury. 2 vols. St. P.
TODOROV, Tzvetan (1972)
"Introduction à la symbolique," *Poétique*, 11.
TODOROV, Tzvetan (1977)
Théories du symbole. Paris. 1977.
TOLSTAJA-SUCHOTINA, T.L. (1973)
"Vblizi otca," *Novyj mir*, 12.
TOLSTOJ, L.N. (1942)
War and Peace. Translated by Louise and Aylmer Maude. London.
TOMAŠEVSKIJ, B. (1956)
Puškin. Bk. 1. M – L.
TOMASEVSKIJ, B.V. (1960)
Puškin i Francija. L.
TOPOROV, V.N. (1975)
"K ob"jasneniju nekotorych slavjanskich slov mifologičeskogo charaktera v svjazi s vozmožnymi drevnimi mifologičeskimi paralleljami." In, *Slavjanskoe i balkanskoe jazykoznanie. Problemy interferencii i jazykovych kontaktov.* M.
TURGENEV, N.I. (1921)
"Dnevniki N. Turgeneva. Vol. III." In, *Archiv brat'ev Turgenevych*, 5. Prague.
TURGENEV, N.I. (1936)
Dekabrist N.I. Turgenev. Pis'ma k bratu S.I. Turgenevu. M – L.
TYNJANOV, Ju.N. (1946)
"Sjužet 'Gorja ot uma'." In, *Literaturnoe nasledstvo*, 47 – 48.
USPENSKIJ, B.A. (1968)
Archaičeskaja sistema cerkovnoslavjanskogo proiznošenija. *(Iz istorii liturgičeskogo proiznošenija v Rossii).* M.
USPENSKIJ, B.A. (1977)
"Historia sub specie semioticae." In, *Soviet Semiotics*, ed. D.P. Lucid, Baltimore and London. Russian text in, *Kul'turnoe nasledie Drevnej Rusi. Istoki, stanovlenie, tradicija.* M. 1976.
USPENSKIJ, B.A. (1978)
"Kul't Nikoly na Rusi v istoriko-kul'turnom osveščenii. (Specifika vosprijatija i transformacija ischodnogo obraza)," *UZ TGU* 643 *(Trudy po znakovym sistemam X).*
USPENSKIJ, B.A. (forthcoming)
"Choženie za tri morja" Afanasija Nikitina na fone jazykovoj i kul'turnoj situacii Drevnej Rusi.
USPENSKIJ, G.I. (1956)
"Vlast' zemli." In, *Sobranie sočinenij v 10-i tomach*, Vol. V. M.
USPENSKIJ, N.D. (1965)
Drevnerusskoe pevčeskoe iskusstvo. M.
USTRJALOV, N. (1859)
Skazanija sovremennikov o Dimitrii Samozvance. 2 parts. 3rd ed. St. P.
VACURO, V.È. (1977)
"'Velikij melancholik' v 'Putešestvii iz Moskvy v Peterburg'," *Vremennik*

Puškinskoj komissii 1974. L.

VAHROS, Igor (1966)
Zür Geschichte und Folklore der grossrussischen Sauna. Helsinki. *(Folklore Fellows Communications*, LXXXII N 197).

VAILLANT, A. (1935)
"Les 'lettres russes' de la vie de Constantin," *Revue des études slaves*, 15, 1–2.

VAJTOVIČ, N.T. (1977)
Barkalabauski letapis. Minsk.

VAL'DENBERG, V. (1916)
Drevnerusskie učenija o predelach carskoj vlasti. Očerk russkoj političeskoj literatury ot Vladimira Svjatogo do konca XVII veka. Pgd.

VAL'DENBERG, V.E. (1929)
"Ponjatie o tirane v drevnerusskoj literature v sravnenii s zapadnoj," *Izvestija po russkomu jazyku i slovesnosti*, II, 1.

VELIKIE MINEI ČETII
Velikie Minei Četii, sobrannye Vserossijskim mitropolitom Makariem. October 1-3, St. P. 1870; October 19-31, St. P. 1880. *(Pamjatniki slavjano-russkoj pis'mennosti, izdannye Archeografičeskoj komissiej)*.

VEL'JAMINOV-ZERNOV, V.V. (1863–1866)
Issledovanie o kasimovskich carjach i carevičach. 3 parts. St. P. *(Trudy Vostočnogo otdelenija imp. Archeologičeskogo obščestva*, 9–11).

VERCHOVSKOJ, P.V. (1916)
Učreždenie Duchovnoj kollegii i Duchovnyj reglament. K voprosu ob otnošenii cerkvi i gosudarstva v Rossii. Issledovanie v oblasti istorii russkogo cerkovnogo prava. 2 vols. Rostov on Don.

VERESAEV, V. (1929)
"V studenčeskie gody," *Nedra* XVI.

VESELOVSKIJ, A.N. (1866)
"Dante i simvoličeskaja poèzija katoličestva," *Vestnik Evropy*, IV.

VESELOVSKIJ, A.N. (1875)
Opyty po istorii christianskoj legendy. *(Žurnal Ministerstva narodnogo prosveščenija*, CLXXVIII–CLXXIX).

VESELOVSKIJ, S.B. (1963)
Issledovanija po istorii o pročniny. M.

VESELOVSKIJ, S.B. (1969)
Issledovanija po istorii klassa služilych zemlevladel'cev. M.

VIGEL', F.F. (1928)
Zapiski. M.

VINOGRADOV, V.V. (1938)
Očerki po istorii russkogo literaturnogo jazyka XVII–XIX vv. M.

VJAZEMSKIJ, P.A. (1854)
[Contribution], *Moskvitjanin*, 6, section IV.

VJAZEMSKIJ, P.A. (1929)
Staraja zapisnaja knižka. L.

VODOFF, W. (1978)
"Remarques sur la valeur du terme 'tsar' appliqué aux princes russes avant le milieu du XVe. siècle," *Oxford Slavonic Papers*, New Series, XI.

VOLKONSKAJA, M.N. (1914)
Zapiski Kn. Marii Nikolaevny Volkonskoj. 2nd ed. St. P.

VOLKOV, M.Ja. (1973)
"Monach Avraamij i ego 'Poslanie Petru I'." In, *Rossija v period reform Petra I*.

M.
VOPROŠENIE
"Voprošenie knjazja Izjaslava, syna Jaroslavlja, vnuka Volodimirova, igumena Pečerskago velikago Feodosija o Latine." In, Andrej Popov, *Istoriko-literaturnyj obzor drevnerusskich polemičeskich sočinenij protiv latinjan (XI-XV v.)*. M. 1875.

VOSSTANIE
Vosstanie dekabristov. 11 vols. M-L. 1925-1958.

VRANGEL', Baron N.N.
Istorija skul'ptury. M. [n.d.]

WITTRAM, R. (1964)
Peter I. Czar und Kaiser. Zür Geschichte Peters des Grossen in seiner Zeit. 2 vols. Göttingen.

ZAKONY (1903-1905)
Polnyj svod zakonov, ed. G.G. Savič. 16 vols. St. P.

ZAVALIŠIN, D.I. (1908)
Zapiski dekabrista D.I. Zavališina. St. P.

ZAVOJKO, G.K. (1914)
"Verovanija, obrjady i obyčai velikorossov Vladimirskoj gubernii," *Ètnografičeskoe obozrenie*, CIII-CIV, 3-4.

ZAVOJKO, K. (1917)
"V Kostromskich lesach po Vetluge reke. (Ètnografičeskie materialy, zapisannye v Kostromskoj gubernii v 1914-1916 gg.)," *Ètnografičeskij sbornik*. Kostroma. (*Trudy Kostromskogo naučnogo obščestva po izučeniju mestnogo kraja*, VIII).

ŽDANOV, I.N. (1904)
"Slovo o Zakone i Blagodati i Pochvala kaganu Vladimiru." In, I.N. Ždanov, *Sočinenija*, I, St. P.

ZELENIN, D.K. (1914)
Velikorusskie skazki Permskoj gubernii. S priloženiem dvenadcati baškirskich skazok i odnoj meščerjakskoj. Pgd. (*Zapiski imp. Russkogo Geografičeskogo Obščestva po otdeleniju ètnografii*, XLI).

ZELENIN, D.K. (1914-1916)
Opisanie rukopisej Učenogo archiva imp. Russkogo geografičeskogo obščestva. 3 vols. Pgd.

ZELENIN, D.K. (1916)
Očerki russkoj mifologii. I. *Umeršie neestestvennoj smert'ju i rusalki.* Pgd.

ZELENIN, D. (1927)
Russische (Ostslavische) Volkskunde. Berlin and Leipzig.

ZELENSKIJ, V. (1887)
Russkaja kritičeskaja literatura o proizvedenijach A.S. Puškina. M.

ŽELJABUŽSKIJ (1840)
Zapiski Željabužskogo s 1682 po 2 ijulja 1709. Ed. D. Jazykov. St. P.

ŽIVOV, V.M. & USPENSKIJ, B.A. (1981)
"Car' i bog. Jazykovye aspekty sakralizacii monarcha v Rossii." In, *Tri epochi pol'sko-russkogo literaturnogo obščenija.* I. *Kul'tura Barokko.* (In preparation.)

ZOBNIN, F. & PATKANOV, S. (1899)
"Spisok tobol'skich slov i vyraženij," *Živaja starina*, IX, 4.

ZUMMER, V.M. (1925)
"Problematika chudožestvennogo stilja Al. Ivanova: stil' 'biblejskich èskizov',"

Izvestija Azerbajdžanskogo Gos. Universiteta, 2-3 (*Obščestvennye nauki*).

ŽURNAL
Žurnal, ili Podennaja zapiska, blažennyja i večnodostojnyja pamjati gosudarja imperatora Petra Velikago s 1698 goda, daže do zaključenija Nejštatskago mira. Part I. St. P.

ZYZYKIN, M.V. (1931–1939)
Patriarch Nikon. Ego gosudarstvennye i kanoničeskie idei. 3 parts. Warsaw.

Mably, Abbé, 27
Magarshak, D., 213, 299
Magic, 9, 41, 47, 125-6, 127, 253, 297, 298
Makogonenko, G. P., 228
Makar'ev fair, 217 &n.
Makarij, Metropolitan, 32, 33
  Menology of, 11, 293, 294
Makarov, N., 281-2
Maksimov, S. V., 32, 35, 51, 287, 289, 290
Maltese Order, 27, 46
Mamaj, King, 253
Mamonov (member of "Russian Knights"), 112
Mandel'štam, O., 67, 134, 139
  Stone, 67
Man'kov, A. G., 31
Marfa Boreckaja, Mayor of Novgorod, 101, 248, 251; see also F. F. Ivanov, Karamzin
Margeret, J., 260-1, 278
Marianus Gospel, 65
Marija Fedorovna, Dowager Empress, 96, 120
Marin, S. N., 156, 243-4
Marinuška, see Mniszech, Marina
Marks, royal, 202, 264-5, 280
Marriage rituals, 9, 12, 31, 32
Martin, E. M., 86
Martos, I. P., 143 &n.
Marx, K.,
  The Eighteenth Brumaire of Napoleon Bonaparte, 147
Mary, Blessed Virgin (Mother of God), 5, 8, 29, 30, 106, 261, 265, 278, 281, 297-9, 300
——, Intercession of, see pokrov
Maskevič, S., 51
Massa, I., 278
Maturin, C.,
  Melmoth the Wanderer, 150
Maxim the Greek [Maksim Grek], 55, 66, 280
Maximilian, Tsar, 253
Medoks, R., 193-200, 201, 206, 211
Melmoth, see Maturin
Mel'nikov, P. I., 32, 66, 279
Memory, cultural role of, xii, 3, 4, 12, 16, 26, 28
Mendacity, 180ff. See also Chlestakovism
Menology, 11 n.

Men'šikov, A. D., 57, 209
Mérimée, P., 148
Merzljakov, A. F., 90, 230
Meščerskaja, Princess, see Basargina
Meščerskij, N. A., 139
Michael, Archangel, 58, 279
Michael, Prince, 279
Michail Fedorovič, Tsar, 262, 266-7, 279
Michajlovskij-Danilevskij (censor), 243
Michigan Slavic Publications, 33
Middle Ages, in Russia, 4,5
——, in West, 4, 5
Miljutin, D. A., 255
Miller, Vs. F., 290
Milonov, M. V., 79, 80, 244
Miloradovič, M. A., 172, 173, 255
Minin, K., 143n., 150n., 193 &n.
Mithridate, 198, 199
Mithridates, 198
Mniszech, Marina, 274, 275
Model, art as, 142, 145, 178, 252
——, cultural, 3, 19, 24-6
——, life as, 142, 156
——, theatrical, for behavior, 141, 145, 147, 160, 165-9, 171, 173, 234, 237-40, 241, 248-52
Models, literary, for behavior, 86, 87, 90-91, 93, 94-6, 119, 145, 146, 147, 150, 156, 161, 170, 204, 207, 208, 241-2, 245
——, socio-cultural, 125, 127
Modzalevskij, B. L., 102, 121
Moiseeva, G. N., 65
Mokoš, 8, 299
Mokul'skij, S., 175, 176
Molčalin (character from Woe from Wit), 76, 83, 106
Molière, 80, 151
  Tartuffe, 151
Molostvov, friend of Puškin, 109
Mons, W., 237
Montage, 168
Montesquieu, 255
Mordvinov, A. N., 200
Mordvinov, Admiral N. S., 183
Morris, C., ix, 191
Moscow, 86, 88, 102, 113, 144, 151, 166, 177, 184, 193, 197, 198, 199, 200, 217, 235, 259, 267, 269, 271, 272, 274, 279, 282, 283, 284, 287, 289
Moscow Historical Museum, 266

Pletnev, P. A., 169, 214
Plot, as interpretation of behavior, 85, 86, 87, 93, 156, 245, 252
Plutarch, 146, 187, 244, 249
Poetry and other arts, 171-2
Pogodin, M. P., 158, 213
pokrov, 298
Pokrovskij, N. N., 30, 279
Poland, attitudes to, 43
———, Russian administration of, 115
Polarity, in Russian culture, 4; see also Oppositions
Polevoj, N., 80, 119
Polevoj, N., 213, 228
Poležaev, A. I., 97
Polish uprising, 111
Polockij, S., 134, 278
Polonisms in Russian royal titles, 65, 260
Polosin, I. I., 52, 281, 288
Poltava, 62, 132, 149, 170, 171, 282, 285, 286
Poltorackij archive, 229
Polubenskij (Ivan the Terrible's courtier), 55
Popov, A., 30, 31, 280, 283
Popriščin (character in Dostoevskij's *The Diary of a Madman*), 189, 196-7, 204, 210
Popruženko, M. G., 67
Porošin, S., 45, 52, 290
Portnjagin, General, 194
Posa, Marquis of, in Schiller's *Don Carlos*, 90, 91, 92, 93, 121
Potemkin, G. A., 21, 34, 179 &n., 242-3
Potocki, J.
   The Manuscript found in Saragossa, 219
Povest' vremennych let, see *Tale of Bygone Years*
Požarskij, D., 143n., 150 &n., 193
Pragmatics, of literary character, 177-212
———, of text, 191-2, 193, 208
Praskov'ja Fedorovna, Tsarina, 65
Predtečenskij, A. V., 121, 163
Preobraženskoe, 284
Presburg, 284, 285
Pretenders, religious, 261-2
———, royal, 259-292
Print, popular *[lubočnaja kartinka]*, 45, 234, 240, 242
Priselkov, M. D., 29

Prochorov, G. M., 284
Prokof'ev, E. A., 163
Prokopij of Ustjug, St., *Life* of, 48, 52
Prokopovič, F., 18, 19, 20, 34, 58, 59, 62-3, 65, 66, 135, 139, 149, 161, 278, 285-6
Prokopovič, N. Ja., 214
Prostakova, 25
Protestantism, 59, 61
Prozorovskij, P., 285
"Prus," 53
"Prutkov, K.," 252
Pskov, 57, 280, 299
PTL. A Journal for Descriptive Poetics and Theory of Literature, 230
Puffendorf, S. von, 135
Pugačev, E. I., 202, 218 &n., 226, 262 & n.-263, 266, 280, 281, 291
Puppet shows, 152, 176, 178, 237, 240, 253
Purgatory, 4
Puščin, I. I., 104, 122, 194-5, 211
Puškin, A. M., 151, 162
Puškin, A. S., 23, 36, 63, 76, 78, 79, 80, 86, 87, 88, 90, 98, 101, 102, 103, 104, 105, 108, 109-10, 114, 116, 117, 118, 119 &n., 121, 122, 134, 138, 147, 152, 154, 155, 159, 163, 167, 169-70, 170-1, 172, 176, 189, 197, 208, 209, 210, 211, 214-24, 225, 227, 229, 242, 243, 244, 246, 247, 250, 255, 256
   The Bridegroom, 216
   The Bronze Horseman, 63, 64, 155, 171
   The Captain's Daughter, 219, 222, 226
   The Captive of the Caucasus, 216, 219-20
   The Covetous Knight, 230
   Dubrovskij, 219, 220, 222, 224, 226
   Eugene Onegin, 76, 138, 208, 216-8, 219
   The Fountain of Bachčisaraj, 23, 216
   The Gipsies, 118
   The Golden Fish, 210
   A History of the Village of Gorjuchino, 237
   My Genealogy, 209
   The Negro of Peter the Great, 138
   "A Novel at the Caucasian Waters," 219, 220, 229

CPSIA information can be obtained at www.ICGtesting.com
Printed in the USA
BVOW030057280212

283939BV00005B/2/P